# The Propaganda Model Today:
# Filtering Perception and Awareness

Edited by
Joan Pedro-Carañana, Daniel Broudy
&
Jeffery Klaehn

University of Westminster Press
www.uwestminsterpress.co.uk

Published by
University of Westminster Press
115 New Cavendish Street
London W1W 6UW
www.uwestminsterpress.co.uk

Text © the editors and several contributors 2018

First published 2018

Series cover concept: Mina Bach (minabach.co.uk)
Print and digital versions typeset by Siliconchips Services Ltd.

ISBN (Paperback): 978-1-912656-16-5
ISBN (PDF): 978-1-912656-17-2
ISBN (EPUB): 978-1-912656-18-9
ISBN (Kindle): 978-1-912656-19-6

DOI: https://doi.org/10.16997/book27

This work is licensed under the Creative Commons Attribution-NonCommercial-NoDerivatives 4.0 International License. To view a copy of this license, visit http://creativecommons.org/licenses/by-nc-nd/4.0/ or send a letter to Creative Commons, 444 Castro Street, Suite 900, Mountain View, California, 94041, USA. This license allows for copying and distributing the work, providing author attribution is clearly stated, that you are not using the material for commercial purposes, and that modified versions are not distributed.

The full text of this book has been peer-reviewed to ensure high academic standards. For full review policies, see: http://www.uwestminsterpress.co.uk/site/publish/

Suggested citation:
Pedro-Carañana, J., Broudy, D. and Klaehn, J. (eds.). 2018. *The Propaganda Model Today: Filtering Perception and Awareness*. London: University of Westminster Press. DOI: https://doi.org/10.16997/book27. License: CC-BY-NC-ND 4.0

To read the free, open access version of this book online, visit https://doi.org/10.16997/book27 or scan this QR code with your mobile device:

# Dedication

*The editors dedicate this collection to the memory of Edward S. Herman (7 April 1925 – 11 November 2017), the principal architect of the Herman-Chomsky Propaganda Model.*

# Competing interests

The editors and contributors declare that they have no competing interests in publishing this book.

# Contents

1. Introduction — 1
   *Joan Pedro-Carañana, Daniel Broudy and Jeffery Klaehn*

## Part I: Theoretical and Methodological Considerations — 19

2. Interview with Edward S. Herman: Ideological Hegemony in Contemporary Societies — 21
   *Jeffery Klaehn, Joan Pedro-Carañana, Matthew Alford and Yigal Godler*
3. What the Propaganda Model Can Learn from the Sociology of Journalism — 25
   *Jesse Owen Hearns-Branaman*
4. Journalism Studies' Systematic Pursuit of Irrelevance: How Research Emphases Sabotage Critiques of Corporate-Run News Media — 37
   *Yigal Godler*
5. Does the Propaganda Model Actually Theorise Propaganda? — 53
   *Piers Robinson*

## Part II: The Internet and New Digital Media — 69

6. Propaganda 2.0: Herman and Chomsky's Propaganda Model in the Age of the Internet, Big Data and Social Media — 71
   *Christian Fuchs*
7. System Security: A Missing Filter for the Propaganda Model? — 93
   *Daniel Broudy and Miyume Tanji*
8. From #15M to *Podemos*: Updating the Propaganda Model for Explaining Political Change in Spain and the Role of Digital Media — 107
   *Miguel Álvarez-Peralta*
9. Anti-Communism and the Mainstream Online Press in Spain: Criticism of Podemos as a Strategy of a Two-Party System in Crisis — 125
   *Aurora Labio-Bernal*

## Part III: Screen Entertainment and Broadcast Media — 143

10. A Screen Entertainment Propaganda Model — 145
    *Matthew Alford*
11. American Television: Manufacturing Consumerism — 159
    *Tabe Bergman*
12. The Sport of Shafting Fans and Taxpayers: An Application of the Propaganda Model to the Coverage of Professional Athletes and Team Owners — 173
    *Barry Pollick*

## Part IV: Case Studies on Media and Power: The Interplay Between National and Global Elites — 191

13. The 2008 Financial Crisis, the Great Recession and Austerity in Britain: Analysing Media Coverage Using the Herman-Chomsky Propaganda Model — 193
    *Andrew Mullen*
14. Corporate-Market Power and Ideological Domination: The Propaganda Model after 30 Years – Relevance and Further Application — 223
    *Florian Zollmann*
15. Imperialism and Hegemonic Information in Latin America: The Media Coup in Venezuela vs. the Criminalisation of Protest in Mexico — 237
    *Francisco Sierra Caballero*
16. 'Dynamic' Obama Lectures 'Bumbling' Castro on Race Relations in Cuba, While Wilfully Blind to Black Lives Matter Movement in the US — 249
    *James Winter*
17. Thinking the Unthinkable about the Unthinkable – The Use of Nuclear Weapons and the Propaganda Model — 263
    *Milan Rai*
18. Conclusion — 279
    *Joan Pedro-Carañana, Daniel Broudy and Jeffery Klaehn*

Index — 293

CHAPTER 1

# Introduction

Joan Pedro-Carañana, Daniel Broudy
and Jeffery Klaehn

If you're not careful, the newspapers will have you hating the people who are being oppressed, and loving the people who are doing the oppressing.

–*Malcolm X*

The propaganda system allows the U.S. leadership to commit crimes without limit and with no suggestion of misbehaviour or criminality.

–*Edward S. Herman*

The smart way to keep people passive and obedient is to strictly limit the spectrum of acceptable opinion, but allow very lively debate within that spectrum.

–*Noam Chomsky*

Often, 'freedom of expression' is mistaken with 'freedom of pressuring'… It is no longer necessary for the ends to justify the means since

---

**How to cite this book chapter:**
Pedro-Carañana, J., Broudy, D. and Klaehn, J. 2018. Introduction. In: Pedro-Carañana, J., Broudy, D. and Klaehn, J. (eds.). *The Propaganda Model Today: Filtering Perception and Awareness*. Pp. 1–18. London: University of Westminster Press. DOI: https://doi.org/10.16997/book27.a. License: CC-BY-NC-ND 4.0

the means, the means of communication – the mass media – justify the ends of a power system that imposes its values on a global scale ... [The] many are being held incommunicado by the few.
–Eduardo Galeano

## 1. Reception of the Propaganda Model

Edward Herman and Noam Chomsky first proposed their 'propaganda model' (PM hereafter) of media operations in *Manufacturing Consent: The Political Economy of the Mass Media* in 1988.[1] Since then, the PM has seen noteworthy modifications[2] and has attracted significant scholarly attention from around the world.[3] While the individual elements of the propaganda system (or 'filters') identified by the PM (ownership, advertising, sources, flak and anti-communism) had previously been the focus of much scholarly attention, their systematisation in a model, empirical corroboration and historisation have made the PM a useful tool for media analysis across cultural and geographical boundaries.

Despite the wealth of scholarly research Herman and Chomsky's work has set into motion over the past decades, the PM has been subjected to marginalisation;[4] poorly informed critiques;[5] and misrepresentations.[6] Interestingly, while the PM enables researchers to form discerning predictions as regards corporate media performance, Herman and Chomsky had further predicted that the PM itself would meet with such marginalisation and contempt.

In current theoretical and empirical studies of mass media performance, uses of the PM continue, nonetheless, to yield important insights into the workings of political and economic power in society, due in large measure to the model's considerable explanatory power. Its appeal also appears to come from the simplicity with which it may be used to investigate and elucidate how dominant institutional forces in society shape mass media performance. By illuminating ways in which power structures and privileged actors routinely impact patterns of media behaviour, the PM serves as a highly effective means of clarifying how dominant systems of propaganda and manipulation can affect capitalist societies, characterised by the increasing control of democratic institutions by financial and political-State forces to the detriment of the general population.

In academic contexts currently marked by the de-politicisation of Cultural and Media/Communication Studies,[7] this collection aims to introduce readers to the PM, to present cutting-edge research demonstrating the model's general validity and to critically update, expand, and refine it.[8] To these ends, we have brought together international researchers to analyse the continuities and new developments in media environments throughout various regions of the world. This volume, thus, endeavours to serve as a benchmark text for anyone interested in the PM, including students, scholars and researchers, concerned citizens, social, political and media activists as well as policymakers across a range of disciplines, such as communication/media studies, sociology, political science/international relations, peace/war studies and political economy. While this collection is aimed primarily at a particular audience, it is also constructed in a way that remains widely accessible to a more general readership concerned about the influence of propaganda on the public mind and the mechanisms through which the power elites exert control over society through media.

The volume locates these latest studies on media systems within the wider body of work already built on the PM so as to contextualise, refine, clarify and improve the model's utility and validity. By bringing together a number of leading scholars on the PM at an international level, we strive to give greater shape to a school of thought rooted in Herman and Chomsky's original work, which has seen various developments throughout the years via theoretical reflection and application to specific case studies. An example of the development of PM scholarship, and predecessor of this volume, is the work undertaken by Klaehn, which focused on the model's theoretical, methodological, applied, and practical dimensions.[9]

## 2. The Propaganda Model and the Political Economy of Media

The political economy approach and institutional analysis of the mass media that the PM follows is embedded in the tradition of radical mass media criticism.[10] The PM connects directly with the US tradition of critical, empirical studies[11] and draws upon previous research on the historical evolution of the media, including in the UK.[12] The PM shares with Marxian analysis the materialist criticism of domination and of the power structures that affect the media, as well as a historical perspective. However, Herman and Chomsky did not specifically position the PM within the Marxian scholarship of media and communication. The original conceptualisation of the model differs from Marxian analyses that specifically focus on contradictions affecting the media and the possibilities of journalism to contribute to social justice.[13] Instead, the book *Manufacturing Consent* emphasised the key dimensions of elite power that restrict media performance and drastically reduce the possibilities of promoting egalitarian change. However, the PM is also attentive to divisions among the elites and the emergence of strong social movements to explain the opening of the range of opinion in the media. Moreover, this volume shows that PM scholarship is also analysing the role played by journalists and professionalism, the changes that digital technologies are prompting, national contexts, and the influence of audiences and media activism on news production.

The PM perspective coincides with Marxian analysis of the media as part of a wider capitalist system oriented toward profit maximisation and the incessant accumulation of capital in increasingly oligopolistic contexts. The PM understands media structures and contents, thus, to be shaped by corporate-State powers and oriented toward the production of profits and the reproduction of class societies. Therefore, the PM would not apply to nations, societies, and communities where alternative forms of organisation and values appear. In so-called 'communist' states of the present (and past) while capital doesn't (and didn't) rise above the authority and power of the decision-making central authority, obvious social and economic inequities and inequalities appeared, and these gaps necessitated the use of various forms of consent and compliance with the system. However, these propaganda systems differ from Western systems of propaganda because the dictatorial State plays the central role in determining media contents, there is prior censorship and physical repression of dissidents, and the media opinion is much more monolithic.

The PM clearly does not apply to societies where the manufacture of consent isn't necessary for the maintenance of a capitalist order that generates and maintains inequality, inequity, and oppression. The earliest kibbutz of Israel, for example, approximated most closely societies in which the manufacture of consent was subsumed by the high value its members placed upon common goals. Today, peace journalism and communication for conflict resolution provide a different perspective for journalistic practice. Alternative media outlets based on workers' cooperatives and reader-supported news provide information which differs significantly from mainstream contents. For example, Amy Goodman of *Democracy Now!* was the only journalist who covered the first protests of indigenous people against the construction of the pipeline in their lands in North Dakota. She was disciplined through serious flak as she faced riot charges that were, ultimately, rejected by the judge. Alternative forms of communication are also being practiced by indigenous peoples throughout Latin America through community media that promote values of living in common, social justice, mutual understanding and harmony with nature. For example, communication based on the cosmovision and practice of Sumak Kawsay (Good Living) appeals to harmony between individuals, individuals with society, and both with nature as part of the same totality.

## 3. The (Ideal) Democratic and Egalitarian Role of the Media

At a time when grassroots movements and emerging political forces are aiming to intervene in the privatized media sphere and eventually transform it, a necessary step before any meaningful change can be achieved is a better understanding of the functioning and functions of media, i.e. how and why mass media contribute to the (re)production of the existing order with its unjust class structure, its increasing inequalities and inequities, the manifest reality of perpetual war, the structural limitations to rights and freedoms, and the accelerated erosion of democratic institutions that societies are witnessing across the globe.

As so many of the perceptions that people gather of events unfolding from place to place around the world are developed through vicarious experiences manufactured by media systems, their centrality to the configuration of our minds and worldviews cannot be understated. This mediating function permits populations to be in touch with real and fictional universes of reference and to (re)orient their attitudes and behaviours according to symbolic imaginaries and images that serve to mould their cognitive and emotional frameworks. While the PM does not offer a specific method of measuring precisely the quantitative emotional impact media have on the public mind, one underlying assumption is that, even as resistance to media influence is quite common, the systems of propaganda in place have historically tended to play a significant role in achieving in the public both conformity and consensus across sites of social conflict. Accordingly, mass media have traditionally been expected to perform a fundamental democratic function in the control of powerful institutions and in the development of a rational, deliberative and pluralistic public sphere[14]—and certainly more so in today's hyper-mediated societies. In an ideal society, media would, by performing their fourth and fifth-estate function, act as instruments used for citizen empowerment and as the primary citizen watchdog over the ruling powers.

Instead of deploying power over citizens to cultivate their views on issues central to their individual and collective lives, traditions born of the Enlightenment and of the working-class struggle have called for media systems that foster citizens' capacity to engage in critical thinking and contribute consciously to their own social awareness and emancipation. Media systems freed from external pressures and constraints would, thus, feed the very freedom of thought necessary for the democratic functioning of societies. Historically, democratic media have been developed and continue to be employed as useful tools for resistance and social change, especially through the so-called 'new' or alternative media, though they appear mostly ineffective in counteracting the current hegemony held by the mainstream media. A political economy approach suggests that it is not possible to develop a genuine public sphere in conditions established by already existing capitalist influence. Therefore, the possibility of creating democratic and egalitarian media systems lies to a great extent in sweeping transformations that circumvent the influence of the filters identified by the PM, as well as the dismantling of other oppressive social and political structures.

## 4. Propaganda and Power

Next to the ideal conception of media performance, the opposite perspective has been defended and put into practice by state and corporate elites. Already Aristotle developed a systematic analysis of rhetoric as the art of persuasion, arguing that rhetoric had often been used to manipulate emotions, hide crucial facts, and seek to convince the other party of ideas and concepts contrary to their own interests, but which could also be developed into modes of persuasion based upon philosophical knowledge for enlightenment and the common good.[15] In the early sixteenth century, Niccolò Machiavelli understood (and practiced) clearly how power operates as a social relation and depends, to an important extent, on the development of ideological instruments for the control of one group over another.[16]

One of the first intellectuals to develop an in-depth analysis of the role of communication, sociology and 'publicity' in (emerging) industrial societies was Auguste Comte.[17] The French sociologist broke with humanist-Enlightenment social knowledge that conceived progress as human development and happiness as self-realisation to identify them with industrial productivity and security based upon obedience. In the Comtian dystopia, the 'spiritual power' (the media, education, publicists, social science) of the ruling elites would become fundamental so that the societal, 'changes that are inevitable [would] seem desirable to those who will [invariably] suffer the misery, fatigue, illness, and unhappiness that are the unavoidable costs of progress.'[18] Comte's positivist sociology, or 'social physics', sought to abandon the idea of developing knowledge based on ethical principles in favour of allegedly value-free knowledge that would be better suited to defining and organising the nascent industrial society. An exact knowledge of society would allow objective social action, i.e. action adapted to the needs of the economic system for techno-industrial development, irrespective of human values or its convenience for the majority of the population. For Comte, the public mind needed to be readapted to the developing demands of industrial capitalism in a manner that would make the people's brain a mirror image of the external order. Thus, there would no longer be sufficient time or space for men and women to contemplate the possibilities of social change based upon shared human values, but merely the manufactured need for them to attend, against their own interests, to the new capitalist system, its perpetual maintenance, and the new alliance of the industrial bourgeoisie with the Restored monarchies.

In the same vein, the transition to an industrial system that generated great suffering in the US was guided long ago by a State-Corporate nexus promoted by those who Jefferson labelled the *Aristocrats*, i.e. the elite sectors of society that distrust and fear the common people (pejoratively referred to as the 'rabble' or the 'mob') and aim to constrain its power and transfer it to the dominant classes.[19] Needless to say that they succeeded in imposing their designs on the *Democrats*, who had viewed the people as the safest depository of the public interest and the legitimate safeguard of democracy against corruption and abuses of power by government and corporate institutions.[20] Propaganda and miseducation would serve as the principal tools in re-engineering the desires and tastes of a largely rural, self-organised and cooperative population and presenting to it a specific form of industrialisation centred around a system of wage-labour promoted by the *aristocratic* State, bankers, and other corporate leaders.

In the early twentieth century, the Italian militant communist Antonio Gramsci contended that any social order and dominant historical bloc relies not only on violence and coercion, but also on the production of cultural hegemony, which leads to the attachment of the subordinate classes to the worldview and interests of the dominant classes.[21] A very similar line of thought was developed by several founders of media and Communication Studies in the United States, such as Edward Bernays, George Creel, Walter Lippmann, Paul Lazarsfeld and Harold Lasswell: a sophisticated system of propaganda was needed to persuade the masses to comply with the interests of the dominant classes.[22] In turn, their theories provided the intellectual and historical foundation upon which Herman and Chomsky constructed the propaganda model. As is well known, the title of the book in which the authors originally propound the propaganda model, *Manufacturing Consent*, references a passage in Lippmann's classic work on public opinion and propaganda. From a positivist-behaviourist-functionalist perspective, these founding figures offered elaborated theories for alternative terms of the 'engineering of consent', 'crystallisation of public opinion', 'management of the public mind', or 'public relations'. In their view, regarding the governance of society, since there remain many fundamental issues evidently too important and complicated to be left in the hands of what they saw as the ignorant masses, the ruling classes would need effective ideological and axiological tools to maintain their dominance in an increasingly complex world that might otherwise see the widespread emergence of movements toward genuine social justice. Elemental to these conceptual tools were Sigmund Freud's theories of psychoanalysis, which would serve to hasten public consent to new behaviours (e.g. consumerism and indebtedness), to the establishment of repressive policies (e.g. curbing workers' rights) and to decisions the population did not originally desire (e.g. war).

According to Chomsky, the underlying position of the social engineering perspectives is synthesised in the idea that 'propaganda is to a democracy what the bludgeon is to a totalitarian state,'[23] i.e. with the transition from absolutist and dictatorial systems to formally democratic and mass-consumerist societies, the use of violence for the control of the population ceases to be legitimate and thus ideological means of domination must be devised and deployed. The great victory for the masses that saw the establishment of democracy could, in effect, be counteracted by enlarging the distance between the people and their elected representatives through media manipulation. As Machiavelli had already shown, the institutions in charge of exercising power are not usually the great safeguard of the general interests as it is widely claimed, but they, instead, function in favour of special interests.[24] That is, representative institutions today operate to satisfy the interests of the political and state elites, which, in turn, work in symbiosis with the financial and economic elites, who exercise tighter controls over the economy and government policy-making. In Lippmann's words, a 'spectator democracy,'[25] instead of a democracy of informed and engaged participants, has widely developed through the production of redundant misinformation, the development of a culture of fear ('Danger!

Danger!, shouts the dangerous', as Galeano ironised) and an overabundance of trivial entertainment framed within elite perspectives—all of which work in concert to frustrate the efforts of the general public to make full sense of the wider world of which they are members, the position they occupy, and the real possibilities available to those who seek to organise for social change.

With the hijacking of democracy by state and financial powers that started in the 1970s-80s, there is an ongoing trend of upward transference of wealth, intensification of inequality, and reduction of social and human rights. This trend is also clearly reflected in the increasing concentration of mass media ownership, which has come with the demise of an historically egalitarian distribution of media power which any democracy naturally requires for its proper functioning. We can observe the results at present in the appearance of an ever-widening chasm between the majority of the population and the political and economic elites.

These gaps have certainly not gone unnoticed. Alongside the movements of resistance that develop against this kind of domination exerted by the ruling classes there have also been significant responses brought to that resistance by the elites. A paradigmatic example of such a response can be found in the strategic development of an international organisation of neoliberal elites. Founded by David Rockefeller and Zbigniew Brzezinski, the Trilateral Commission produced its first significant analysis of the 'democratic surge' of the 1960s, which provoked, 'a reassertion of the primacy of equality as a goal in social, economic, and political life' and 'a general challenge to existing systems of authority, public and private,' including, hierarchy and wealth. The commission's inaugural analysis outlined in *The Crisis of Democracy* [26] casts the problem as an 'excess of democracy,' which prescribes 'a greater degree of moderation in democracy' both at the social and media levels.[27] This moderation would entail the reaffirmation of anti-democratic principles and the marginalisation of the ideas propagated during the 1960s, which 'only frustrate the purposes of those institutions.'[28] In synthesis, the solution would be to establish 'desirable limits to the indefinite extension of political democracy.'[29] The political and economic powers should, thus, employ their influence to control the type of communication and education provided to citizens so as to reduce their capacity to engage in egalitarian and democratic social change.

According to the propaganda perspective, the threat for the power elites posed by an educated and informed populace can be counteracted without overt coercion that would seem unacceptable in a democracy. This is the reason that media work to manage the fiction of promoting plural debates and even of being critical of established powers. But this strategy allows only for lively debate within very narrow boundaries that do not question the overall oppressive structure of contemporary societies and marginalise critical-emancipatory views. And, very often, debates only reflect the tactical divisions among the different sectors of the elite that want their views to be heard and disseminated (e.g. Watergate).[30] Moreover, spaces for more freedom of thought and critical comment can occasionally be found—even as they tend to be closed in a short period of time—when the media face important contradictions, including widespread citizen mobilisation opposing certain government activities (like launching a preventive war against a defenceless nation) and pressuring for more reliable information.[31]

## 5. Social and Media Structures and Contents

The most effective way to control the media is, thus, not through direct control in fascist or Soviet-style, totalitarian systems. Instead, the media are subject to less visible, market and political mechanisms that tend to filter the information that is *fit to print* in a non-conspiratorial way—even as agency of concrete people is fundamental. This book explains the mechanisms through which structures of wealth and corporate-State power filter media production, exclude many critical journalists, and limit the democratic possibilities of mediated communication. Moreover, it identifies the relations between the structural conditions within which the media operate and the contents they elaborate for both elite and mass consumption.

The systematic analysis proposed by the PM, thus, enables us to assay media systems at two interrelated levels. At one level, the filters allow for identifying the economic, political and ideological conditions of media production in milieus marked by a powerful alliance between capital and political-State forces. These filters and relations explain *why* the media perform a propagandistic role oriented toward the reproduction of the existing capitalist, warmongering socio-political order as well as the tactical changes in the system that are required for its further continuity and expansion. At the same time, the PM allows for the rigorous study of *how* the mainstream media undertake this role through content and discourse analysis of the products they deliver to the audience. We employ this comprehensive approach to systematically expose and explain the central role played by the media in contemporary societies marked by increasing instability, chaos and inequality promoted by the dominant powers at both national and global levels. The collection is, therefore, theoretically informed and empirically grounded.

Moreover, while this volume considers new developments in media environments marked by rapid shifts in technology, it also analyses contemporary case studies of international relevance in a period of worldwide, structural dominance of global media moguls.[32] We begin with the recognition that the advent of the internet—as has occurred during preceding technological revolutions—has been underpinned by techno-centric, techno-utopian, and technocratic discourses that marginalise human values and social relations in their analysis of the significance of new media, propagating the fiction that technological advancements in and of themselves engender social and economic utopias.[33]

Accordingly, the emergence of the internet would naturally lead to an historical period marked by human connectivity, intercultural understanding, democratization, equality, peace, and economic development. However, an historical perspective allows for observing the evolution of the internet from its origins as a collaborative tool for the free exchange of information and ideas within an increasingly commodified space now dominated by corporations in search of profit that together with State forces have established a system of massive surveillance, violation of intimacy, and elite influence. The humanist utopia of fostering cooperation and mutual understanding in platforms free from commercial and State control is, thus, giving way to the development of what increasingly appears to be a dystopia in which members of the *global village* are unified by the centralising forces of the market in close alliance with the State. The internet is, thus, being shaped by the intentional actions of elite actors as online citizen social interactions are managed by the algorithms of digital communications that are far from neutral.[34] A critical, political economy approach to the study of new media is, therefore, required for concerned citizens to understand how the internet is shaped by much larger structures that limit their possibilities to engage in positive socio-political change and contribute to the accumulation of capital and the achievement of self-interested political goals.[35]

At the same time, explorations of the transformative potential inherent in digital media and their uses by citizens in popular movements have become necessary. Such analysis must acknowledge that after decades of propaganda conditioning and the increase of oppressive material realities and living conditions, the majority of social uses made of the internet are oriented toward the continued maintenance of prevailing inequities in power relations between different actors. As Morozov has exposed, one can readily observe important incongruities between the *expected uses* of new communication technologies as posited by commercial, State and pseudo-intellectual agents and their *actual uses*.[36] In this vein, McChesney has noted a contradiction that can be located in the proliferation of techno-communicative capacities for social change and a widely de-politicised and de-mobilised citizenry, whose frustration and anger with the existing social order and their deteriorated living conditions are increasingly susceptible to exploitation by populist neo-authoritarian forces.[37]

However, the emergence of new social and political movements has also demonstrated an important capacity to influence the digital media sphere by combining grassroots organisation efforts and social mobilisation in the public squares and the streets with creative and innovative, communicative production in online social networks—even if notable influence has been temporary and susceptible to being assimilated by the system. Even though elite actors currently maintain hegemony on the internet, digital media can be understood as sites of ongoing struggle and contradiction within the framework of the power relations that affect digital media in processes marked by both control and resistance. It is in this sustained tension between forces and counter-forces at both the social and communicative levels that new digital media can be explored as 'spaces of hope'[38]—digital spaces that ought to work in complementary ways with social action on the ground if real and meaningful change is to be achieved.

We employ the PM not only in the context of the rise of digital media, but within the development of new threats to democracy, to the general public, and even to the human species posed by global war, nuclear weapons, climate change, mass surveillance, the advent of populist neo-authoritarian forces, and other related challenges. Accordingly, we also focus on the media's portrayal of emerging social and political movements developing and aiming to counteract the impositions posed by global capitalism, neoliberalism, and so-called policies of austerity.

The collection we have assembled explores how the PM can be applied to analysis not only of contemporary media markets within the United States, but also more importantly beyond the market and media outlets initially examined by Herman and Chomsky. Uniquely, the book features an important underlying aim, which is to understand the PM's generalisability across varied media systems and products, cultures and national boundaries, including the UK, Germany, Canada, Spain, and Latin America, analysing media performance within their respective context and assessing the utility of the PM to explain observed phenomena peculiar to specific media systems.

## 6. Functions of 'Liberal' Media

While *Manufacturing Consent* was famous after its appearance for featuring Herman and Chomsky's critical analysis of the *New York Times*' coverage of certain key historical events, Todd Gitlin suggests in a recent *Times* obituary (November 21, 2017), where he had been interviewed by a *Times* journalist, that the PM emerges from a Manichean view of the world.[39] In another obituary (November 16, 2017) to Herman, Gitlin observes that, 'the whole approach to [*Manufacturing Consent*] is deeply simplistic,'—as if to intimate that the elegant simplicity of a model disqualifies it from serious consideration.[40] Crucially, Gitlin's claim is noteworthy for its misinterpretation—'if you think that the *New York Times* is *Pravda*, which is ... what [Herman and Chomsky are] saying'—as well as its over-simplification—'then what vocabulary do you have left for Fox News?' What the PM encourages and allows anyone to do is to investigate these important differences between so-called 'liberal' newspapers such as *The New York Times* and (ultra-) 'conservative' outlets such as Fox News. Contrary to Gitlin's claim, the PM holds that even as media systems are oriented toward the reproduction of capitalist societies, they do not function in a homogeneous or monolithic way.

For PM scholars engaged in describing and analysing this system, however, one central function observed of the liberal corporate media is the necessity of acceptable limitation placed upon left-leaning opinion, especially in terms of the dimensions and depth of social transformation. While feigning favour for social equality, the so-called 'liberal media' evade and ignore the need for fundamental transformations in the economic system. (Ultra)conservative commentators at work in corporate news manufacturing entities respond by reproducing audacious (and ironic) claims when they criticise mainstream media as being liberal—i.e. too socially progressive. What continued to fascinate Edward Herman was, 'how the conservative critics of the media who allege that the media are liberal have a tendency to ignore ownership. They sort of pretend that the media are controlled by Dan Rather and Peter Jennings and these people down at the bottom of the power hierarchy in the media.'[41] Relations of ownership continue to be fundamental both in the media and in the broader social system, but they are hardly questioned in the media—whether conservative or liberal.

The liberal media are also attentive to issues of gender and racial equality, but inattentive to representing the interests of the working class.[42] They embrace sexual diversity but promote its commodification and categorical separation from class equality, which is required for the real materialisation of sexual diversity.

In the words of Nancy Fraser, liberal media have adopted the position of 'progressive neoliberalism.'[43] Blithely coexisting in this oxymoronic milieu has been possible in the USA, Frazer notes, because of the late alliance of multiculturalist and pro-diversity social justice movements with the corporate forces of cognitive capitalism (Wall Street, Silicon Valley, Hollywood, the liberal media…)—an alliance which has been mediated by, reproduced, and materialised in the drone-warfare figures of the Clintons and the Obamas. The limitations of such approaches are represented in media support for corporatised versions of feminism. Instead of working to disassemble dominant patriarchal social relations and the inequitable distribution of power, corporate feminism favours women's struggles for power while ignoring the long-existing hierarchical corporate and political structures.

Progressive neoliberalism uses diversity, with its positive connotations, as a strategic marketing tool for creating vacuous images of the corporate cool— the icons of a new 'cosmopolitan' age in which broader societal economic inequality and cultural imperialism continue to rise. While such a self-image of diversity is used as a self-legitimising strategy in terms of its public face and internal rationalisations, the liberal media watchdogs have left militarism and imperial expansion unchecked while uncritically supporting so-called 'free trade agreements' that grant even more power to economic globalist elites. Furthermore, as so-called liberal media have abandoned peace journalism, they have failed to examine the structural and cultural causes of violence as well as contemplate and offer possible solutions for peace-building and conflict resolution across cultures.[44]

Liberal media establish the limits of economic discourse by featuring and promoting neo-Keynesian economists such as Krugman and Stiglitz while paying scant attention to the importance of workers' cooperatives and Marxist economics. There is surely a significant difference between the systematic denial of climate change in ultra-conservative media on one hand and reports of liberal media based on empirical facts and alarming images on the other. But the problem with liberal media is that climate change is scarcely ever connected to capitalism, consumerism, extractivism, or their externalities, so these media ignore or fail to explore possible post-capitalist alternatives. Liberal media, colonised by neoliberal ideology, act as a governor that wields tight control over the definitions of key terms and concepts and, thus, prevents the public from imagining alternative social or economic realities.[45]

Crucially, liberal media ignore important analysis of the oligarchic superstructure of the media system itself and the negative consequences on journalism that critical scholars have already identified.[46] Media owners and advertisers are content to commodify social movements and diversity only insofar as their packaging produces real profits. A range of ideologically acceptable sources is presented to signify plurality and diversity of opinion—so long as they maintain a refusal to question the corporate system itself. Sources and journalists who work outside of the boundaries of this framework are framed as radicals. The ideology of corporate diversity disregards the intersections of class with gender, race and sexuality and leaves little room for critiques of free-market capitalism and for socialism. The possibility of nationalising, for example, key sectors of the economy is hardly considered.

Having fully embraced the neoliberal agenda and its attendant austerity policies, the liberal media display little regard for 'the losers of globalisation', namely, the industrial working class or the exploited workers clinging to a life of slave wages. Instead of analysing in-depth why Trump's fake populist appeals to the working class have been successful and what key roles these appeals have played, the liberal media have turned to ridicule and parody rather than to offer anything of substance to voters seeking potentially viable alternatives. Moreover, perhaps because of the conspicuous absence of a thoughtful alternative narrative, liberal media enable Trump to set the agenda in the public discourse while diverting Main Street attention away from the long-overdue need to enact reforms in the pro-Wall Street political landscape.

Liberal media outlets include alternative reporting by critical journalists and intellectuals which are demanded by critical news consumers. Even as their reports play a fundamentally important role in keeping concerned citizens informed, such journalists represent a minority in newsrooms. Their appearance and effort might influence the development of their public star power (celebrity), but their minority position indicates that they are meaningless tokens used with pre-determined futility to challenge the general pro-corporate approach to reporting in liberal media. Engaging in the charade, liberal media conjure up the necessary illusions of plurality while neglecting potential transformations of the overall corporate structure that establishes the editorial line with its important influence on key decisions. Even as it is always better to feature more diversity, to adopt Marcuse's term, the media use diversity as a form of 'repressive tolerance:'[8] a few drops of alternative views easily diluted by the structural conditions of a vast mass media ocean.

In sum, liberal media function under the conscious or unconscious sway of progressive neoliberal ideology, which serves as a form of self-legitimisation and self-gratification. Perhaps the greatest achievement realised in contemporary liberal media has been the re-engineering of liberalism itself, its positive connotations, and the narrowing, even further, of the range of thinking, speaking, and writing in progressive ways that challenge the hegemonic order. Seeing these alterations will provide readers of this volume insights into the rebranding of the left and how this insidious process has led substantially to the crisis of progressive politics and what this means for the working classes, the marginalised and the dispossessed.

## 7. Organisation of the Book

This volume features four major divisions. Part I addresses the theoretical and methodological dimensions of the Propaganda Model. It begins with an interview with Edward Herman on the model itself, its place within academia, its usefulness to analysts and practitioners across disciplines, and its applicability to understanding both traditional and digital modes of media performance and output. Authors in this section of the volume discuss the functional utility as well as the ongoing marginalisation of the Propaganda Model within academic journalism studies, its consequences to professional practices, and the rationalisations that journalists make in reporting. Authors explore questions of how journalists are socialised within institutional cultures, how Journalism Studies have systematically avoided subjecting journalistic practices to analysis that could expose structural power inequalities. The section extends methodological considerations of the Propaganda Model from corporate media performance to the actual propaganda apparatus that shape the information environment.

Part II reflects on propaganda as a concept and practice within new mediated digital communications systems and interfaces. Authors apply the elements of the Propaganda Model to corporate media as components of a larger System of social and ideological influence and coercion. They examine the characteristics and possibilities of digital activism in connection to physical activism for challenging the prevailing political order, as well as the responses they have received. Power relations, popular resistance, and concepts of democracy are carefully examined in the behaviour and language used by elites to guard the System against attacks.

Part III features applications of the Propaganda Model to forms of media and content not previously analysed within this theoretical framework. It presents analysis and arguments for expanding the scope of the model to include the entertainment industry through the analysis of television, professional sports, Hollywood movies and videogames. Quantitative and qualitative research methods are also presented for analysis of empirical evidence of political content in entertainment products. Authors argue that the PM with a broadened analytical range of media remains to be a strong conceptual tool for explaining and predicting media performance.

Finally, Part IV presents case studies of corporate media and reporting practices as reflections of elite power. Authors investigate the institutional structuring of the media environment, its ideological influences and market constraints, its pro-capitalism and pro-militarism bent, and its performance in moulding, predicting, and controlling the behaviour of the masses. Authors examine how the Propaganda Model helps unfold the contradictions of policies and practices seen in massive public expenditures during periods of forced economic austerity, in imperialist activities cast as humanitarian and human rights interventions, and in the limitations placed on the public debate surrounding nuclear deterrence.

In the concluding section, the editors pull together the plurality of theoretical and empirical studies presented in the collection to measure the validity of the three main hypotheses of the PM. We identify the fundamental dimensions of the PM, the key modifications and expansions that are suggested—such as the inclusion of new filters—and the model's value for conducting research in different geographical contexts and media systems and products. In this conclusion, as in the rest of the book, we seek to contribute to elucidating the functioning and functions of the media in contemporary societies hoping that systematic knowledge about media structures and contents will further promote reflection among media practitioners, students and scholars as well as within broader sectors society. If our analysis is correct and the media engage in the production of diverse forms of symbolic violence, it becomes apparent that broad movements for the deep transformation of the media systems are required—movements which to be successful, of course, require wider transformations in the social and political order, especially regarding its class structure.

## Notes and Bibliography

[1] Edward S. Herman and Noam Chomsky, *Manufacturing Consent: The Political Economy of the Mass Media*. New York: Pantheon, 1988, 2002.

[2] Herman and Chomsky, *Manufacturing Consent*; Edward S. Herman, 'The Propaganda Model: A Retrospective,' *Journalism Studies* 1, no. 1 (2000): 101–112.

3 Joan Pedro, 'The Propaganda Model in the Early 21$^{st}$ Century – Part 1,' *International Journal of Communication* 5, (2011a): 1865–1905; Joan Pedro, 'The Propaganda Model in the Early 21$^{st}$ Century – Part 2,' *International Journal of Communication* 5, (2011b): 1906–1926; Jeffery Klaehn, 'A Critical Review and Assessment of Herman and Chomsky's Propaganda Model,' *European Journal of Communication* 17, no. 2 (2002): 147–182; Klaehn, Jeffery (ed.). *Filtering the News: Essays on Herman and Chomsky's Propaganda Model*. Montreal: Black Rose, 2005; Klaehn, Jeffery (ed.). *The Political Economy of Media and Power*. New York: Peter Lang, 2010; Kiyomi Maedomari-Tokuyama, 'Complicit Amnesia or Willful Blindness? Untold Stories in US and Japanese Media,' in *Under Occupation: Resistance and Struggle in a Militarised Asia-Pacific*. (Eds. Broudy, D., Simpson, P., & Arakaki, M.). Newcastle upon Tyne: Cambridge Scholars Publishing, 2013: 98–125; Tabe Bergman. *The Dutch Media Monopoly*, Amsterdam: VU University Press, 2014; SourceWatch, 'Propaganda Model,' 2011.

4 Andrew Mullen, 'Twenty Years On: The Second-Order Prediction of the Herman-Chomsky Propaganda Model,' *Media, Culture and Society* 32, no. 4 (2010a): 672–690; Andrew Mullen, 'Bringing Power Back In: The Herman-Chomsky Propaganda Model, 1988–2008' in *The Political Economy of the Media and Power*, edited by Jeffery Klaehn. New York: Peter Lang, (2010b): 207–234.

5 Noam Chomsky, *Necessary Illusions: Thought Control in Democratic Societies*. Cambridge, MA: South End Press, 1989; Herman, 'A Retrospective,' Mullen, 'Twenty Years On.'

6 Jeffery Klaehn and Andrew Mullen, 'The Propaganda Model and Sociology: Understanding the Media and Society,' *Synaesthesia: Communication Across Cultures* 1, No. 1 (2010): 10–23; Andrew Mullen and Jeffery Klaehn, 'The Herman-Chomsky Propaganda Model: A Critical Approach to Analyzing Mass Media Behaviour,' *Sociology Compass* 4, No. 4 (2010): 215–229.

7 Natalie Fenton, *Digital Political Radical*. Cambridge, UK: Polity, 2016.

8 See also Collin Sparks, 'Extending and Refining the Propaganda Model,' *Westminster Papers in Communication and Culture*, 4(2) (2007): 68–84.

9 Jeffery Klaehn, *Filtering*; Klaehn, Jeffery (ed.). *Bound by Power: Intended Consequences*. Montreal: Black Rose, 2006; Klaehn, *The Political Economy*.

10 Berry, D., & Theobald, J. (Eds.), *Radical Mass Media Criticism*. London: Black Rose Books, 2006.

11 Ben Bagdikian, *The Media Monopoly*, 2nd ed. (Boston, MA: Beacon Press, 1987); Herbert I. Schiller, *Communication and Cultural Domination* (White Plains, NY: International Arts and Sciences Press, 1976).

12 James Curran and Jean Seaton, *Power Without Responsibility: The Press and Broadcasting in Britain*, 2nd ed. (London: Methuen, 1985).

13 Des Freedman, *The Contradictions of Media Power*. London: Bloomsbury, 2014; Sparks, 'Extending and Refining the Propaganda Model,' *Westminster Papers in Communication and Culture*, 4(2) (2007): 68–84.

14 Jürgen Habermas, *The Structural Transformation of the Public Sphere: An Inquiry into a Category of Bourgeois Society*. Cambridge, UK: Polity, 1989.

15 Aristotle. *Art of Rhetoric*. Cambridge: Harvard University Press, 1926.
16 Niccolò Machiavelli. *The Prince*. Online: The Project Gutenberg, 2006.
17 August Comte. *The Positive Philosophy*. Kitchener, ON: Batoche Books, 2000.
18 Martín-Serrano, Manuel. *Comte, el Padre Negado*. Madrid: Akal, 1976, 145.
19 Thomas Jefferson, 'Times and Methods Change But Not the Rights of Man'. In Mayo, B. (1970). *Jefferson Himself: The Personal Narrative of a Many-Sided American*, pp. 338–339. Charlottesville, VA: University of Virginia Press, 1824, 338.
20 Noam Chomsky, 'Force and Opinion,' *Z Magazine*, July-August, 1991; Chomsky, Noam. *Chomsky on Miseducation*. Maryland: Rowman & Littlefield, 2000; Zinn, Howard. *A People's History of the United States: 1492-Present*. New York: Harper Perennial Modern Classics, 2005.
21 Antonio Gramsci. *Prison Notebooks*. New York: Columbia University Press, 1992.
22 Noam Chomsky, *Media Control: The Spectacular Achievements of Propaganda*. New York: Seven Stories Press, 1997; Herman, 'A Retrospective'; Herman and Chomsky, *Manufacturing*.
23 Chomsky, *Media Control*, 20.
24 Herman and Chomsky, *Manufacturing*.
25 Chomsky, *Media Control*, 17.
26 Michel Crozier, Samuel Huntington and Joji Watanuki. *The Crisis of Democracy. Report on the Governability of Democracies to the Trilateral Commission*. New York: New York University Press, 1975: 61-2, 74.
27 Crozier, Huntington and Watanuki, *The Crisis*, 113.
28 Ibid, 114.
29 Ibid, 115.
30 Herman, 'A Retrospective'; Herman and Chomsky, *Manufacturing Consent*.
31 Des Freedman, *The Contradictions of Media Power*. London: Bloomsbury, 2014; Herman, 'A Retrospective'; Herman and Chomsky, *Manufacturing Consent*.
32 Edward S. Herman and Robert W. McChesney, *The Global Media: The New Missionaries of Corporate Capitalism*. New York: Continuum International, 1997.
33 James Curran, Natalie Fenton and Des Freedman, *Misunderstanding the Internet*. London: Routledge, 2016; Morozov, Evgeny. *The Net Delusion: The Dark Side of Internet Freedom*. New York: PublicAffairs, 2010; Mosco, Vincent. *The Digital Sublime: Myth, Power, and Cyberspace*. Cambridge, MA: MIT Press, 2004.
34 José van Dijck, *The Culture of Connectivity: A Critical History of Social Media*. Oxford: Oxford University Press, 2013.
35 Christian Fuchs and Vincent Mosco, 'Introduction: Marx is Back–The Importance of Marxist Theory and Research for Critical Communication Studies Today.' *tripleC: Communication, Capitalism & Critique*. 10.2 (2012): 127–140.
36 Morozov, *The Net Delusion*.
37 Robert W. McChesney, *Rich Media, Poor Democracy*. Urbana: University of Illinois Press, 1999.

[38] David Harvey, *Spaces of Hope*. Berkeley, CA: University of California Press, 2000.

[39] Todd Gitlin cited in Sam Roberts, (November 21, 2017). 'Edward Herman, 92, critic of U.S. media and foreign policy dies,' *The New York Times*, accessed at https://www.nytimes.com/2017/11/21/obituaries/edward-herman-dead-critic-of-us-media-and-foreign-policy.html.

[40] Todd Gitlin cited in Harrison Smith. (November 16, 2017). 'Edward S. Herman, media critic who co-wrote 'Manufacturing Conset', dies at 92,' *The Washington Post*, accessed at https://www.washingtonpost.com/local/obituaries/edward-s-herman-media-critic-who-co-wrote-manufacturing-consent-dies-at-92/2017/11/16/7cab93ca-cade-11e7-aa96-54417592cf72_story.html?utm_term=.0eb671d9d70b.

[41] Edward Herman, 'The Myth of the Liberal Media: The Propaganda Model of News,' interview by Justin Lewis, Media Education Foundation, 1997, transcript, http://www.mediaed.org/transcripts/Myth-of-The-Liberal-Media-Transcript.pdf.

[42] David Hesmondhalgh, *Media Production*. Milton Keynes, Open University Press, 2005, 11. Hesmondhalgh, David. 'The Media's Failure to Represent the Working Class: Explanations from Media Production and Beyond'. In *The Media and Class*, edited by June Deery and Andrea Press. New York: Routledge, 2017, 21–37.

[43] Nancy Fraser. (January 2, 2017). 'The end of progressive neoliberalism,' *Dissent Magazine*, https://www.dissentmagazine.org/online_articles/progressive-neoliberalism-reactionary-populism-nancy-fraser.

[44] Robert Hackett, 'Is Peace Journalism Possible? Three Frameworks for Assessing Structure and Agency in News Media,' *Conflict & Communication Online*, (5)2, 2006. http://www.cco.regener-online.de/2006_2/pdf/hackett.pdf; Galtung, Johan. 'Peace Journalism and Reporting on the United States,' *Brown Journal of World Affairs*. (22)1, 2015. https://www.brown.edu/initiatives/journal-world-affairs/sites/brown.edu.initiatives.journal-world-affairs/files/private/articles/Galtung.pdf.

[45] Herbert I. Schiller, 'U.S. as Global Overlord: Dumbing down, American-style,' *Le Monde Diplomatique*, August 1999.

[46] Serrano, Pascual, La historia oculta de los grupos de comunicación españoles. Madrid: Foca Investigación, 2010.

# PART I

# Theoretical and Methodological Considerations

CHAPTER 2

# Interview with Edward S. Herman: Ideological Hegemony in Contemporary Societies

Jeffery Klaehn, Joan Pedro-Carañana, Matthew Alford and Yigal Godler

### 1. Has social control always been naturalised?

In modern societies, surely. People with wealth and political and social power want to protect and expand their interests, and this requires command over the means of communication that will allow these privileges to be sustained and grow. The growth of inequality enlarges the need and ability to dominate the flow of information and inculcate proper values.

---

How to cite this book chapter:
Klaehn, J., Pedro-Carañana, J., Alford, M. and Godler, Y. 2018. Interview with Edward S. Herman: Ideological Hegemony in Contemporary Societies. In: Pedro-Carañana, J., Broudy, D. and Klaehn, J. (eds.). *The Propaganda Model Today: Filtering Perception and Awareness.* Pp. 21–24. London: University of Westminster Press. DOI: https://doi.org/10.16997/book27.b. License: CC-BY-NC-ND 4.0

**2. The PM is concerned with the question of how ideological power and material power intersect and reinforce one another and assumes interrelations between state, corporate capitalism and the corporate media. How does academia factor into the equation, with regard to the dialectic between ideology and power?**

Academia is an important institutional segment of information and ideology production and dissemination. As such, it has always been controlled by and in service to elite interests. But because of its functions in teaching and research it is granted a degree of independence beyond that accorded workers in profit-making and governmental bodies. However, this independence is limited by fund-raising imperatives and the pressures to conform to conventional wisdom. As the propaganda model departs from the conventional wisdom that the mainstream media (MSM) are not a part of the power structure but are independent servants of the general public, not the elite, the PM will not be favoured by the general run of academics. Some hard evidence on this point was provided by Andrew Mullen in a 2010 study which reviewed the performance of ten communications and media journals in Europe and North America for the years 1988 through 2007, and which found that only 79 of 3,053 articles (2.6 per cent) even mentioned the PM, a majority of these only citing it without discussion.[1]

**3. Would you characterise the PM as being grounded in a democratic approach specifically oriented toward public relevance?**

Yes. It assumes that high relevance will attach to a model that shows the MSM to be an arm of the elite, and on crucial issues to be serving elite interests rather than those of the general public. On some of these issues, such as 'free trade' agreements (really investor-rights-expansion agreements) polls have regularly showed the public hostile but the MSM dependably supportive of such agreements in accord with elite preferences. The PM helps explain why.

**4. The PM was originally designed to focus on elite, agenda-setting newspapers in the United States. How useful is the model in terms of studying patterns of media performance in non-US countries?**

It should be useful where basic structural conditions fit the model, as that of the United States does. That is, where they have a dominantly private ownership economy, a mainly commercial media depending heavily on advertising, and substantial inequality. Global trends have tended to strengthen the necessary conditions, and the model has been shown to hold quite well in Britain, Germany and other countries.

## 5. How does the model position television and the internet in relation to social and political change?

TV was well entrenched in 1988, and its development was perfectly compatible with the workings of the PM (perhaps most notable was the importance of advertising as the funding source). The growth of the internet seemed to hold forth the promise of a more democratic media, but, as it has evolved, a remarkable and rapid concentration of effective platforms has come into existence, with Google and Facebook on top, capturing a very large fraction of advertising revenue and patronage by the general public.[2] These are not news organisations, and how their monopoly power will eventually work out as regards the journalism function is unclear, but they are very much advertising based, and they have already shown great deference to the wishes of power entities like the CIA, NSA, FBI and State Department. Thus, the likelihood that they will serve the public interest as a democratic force seems extremely slim.

## 6. In what ways can media foster indifference and how does this serve power?

They can foster indifference by systematically failing to provide information and perspectives that address the public's concerns and ultimately showing the public that they are not on the public's side and that what the public may want is not attainable. The MSM do a better job of amusing and otherwise entertaining than dealing credibly with substantive issues. This will help leave the status quo unthreatened.

## 7. How is fear used to achieve ideological hegemony, in your view?

It focuses attention on an approved target, diverting the public from real problems that the elite is not prepared to address. Back in 1904, Thorstein Veblen featured the value of a warlike policy in 'directing the popular interest to other, nobler, institutionally less hazardous matters than the unequal distribution of wealth and of creature comforts.'[3]

### 8. What does the PM have to say about the media coverage of Trump's election campaign and first months as President?

The MSM clearly favoured Hillary Clinton, but many of the elite were pleased with Trump's anti-regulatory and tax 'reform' plans. They also gave Trump a great deal of free media space because his demagoguery resonated with large numbers and playing him up raised media audience sizes. Since the election the MSM have been much more hostile to him and have teamed with the Democrats in creating a Russo-phobic environment, in good part to squelch any attempt on his part to soften policy on confronting Russia and keeping the war party happy and profitable. This all fits nicely into the PM framework.

### 9. How would you reply to a critic who suggests that the PM's explanatory filters are simply an arbitrary list of possible causes for the declawing of media?

The filters are all tied to institutions and processes that experience and evidence show decisively influence media choices, and that are embodied in the five named elements of the PM.

### 10. If 'flak' requires conscious activity, how can it be considered a 'filter'?

Media decisions entail conscious activity, so that the conscious effort of protesters to influence those decisions does not seem incompatible with filtering.

### 11. So, do you think the PM is still a useful tool to analyse the media in the twenty-first century?

Yes, certainly in the short and medium term, with the commercial media and the power of advertising increasing in strength almost everywhere. The longer-term outlook is hazier with the threat of nuclear and climate-based disaster, the growth of inequality and the possibility of severe social disruption and greater centralisation of political power, militarism, and a new era and new forms of fascism.

### Notes and Bibliography

[1] Andrew Mullen, 'Twenty Years On: The Second Order Predictions of the Herman-Chomsky Propaganda Model,' *Media Culture and Society*, 2010.
[2] Jonathan Taplin, *Move Fast and Break Things*, New York: Little Brown, 2017.
[3] Thorstein Veblen, *The Theory of Business Enterprise*, Charles Scribner, 1904, 393.

# CHAPTER 3

# What the Propaganda Model Can Learn from the Sociology of Journalism

Jesse Owen Hearns-Branaman

## 1. Introduction

This chapter will attempt to resolve one of the major conflicts surrounding Herman and Chomsky's Propaganda Model (PM). This conflict is the result of the political-economic focus of the model, achieved by leaving out consideration of journalists themselves. I argue that incorporating sociological theory about journalism, specifically professionalism, self-censorship, and secondary socialisation, will better enhance the PM's explanatory power and help address concerns about its limitations. Such sociological aspects function as 'filters' in a similar way to the five described in the PM and are, in fact, implied heavily in the PM, especially in the sourcing and ideology filters.

This analysis will hearken back to advice given in the 1970s, that 'any sociological analysis of the ways in which the mass media operate as ideological agencies which fails to pay serious attention to the economic determinants framing production is bound to be partial.'[1] We might state the opposite as well, that any political-economic analysis which 'fails to pay serious attention' to sociological aspects of news production is 'partial.' The flow must go both ways; neither approach can offer rounded and robust explanations in isolation.

---

**How to cite this book chapter:**
Hearns-Branaman, J. O. 2018. What the Propaganda Model Can Learn from the Sociology of Journalism. In: Pedro-Carañana, J., Broudy, D. and Klaehn, J. (eds.). *The Propaganda Model Today: Filtering Perception and Awareness.* Pp. 25–36. London: University of Westminster Press. DOI: https://doi.org/10.16997/book27.c. License: CC-BY-NC-ND 4.0

Historically speaking, 'industry self-regulation assumed the form of professional journalism' in the early twentieth century, relying on the notion that 'journalists would learn to sublimate their own values' so that the audience 'could trust what they read and not worry about who owned or worked on the newspaper,' and thus 'press concentration would become a moot issue.'[2] Professional ethical standards for journalists are intimately tied to the political economy of the press, acting as a smoke screen for the economic interests of the owners. Professionalism and journalistic socialisation are therefore the consequences of media concentration, not the cures for it, and must be viewed in this context, not as a separate, neutral element serving only to give 'objective' news. McChesney's main points to support this are very PM-related; sourcing patterns and the reliance on official sources, the 'avoidance of contextualisation' outside of the elite debate on issues, and the avoidance of critical examination of big businesses, instead focusing on entertainment, crime, and government.[3]

Before going more fully into professionalism and socialisation, I will describe the ways in which ambiguity about the role of journalists in political-economic analysis such as the PM occurs. I will then elaborate on research into professionalism and secondary socialisation. This will then be applied to critiques that the PM is a 'conspiracy theory' in order to show how such sociological research will bolster, not refute, the findings of the PM and related political-economic research.

## 2. PM and Journalists

One point of criticism for the PM comes from its lack of consideration of the sociology of journalists.[4] That is to say, its analysis is of the political-economic roots of news media organisations and the subsequent texts produced, not the practices of journalists. As Klaehn notes, the PM 'is not concerned to analyse practical, organisational, or mundane aspects of newsroom work' because 'deliberate intent ('conspiracy') and unconscious hegemony ('professional ideology') are for the most part unknowable and unmeasurable.'[5] The purpose of the PM is to measure what can be measured, the texts the journalists write, because it is impossible to differentiate between the conscious and unconscious drives behind journalists' activities. It also extends from Chomsky's own perspective on the role of journalists within the news media industry: 'this analysis tends to downplay the role of individuals: they're just replaceable parts.'[6] The argument is, therefore, that it is a waste of time to analyse these 'replaceable parts' of a machine. The reason the machine was made, what the machine makes, the political and economic context in which the machine operates, all of these elements are what *can* and *should* be examined.

This exclusion leads to several different criticisms. Comeforo, for example, argues that the PM has two incompatible points of view when describing the activeness and agency of journalists. It casts them as being *too active* when in fact they are *passive*.[7] Journalistic routines, the hierarchy of the newsroom and influence of the editor, the news company's organisational culture, the sourcing patterns for their information, and other elements outside of the journalists' control are far more important and influential than active subversion by or the inherent subjectivity of the journalists. At the same time, Comeforo argues that the PM casts them as *too passive* when in fact they are often very active and have a large measure of control. This includes journalists' maintenance of relationships with politicians and suppression of stories to maintain these relationships, and also examples of the CIA infiltrating newsrooms to actively spread disinformation.[8]

This duality is, however, not a problem only of the PM itself but of Journalism Studies in general, and perhaps is an underlying dialectic that grounds journalism. Blumler and Gurevitch previously noted as much, that journalists have control over some areas and not others and thereby have to negotiate and adapt depending on the circumstances.[9] Journalists can be very active about, for example, finding 'alternative' sources of information, or can passively relay the same old elite perspectives, as long as it remains in the realm of legitimate debate about that specific topic.

Responding to a similar critique made by Lang and Lang,[10] Herman and Chomsky reply:

> We believe that our focus on media performance as opposed to journalists' thoughts and practices is fully justified. If a reporter deals entirely differently with an election supported by his or her government and one opposed by it, we do not feel that it is urgent to try to find out what goes on in that reporter's (or the editor's) head in following this dichotomous agenda; those facts speak for themselves and the reporter's explanations and rationalisations are of far lesser interest.[11]

However, as Thompson points out, 'there is plenty of empirical evidence from sociological studies of media organisations available to support the proposition that the various filters can and do shape news content.'[12] The PM's study itself only uses a mixed qualitative and quantitative content analysis to produce evidence of the different treatment that American media gives to the government's official enemies, and this data could not have been gathered sociologically.

It is, thus, not fair to hastily dismiss the findings of the PM because they did not conduct interviews with journalists or do focus groups or use other sociological methods. That was simply not the purpose of the PM. However, my argument is that that the inclusion of such sociological research on news media professionals would not refute the PM and can, in fact, greatly assist in the robustness of the model.

Counter to Herman and Chomsky's rejection of sociological methods,[13] I argue that including research gathered through interviews with journalists and ethnographic work does not simply give the journalists' 'rationalisations' for their work.

This is a very narrow interpretation of what vigorous sociological research does. Much like the content analysis of the original PM, the surface-level expressions of these professionals cannot be taken at face value. As this discourse is a result of the system in which the journalists operate, their talk must be viewed in this way.

Linguists, such as Potter and Wetherell, argue that consistency in a discourse could indicate the same 'function' of language in that 'two people may put their discourse together in the same way because they are **doing the same thing with it.**'[14] Similarly, Fairclough argues that 'institutions construct their ideological and discoursal subjects' in that 'they impose ideological and discoursal constraints upon them as a condition for qualifying them as subjects.'[15] Thus, we can say that if journalists give a more or less unified take on certain issues this does not mean that they all agree or 'believe' this position is true; it means that they are required, as members of the institution of journalism, to produce the same discourse. Thus, the 'rationalisations' their discourse provides are not useless; they indicate the ways in which they have been socialised into the journalistic discourse. If a journalist says, for example, that they are not under the influence of their owners or advertisers, this assertion does not necessarily mean that they are not under such influence but that, instead, admitting to that influence is not permissible within journalistic discourse.

Others have argued that 'it is social and economic interests which are embodied by the institutions created and operated by real humans which provide the link between the economic and the ideological.'[16] This link is missing from the PM and inclusion of the talk of professionals embedded in the journalistic discourse can only further enlighten how the political economy and ideology of the news media is linked.

## 3. Journalistic Professionalism

Journalism as a profession is a notion that is not covered well in the PM. Yet research about professionalism in general gives a lot of support to PM's thesis. Professionalism has a conflicting relationship with 'democracy' because it involves 'formal' or 'elite' knowledge which is 'not open to the active participation of all' and could be 'seen as a threat to democracy.'[17] While this is talking about professions in general, it seems even more suitable to journalism. Medical professionals, for example, possess 'formal' and 'elite' knowledge, yet they are not considered to be an integral aspect of democratic forms of governance. Journalism, on the other hand, is intimately connected with democratic processes to a degree surpassing all other professions, except perhaps politics and public service jobs to the extent that they can be considered professions.

Additionally, a major aspect of the growth of professions was 'its traditional connotations of disinterested dedication and learning provided political legitimation.'[18] Such 'disinterested dedication' is also a hallmark of professional journalism, implicating such important journalistic concepts of ethical behaviour, objectivity and a corresponding lack of subjectivity, and standardised routines and practices.

Speaking of journalism as a profession, Deuze argues that 'ideology can be seen as a system of beliefs characteristic of a particular group, including – but not limited to – the general process of the production of meanings and ideas (within that group).'[19] It is thus 'possible to speak of a dominant occupational ideology of journalism,' one that is still open to interpretation and different usage, but it still based on 'a collection of values, strategies and formal codes' which are 'shared most widely' in the journalistic field.[20] The critique of the PM as a conspiracy theory, as will be discussed later, would then need to apply to *all* such professions. While fringe groups would see the medical field as a conspiracy, such a critique is not sustainable. Doctors, surgeons, nurses, etc., certainly have a 'system of beliefs' and hopefully have a 'disinterested dedication' to their profession. Medical professionals are part of an institutional structure that operates more or less uniformly and with the same results in the same way as journalism, thus describing the political-economic structure of journalism in such a manner is highly consistent with that of other professions.

Bourdieu criticised political-economic approaches in general, arguing that 'to understand what happens in journalism, it is not sufficient to know who finances the publications, who the advertisers are, who pays for the advertising [...] and so on,'[21] such as what the PM does. He argues that 'what is produced in the world of journalism cannot be understood unless one conceptualises this microcosm as such and endeavours to understand the effects that the people engaged in this microcosm exert on one another,'[22] that is, the interactions within the field of journalism. The latter does not disprove the former, it can only help support it. An 'individual's predispositions, assumptions, judgements, and behaviours are the result of a long-term process of socialisation, most importantly in the family, and secondarily, via primary, secondary, and professional education.'[23] Hand in hand with professionalism is the secondary process of socialisation that occurs when journalists enter the profession, a process that will now be discussed in further detail.

## 4. Socialisation of Journalists

> [M]ost of the people at the [*New York*] *Times* who make it to be correspondent or editor or whatever tend to be either very obedient or very cynical. The obedient ones have adapted – they've internalized the values and believe what they're saying.[24]

While primary socialisation takes place during childhood, at home with input from parents and immediate family, secondary socialisation occurs outside the first close-knit group we spend time with.[25] This includes, initially, school and other social activities. When we enter the workplace, secondary socialisation continues to occur throughout our careers.

As Shoemaker and Reese note, this happens through a process of filtering out people unsuitable for the job: 'Because they strive to be taken seriously, reporters are vulnerable to pressure to conform. If they start saying things that diverge from the common wisdom, they are noticed. Editors may doubt their credibility and wonder if they can be trusted – it's safer to hew to the common wisdom.'[26] Hiring, firing, promotions, demotions, prestigious and non-prestigious assignments, all of these factors contribute to the secondary socialisation of journalists, as well as all other professions.

One example of socialisation comes from Gans' study conducted via newsroom ethnography, which examined television and magazine journalism in the 1970s.[27] He argues this is expressed through self-censorship or 'anticipatory avoidance' in which 'journalists are restrained from straying into subjects and ideas that could generate pressure, even if their own inclinations, as professionals or individuals, do not often encourage them to stray in the first place.'[28] These rules for performance are learnt both through education and on the job, although the latter is ultimately more important.

This occurs at two levels, conscious and unconscious. While journalists define self-censorship as 'the conscious response to anticipated pressure from non-journalists,' it can also be 'unconscious, in which case journalists may not be aware they are responding to pressure.'[29] The consequence of this is, however, that it becomes hard for researchers to distinguish between conscious and unconscious choices made by media professionals, and it is nearly impossible for media professionals themselves to distinguish, let alone relay that information to researchers. For example, '[s]urrender to pressure is viewed as an act of cowardice and a sign of powerlessness, and those who must surrender are loath to discuss it.'[30] Even if a journalist is consciously bowing to pressure, they are unlikely to reveal it to researchers.

This indicates why Herman and Chomsky are reluctant to consider primary sociological research on journalists, due to the limits of certain versions of that method into gaining insight into journalists' thoughts and performance. Yet they still give plenty of hypothetical examples of socialisation and self-censorship and implicitly rely on it to deal with the notion of individual journalists' performance.

For example, the 'learned and understood limits of subject matter, tone, balance and the like' are what teach journalists how to self-censor.[31] As Chomsky notes, 'The general subservience of the media to the state propaganda system does not result from direct government order, threats or coercion, centralized decisions, and other devices characteristic of totalitarian states, but from a complex interplay of more subtle factors.'[32] These 'subtle factors' include secondary socialisation, professionalism, and self-censorship, as discussed above. Chomsky gives a detailed hypothetical example of this:

> Suppose that as a reporter you start going outside of vested interests. You will find, first of all, that the level of evidence that's required is far higher. You don't need verification when you go to vested interests, they're self-verifying. Like, if you report an atrocity carried out by guerrillas, all you need is one hearsay witness. You talk about torture carried out by an American military officer, you're going to need videotapes. […] if a journalist quoted an unnamed 'high U.S. government official,' that suffices as evidence. What if they were to quote some dissident, or some official from a foreign government that's an enemy? Well, they'd have to start digging, and backing it up, and the reporter would have to have mountains of evidence, and expect to pick up a ton of flack, and maybe lose their job, and so on. With factors of that kind, it's predictable which way they're going to go.[33]

We, thus, can see the direct connection between socialisation via 'flak' and the potential to 'lose their job' and the effect of those processes on the selection of sources, framing of events, and the sphere of legitimate consensus.

Chomsky often connects this process to ideological control in society in general and the specific expression of that on journalism

> [I]f you're, say, a young person in college, or in journalism, or for that matter a fourth grader, and you have too much of an independent mind, there's a whole variety of devices that will be used to deflect you from that error – and that if you can't be controlled, to marginalize or just eliminate you […] If you're a young journalist and you're pursing stories that the people at the managerial level above you understand, either intuitively or explicitly, are not to be pursued, you can be sent off to work at the Police Desk, and advised that you don't have 'proper standards of objectivity' […][34]

The institutional necessity for professionalism and the practice of socialisation of journalists can explain why the 'media' perform the way they do. This provides a better basis for a defence of the PM against attacks that it is a conspiracy theory.

## 5. Institutional Ideology vs Conspiracy Theory

As Herman puts it, the PM is 'a model of media *behaviour and performance*, not of media effects,'[35] yet this metonymic use of 'media' creates additional ambiguities. Removing the separation between journalists as individuals and journalists as inculcated in the news media system is necessary for the PM's fundamental thesis. The result, however, leaves the PM open to charges that it is nothing more than a conspiracy theory. How can an international system which consists of millions of individuals, the 'media,' act in a consistent manner without being directed by a single hand?

This leads to another critique of the PM and why, unfairly, it is difficult for it to be accepted in the mainstream debates about media performance. Lester points out that many institutions in the USA 'teach that the press and news media generally are our check on the abuses of power, assuring a continuing adversarial relationship between the governed and the governors and between the "little guy" [...] and big business.'[36] Because the PM takes a position highly contrary to this, it automatically faces an uphill battle to make its point. If the media is not free and independent, it must mean that there is a conspiracy between the government, media organisations, and journalists for some ulterior motive.

Chomsky, of course strongly refutes this: 'With equal logic, one could argue that an analyst of General Motors who concludes that its managers try to maximize profits (instead of selflessly labouring to satisfy the needs of the public) is adopting a conspiracy theory.'[37] The news media live and die by remaining profitable, more so now than in the 1980s when the PM was conceived. As the PM highlights the ways in which this effort to remain profitable leads to practices which structurally filter out a lot of potential media content, this is conceptually the same as the way General Motors or any other company would make efforts to increase their profitability.

Corner responds to Chomsky's defence, arguing that 'few managers at General Motors would find it at all surprising or disturbing that their corporate system worked with such an imperative, however much they might want to understate the social harm caused,' while 'media managers, editors and journalists will strongly disagree that their efforts are essentially in the service of the rich and powerful and systematically against democratic values.'[38] In other words, Corner is stating that the PM assumes there must be a great deal of self-delusion amongst news media professionals for them not to view their business the same way car manufacturers do so. There must be many mechanisms in place to fool journalists into doing the opposite of what they want to do. A criticism of Corner's criticism of Chomsky's defence would be that it does not really matter if news media professionals agree or disagree with a certain characterisation of their job, the evidence points that way and so it is that way we must follow. As discussed above, their talk indicates more their expression of an institutional discourse than their 'real' thoughts and feelings.

A better example to counter Corner and defend the PM would be to point out that, for example, assembly-line workers at a factory would not talk about their work contributing to climate change and pollution. They simply focus on their next task at hand and not on the larger damage done to the environment from the carbon emissions their vehicles produce. Similarly, potential managers at a car company who worried about such issues would never successfully climb to the top of the business ladder; their concerns for the environment over the profitability of the company would preclude them from being promoted over those without such qualms. In a similar way, the socialisation processes at news organisations filter out troublesome journalists who never rise to being editors.

Herman notes that the PM 'suggest[s] that the mainstream media, as elite institutions, commonly frame news and allow debate only within the parameters of elite perspectives.'[39] However, Herman does not elaborate on how 'media,' an abstract noun implicating not just 'institutions' but those who work within those institutions, frame events. To say that 'media frame news' is conceptually the same as saying 'plants grow' or 'the sun shines'? Why not say that 'journalists frame news'? That would implicate specific journalistic actors and imbue them alone with the power to frame, and thus be highly inaccurate. Plants grow because those plants that do not grow die and thus cannot perpetuate their genome; journalists that do not frame events 'within the parameters of elite perspectives' are eventually socialised out of journalism and, thus, are no longer journalists. Asserting the position that 'media frame news' seems to remove the actions of the journalists themselves when those institutionally approved actions are what make them part of the mainstream media.

## 6. Conclusion

This chapter has examined the weaknesses within the PM for dealing with the performance of individual journalists. The inclusion of sociological research on journalists is fully compatible with the PM's argument. Unlike others' critiques, examining the discourse of journalists themselves does not refute the PM; in fact, it can more fully explain media performance. Journalists have to adhere to professional standards and face secondary socialisation when they enter the workplace. This, perhaps, gives the appearance of an ugly and anti-normative 'conspiracy,' yet from many different angles, this is the basic institutional functioning of the news media.

> I do not wish to present the newspaper industry as deliberately and cynically working [...] to disseminate official ideology for commercial gain; to mystify the actions and the motive of government and industry; and to discredit opponents and silence the majority. Though these are indeed the goals and effects of the media, they need not be consciously formulated and strategically planned, because their implementation takes place automatically.[40]

Even critical linguists such as Fowler make this basic argument. It is not a matter of conspiracy among journalists, editors, ownership, and outside businesses to present non-capitalist ideas in an inevitably negative light; it is the way the system has been designed by those capitalist media owners to legitimate capitalism, again done through professionalism and secondary socialisation.

Future research from both political-economic and sociological or linguistic perspectives should better incorporate each other's perspectives. For example, my earlier research involved linguistic analysis of media texts to show how foreign policy positions are replicated in the coverage of the Iran nuclear 'crisis'.[41] This involved an analysis of the transitivity of verbs used by American, British, Iranian, and Chinese news texts to illustrate how the PM's concept of 'official enemies,' a notion inculcated in the socialisation of journalists, are expressed. For example:

> American and British media [the *New York Times* and the *Guardian*] de-emphasize Western (United States, Israel, European Union) material actions while strongly emphasizing Iranian ones, while *Fars* and the *Tehran Times* underplay Iran's material actions but strongly emphasize those of Western countries.[42]

Additionally, my study on applying the PM to Chinese media included sociological research on journalists in China.[43] This helped show how differing political-economic structures are expressed in the discourse of the respective journalists.

By better incorporating a diversity of research, political-economic studies in line with the PM will further bolster their important critical implications. Sociological and linguistic research, similarly, need to feature a firmer political-economic grounding from studies like the PM. This will help give an increased critical edge by connecting how those media structures affect the discourse and practice of journalists.

## Notes and Bibliography

[1] Peter Golding and Graham Murdock, 'Ideology and the mass media: The question of determination,' in eds. Michèle Barrett et al, *Ideology and Cultural Production* Beckenham: Croon Helm, 1979, 198

[2] Robert McChesney, *The Problem of the Media*, New York: *Monthly Review*, 2004, 64

[3] McChesney, *Problem of the Media*, 67–77

[4] Kristin Comeforo, 'Review Essay: *Manufacturing Consent: The Political Economy of the Mass Media*,' *Global Media and Communication* 6(2) (2010); John Corner, 'The Model in Question: A response to Klaehn on Herman and Chomsky,' *European Journal of Communication*, 18 (2003); Jesse Owen Hearns-Branaman, 'A Political Economy of News Media in the People's Republic of China: Manufacturing Harmony?', *Westminster Papers in Communication and Culture* 6(2) (2009); Jesse Owen Hearns-Branaman, *The Political Economy of News in China: Manufacturing Harmony*, Lanham, MD: Lexington, 2014

[5] Jeffery Klaehn, 'A Critical Review and Assessment of Herman and Chomsky's "Propaganda Model,"' *European Journal of Communication*, 17 (2002), 149
[6] Noam Chomsky, *Understanding Power*, eds. Peter R. Mitchell and John Schoeffel, New York: The New Press, 2002, 26
[7] Comeforo, 'Review Essay'
[8] Ibid
[9] Jay Blumler & Michael Gurevitch, *The Crisis of Public Communication*, New York: Routledge, 1995
[10] Kurt Lang and Gladys Engel Lang, 'Noam Chomsky and the Manufacture of Consent for American Foreign Policy,' *Political Communication* 21(1) (2004)
[11] Edward S. Herman and Noam Chomsky, 'Reply to Kurt and Gladys Engel Lang,' *Political Communication*, 21(1) (2004), 106
[12] Peter A. Thompson, 'Market Manipulation?: Applying the Propaganda Model to Financial Media Reporting,' *Westminster Papers in Communication and Culture* 6(2) (2009), 76.
[13] Herman and Chomsky, 'Reply'
[14] Jonathan Potter and Margaret Wetherell, *Discourse and Social Psychology: Beyond Attitudes and Behaviour* (London: Sage, 1987)
[15] Norman Fairclough, *Media Discourse*, London, Arnold, 1995, 39
[16] David Miller and William Dinan, *A Century of Spin*, London: Pluto, 2008, 173
[17] Eliot L. Freidson, *Professional Powers*, London: University of Chicago, 1986, 4–5
[18] Freidson, *Professional Powers*, 33
[19] Mark Deuze, 'What is Journalism?: Professional Identity and Ideology of Journalists Reconsidered,' *Journalism* 6(4) (2005), 445
[20] Ibid, 445
[21] Pierre Bourdieu, 'The Political Field, the Social Science Field, and the Journalistic Field,' in eds. Rodney Benson and Erik Neveu, *Bourdieu and the Journalistic Field*, (Cambridge: Polity, 1995 [2005]), 33
[22] Ibid, 33
[23] Rodney Benson and Erik Neveu, 'Introduction: Field theory as a Work in Progress,' in eds. Rodney Benson and Erik Neveu, *Bourdieu and the Journalistic Field*, Cambridge, Polity, 2005, 3
[24] Chomsky, *Understanding Power*, 114
[25] Jesse Owen Hearns-Branaman, 'Journalistic Professionalism as Indirect Control and Fetishistic Disavowal.' *Journalism* 15(1) (2014)
[26] Pamela J. Shoemaker and Stephen D. Reese, *Mediating the Message*, 2nd ed, London: Longman, 1996, 170
[27] Herbert J. Gans, *Deciding What's News*, (Evanston, IL: Northwestern University, 1979 [2004])
[28] Ibid, 276
[29] Ibid, 251

30 Ibid, 251
31 Edward S. Herman and Noam Chomsky, *The Washington Connection and Third World Fascism*, Montreal, Black Rose Books, 1979, 78
32 Noam Chomsky, *Towards a New Cold War*, London, Sinclair Brown, 1982, 14
33 Chomsky, *Understanding Power*, 25–26
34 Ibid, 237–238
35 Edward S. Herman, 'The Propaganda Model: A Retrospective,' *Journalism Studies* 1(1) (2000), 103
36 Elli Lester, 'Manufactured Silence and the Politics of Media Research: A Consideration of the "Propaganda Model",' *Journal of Communication Inquiry* 16(1) (1992): 46
37 Chomsky, *New Cold War*, 94
38 Corner, 'The Model in Question', 372
39 Herman, 'A Retrospective', 103
40 Roger Fowler, *Language in the News*, London, Routledge, 1991, 24
41 Jesse Owen Hearns-Branaman, 'Official Enemies in Commercial and Soft Power Media,' *Journalism Studies (18)4* (2017)
42 Hearns-Branaman, 'Official Enemies', 464
43 Hearns-Branaman, *Manufacturing Harmony*

CHAPTER 4

# Journalism Studies' Systematic Pursuit of Irrelevance: How Research Emphases Sabotage Critiques of Corporate-Run News Media

Yigal Godler

## 1. Introduction

A sociological truism is that institutional structure always has some social consequences. Consider the following examples of institutional structure: a kibbutz (or a collective) organises social life in some ways and not in others, as does a business enterprise. On the assumption that the social sciences seek to understand why society is organised in some ways and not in others, social scientists will have to at least consider the explanatory potential of some institutional structures. Since empirical questions cannot be prejudged, perhaps no institutional explanation will be up to the task of explaining this or that social phenomenon. However, assuming that the social sciences truly seek to understand social phenomena, one would not expect social scientists to refuse out-of-hand to even consider institutional structures as potential explanations for social phenomena. And yet some social scientific fields seem to do just that.

---

How to cite this book chapter:
Godler, Y. 2018. Journalism Studies' Systematic Pursuit of Irrelevance: How Research Emphases Sabotage Critiques of Corporate-Run News Media. In: Pedro-Carañana, J., Broudy, D. and Klaehn, J. (eds.). *The Propaganda Model Today: Filtering Perception and Awareness*. Pp. 37–51. London: University of Westminster Press. DOI: https://doi.org/10.16997/book27.d. License: CC-BY-NC-ND 4.0

This chapter deals with one such case. It is the case of a field known as Communication Studies (and more specifically, the subfield of Journalism Studies). Although scholars of communication are no strangers to the institutional explanation of media phenomena, they often exhibit the curious tendency of playing down or resisting such explanations. Interestingly, this resistance does not appear only before these scholars attempt empirical research into aspects of media behaviour but also after the empirical research has been carried out (usually, though not always, by others)[1] and has yielded confirmatory findings.

An illuminating case of communication scholars' resistance to institutional explanations has been previously studied. This is the case of the reaction of mainstream communication scholars to Edward Herman and Noam Chomsky's work on media behaviour.[2] Herman and Chomsky offered a formal institutional explanation for the behaviour of the American elite media, known as the Propaganda Model (PM). They hypothesised that the corporate ownership, size and profit orientation of the mainstream media, as well as their dependence on advertisers' money and their reliance on cost-free official sources (alongside pro-establishment experts), would produce a systematic pro-business and pro-government bias in media coverage, when crucial interests of these institutions were at stake. Herman and Chomsky then proceeded to test their hypothesis by analysing the coverage of paired examples of near-identical events with varying consequences for business and government interests, and by assessing the range of debate in the media on several key issues. The media were conclusively found to serve business and government interests when these could be threatened by certain angles and information (which were accordingly excluded from media coverage, played down or distorted).

Mainstream communication scholars reacted to these conclusions with suspicion and hostility. Whereas some of them acknowledged that the specific cases presented by Herman and Chomsky made telling points,[3] they falsely attributed to Herman and Chomsky a series of claims they have never made and committed other logical fallacies.[4] However, evidence suggests that these logical fallacies have also been overlooked by scholars in subsequent mainstream communications studies.[5] The implications of overlooking these logical fallacies for theory and empirical research constitute the story unfolded in the present chapter.

This chapter begins by dissecting research which falsely presented itself as having a bearing on the validity of Herman and Chomsky's work. Next, it follows the trail of scholarly citations to prominent examples of contemporary empirical and theoretical work and analyses its explanatory and analytical validity. These exercises will hopefully illuminate the significance of the documented scholarly practices for the course taken by the discipline of Journalism Studies (a subfield of Communication Studies).

## 2. Challenging the PM or Simply Bracketing the Business Institution?

An influential study by Thomas E. Patterson and Wolfgang Donsbach sought to document and account for partisan bias in the news. To do so, the authors administered questionnaires to journalists across five countries (United States, Great Britain, Germany, Italy and Sweden).[6] These questionnaires were no regular survey. Rather, they were intended as a quasi-experiment of partisan bias. It should be noted that despite the radical differences between their methodology and that of Herman and Chomsky, Patterson and Donsbach believed their findings had a bearing on the validity of Herman and Chomsky's study, including the PM. Indeed, as will be demonstrated in the following text, Patterson and Donsbach were convinced that the PM was belied by their (i.e. Patterson and Donsbach's) empirical work.

The questionnaires in Patterson and Donsbach's study were so constructed as to detect journalists' political/ideological views, as well as to simulate a series of news decisions, such as the determination whether a particular story was newsworthy, what would be an appropriate headline for it and what would be a fitting visual. Once the questionnaires were completed, the scholars were in a position to test correlations between journalists' ideological views and their mock news decisions. Such a correlation was found. On the basis of this data, Patterson and Donsbach concluded that journalists' ideological views produce a moderate bias in news decisions, with some variations between countries.

Crucially, Patterson and Donsbach have contrasted their findings against previous studies of partisan bias. One of the studies mentioned is Herman and Chomsky's *Manufacturing Consent*. As Patterson and Donsbach conclude:

> Gans's perspective [that most journalists hold 'progressive' but 'safe' views]… seems to be more convincing than the claim that journalists serve conservative interests of state and established elites (Herman and Chomsky, 1988). This claim may have some validity when applied to news organisations and their owners but cannot be easily reconciled with the evidence presented here. Journalists are not radicals, but neither are they conservatives. They are best described as a mainstream group with liberal tendencies. Indeed, journalists can act as a partisan counterbalance to the news organisations in which they work (465).

But Herman and Chomsky paid virtually no attention to journalists' individual political preferences, as their view was indeed much closer to the idea that 'news organisations' qua institutions and corporate 'owners' were the genesis of the bias. Herman and Chomsky's study was carried out on the assumption that in a media system which is business-run, the personal views of journalists are causally irrelevant to the nature of media behaviour when crucial systemic or major corporate interests are at stake, as journalists do not control the media, either individually or collectively. However, for Patterson and Donsbach to acknowledge this crucial distinction between the two studies would be to acknowledge the inexorable power dynamic that obtains between the *business* of news and the *industry* of news,[7] whereby business necessarily constrains journalism's truth-seeking potential and its capacity to engage the public in politics. But this would immediately undermine the significance of Patterson and Donsbach's focus on journalists' individual political views. As it would become self-evident that their research design omits the most crucial implications of the business control over journalism.[8] Although Patterson and Donsbach do mention the business element in passing, they do not regard it as an inexorably biasing force. The reader should recall Patterson and Donsbach's claim that 'journalists can act as a partisan counterbalance to the news organisations in which they work.'

In essence, the quasi-experimental design of Patterson and Donsbach's study creates a reality which is unheard of in the mainstream corporate media. That is, a reality of journalists making news decisions under conditions of perfect autonomy from newsroom pressures and constraints. Moreover, even if we ignore this crucial point for the sake of argument, and we assume that journalists' decisions in Patterson and Donsbach's study were indeed reflective of their actual news decisions and consistent with the ultimate decisions made by editors in real existing news organisations, that still wouldn't salvage their case for a causal nexus between journalists' attitudes and news content. And for good reason. For their case to follow, the possibility that journalists' mock decisions correspond to their actual decisions simply because these journalists were more likely than average to accept the institutional dictates of news organisations, would need to be eliminated.[9]

But, perhaps, the fact that Patterson and Donsbach failed to demonstrate the actual explanatory power of journalists' attitudes vis-á-vis news content does not mean such a demonstration is impossible. As senior researchers David Weaver and Cleveland Wilhoit point out '[...] it would be a mistake to think that individual journalists have little freedom to select and shape news stories, or to change the nature of the news organisations for which they work.'[10] Thus, we would need to look at other attempts to demonstrate the causal nexus between journalists' attitudes and news content.

## 3. Contemporary Research

### 3.1 Role Conceptions as Causal Factors

The debate about the causal nexus between journalists' individual attitudes and news content is often cast in the language of 'role conceptions.'[11] Role conceptions are essentially purported social goals which journalists ascribe to themselves in their capacity as journalists, such as informing the public, serving as democracy's watchdog, entertaining the public, etc.[12] Consider how one of the scholarly works citing Patterson and Donsbach – without pointing to the problems addressed in the previous section – by van Dalen, de Vreese and Albaek, makes the case for the explanatory power of role conceptions in a leading periodical of journalism studies, *Journalism: Theory, Practice and Criticism*:[13]

> Studies of cross-national role conception variation presumes [sic] that variation in role conceptions causes variation in content[...] while cross-national studies of content speculate that content variation is caused by variation in role conceptions [....][14]

Thus, at issue is what causes news content to be the way it is. This has obviously been a long-standing concern of media and journalism studies.[15] Since one major product of the media, on which the public relies for trustworthy information, is the news, it is a high-priority task for enlightened and democratically-oriented scholarship to illuminate the mechanisms behind news products.

Hence, the authors identify an empirical lacuna in the literature which they set out to address: '[...]the study of role conceptions by means of journalism surveys and the study of news content by means of content analysis are generally not combined'.[16] Although Patterson and Donsbach are viewed as one of the 'exceptions'[17] to this disconnect between journalism surveys and content analyses, the reader should recall, once again, that actual news content did not figure at all in Patterson and Donsbach's study. Still, it is worth pondering the question of what the significance would be of combining journalism surveys data and content analysis. In my discussion of Patterson and Donsbach's work, I have remarked that even if the mock news decisions they simulated in their study were found to be consistent with actual news products, it would still be impossible to tell whether one of the variables was causally related to the other, or what was the directionality of the causation. This is *a fortiori* the case with respect to a prospective correlation obtained between journalistic role conceptions and news content, in a study which does not even pretend experimental validity. Thus, a study finding such correlations would be a still weaker case for causal relations, even without going into further detail.

But Van Dalen et al. are mindful of the problem of causation. As they correctly note (citing Donsbach), 'cross-national comparisons do not provide a rigid test for causal relations in the same way as experiments or large N-studies.'[18]

> In this comparative study of roles and content, we search for regularities and 'on the basis of prior research or theory (...) place causal interpretations on those observations' (Jackman, 1985: 172). Studies showing a relation at the individual level are ultimately a prerequisite to explain similar relations found at the macro-level studies. This study therefore builds on journalism studies of the professional attitude–behaviour relation at the individual level and extends these to explain the role–content relation on the macro level.[19]

Thus, the authors acknowledge that their causal account of news content by recourse to role conceptions, is purely speculative. But there is a more fundamental problem here. Role conceptions are not specific about what goes on in the reporters' minds. They are rather generalised beliefs about broad societal roles journalists ascribe to their own work, such as informing the public, rousing it, entertaining it, etc. There are presumably various different ways of understanding and performing these roles. A journalist uncritically echoing powerful sources and a critical investigative journalist might both see their work as commensurable with the rather broad role of 'informing the public.' But the survey questions – asking journalists to indicate their level of agreement or disagreement on a 5-point scale – posed by Van Dalen et al. were even more general, as they did not capture one specific role conception at a time:

> [...] national politics is newsworthy by definition; [...] mass media should report about national politics in full detail [...] The medium I work for has a specific political colour which guides me in how to do my work;[...] In the news section, my medium keeps a neutral position in partisan or policy disputes[...].[20]

The responses to these rather general questions were correlated against a number of content features of a sample of published news stories. I juxtapose in the following table the above survey items against excerpts from the corresponding content analysis codebook.

| Survey Item | Content Analysis Item |
|---|---|
| National politics is newsworthy by definition; ... mass media should report about national politics in full detail…( 910) | Visibility of political news was operationalised as the proportion of stories on the front page which cover national politics (compared to the total number of stories on the front page). Coders coded whether the story was framed in terms of conflict (focusing on disagreement between politicians) (de Vreese et al., 2001) or presented politics as a game (focusing on a politician winning or losing) …(911) |
| The medium I work for has a specific political colour which guides me in how to do my work;... In the news section, my medium keeps a neutral position in partisan or policy disputes…(910) | The presence of coverage bias was measured by comparing the visibility of political actors belonging to the largest left leaning and right leaning political party<br><br>The presence of statement bias was measured by comparing the mean tone towards politicians of these two parties. The tone can range from positive (when the emphasis in the story is on the actor's merits, successful solutions, solved problems or abilities) to negative (when the emphasis is on the actor's failures, unresolved problems or inabilities). (911) |

**Table 4.1:** Survey questions versus content codebook in van Dalen et al. (2012).

As should be apparent, the attitude-behaviour parallels drawn by van Dalen et al. are quite problematic. As the authors' own data shows, journalists who think national politics are newsworthy by definition[21] may well decide to use conflict and game frames (913, Table 4.2). The only way in which the use of these frames could be exclusively indicative of journalists' denial of the inherent newsworthiness of national politics, is if journalists could only draw on one criterion of newsworthiness at a time. But this is plainly not the case. Why can't a journalist think politics are inherently newsworthy and simultaneously think the same about conflict or game-like competitiveness among politicians?

In contrast, decisions about the proportion of articles on the front page which deal with national politics may indeed correspond to some news personnel's attitudes about the newsworthiness of national politics, but those decisions typically fall within the jurisdiction of the editor, not of individual journalists. However, by their own account, Van Dalen et al. have surveyed parliamentary reporters, not editors.

Still more problematic are the attitude-behaviour parallels having to do with partisan bias. The survey questions already reveal that journalists are not being asked exclusively about role conceptions, but about the behaviour of their news organisations. This is a tacit, albeit inadequate, backdoor reintroduction of the institutional structure into a study of role conceptions. Consider, once again, the following statement: 'The medium I work for has a specific political colour which guides me in how to do my work.' This is plainly not merely a question about a journalist's attitude or role conception, but also a proposition about the political bent of the news organisation in which she or he is employed.

Similarly, it doesn't follow from the quantitative content measurements which Van Dalen et al. offer that the news coverage is either biased or unbiased. The proportion of coverage afforded each political party can be meaningful only on the assumption that the parties markedly differ from one another on policy issues. If the two parties converge on major policy issues, then an equal level of attention given these two parties in the news coverage wouldn't indicate an absence of bias.[22] It is possible that in some of the countries surveyed the political parties did markedly differ, but no information is provided about an attempt, on the authors' part, to ascertain a meaningful level of political difference between the two largest political parties taken to be representative of both sides of the political spectrum in each one of the countries. Instead, the applicability of the terms 'left-wing' and 'right-wing' to these parties is taken for granted.

But let us assume for the sake of argument that the political parties in each country are markedly different in the policies they promote. Even if one political party is disproportionately represented in one of the newspapers, that still doesn't mean the disproportionality is the result of the political orientation of the newspaper. Indeed, the level of attention afforded each party may have more to do with the party's or party members' conduct, than with the newspaper's political bent. Unless the specific conduct of political parties is held constant, the claim of bias in cases of disproportionate attention remains speculative.[23]

Relatedly, the analysis of the tone adopted toward political actors has apparently much more to do with the behaviours of political actors than with the intentions of journalists (even if we assume they are the ultimate shapers of content). If politicians, either from the self-identified left or from the self-identified right, act egregiously, it is their behaviour rather than the political bent of news personnel/news organisation that would account for the positive or negative tone. Only by controlling in some manner for the potential variance in the behaviours of politicians could van Dalen et al. hope to document bias. But this was not the route taken.

### 3.2 Non-Causal Role Conceptions

But not all role conception research presupposes the explanatory power of role conceptions. Mellado and Van Dalen[24] have begun in recent years research into the gap between role conceptions and news content. Although this research rightly questions the direct causal relationship between role conceptions and news content, it uses an equally problematic methodology as studies which presupposed such an influence. Combining general survey questions with a similarly general content analysis codebook, this research seeks to measure the discrepancy between the survey data and the content analysis data. And indeed, it finds such gaps.

Thus, for instance, one of the most (apparently) dramatic findings is that journalists' ratings of the importance of the watchdog role do not jib at how much criticism their actual coverage directs toward politicians, businessmen and other groups.[25] Leaving aside that it is easy for journalists to exaggerate their commitment to the watchdog role (what could at least partly account for the gap) and that the amount of criticism toward various actors may depend on the realities of the studied country (e.g. researchers would have to control for the potential confounding variables of the incidence of egregious government and business practices), even a hypothetical alignment of a journalist's watchdog role conception with his or her actual news content would not indicate the journalist is free to act as watchdogs, which is how Mellado and Van Dalen interpret their findings. As they write

> […]the results of this study confirm the view of scholars who argue that a disconnect between roles and content is inevitable, since journalists lack sufficient autonomy to live up to their ideals.[26]

Although the argument itself is essentially correct, it does not follow from the study's findings. And for relatively simple reasons. Beyond the trivial distinction between correlations and causality (i.e. role conceptions being correlated with news content wouldn't suggest they cause news content), there is also the somewhat less obvious matter of the systemically innocuous character of the kind of criticism that Mellado and van Dalen's content analysis captures. Consider the following codebook items:

> Act as watchdog of business elites: Questioning de facto powers (the journalist): By means of statements and/or opinions, the journalist questions the validity or truthfulness of what individuals or groups in power say or do; Act as watchdog of political parties; Questioning de facto powers (the source): Questioning of individuals or groups of power through quotes, statements and/or opinions given by someone other than the journalist.[27]

On occasion, businesses attack one another and quite often attack the government. News businesses are no exception.[28] Yet per Mellado and Van Dalen's content analysis these instances would register as the realisation of the watchdog role. Thus, while journalists may be doing wittingly or (more likely) unwittingly their publishers', editors' or advertisers' bidding, journalism scholars sympathetic to Mellado and Van Dalen's empirical operationalisation would regard them as fully autonomous from extraneous influences. The fact that these are hypothetical scenarios does not detract from the validity of the critique, because Mellado and van Dalen take their study to be indicative of reporters' level of freedom.[29]

Thus, unlike Herman and Chomsky who posit rather neatly delineated explanatory variables[30], and conclusive content-based evidence of media bias, Van Dalen et al. and Mellado and Van Dalen provide thoroughly murky variables, including uninformative content data which is simply *assumed* to be indicative of bias and journalists' level of freedom.

### *News Practices*

So far, we have seen that the study of role conceptions diverts scholarly attention away from the power realities of journalism. But this is only half the story. The ascription of explanatory power to and excessive focus on journalists' 'role conceptions' are not the only ways in which mainstream scholars conceal the institutional realities of journalism. Instinctively suspicious about institutional explanations, the literature tends to lionise the scholarly interest in journalists' institutionally de-contextualised everyday routines and practices.

In a recent volume co-edited by Wolfgang Donsbach, who has passed from the scene in the meantime, a prominent media theorist by the name of David Ryfe, announces that the study of institutional sources of power which shape journalistic practices is passé.[31] How he arrives at this conclusion, though, ought to be retraced, if we are to understand the contemporary mode of reasoning about 'news routines' and 'news practices' among mainstream journalism scholars.

Ryfe begins by situating his discussion between two waves of Journalism Studies research. A first wave of ethnographies from the 1960s and 1970s which, according to Ryfe, contend that 'news is best explained as an outcome of organisational and economic pressures.'[32] And a second wave of ethnographies from the 1980's and 1990's finding that

> [...] reporters constantly argued about which routines applied in what context, and even about how to perform a given routine. They took from this finding that reporters have far more latitude to interpret routines— over and against organisational and economic pressures—than the earlier work implied.[33]

Ryfe takes the significance of this debate to be anchored in 'a series of severe economic and symbolic disruptions'[34] which journalism faces today. For Ryfe, at issue here is 'whether and the extent to which journalists can adapt their routines.'[35] A few pages later Ryfe clarifies the severity of the crisis facing journalism and what he means by his reference to journalists' ability to adapt:

> From roughly 2006 forward, the advertising revenue generated by American newsrooms (which employ the great majority of working journalists) began to plummet. With it went jobs. In the 7 years between 2006 and 2013, roughly 30% of American journalists were laid off or took buyouts. Today, revenue generated by American newspapers sits at levels last seen in 1950, and newsrooms are as small as they have been since 1980. This crisis is not as acute in other Western societies. But journalism across the industrialised world is losing readership and viewership, losing revenue, and losing workers.
>
> The crisis in journalism has galvanised scholars to take renewed interest in news production. For the most part, they have sought to understand how journalists are responding to the technological and economic changes facing their industry.[36]

These passages are curious ones. The first paragraph cited above depicts the crisis of journalism in lucid and informative institutional terms: plummeting advertising revenues, layoffs and buyouts. Moreover, newspaper revenues are said to be at the level of the 1950s. Obviously, these institutional processes do not substantially depend on journalists' choices under current power relations. Journalists do not decide on their news organisation's revenue, on whether they are going to keep their jobs or on the company that owns or acquires the news organisation in which they are employed. Thus, so far, Ryfe seems to be cognisant of the fact that journalists are not the agents behind or drivers of the developments he describes. But then the second paragraph (cited above) reveals that mainstream scholars of journalism have been primarily concerned with how *journalists* respond to these changes. Not with trying to explain why these institutional changes occurred in the first place. Be it as it may, I take Ryfe's general description of Journalism Studies' scholarly emphases to be robust and accurate. But Ryfe has additional theoretical insights to contribute.

Ryfe qualifies the earlier statement that the ethnographies of the 1960s and 1970s saw 'news' as 'best explained as an outcome of organisational and economic pressures.' Instead, he now argues:

> Most of this early literature understood that reporters had some degree of flexibility in adapting their routines to circumstance. For instance, Tuchman ...calls news routines 'typifications' as a way of allowing that they 'leave room for a great deal of reportorial flexibility.' In a similar vein, Gans ... refers to routines as 'considerations' that reporters take into account when deciding which stories to run and how to report them.[37]

Only that now Ryfe notes that this earlier work also didn't include evidence of as much uniformity (in journalistic routines) as the authors of this work had implied.[38] Ryfe suggests that the uniformity was 'implied' by such phrases as 'organisation men' and 'manufacturing the news'[39] (in Fishman's work).

However, Ryfe makes clear that the said 'uniformity' is, in any event, not the consequence of power inequalities within the news organisation or the news business, but of mere consensus among journalists: 'According to this literature, reporters share a largely implicit consensus about how to report the news.'[40] But if reporters merely share a consensus why can't the consensus simply change if reporters (collectively, if not individually) wish it to change? Why does such uniformity limit journalists' 'latitude'?[41] This set up reveals the false dichotomy, in Ryfe's rendering, between flexibility and uniformity. Both concepts are consistent with a journalism unmarred by hierarchical power relations.

Political Economists of the media, however, reached rather different conclusions about the same literature. As Herman and Chomsky write about Gans, he '[...]greatly understates the extent to which media reporters work within a limiting framework of assumptions' (F2 332-333, citing specific statements from Gans's book).[42] Similarly, McChesney has referred to Fishman, Tuchman and Gans's research as work which

> tended to accept the dominant institutional arrangements as a given. The institutions were unassailable, and the work tended to concentrate upon newsroom organisation, professional practices, and the implications for content.[43]

A major assumption in Ryfe's resistance to a power analysis of journalism is the claimed usefulness of what he calls 'practice' theories, which recent prominent studies of journalism have presumably demonstrated.[44] The term 'practice theories' is a reference to a collection of ideas by several theorists whose work is 'designed to overcome the conceptual impasse'[45] between structure and agency.[46] Here are some of the tenets Ryfe draws from 'practice' theories:

> Within practice theory, routines are *properly* understood not as expressions of external pressures on journalists (whether understood as organisational, political, or economic pressures)[...][47] (emphasis added).

And once again,

> [...] there is no need to impute a structure to social action (economic, political, or otherwise) beyond the conditions of practice (132, emphasis added).

Thus, for Ryfe, the idea that structure has anything to do with practice is invalid a priori. There is no need to admit structure into the explanatory calculus. Instead, it should be enough – or so Ryfe would argue – to meticulously document the details of how reporters cope with their changing economic and technological environment.

## 4. Conclusion

I have argued that the aversion of mainstream journalism scholars to the analysis of journalism in terms of institutional structures expresses itself not merely in particular dogmas, but also in scholarly practices and emphases, both in the kinds of methodologies adopted and in the data which is deemed meaningful. Specifically, I have provided examples of how mainstream scholars drew on journalists' political beliefs, journalists' conceptions of their own professional roles and newsroom practices, to obscure the power relations in journalism.

I tried to illustrate the severe analytical and methodological problems inherent in this scholarly work. Thus, I have noted the tendency to construct research designs which eliminate or obfuscate the hierarchical relationship between the business side and the production side of news, the unsatisfactory quality of the evidence used to infer the general features of the news content, and the refusal to consider news practices in the context of institutional power mechanisms.

## Notes and Bibliography

[1] See note 2. Daniel C. Hallin, for instance, tended to resist the institutional explanation even after his own research lent support to it. See also Footnote 3 for Eric Herring and Piers Robinson's work which provides additional examples of this phenomenon.

[2] Edward Herman and Noam Chomsky, *Manufacturing Consent: The Political Economy of the Mass Media* (New York: Pantheon Book, 1988).
[3] Daniel C. Hallin, *We Keep America on Top of the World: Television Journalism and the Public Sphere* (New York and London: Routledge, 1994). Michael, Schudson, 'The Sociology of News Production,' *Media, Culture & Society* (1989) *11*(3): 263–282.
[4] Edward S. Herman, 'The Propaganda Model: A Retrospective,' *Journalism Studies* (2000) *1*(1): 101–112). Andrew Mullen and Jeffery Klaehn, 'The Herman-Chomsky Propaganda Model: A Critical Approach to Analysing Mass Media Behaviour,' *Sociology Compass* (2010) *4*(4), 215–229.
[5] Eric Herring and Piers Robinson, 'Too Polemical or Too Critical? Chomsky on the Study of the News Media and US Foreign Policy,' *Review of International Studies* (2003) *29*(4) 553–568; Yigal Godler, 'Why Anti-Realist Views Persist in Communication Research: A Political Economic Reflection on Relativism's Prominence,' *Critical Sociology* (2016) 0896920516645935; Andrew Mullen, 'Twenty Years On: The Second-Order Prediction of the Herman-Chomsky Propaganda Model,' *Media, Culture & Society* (2010) *32*(4), 673–690.
[6] Thomas E. Patterson and Wolfgang Donsbach, 'News Decisions: Journalists as Partisan Actors.' *Political Communication* (1996) *13*(4), 455–468. Unless stated otherwise, all quotes and citations in this section are taken from Patterson and Donsbach's 'News Decisions' .
[7] Jonathan Nitzan and Shimshon Bichler, *Capital as Power: A Study of Order and Creorder* (London and New York: Routledge, 2009). I am drawing here on Thorstein Veblen's distinction between business and industry and, in particular, on Nitzan and Bichler's conceptual elaboration of this distinction. On this view, business is an institution of control, and industry is the realm in which knowledge and creativity are applied. References to Veblen's important works can be found in Nitzan and Bichler's book.
[8] A point to which I return in the next paragraph.
[9] Schmidt, 'Disciplined Minds'. A related fact about Patterson and Donsbach's study, which reveals their tendency to prejudge the investigation against the finding of power relations, is the nature of their sample. According to Patterson and Donsbach, the sample pooled together reporters, editors and even some managers and owners (456) in unknown proportions. The uneven opportunities of these actors to shape news content was not regarded as problematic.
[10] David H. Weaver and Cleveland Wilhoit, *The American Journalist in the 1990s: U.S. News People at the End of an Era* (1996) Mahwah, NJ, Lawrence Erlbaum Associates Publishers, 191.
[11] Claudia Mellado, Lea Hellmueller and Wolfgang Donsbach, 'Journalistic Role Performance: A New Research Agenda in a Digital and Global Media Environment,' in *Journalistic Role Performance: Concepts, Contexts and Methods* eds. Mellado et al. (New York: Routledge, 2017), 4.

12. Daniel C. Hallin, 'Preface,' *Journalistic Role Performance: Concepts, Contexts and Methods* eds. Mellado et al. (New York: Routledge, 2017), xi-xvii.
13. Arjen van Dalen, Claes H. de Vreese, and Erik Albaek, 'Different Roles, Different Content? A Four-Country Comparison of the Role Conceptions and Reporting Style of Political Journalists,' *Journalism: Theory, Practice and Criticism* (2012) 13 (7), 903–922. Despite recent changes in the study of role conceptions (See Mellado, Hellmueller and Donsbach, 'Role Performance'), van Dalen et al. were correct in that, at the time of writing, 'Studies of journalistic cultures generally study either role conceptions or news content' (904). Thus, van Dalen et al. is the closest that studies of role conceptions ever came to making an empirical case for the explanatory power of role conceptions vis-á-vis news content. Hence the choice to analyse this specific article.
14. van Dalen et al., 'Different roles, different content?' 904.
15. Pamela J. Shoemaker and Stephen D. Reese, *Mediating the Message: Theories of Influences on Mass Media Content* (Toronto: Longman, 1996). Among other things, the book provides historical background on the scholarly attempts to explain news content.
16. van Dalen et al., 'Different roles, different content?,' 904.
17. Ibid. Unless stated otherwise all subsequent citations in this section are from van Dalen et al. Page numbers are provided in the text.
18. Arjen van Dalen, Claes H. de Vreese, and Erik Albaek, 'Different Roles, Different Content? A Four-Country Comparison of the Role Conceptions and Reporting Style of Political Journalists,' *Journalism: Theory, Practice and Criticism* (2012) 13 (7), 905.
19. Ibid.
20. Ibid.
21. The authors use the term 'sacredotal' to describe such a hypothetical role conception, and counterpose it to a 'pragmatic' role conception, which sees news values only in conflict and game frames.
22. Thus, for instance, some scholarly literature provides grounds for questioning the left-wing credentials of both the Labour Party in the UK and the German SPD. See Luke March and Cas Mudde, 'What's Left of the Radical Left? The European Radical Left After 1989: Decline and Mutation,' *Comparative European Politics* (2005) 3, 23–49 (See specifically: 36) ; Leo Panitch and Colin Leys, *The End of Parliamentary Socialism: From New Left to New Labour* (London and New York: Verso, 2001).
23. Notably, the authors found no evidence of disproportionate media attention vis-a-vis any of the political parties (914, Table 3).
24. Claudia Mellado and Arjen van Dalen, 'Between Rhetoric and Practice: Explaining the Gap between Role Conception and Performance in Journalism,' *Journalism Studies* 2014 15 (6), 859–878.
25. Mellado and Van Dalen, 'Rhetoric and Practice,' 868.
26. Ibid, 873.

27 Ibid, Appendix A, 877.
28 Herman and Chomsky, 'Consent.'
29 Mellado and van Dalen, 860.
30 The only analytically problematic feature of the model is 'anti-communist ideology'. Edward Herman and Noam Chomsky, *Manufacturing Consent: The Political Economy of the Mass Media*, (New York: Pantheon Books, 2002), xvii.
31 David Ryfe, 'News Routines, Role Performance and Change in Journalism,' in *Journalistic Role Performance: Concepts, Contexts and Methods* eds. Mellado et al. (New York: Routledge, 2017). Ryfe (2017) uses the concept of power twice in this essay (127, 132), but not in the context of institutions being shapers of practices. Unless stated otherwise, all subsequent citations are from Ryfe, 'Change in Journalism.'
32 Ibid., 127.
33 Ibid., 127.
34 Ibid., 128.
35 Ibid., 128.
36 Ibid., 130-1.
37 Ibid., 197.
38 Ibid., 129.
39 Ibid., 129.
40 Ibid., 129.
41 Ibid., 127.
42 Herman and Chomsky, 'Manufacturing Consent'.
43 McChesney, 'Media,' 128.
44 Ryfe mentions the recent works of the following journalism scholars: Anderson, Benson, Lowrey, Ryfe, Turner, Usher, Willig. I take these to be representative of contemporary mainstream (and indeed influential) journalism studies.
45 Ibid., 128.
46 Ryfe uses the terms 'objectivism and subjectivism' on page 128. However, he clarifies on the preceding page that these are equivalent to 'structure and agency' respectively. I adopt the latter concepts on the assumption they are more familiar to the reader.
47 Ibid., 128.

CHAPTER 5

# Does the Propaganda Model Actually Theorise Propaganda?

Piers Robinson[1]

## 1. Overview

The Propaganda Model (PM), first published in *Manufacturing Consent: The Political Economy of the Mass Media*[2] and describing how corporate media serve as conduits for business and government propaganda, has weathered many criticisms over the years. Derided by some as 'simplistic' or 'conspiratorial', shunned by the 'respectable' academy and, perhaps more often than not, simply ignored, the model has, however, stood the test of time and, at least to this writer, it seems that there is little in the way of substantial disagreement amongst many scholars with the basic claims put forward in the model. The way in which the model has been adopted by researchers has not been optimal, however, and this chapter puts forward the case for a significant expansion of the model and the way it is employed so as to provide a more thorough-going analysis of the strategies and organisations actually involved in the creation of propaganda: as such, I argue for an expansion to the model which would allow it to live up to its name. To be clear, this is not necessarily a criticism of

---

How to cite this book chapter:
Robinson, P. 2018. Does the Propaganda Model Actually Theorise Propaganda? In: Pedro-Carañana, J., Broudy, D. and Klaehn, J. (eds.). *The Propaganda Model Today: Filtering Perception and Awareness*. Pp. 53–67. London: University of Westminster Press. DOI: https://doi.org/10.16997/book27.e. License: CC-BY-NC-ND 4.0

Herman and Chomsky given that they always saw the Propaganda Model of the media as one part of a much broader set of structures and processes through which dominant ideologies are communicated and vested political and economic interest protected: but it is a criticism of the way in which the model has tended to draw attention to the corporate media at the expense of a more detailed consideration of the strategies and organisations that function to create a propagandised information environment in the first instance.

The chapter proceeds in three stages: section two briefly recaps the core claims of the Propaganda Model as well as summarising initial criticisms and then noting the extent to which the model is now accepted and indeed endorsed by many critical scholars. Section three then sets out the argument that, in significant ways, the model captures only a portion of the processes involved in the production of propaganda. In this way, perhaps ironically, the model shares the same shortcomings as other more mainstream models of media-state relations. Section four then sets out the processes which should be incorporated into a revised and expanded Propaganda Model. The chapter concludes with a brief discussion of the importance of this suggested expansion with respect to assessing the democratic health of contemporary liberal democracies and identifies some areas for future empirical research.

## 2. From Outcast to Mainstream: A Short History of the Propaganda Model

The original model developed by Herman and Chomsky detailed the now well-known five filters (size, concentration and profit orientation of the mainstream media, their reliance upon advertising and official sources, flak and the ideology of anti-communism) which worked together in order to shape the news output of corporate US media.[3] Early reactions to the Propaganda Model from the academy were largely dismissive, arguing variously that the model was inaccurate, simplistic or counter-productive[4] whilst frequent 'off the record' conversations experienced by this writer suggested their work was polemical or unscholarly. Indeed, two academics reported that they had experienced suggestions to remove references to Chomsky's work write:

> these have been made by those who say that they agree with Chomsky but were concerned to protect us from the costs of being associated with him. On one occasion, it was suggested that, even though a manuscript written by one of us indicated concurrence with Chomsky's analysis on a particular issue, references to Chomsky should remain in the manuscript only when disagreement with Chomsky was being registered. The point was made an argument would be dismissed merely for having Chomsky's name attached to it, whereas if it had a mainstream big name as the source, it would be applauded for its great wisdom.[5]

Such prejudice has led, over time, to a remarkable silencing of their work across significant swathes of mainstream academic research on media and politics. Herring and Robinson reviewed eight significant studies of media-state relations, all of which shared similar analyses of the relationship of mainstream media to power, but none of which referenced *Manufacturing Consent*.[6] Woods identified a similar pattern across a corpus of introductory texts to International Relations.[7] Since then, however, many important mainstream accounts of media-state relations have, to varying degrees, reflected or concurred with many of the basic claims made in the Propaganda Model[8] whilst others have continued to draw attention to the importance of their work for understanding media-state relations[9]. It is perhaps possible then that there might now be some kind of generalised academic acknowledgement of the analysis they provide, at least for those who accept that there are powerful and significant constraints acting upon media autonomy such that their ability to speak truth to power and hold the powerful to account are not being met. In addition, other scholars are continuing the media critique epitomised by the Propaganda Model[10] and earlier Marxist-inspired analyses of the media. So, in sum, the challenge and resistance to power represented in the work of Herman and Chomsky has then been far from futile.

## 3. Identifying Theoretical Limitations to the Propaganda Model and its Elite-driven Bedfellows

As mentioned above, the central claims of the Propaganda Model are largely compatible with the body of critical literature, the *elite-driven paradigm*, which theorises media-state relations and identifies the great extent to which corporate media are closely located to political and economic power. Lance Bennett's oft-cited *indexing hypothesis*,[11] Daniel Hallin's *media spheres*,[12] Robert Entman's *cascading activation model*,[13] Gadi Wolfsfeld's *political contest model*[14] and my own *policy-media interaction model*,[15] all are compatible with the central claims set out in the Propaganda Model. All of these accounts focus on theorising, with sometimes relatively subtle differences, the forces that act on media in order to create their 'close proximity' to political and economic power. In particular, they all place great significance on the role of media reliance upon official sources when defining the news agenda (i.e. the sourcing filter described in the Propaganda Model). However, in doing so, they all share a particular weakness: they fail to go beyond this official source-media linkage into a deeper exploration of ways in which officials, and the governments and business interests that they represent, engage in the systematic manipulation of information. To put this another way, before the point is reached at which an official source passes information to the journalist, all of the elite-driven paradigm models provide minimal insight into the processes of 'information management' and propaganda production.

This is an important shortcoming, especially for a model with the title 'propaganda'. The PM asserts that a highly propagandised worldview is being communicated to media precisely because they are so dependent upon official sources and that this worldview serves elite interests. But the model provides little or no insights into how this distorted worldview is created in the first instance. In a sense, the PM and other elite-driven paradigm models are only presenting us with half the picture of what is going on. There are several reasons why this is a problem; some minor, some major. First, to the extent that the Propaganda Model focuses attention on the media, and why they come to fail, the attention and blame is focused upon journalists and editors. This might be fair enough for some, but it does take attention and blame away from the governments and corporations involved in actively manipulating and distorting information: it takes two to tango and one might reasonably expect governments and corporations to take an even greater share of the responsibility in this relationship. Second, in theoretical terms, there is a tension between the fifth filter (ideology) and the fact that there is also active production of propaganda. The ideology filter posits the existence of a fixed system of ideas which fix or shape understandings, closing off some ways of thinking about the world and enabling others. Ideology, as it is commonly understood and presented in the PM, is not a particularly active process and is normally assumed to function in a way that does not involve conscious and intentional actions:[16] the ideology of anti-communism, for example, referred to a widely shared perspective that assumed communism was inherently bad, whilst capitalism was morally superior. Journalists, editors and officials simply shared this outlook, so, for example, when it came to the Vietnam War, all understood the 'right' way of interpreting the conflict and without having to think about it. But there this is more to it than that. Those ideologically driven anti-communist impulses did not spontaneously occur; they had to be constructed and promoted at some point, and that is where an understanding of propaganda can help make greater sense of the ideology filter. Propaganda understood as the active promotion of particular world views can be seen as, in the first instance, the establisher of particular ideological constructs. In the US, a large part of the propaganda which helped cement the ideology of anti-communism presumably emerged with the infamous 'red scares' of the 1950s and McCarthyism as well as exaggerated intelligence claims regarding the threat posed by the Soviet military. In sum, the point here is that bringing propaganda production into the frame helps us to understand better how ideological frameworks get to be constructed in the first instance.[17]

There are even more important reasons why we should take the 'propaganda short-coming' of the PM seriously. The scale of the euphemistically titled 'public relations' industry is vast and indeed represents one of the largest industries in the world, and with massive impacts. For example, the US federal government spent $16 billion on 'outside PR, ads' between 2002 and 2012. In the recent past persuasion and manipulation of public perceptions has been conducted by the tobacco industry about the dangers of smoking, causing 100 million deaths in the twentieth century,[18] and also by the fossil fuel industry attempting to obfuscate understanding of climate change.[19] At the same time, sophisticated strategies are involved in manipulating perceptions and behaviours and which, together, constitute a clear set of doctrines and practices. Propaganda production also involves co-ordination with think tanks, academia and NGOs. For all these reasons, one can reasonably assume that the production of propaganda is a process involving very significant resource allocation, intensive activity, and one which is extremely important. Indeed, the resources allocated and the intensiveness of the activity far outstrips those related to corporate media. For example, as recent Pew studies have shown and others have commented upon, the imbalance between journalists and PR workers is even greater now than before with the latter outnumbering the former three to one.[20] Suffice to say, if we want to fully understand how and why the media come to present such a distorted worldview, we need to examine all of these dimensions related to the production and dissemination of propaganda: And this means moving beyond a focus on corporate media and expanding analysis to include examination of propaganda strategies and sites of production. And it is to this task that we now turn.

## 4. Extending the Explanatory Reach of the Propaganda Model through an Examination of Propaganda Production

If we are then to fully understand the way in which media function as a propaganda arm for powerful interests, it is necessary to expand the existing model in ways which might do greater justice to the actual production of propaganda. What follows is no more than an approximate sketch of the kinds of issues which should be incorporated into an expanded version of the existing Propaganda Model. But taking the issues identified above, I want to discuss first the matter of the persuasion strategies employed as part of propaganda campaigns, and second the range of actors involved in propaganda production.

### 4.1 'Strategies of Propaganda and Persuasion'

The term propaganda is actually widely disputed. For some, propaganda is understood to refer to any kind of persuasion[21] whilst for others it is understood to refer to only manipulative forms of persuasion.[22] Clearly, in terms of how Chomsky employs the term propaganda, he is understanding it to involve manipulative forms of persuasion and it is certainly the case that most working definitions of propaganda employ some notion of manipulation. It is also important to note that actors involved in propaganda production are likely to hold a variety of self-perceptions about what they are engaged in: some will be fully aware that their activity involves intentional manipulation of beliefs and behaviours; others might have already internalised a particular world view and believe that they are telling the truth; and for others it might be the case that attempts to manipulate opinions and behaviours is a necessary and acceptable part of contemporary society. The common feature across all of these self-perceptions is the organised, systematic and intentional manipulation of information in ways that either distorts peoples' perception of reality or pushes them to behave in ways they would not otherwise do.

But how does persuasion and influence become manipulative and what constitutes manipulation? Neither the literature on propaganda, nor the Propaganda Model as currently formulated, give much in the way of insight to this question. The existing and most widely adopted definition of propaganda involves demarcating propaganda into white, grey and black categories.[23] This is actually a rather crude and inadequate formulation because it falls into the trap of equating white propaganda, whereby one-sided but factually accurate claims are made in order to persuade, with truthful communication. However, as Bakir et al. explain,[24] stating only half the truth can itself be fundamentally deceptive and, therefore, manipulative. A more productive approach is to conceptualise clearly the ways in which communicative processes of persuasion and influence can become manipulative. For example, Herring and Robinson[25] developed a conceptual framework which mapped the key ways through which the propaganda strategy of *deception* works. Deception might occur through lies: statements of fact known to be untrue which are nonetheless communicated in order to deceive. However, although many associate propaganda with lying, and it is certainly the case that many people interpret Chomsky's position, and that of the PM, with this form of deception, it is also the case that 'lies have short legs'[26] and, moreover, are a high-risk political strategy. In other words, getting caught out in a lie is normally fatal in political terms. More common ways in which deception occurs is through strategies of omission and distortion. Omission involves selecting some facts, and ignoring others, in a way that makes your case more likely to persuade. This is more than a matter of simply trying to persuade someone based upon how you might see an issue. It is a matter of deliberate omission of information that might be critical to whether or not someone is likely to be persuaded. Another frequently employed tactic is to distort or exaggerate facts. As Herring and Robinson[27] describe, the now infamous deception over Iraq's alleged possession of WMD in the run-up to the Iraq War involved a fundamental distortion of intelligence estimates: through distortion of information an actual intelligence assessment that described Iraq as a potential future threat, perhaps five years down the line, was distorted to say that Iraq was currently capable of launching WMD within 45 minutes of an order.

It is also important to recognise that propaganda strategies involve more than the deceptive manipulation of information in the three ways described. It also frequently involves misdirection[28] which entails producing and disseminating true information but which is intended to direct public attention away from problematic issues. Beyond the management and shaping of the information environment, propaganda can also involve action in the real world or, to be more precise, shaping material contexts through the use of incentives and, at times, influencing conduct via threats.[29] For example, sanctions against regimes involving the targeting of populations and governments in order to alter their behaviour are examples of incentivising strategies aimed at organising conduct. Again, strategies such as the 'shock and awe' campaign witnessed at the start of the 2003 invasion of Iraq, involving highly visible and dramatic bomb attacks on Iraqi government buildings right in the centre of Baghdad, are designed to communicate powerful coercive messages to populations largely revolving around a message to surrender and comply with invading forces!

Overall, analysing and understanding the precise strategies of persuasion and influence that are employed in any given case can help to provide a richer and deeper understanding of the ways in which information, which is then passed through the media and on to the public, comes to be profoundly distorted in the ways claimed by Herman and Chomsky. The concepts of incentivising and coercing propaganda messages,[30] add important additional layers to our understanding of the propaganda techniques used by powerful actors.

## 4.2 Sites of Propaganda Production

The production of propaganda involves more than government and corporation 'spin doctors' and 'PR' agents, it also involves a variety of entities, including think tanks, NGOs, and even academia. It also involves actors from within the so-called 'deep state' including the intelligence services.

For example, think tanks can be used as vehicles in order to generate information and, frequently, operate in ways which reflect the interests and agenda of their sponsors.[31] Although not necessarily always part of contributing towards manipulated and propagandised representations of particular issues, sometimes they are. So, for example, *Spinwatch* recently produced a report on the Henry Jackson Society, a think tank founded in 2005 and presented as bipartisan. As they document in their report,[32] this think tank, funded by an array of undisclosed donors, has been active in 'promoting a strongly pro-Israel agenda, organizing anti-Islam activities … (and) advocating a transatlantic military and security regime'.[33] Interestingly, and as revealed in a leaked document, HJS, also planned co-ordinated activities aimed at discrediting Noam Chomsky via influencing mainstream media journalists.[34] Clearly, shaping the information environment and manipulating opinions (aka propaganda) would appear to have been a key objective of this think tank.

NGOs have also been implicated, on occasion, in the unintentional circulation of propagandistic information. For example, during the Libyan war in 2011, human rights-related claims against the Libyan government circulated prior to the intervention, including in an AI press briefing.[35]

After the intervention, however, an AI investigation could not corroborate allegations of mass human rights violations by Gaddafi regime troops.[36] In the case of the 2011-present war in Syria, the White Helmets group are presented as an independent organisation set up to save civilians. However, one government document indicates that the organization has been funded as part of broader attempts to support 'moderate opposition to provide services for their communities and to contest new space', and to empower 'legitimate local governance structures to deliver services [and giving] credibility to the moderate opposition'.[37] As such, the White Helmets would appear to be part of a broader US/UK regime change strategy which has supported the overthrow of the existing Syrian government. At the same time, the White Helmets have served an important public relations purpose by providing 'an invaluable reporting and advocacy role' and 'confidence to statements made by UK and other international leaders made in condemnation of Russian actions'.[38] Because the White Helmets only operate in areas held by opposition groups, they can only present a partial picture of events. The utility of this organization, intentional or not, for propaganda purposes is without question. Indeed, a film about the White Helmets was even awarded an Oscar in 2016.

Academia is not immune from propaganda activities and can itself become part of the broader propaganda apparatus. For example, Herring and Robinson[39] argued that, to a large extent, the filters identified in the Propaganda Model as acting upon the media are also relevant to academia. Reliance upon grants, wishing to curry favour with official sources, as well as ideological imperatives, all mean that academia is far less free from the influence of power than is often assumed by those outside the academy, and also many within academia.[40] For example, Simpson's *Science of Coercion* draws upon a variety of sources, including FOI'd documents, and carefully documents the relationship between the fledgling academic discipline of communication science/studies and US psychological operations (psy ops).[41] He highlights powerfully the interdependence between the academy and the US government and makes a powerful case that, in a very fundamental sense, communication science/studies are shaped, to this day, by the imperatives of political power.

Finally, the intelligence services are key producers and disseminators of propaganda in contemporary liberal democracies. For example, long before the now notorious intelligence-based WMD allegations made against Iraq during the run-up to the 2003 invasion of Iraq, British intelligence was involved in manipulating evidence in order to promote the impression that Iraq had an ongoing WMD programme. From 1991 onwards the MI6 Operation Rockingham was involved in cherry picking intelligence from the UN weapons inspections (set up after the Persian Gulf War) in order to, as a former chief UN weapons inspector put it, skew 'UK intelligence about Iraqi WMD towards a preordained outcome that was more in line with British government policy that it was reflective of the truth'.[42] Such activities were geared toward influencing the UN Security Council but also most likely designed to help maintain public support for the UK sanctions regime against Iraq. Operation Mass Appeal, initiated in the late 1990s, was precisely geared towards influencing public opinion by exaggerating the threat posed by Iraqi WMD.[43] Finally, propaganda activities extend beyond attempts to influence publics via mainstream media and include popular culture propaganda. For example, Schou has documented the close involvement between the CIA and Hollywood.[44] The relationships here range from mutual exploitation, through co-optation, and on to more direct patterns of censorship. The overall net objective is to manipulate beliefs and attitudes in ways that are conducive to the interests of the US government.

In sum, a full analysis of propaganda requires identification and critical examination of the various sites of propaganda production which, in practice, extend well beyond the communications officials and PR offices of governments and major corporations to include think tanks, NGOs, academia and the intelligence services. In extending the Propaganda Model to include analysis of these sites of production, it is also essential to maintain a weather eye on the potential overlap between, and even integration of, these apparently discrete sites of propaganda production. For example, there is evidence that some journalists working in the media have been either intelligence service assets or, indeed, members of the intelligence services themselves.[45] At the same time academics have become involved with intelligence-military activities on many occasions; for example, anthropologists have become, controversially, involved in the human terrain system (HTS) project aimed at using 'local' knowledge in order to, in the broadest sense, win hearts and minds and organise conduct in countries that Western governments have invaded and occupied.[46] A similar phenomenon emerged with the involvement of psychologists in the US post 9/11 torture programme.[47] It is also worthwhile addressing the question of the extent to which networks connecting think tanks, NGOs, and perhaps even some individuals within academia, might be involved in propaganda activities. For example, in relation to the current Syrian conflict, in 2012, the then US Secretary of State Hilary Clinton authorised the 'training for more than a thousand (Syrian) activists, students, and independent journalists'[48] in order to promote her regime change preference. The question begged by the revelation from Clinton is how many of those apparently recruited are working in support of NGOs, for example the White Helmets discussed above, and have become either connected or involved with think tanks or perhaps even exist now within academia. In sum, these sites of propaganda should not be investigated only as discrete sites of propaganda production, but also, potentially, as part of broader propaganda networks.

## 5. Concluding Comments: Propaganda, the Exercise of Power, and the Health of Contemporary Liberal Democracy

We know much about the media and why it so frequently fails to speak truth to power, fails to relay accurate information on the most important issues of our day, and frequently ends up relaying propaganda designed to manipulate beliefs and behaviour. Herman and Chomsky's Propaganda Model has played an important role in raising awareness of these failures amongst both academics and the public at large. The model and their work have been a major service to critical thinking and, ultimately, democracy. It is the experience of this author, with 20 years teaching in higher education, that many more students today are aware of the structural failings of mainstream media than was the case in the 1990s. Referencing and talking about the Propaganda Model seems to elicit fewer smirks and knee jerk reactions than was the case 20 years back. Progress *has* been made.

However, moving understanding and critical awareness forward means extending and widening the Propaganda Model, refocusing attention away from the well-documented failings of the mainstream media and on to those actors who are, ultimately, the source of propaganda. Some of this work involves the examination of propaganda tactics and strategies, or doctrines, which make up the tool kit of the propagandist. Some of these tactics involve processes of information manipulation whereby deception can occur through lying, distortion, omission and misdirection. But some are more physical and 'real world' involving incentivisation and coercion. Propaganda is about winning hearts and minds and also about organising conduct and this can involve shaping material contexts and action in the real world.[49] Beyond tactics and strategies, we also need to extend analysis to include the array of entities, from think tanks to the academy, which can become involved in propaganda activities and the way in which these might sometimes overlap and be interconnected.

Such an expansion of the Propaganda Model would help us to much better understand how the propaganda, which is relayed by mainstream media so readily, is produced and the ways in which the minds and behaviour of people in contemporary liberal democracies might come to be manipulated and conditioned. Shining a light on those involved in the actual creation of propaganda would also serve to increase public accountability of those actors and organisations who are involved in these activities, just as the original Propaganda Model has helped increase the accountability of corporate media. Finally, mapping these activities across multiple cases and through detailed empirical research will serve to elucidate hidden agendas, interests and networks, and the way in which propaganda is employed in order to exercise power in ostensibly accountable and democratic political systems. Establishing just how far this propaganda extends, and the extent to which there has been a 'major and permanent adjustment or displacement of reality',[50] will provide vital insights to the democratic health, or ill-health, of contemporary liberal democracies.

Seventeen years in to the twenty-first century, the liberal democracies of the West have experienced multiple wars initiated and led by the US, profound economic crisis and a continued hesitation to confront some of the most pressing issues of our time such as global poverty and environmental crisis. As Chomsky himself has noted on many occasions in recent years, we are on a precipice, facing the potential even of extinction due to climate change or nuclear war.[51] Propaganda has undoubtedly had much to do with facilitating this state of affairs, whether through persuading publics of non-existent WMD threats (in the case of Iraq), mobilising consent for a 'war on terror'[52] or helping powerful vested interests such as the fossil fuel industry sow seeds of doubt about climate change.[53] We must fully understand, expose and critique propaganda in order to regain accountability and control over our course. Extending the Propaganda Model in order to do this is a pressing,[54] urgent, matter.

## Notes and Bibliography

[1] Thanks to an anonymous reviewer, Daniel Broudy and Stefanie Haueis for feedback and comments on earlier drafts.

[2] Edward Herman and Noam Chomsky, *Manufacturing Consent: The Political Economy of the Mass Media* (New York: Pantheon; 1988).

[3] The first filter identified the importance of the fact that US corporate media were owned by a relatively small number of extremely large and powerful corporations: in effect, ownership equates to control and means that news stories that challenged the interests of those corporations are far less likely to surface. The detailed process by which this works includes strategic interventions by owners, self-censorship by employees, and the internalisation of the values, ethos and worldview of a corporation by its employees. The second filter identified the importance of advertising: because mainstream media are so reliant upon advertising revenue in order to be profitable, they become constrained by the need to appeal to affluent audiences, the risk-averse nature of sponsoring corporations and the bottom line that stories running against the interests of any corporation that is sponsoring adverts might lead to that same corporation threatening to withdraw. The third filter identified the tendency of journalists to rely upon, and defer to, official sources when reporting stories. Whether due to time and money pressures pushing journalists towards reliance upon press releases, or the instinct to talk to those in powerful positions when trying to understand what is going on, studies of journalist-source relations consistently show that, when it comes to political news, journalists only relatively rarely move beyond government officials and elected representatives when sourcing their stories. The fourth filter, flak, notes the importance of disciplining attacks on journalists who do stray beyond the boundaries of 'acceptable' criticism. Whether from 'spin doctors' or the array of think tanks that now exist, journalists who published very critical stories can be subjected to smear

campaigns and excessive criticism which serve to induce caution when deciding what kind of stories to cover and write about. The fifth filter of the Propaganda Model, the ideology filter, describes the importance of anti-communist ideology which worked, at least during the Cold War, to create an ideological bond, or shared world view, between journalists and political elites. Because of this ideological bond, conflicts around the world were readily perceived in terms of 'the struggle against communism' and divided the world 'neatly' into 'good guys' and 'bad guys'. Of course, and as Herman has pointed out, 'anti-communism' should be understood as part of a much broader agenda regarding 'free market rhetoric, US economic access and massive states subsidies to private corporations' which opposed 'any challenge to elite interests and US economic penetration of any state be it of the left or the right'. As such, the ideology filter is still in play.

4 Daniel Hallin, *We Keep America on Top of the World* (London: Routledge, 1994); Robert Entman,'News as Propaganda: Review of Manufacturing Consent' *Journal of Communication* (4): 124–127; Peter Golding and Graham Murdock (1996) 'Culture, Communications and Political Economy', *Mass Media and Society* (London: Arnold), pp.11–30.

5 Eric Herring and Piers Robinson (2003) 'Too Polemical or Too Critical? Chomsky on the Study of the News Media and US Foreign Policy.' *Review of International Studies* 29(3): 561.

6 Ibid.

7 Lawrence Woods (2006) 'Where's Noam? On the Absence of References to Noam Chomsky in Introductory International Relations Tectbooks,' *New Political Science*, 28(1): 65–79.

8 Lance W. Bennett (1990), 'Toward a Theory of Press-State Relations in the United States', Journal of Communication, 40(2): 103-25; Robert Entman (2004) *Projections of Power: Framing News, Public Opinion and US Foreign Policy* (Chicago, IL: University of Chicago Press); Gadi Wolfsfeld (1997) *The News Media and Political Conflict* (Cambridge: Cambridge University Press).

9 Alison Edgley, (2005) 'Chomsky's Political Critique: Essentialism and Political Theory' *Contemporary Political Theory* 4: 129–153; Herring and Robinson, 'Too Polemical or Too Critical'; Jeffery Klaehn (2002), 'A Critical Review and Assessment of Herman and Chomsky's 'Propaganda Model' *European Journal of Communication* 17: pp. 147–182; Jeffery Klaehn (2003), 'Behind the Invisible Curtain of Scholarly Criticism: Revisiting the Propaganda Model' *Journalism Studies* 4(3): 359-369; Jeffery Klaehn and Andrew Mullen (2010), 'The Herman-Chomsky Propaganda Model: A Critical Approach to Analysing Mass Media Behaviour' *Sociology Compass* 4(2): 215–229; Andrew Mullen (2010), 'Twenty Years On: The Second Order Prediction of the Herman and Chomsky Propaganda Model' *Media, Culture and Society* 32(4): 673–90; Joan Pedro (2009), 'A Critical Evaluation

of Herman and Chomsky's Propaganda Model' *Revista Latina de Comunicacion Social* 64: 210–233; Piers Robinson 'The Propaganda Model: Still Relevant Today' in Alison Eagley (2017) ed. *Noam Chomsky* (London: Palgrave, Macmillan).

[10] Christian Fuchs, (2012) 'Critique of the Political Economy of Web 2.0 Surveillance', pp. 31–70 in C. Fuchs, K. Boersma, A. Albrechtslund and M. Sandoval (eds) *Internet and Surveillance: The Challenges of Web 2.0 and Social Media*. London: Routledge; Desmond Freedman, *Contradictions of Media Power* (2014: Bloomsbury Press); Robert W. McChesney, (2008) *The Political Economy of Media: Enduring Issues, Emerging Dilemmas*. New York, NY: Monthly Review Press.

[11] Bennett, (1990) 'Toward a Theory of Press-State Relations'.

[12] Daniel Hallin, *The Uncensored War: The Media and Vietnam* (1986, Berkeley: University of California Press).

[13] Entman, *Projections of Power*.

[14] Wolfsfeld, *The Media and Political Conflict*.

[15] Piers Robinson (2002), *The CNN Effect: The Myth of News, Foreign Policy and Intervention* (Routledge: London and New York).

[16] David Miller, 'Media Power and Class Power: Overplaying Ideology' in L. Panitch and C. Leys (2002) (eds), *Socialist Register* (Woodbridge: Merlin Press) 245–264.

[17] Ibid.

[18] David Michaels (2008) *Doubt is Their Product: How Industry's Assault on Science Threatens Your Health* (Oxford: Oxford University Press).

[19] Naomi Oreskes and Erik M. Conway, (2011), *Merchants of Doubt: How a Handful of Scientists Obscured the Truth on Issues from Tobacco Smoke to Global Warming* (New York: Bloomsbury Publishing).

[20] Robert McChesney and John Nichols (2010). *The Death and Life of American Journalism: The Media Revolution That Will Begin the World Again* (Philadelphia, PA: Nation Books).

[21] For example see Philip M. Taylor (1992), 'Propaganda from Thucydides to Thatcher', Address to the annual conference of the Social History Society of Great Britain.

[22] For example see Jowett, G. S. and O'Donnell, V. J. (2012), *Propaganda and Persuasion*, 5th edn. (Sage: London and Thousand Oaks).

[23] Ibid.

[24] Vian Baker, Eric Herring, David Miller and Piers Robinson (2018) 'Strategies of Deception, Incentivisation and Coercion: A New Conceptual Framework for Understanding Propagandistic Persuasive Communication' *Critical Sociology*. Available online first.

[25] Eric Herring and Piers Robinson (2014) 'Report X Marks the Spot: the British Government's Deceptive Dossier on Iraq and WMD', co-authored with Eric Herring. *Political Science Quarterly*, 129 (4): 551–584.

26 Friedrich, C. J. (1943). Issues of Informational Strategy. *Public Opinion Quarterly* 7(1): 77: pp. 78–79.
27 Op cit.
28 Vian Bakir (2013), *Torture, Intelligence and Sousveillance in the War on Terror: Agenda-Building Struggles.* (Farnham: Ashgate).
29 Op cit. Note xxiii.
30 Op cit. Note xxiii.
31 James A. Smith (1993), *Idea Brokers: Think Tanks and the Rise of the New Policy Elite* (New York: The Free Press).
32 Tom Griffin, Hilary Aked, David Miller and Sarah Marusek (2015), *The Henry Jackson Society and the Degeneration of British Neoconservatism: Liberal Interventionism, Islamophobia and the 'War on Terror'* (Spinwatch, Public Interest Investigations). Available at http://www.spinwatch.org/index.php/issues/more/item/5777-new-report-on-the-henry-jackson-society. Download date 23 June 2017.
33 Ibid., p. 74.
34 Theodore Sayeed (2016), 'Chomsky and his Critics' in *Mondoweiss*, 19 February 2016. http://mondoweiss.net/2016/02/chomsky-and-his-critics/. Download date 23 June 2015.
35 Amnesty International (2011) 'Libya: Organization Calls for Immediate Arms Embargo and Assets Freeze' Amnesty International Statement: 23 February 2011.
36 House of Commons Foreign Affairs Committee (2016) 'Libya: Examination of Intervention and Collapse and the UK's Future Policy Options' (Houses of Parliament).
37 UK Gov summary document available at https://assets.publishing.service.gov.uk/government/uploads/system/uploads/attachment_data/file/630409/Syria_Resilience_2017.pdf. Download date 9 May 2018.
38 Ibid.
39 Herring and Robinson (2003) 'Too Polemical or Too Critical'.
40 For accounts detailing the limits to academic autonomy see Lewis Coser, (1965), *Men of Ideas* (New York: Simon and Schuster: New York), p. 140 and p. 337; C. Wright Mills (1968), *Power, Politics and People: Collected Essays* (Oxford: Oxford University Press); Dick Flacks, 'Making History and Making Theory: Notes on How Intellectuals Seek relevance' in Charles Lemert ed., (1991), *Intellectuals and Politics: Social Theory in a Changing World* (Newbury Park, CA: Sage); Russell Jacoby (1987), *The Last Intellectuals: American Culture in the Age of Academe* (New York: Perseus Books); Peter Eglin 'Partnership in an Evil Action: Canadian Universities, Indonesia and East Timor and the Question of Intellectual Responsibility Again' pp217-30 in Jeffery Klaehn ed., (2005) *Bound by Power: Intended Consequences* (2005; Montreal: Black Rose); Robert Jensen, 'The Faculty Filter: Why the Propaganda Model is Marginalized in U.S. Journalism Schools' in Jeffery Klaehn ed., (2010) *The Political Economy of Media and Power* (New York: Peter

Lang); David Cromwell 'Absurd Silence and Misplaced Pragmatism: How Dissent is Kept to Manageable Levels' pp 90-104 in Klaehn (ed.), *Bound by Power*; See also *Power Over Principle, the Costs of Dissent: An Interview with Brian Martin* in Klaehn (ed.), *Bound by Power*.

[41] Christopher Simpson (1994), *The Science of Coercion: Communication Research and Psychological Warfare, 1945-1960* (Oxford: Oxford University Press).

[42] Mark Curtis (2004), *Unpeople: Britain's Secret Human Rights Abuses* (2004: London:Vintage).

[43] Ibid.

[44] Nicholas Schou (2016), *Spooked: How the CIA Manipulates the Media and Hoodwinks Hollywood* (New York: Skyhorse Publishing).

[45] Joseph Trento (2005), *The Secret History of The CIA* (Rosevill, CA: Prima Publishing). See also Carl Bernstein's 1977 *Rolling Stone* expose available here http://www.carlbernstein.com/magazine_cia_and_media.php. Downloaded 2 July 2017.

[46] C. Sims (2016) 'Academics in Foxholes: The Life and Death of the Human Terrain System', *Foreign Affairs*, 4 February 2016.

[47] Tom Bartlett (2015), 'Psychologist Implicated in APA's Torture Report Resigns Academic Post', *The Chronicle of Higher Education,* 21 July 2015.

[48] Hilary Clinton (2014) *Tough Choices* (New York: Simon and Schuster), p. 393.

[49] David Miller and Piers Robinson (2017), *'Propaganda'*: A Short Introductory Film. Available at https://vimeo.com/219533611. Downloaded 4 July 2017.

[50] John Corner. (2007), 'Mediated Political, Promotional Culture, and the Idea of "Propaganda"', *Media, Culture and Society*, 29(4): 669–677.

[51] David Ray Griffin, *Bush and Cheney: How they Ruined America and the World* (2017: Northampton Press: MA).

[52] Piers Robinson (2017), 'Learning from Chilcot: Propaganda, Deception and the 'War on Terror', *International Journal of Contemporary Iraqi Studies*, Vol. 11, No. 1-2, 1 March 2017, pp. 47–73.

[53] Oreskes and Conway (2011), *Merchants of Doubt*.

# PART II

# The Internet and New Digital Media

CHAPTER 6

# Propaganda 2.0: Herman and Chomsky's Propaganda Model in the Age of the Internet, Big Data and Social Media

Christian Fuchs

## 1. Introduction

Herman and Chomsky's book *Manufacturing Consent: The Political Economy of the Mass Media*[1] was published nearly 30 years ago. Today, not only has the Soviet Union disappeared, but we have also experienced the progressive intensification of neoliberalism and financialization, the 2008 world economic crisis, austerity, constant growth of inequalities, and the extension and intensification of nationalism, new racism, and xenophobia. The news media are in crisis. Advertising has shifted from print towards targeted online ads. Today we not only have the World Wide Web and mobile phones, but also Big Data, Google, Facebook, YouTube, Twitter, Flickr, Instagram, Wikipedia, blogs, etc. have become important means of information and communication. Given these changes, the question arises if and how we can make sense of the propaganda model in the age of the internet and social media.

Herman and Chomsky summarise the propaganda model in the following words:

> The essential ingredients of our propaganda model, or set of news 'filters', fall under the following headings: (1) the size, concentrated ownership, owner wealth, and profit orientation of the dominant mass-media firms;

---

How to cite this book chapter:
Fuchs, C. 2018. Propaganda 2.0: Herman and Chomsky's Propaganda Model in the Age of the Internet, Big Data and Social Media. In: Pedro-Carañana, J., Broudy, D. and Klaehn, J. (eds.). *The Propaganda Model Today: Filtering Perception and Awareness*. Pp. 71–92. London: University of Westminster Press. DOI: https://doi.org/10.16997/book27.f. License: CC-BY-NC-ND 4.0

(2) advertising as the primary income source of the mass media; (3) the reliance of the media on information provided by government, business, and 'experts' funded and approved by these primary sources and agents of power; (4) 'flak' as a means of disciplining the media; and (5) 'anticommunism' as a national religion and control mechanism. These elements interact with and reinforce one another. The raw material of news must pass through successive filters, leaving only the cleansed residue fit to print. They fix the premises of discourse and interpretation, and the definition of what is newsworthy in the first place, and they explain the basis and operations of what amount to propaganda campaigns.[2]

The key aspect is that wealth and power inequalities shape what is considered newsworthy, what gets reported, and what is heard, read and watched. It should be noted that the propaganda model is not a theory. A theory of propaganda and ideology requires a systematic theory of society and capitalism, in which the role of culture, ideology and propaganda is clearly defined. It is for example unclear why exactly there are five elements and how they are theoretically justified. Moreover, entertainment and the spectacle as a filter that displaces and colonises political communication is missing from the model. Jürgen Habermas argues that entertainment is part of the process of the feudalisation and de-politicisation of the public sphere: 'Reporting facts as human-interest stories, mixing information with entertainment, arranging material episodically, and breaking down complex relationships into smaller fragments – all of this comes together to form a syndrome that works to depoliticize public communication.'[3] It is therefore best to view the Propaganda Model (PM) as a not necessarily complete list of elements that are ideologically influencing factors on the agenda of the news media. The fifth element of anti-communism should probably best be generalised in terms of dominant ideologies that influence the media.[4] Also Joan Pedro suggests to term the fifth dimension 'dominant ideology'.[5] In the thirty years since the publication of the book, especially the neoliberal 'belief in the "miracle of the market" (Reagan)'[6] has become dominant.

In respect to criticisms arguing that the model is functionalist and does not take resistance and contradictions into account, Herman argues that 'the system is not all-powerful,'[7] that there are 'uncertain and variable effects' and 'contesting forces.'[8]

## 2. Social Media and Power

One often hears that social media and the decentralised character of the internet overcome hierarchies and foster a participatory culture and democratic communication. Edward Herman has voiced scepticism about this assumption: 'Some argue that the internet and the new communication technologies are breaking the corporate stranglehold on journalism and opening an unprecedented era of interactive democratic media.'[9] He argues that new technologies 'permit media firms to shrink staff even as they achieve greater outputs, and they make possible global distribution systems that reduce the number of media entities.'[10]

### 2.1 Size, Ownership, Profit Orientation

The dominant social media platforms have concentrated ownership. Google-co-founders Larry Page and Sergey Brin own 42.4% and 41.3% respectively of Alphabet's class B common stock. Page controls 26.6% of the voting power; Brin 25.9%.[11] Facebook owner Mark Zuckerberg controls 85.3% of the company's class B common stock and 60.1% of the voting power.[12] Social media is also a highly concentrated market: Google controls 71% of the world's searches, and Facebook and its subsidiary WhatsApp account for 48% of users worldwide of the top 10 social media platforms.[13]

Both Google searches and the Facebook news feed are very important sources of news today. In respect to the 2016 US presidential election, the group of 18–29-year-olds considered social media the most important news source:[14] For all who are 30 or older, TV news was the most important source. Taking the entire adult population together, 78% used television during one week for learning about the election, 65% used digital information sources (48% news websites; 44% social networks), 44% used the radio, while 36% read print newspapers. The data indicate that the internet does not substitute but merely complements traditional news sources. Among younger people, however, it is the most important source of news.

Algorithms determine the ranking of Google's search results and Facebook's news feed. The centralised ownership of these companies (from which users are excluded), combined with the huge market share of users the two companies hold and the fact that both platforms are important news sources, results in the circumstance that ownership also means control over algorithms that determine news sources for a significant part of the population. Both algorithms are intransparent; they are corporate secrets. As capitalist companies, Google and Facebook want to protect themselves from competition. Factors that play a role in Facebook's news feed algorithm e.g. include your closeness to a person posting content (closeness meaning how regularly you interact with them through messaging, likes, etc.), the type of a post or the achieved popularity of a post.[15] It is also possible to boost a particular post by paying for it, or to buy a sponsored ad that targets a specific group of users' news feeds. Google's PageRank algorithm ranks web pages using various criteria, such as the number of sites that link to them – a weight is given to each link. So, if the *New York Times* links to your web page, then this link is likely to have a higher weight than the link your best friend posts on her/his site. Also, on Google is it possible to purchase sponsored links that are boosted to prominent screen positions.

The discussion shows that social media's ownership matters in several respects. Firstly, social media markets tend to be highly concentrated. Private ownership locks users out from the control of algorithms that determine the priorities of how search results and news are presented. The specifics of the algorithms are secret because of the secret nature of intellectual property and because capitalism's laws of competition foster secrecy.

Online advertising is, however, contradictory. On average, users only click on one out of one thousand advertisements.[16] And even then, it is uncertain if they really stay on a linked page and if they buy something there. The effects of targeted online advertising may therefore be overstated. Because of the fetishistic idea that algorithms and Big Data allow perfect interest-based targeting, advertisers gain the impression that they can sell commodities via social media. If it turns out that this is a misconception, then targeted advertising may lose credibility and social media capitalism's financial bubble may burst and cause the next dot-com crisis.

### 2.2 Advertising

Figure 6.1 shows statistics about the development of the distribution of global advertising spending.

The data shows that the share of online advertising has increased from 17.9% to 28.3% in the years from 2010 until 2015. During the same time, newspaper advertising revenue has dropped significantly and its share has decreased from 20.5% to 14.8%. Online advertising has globally become the second most

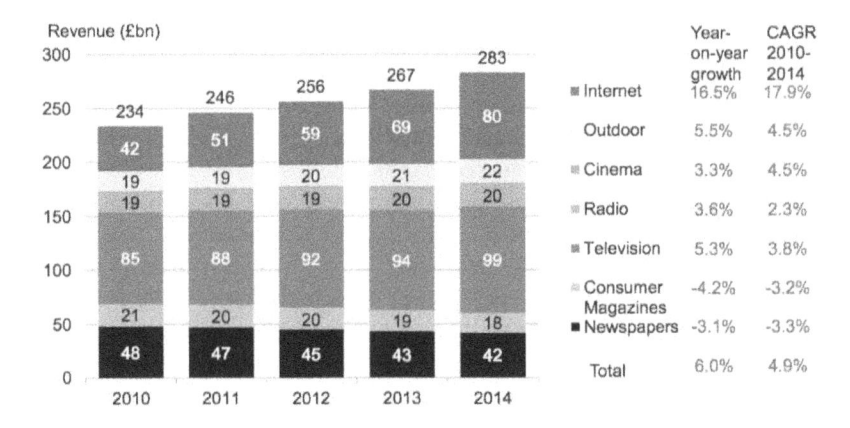

| Revenue (£bn) | 2010 | 2011 | 2012 | 2013 | 2014 | | Year-on-year growth | CAGR 2010-2014 |
|---|---|---|---|---|---|---|---|---|
| Total | 234 | 246 | 256 | 267 | 283 | Total | 6.0% | 4.9% |
| Internet | 42 | 51 | 59 | 69 | 80 | Internet | 16.5% | 17.9% |
| Outdoor | 19 | 19 | 20 | 21 | 22 | Outdoor | 5.5% | 4.5% |
| Cinema | 19 | 19 | 19 | 20 | 20 | Cinema | 3.3% | 4.5% |
| Radio | | | | | | Radio | 3.6% | 2.3% |
| Television | 85 | 88 | 92 | 94 | 99 | Television | 5.3% | 3.8% |
| Consumer Magazines | 21 | 20 | 20 | 19 | 18 | Consumer Magazines | -4.2% | -3.2% |
| Newspapers | 48 | 47 | 45 | 43 | 42 | Newspapers | -3.1% | -3.3% |

**Fig. 6.1:** The development of global ad spending's distribution.[17]

important form of advertising after television advertising. Especially in times of crisis, online advertising seems to appear to advertisers as the more secure option because it is individualised through extensive surveillance of online behaviour and algorithmically targeted. Traditional news journalism is in a crisis of a commercial character, notably in relation to its advertising revenues.

Google, Facebook and Twitter are not just sources of news and information. These websites are also among the world's largest advertising agencies. They are in the business of selling targeted ad space as a commodity and derive their revenues almost exclusively from targeted advertising.[18] Herman and Chomsky remarked in an interview about the PM in respect to the second filter that Google and Yahoo 'are heavily dependent on advertising revenue.'[19] Given their high numbers of users, platforms such as Google and Facebook can expect to attract large shares of ad investments seeing that companies are interested in reaching a large number of people from their targeted audience. Social media advertising allows both broad reach and precision targeting.

Herman and Chomsky argue that advertisers prefer to run ads during TV programmes that are 'culturally and politically conservative,'[20] i.e. entertainment and spectacle oriented programmes and news and discussion programmes that have a right-wing, conservative and pro-capitalist bias. The effect is that media that focus on entertainment and spectacles tend to attract more advertisements, whereas independent media 'suffer from the political

**Fig. 6.2:** Example of a promoted tweet. Data source: twitter.com, accessed on 11 November 2016.

discrimination of advertisers.' On social media, the situation is slightly different, but not necessarily better: on Facebook and Twitter, users can pay to promote postings. Facebook, Twitter and Google allow targeted ads. On Twitter, it is also possible to promote trends. Figure 6.2 shows a promoted posting from Twitter.

Promoted posts show up on Twitter users' news feeds, profiles or tweet detail pages. Figure 6.3 shows that on Twitter, targeting is not only possible based on gender, languages and devices, but also based on search keywords, followers of particular users, interests, TV shows, behaviours, and events. Figure 6.4 shows details of Twitter's behavioural targeting feature.

On television, advertisers target particular audiences who watch specific programmes. In newspapers, they target the typical reading audience. On social media, multiple audiences can be targeted at once because there are micro and niche publics. This makes the logic of advertising different on social media than in traditional media. The overall effect is an online advertising-user-spiral, in which more and more advertising revenue shifts from print to digital due to the targeting possibilities. The advertising-circulation-spiral was first observed in the realm of newspaper advertising,[21] but it certainly also contributes to the monopolisation of online markets. In 2015, the finance and insurance industry, followed by the retail industry, comprised the largest share of ad spending on Google. Amazon was the largest advertiser with investments of US$ 157 million.[22] In 2013, Samsung was with US$ 100 million the biggest advertiser on Facebook.[23]

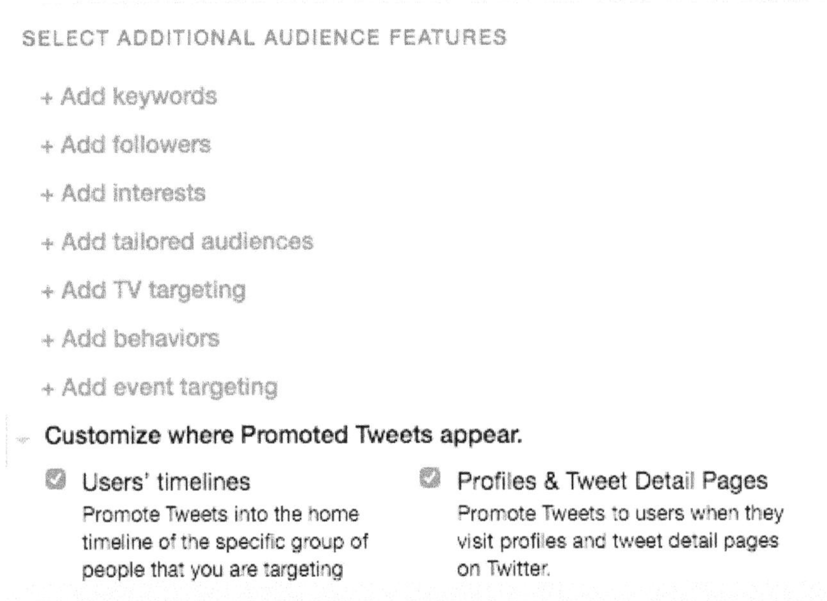

SELECT ADDITIONAL AUDIENCE FEATURES

+ Add keywords

+ Add followers

+ Add interests

+ Add tailored audiences

+ Add TV targeting

+ Add behaviors

+ Add event targeting

- **Customize where Promoted Tweets appear.**

    ☑ Users' timelines
    Promote Tweets into the home timeline of the specific group of people that you are targeting

    ☑ Profiles & Tweet Detail Pages
    Promote Tweets to users when they visit profiles and tweet detail pages on Twitter.

**Fig. 6.3:** Targeting of ads on Twitter.

Browse and select behaviors

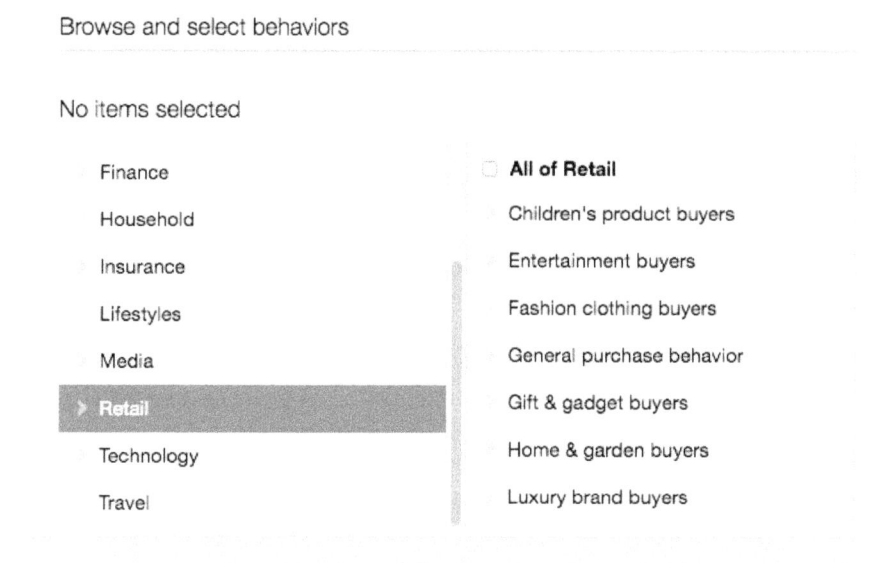

No items selected

| Finance | All of Retail |
| Household | Children's product buyers |
| Insurance | Entertainment buyers |
| Lifestyles | Fashion clothing buyers |
| Media | General purchase behavior |
| > Retail | Gift & gadget buyers |
| Technology | Home & garden buyers |
| Travel | Luxury brand buyers |

**Fig. 6.4:** Behavioural targeting on Twitter.

The discussion shows that online advertising acts as a filter in several ways: (i) It allows large transnational corporations with large ad budgets to confront a large targeted audience with content and ads; (ii) Regular content becomes ever more difficult to discern from advertising. There is no clear temporal or spatial differentiation. Corporations are interested in native online advertising and branded online content as it allows them to deceive users and to almost act like news media, effectively undermining the independence of reporting. Companies can increase reach via social media; (iii) The online advertising-user-spiral increases social media's power in advertising and news-making and advances monopoly tendencies in the online economy; (iv) An important fourth dimension that needs to be added which Herman and Chomsky do not discuss is that advertising means exploitation of audience labour.[24] On social media, users' digital labour produces a data commodity and is exploited by the platforms for selling targeted ad spaces.[25]

### 2.3 Sourcing

Colin Sparks argues for an extension and refining of the PM:

> The central departure from the classical formulations of the PM is that, in place of the stress it gives to the uniformity of the media, we now expect to find diversity. The divided nature of the capitalist class, the presence of powerful critical currents which find legitimate public expression in a capitalist democracy, the need to address the concerns

of a mass audience, political differentiation as a marketing strategy, all point to the necessity for any viable media system to include a range of different opinions. [...] Of course, it is entirely true that the range of dissenting voices is carefully controlled. There tends to be a preponderance of elite voices, and those in turn will tend to reflect the views of powerful groups in economics and politics. [...] Sometimes, however, radical individuals do get regular exposure in the media [...] partly at least for the good business reason that it fits the marketing strategy of particular media to attract the substantial number of radical individuals towards their niche in the market.[26]

Des Freedman[27] discusses the example of the British tabloid the *Daily Mirror* that during the 2003 Iraq war substituted its usual focus on celebrities and scandals with an anti-war campaign. The example shows that also mainstream media, especially in situations of crisis, can take alternative positions, and that such exceptions matter. Freedman argues for giving attention to 'both structure *and* agency, contradiction *and* action, consensus *and* conflict.'[28] Herman and Chomsky acknowledged the possibility for diversity: 'The mass media are not a solid monolith on all issues.'[29]

Sourcing as a filter is different online than in broadcasting because the internet has a decentralised and global architecture. Manuel Castells[30] argues that the internet allows mass-self-communication, which means that a larger number of producers online as compared to the broadcast model can reach a larger audience. The basic difference between computer networks and broadcasting is that the network is a universal machine, at once a technology or production, distribution and consumption. Combined with its global reach and significant bandwidth rates, this allows the phenomenon of user-generated content. User-generated content does however not automatically imply political plurality and diversity. The key question about communication power shifts from the control of production towards the control of attention and visibility. Attention and visibility, however, also need to be produced and are thus aspects of production. Gaining online attention and visibility requires money, time and labour-force. Everyone can in principle produce content online, but in a capitalist society only a minority attracts online visibility and attention.[31]

A *first* online asymmetry concerns the fact that 'the traditional media themselves have occupied the internet and are dominant news providers there; [...] they have the resources and pre-existing audiences to give them a huge advantage over alternative media potential rivals.'[32] In November 2016, the most popular online news site was CNN.com. While CNN was on 11 November, 2016, the 72nd most accessed website in the world, the independent news sites alternet.org and democracynow.org were only ranked in positions 5,967 and 9,493 respectively on the list of the world's most accessed websites.[33] Notwithstanding, alternative online media certainly attract significant audiences. At the same time, they tend to face resource problems because they are not organised as capitalist businesses.

**BUY REAL FACEBOOK FOLLOWERS|COUNTRY TARGETED AT $21**

Get real active and country targeted followers on our profile. We use different marketing techniques to get you active users on facebook. Your profile would be promote on our own facebook network, other social media and websites. Your followers would be interested in your profile and would like to see your posts.

| 1000 FACEBOOK FOLLOWERS | 2000 FACEBOOK FOLLOWERS | 3000 FACEBOOK FOLLOWERS | 5000 FACEBOOK FOLLOWERS | 10000 FACEBOOK FOLLOWERS |
|---|---|---|---|---|
| $21 ONE TIME | $41 ONE TIME | $61 ONE TIME | $91 ONE TIME | $171 ONE TIME |
| FREE SERVICES | FREE SERVICES | FREE SERVICES | FREE SERVICES | FREE SERVICES |

**Fig. 6.5:** An example for online attention as commodity. Data source: http://www.followersandlikes4u.com.

*Second*, money is an important factor in attaining online visibility and attention. It is possible to boost one's online attention by buying likes, followers, re-tweets, etc. Figure 6.5 shows an example of a company that sells Facebook followers. Users with a budget to spend can buy more visibility online. If your number of followers is large enough, then it is also more likely that others start following you because there are reputational hierarchies and the artificially inflated number of likes, re-tweets and followers is a form of psychological impression management.

*Third*, there are reputational inequalities. Social media attention is highly stratified. A small elite group of users dominates online visibility and attention.[34] As an example, table 6.1 shows the Facebook pages that have the largest number of fans.

The data indicate that corporations and entertainment dominate social media attention. News and information therefore tend to focus on popular topics.

| Rank | FB Page | Number of Fans | Type |
|---|---|---|---|
| 1 | Facebook for Every iPhone | 500 300 326 | App |
| 2 | Facebook | 174 559 960 | Corporation |
| 3 | Cristiano Ronaldo | 117 252 364 | Footballer |
| 4 | Shakira | 104 416 196 | Musician |
| 5 | Vin Diesel | 100 378 269 | Actor |
| 6 | Coca-Cola | 99 713 570 | Brand, corporation |
| 7 | FC Barcelona | 94 669 625 | Football team |
| 8 | Read Madrid C.F. | 92 645 690 | Football team |
| 9 | Eminem | 91 308 332 | Musician |
| 10 | Leo Messi | 87 147 610 | Footballer |
|  | Bernie Sanders | 4 653 316 | Politician |
|  | Karl Marx | 1 450 139 | Political theorist |

**Table 6.1:** The most popular pages on Facebook. Data source: https://www.socialbakers.com, http://www.facebook.com, accessed on 12 November, 2016.

Politics is less visible and more marginalised. Bernie Sanders and Karl Marx, two symbols of left-wing politics, have significantly fewer fans. In an interview, Herman and Chomsky point out this development: '[M]uch of the new media on the internet is oriented toward facilitating social connections, with politics secondary at best, and the best of the new alternative media have limited resources and outreach and specialize in critical analysis rather than news-making.'[35]

The tabloidisation of social media is, however, just a tendency, not a determinism or totality. Social movements often use social media because they are not adequately represented in the mainstream media. They tend to understand how to use online communication as a tool for political organisation well. The capitalist online public sphere is not totally, but predominantly, an entertainment sphere, and only to a lesser extent is it a political public sphere.

*Fourth*, political bots play a role in online political communication. A bot is a piece of software code that performs certain online behaviour based on an algorithm. Examples are automatic tweets or re-tweets or the posting of images and texts from a database at particular times. The problem of bots in political communication is that they can appear human-like, can distort attention, harass and scare people, etc. They are an expression of the online automation of human action, the replacement of humans by machines. There are concrete humans who own, control, and programme bots. So, whereas the political bot does not have political attitudes, morals and interests, its behaviour is shaped by human beings who have particular political interests.

Kollanyi, Howard and Woolley have analysed around 10 million tweets mentioning Hillary Clinton and Donald Trump around the time of the third US presidential election debate.[36] They found that political bots posted 36.1% of the pro-Trump tweets and 23.5% of the pro-Clinton tweets. Given that political opinion and sentiment analysis is increasingly conducted on Twitter and with the help of Big Data analytics, political bots can manipulate the public perception of public opinion. Considering that a certain degree of online politics is automated, political attitudes should probably not at all be measured with the help of Big Data analytics. Political bots, Big Data analytics and computational social science methods can colonise, distort, instrumentalise and manipulate the public sphere.

## 2.4 Flak/Mediated Lobbying

Herman and Chomsky do not properly explain the name of the fourth dimension: Flak. This German term stems from military jargon. The Nazis used *Flak* as an abbreviation for ***Fl****iegerabwehr****k****anone*. In a comprehensive overview, Joan Pedro suggests to speak of 'countermeasures to discipline the media'[37] instead of flak. We could also simply speak of mediated lobbying attempts.

Herman and Chomsky define flak the following way: "'Flak' refers to negative responses to a media statement or program. It may take the form of letters, telegrams, phone calls, petitions, lawsuits, speeches and bills before Congress, and other modes of complaint, threat, and punitive action. It may be organized centrally or locally, or it may consist of the entirely independent actions of individuals.'[38] In the digital age, lobbying for certain interests has been extended to social media and is no longer simply aimed at centralised media organisations, but now aims to directly transmit political messages to as many internet users as possible.

At the time of the 2011 Arab Spring and the subsequent Occupy movements, there was much euphoria about protest and revolutionary movements' use of social media for public engagement and political organisation.[39] After the world economic crisis had started in 2008, it seemed like revolution was possible. The role of social media in revolutions and protests was often overstated. Empirical analysis shows that in protests, social media communication tends to interact with other forms of political communication, especially face-to-face-communication.[40] Revolutions and protests are not virtual, but take place offline and online simultaneously.

Political groups and movements from all parts of the political spectrum utilise the internet and social media for political communication. The example of political bots mentioned in the previous section shows that both supporters of Donald Trump and Hillary Clinton used bots for trying to boost their candidate's popularity. Automated lobbying is a particular form of flak in the digital age.

In the early days of the internet, sometimes the impression was conveyed that left-wing and green movements such as the Zapatista solidarity campaigns were very skilled at utilising the internet for political communication because they are grassroots organisations and that far-right groups were very bad at it due to their hierarchical leadership ideology. The basic argument was that grassroots movements as well as the internet have a flat and decentralised structure and therefore are suited for each other. This assumption underestimates the internet's social hierarchies and power structures that are not technically determined. Today right wing lobbying is a large-scale affair on the internet.

In November 2016, Hillary Clinton had 10.9 million Twitter followers, while Donald Trump had 14.6 million. French President François Hollande had 1.78 million followers, the National Front leader Marine Le Pen 1.18 million. In the UK, left-wing Labour Party leader Jeremy Corbyn had 662k followers, Nigel Farage 516k.[41] The data indicate that right-wing groups and individuals are at least just as active and popular on social media as left-wing activists and groups.

Figure 6.6 shows a typical tweet by Donald Trump. It achieved a high number of likes and re-tweets: More than 7,500 likes and 20,000 re-tweets. The example shows that right-wing politics today to a significant extent takes place online and on social media.

Right-wing lobbying is not limited to established parties and politicians, but is to a significant degree carried by right-wing social movements. The alt-right

**Donald J. Trump**
@realDonaldTrump

Thank you NH! We will end illegal immigration, stop the drugs, deport all criminal aliens&save American lives! Watch bit.ly/2embjxvNH

RETWEETS 7,541    LIKES 20,826

Fig. 6.6: A tweet by Donald Trump. Source: twitter.com.

movement is a far-right movement that is predominantly active on the internet. It is racist, white supremacist, anti-Semitic, homophobic, anti-feminist, and Islamophobic. It uses social media, internet memes, and right-wing sites such as Breitbart News. Donald Trump has appointed Breitbart's executive chairman Steve Bannon as his White House chief strategist. The alt-right movement uses hashtags such as #WhiteGenocide, #MAGA (Make America Great Again), #ccot (Conservative Christians on Twitter), #tcot (Top Conservative on Twitter), #WhiteSupremacist, #AltRight, #AntiWhite, #WhiteLivesMatter, #WarOnWhites, #NRx (Neoreaction). *The Guardian* has reported that Trump supporters spread fake news stories and conspiracy theories about Hillary Clinton on social media.[42] Empirical research confirms such tendencies.[43] As dialectical counter-pole to the fact that there are fake online stories, one must also stress that fact-checking organisations that work on professionally revealing truths and falsehoods have emerged. They are organisations such as the International Fact-Checking Network.

The Norwegian Nazi terrorist Anders Breivik was quite digitally savvy. He gathered information online, purchased weapons and bomb equipment online, was an online gaming enthusiast (World of Warcraft, Call of Duty) participated in far-right discussion fora such as Stormfront, nordisku.nu and document.no, gathered more than 9,000 friends on Facebook, and spread propaganda videos with the help of YouTube and Vimeo.[44]

Even if we do not like it, fascism and right-wing extremism on social media are to a significant degree public forms of communication. They constitute a reactionary public sphere that is mediated by the internet, social media, mobile communication, etc. The point is to create a political climate in society that advances democratic and civil public spheres, which is however not just an issue that concerns how we communicate. It is also a political task that needs to aim at overcoming inequality, discrimination exploitation and domination in society. Online fascism is online communication that aims to advance creating a fascist society by spreading hatred, prejudices, authoritarian populism, friend/enemy propaganda, and fetishist political ideology. Right-wing extremism online appropriates certain elements of fascism (e.g. hatred against immigrants and refugees, anti-Semitism, anti-socialism, etc.) in online speech.

In an interview Herman and Chomsky argued that right-wing media, including Fox News, right-wing talk radio and blogs, form 'a right-wing attack machine and echo-chamber'.[45] In the current political climate of nationalism, racism, xenophobia and elements of fascism, social media is certainly a right-wing attack machine. It must, however, also be seen that the political left is skilled at using social media, which maintains online politics as a contradictory space.

## 2.5 Ideologies

Ideology is a complex term with many meanings that range from individual or collective meanings or worldviews to the notion of false consciousness.[46] The advantage of a critical notion of ideology over a general one is that it allows normative judgements about how a good society looks like. Herman and Chomsky speak of neoliberal ideology,[47] Western ideology,[48] anti-Communist ideology,[49] the national-security ideology,[50] right-wing ideology,[51] and the ideology of national security.[52] But they never define the term. Ideology can in a critical manner be understood as a semiotic process in which humans practice the production and spreading of information, meanings, ideas, belief, systems, artefacts, systems, and institutions that justify or naturalise domination and exploitation.[53] Ideology is the semiotic level of domination and exploitation.

In times of crisis, it is highly likely that all sorts of ideologies are expressed and challenged in public communication. There are both ideologies of the internet and ideologies on the internet. Ideologies of the internet are a form of public communication that fetishises instrumental control of online communication. It is instrumental communication about instrumental communications, a meta-form of communication that justifies and defends the application of instrumental reason to the internet. Neoliberal ideologies of the internet present the online world as a frontier for investments that create a better world. They leave out questions of inequality, digital labour, class and exploitation. An example is that Google describes itself as showing that 'democracy on the web works,' reducing democracy and participation to the issue that 'Google search works because it relies on the millions of individuals posting links.' Questions relating to the secrecy of Google's search algorithm, its monopoly power in the search market, users and employees' lack of control of its means, etc. are not asked. State ideologies of the internet justify state surveillance, censorship and control of the internet and leave out questions of privacy and freedom of speech.

Britain's Prime Minister Theresa May said that without advanced surveillance capacities and technologies, 'we run the risk that murderers will not be caught, terrorist plots will go undetected, drug traffickers will go unchallenged, child abusers will not be stopped, and slave drivers will continue their appalling trade in human beings.'[54] Compare this quote to Donald Trump's tweet in figure 6.6. Both present society as being full of illegal immigrants, criminals, drugs, terrorism, child abuse, slavery, and other dangers. The ideological trick is to first create the impression of ubiquitous danger and to then call for quick fixes by calling for deporting or locking up or monitoring scapegoats, enhancing the use of surveillance technologies, etc. The problem is that there is no technological fix to political and socio-economic problems. Categorical suspicion turns the presumption of innocence into a presumption of guilt so that certain humans are automatically considered terrorists and criminal until proven innocent.

Ideology on the internet is the phenomenon of fascism, racism, right-wing extremism, nationalism, classism, sexism, anti-Semitism, etc. online. Given that right-wing ideology is flourishing in many societies, it is also exceedingly present online and on social media. Ideology on the internet tends to make use of visual means and tabloidisation (simplification, using few words, emotionalisation, scandalisation, polarisation, banalisation, manipulation, fabrication, etc.). User-generated ideology is the phenomenon that ideology production is no longer confined to professional ideologues, but has become possible on the level of everyday life. Ideologies are sensational, populist, simplistic, emotional, and speak directly to particular subjects. Because of these features, online ideology tends to attract a lot of attention. Algorithms reward those who gain significant levels of attention by helping to further amplifying them. Therefore, there is a tendency of *algorithmic amplification of online ideologies*.

The 2016 Austrian presidential election saw a run-off between far-right candidate Norbert Hofer representing the Freedom Party of Austria and the Green Party candidate Alexander Van der Bellen. Hofer's supporters mobilised especially on Facebook, where they often spread violent threats against Van der Bellen, refugees, immigrants, and others. An analysis of such comments showed that the important elements of political communication were: (1) authoritarian populism guided by the leadership principle, (2) nationalism, (3) the friend/enemy scheme, and (4) militancy and violent threats.[55]

Herman remarks that the 'fifth filter – anti-communist ideology – is possibly weakened by the collapse of the Soviet Union and global socialism.' The situation has again changed since with various Occupy movements, Jeremy Corbyn, Bernie Sanders, Syriza, Podemos, etc., once again putting the idea of socialism on the political agenda. We see both liberal and right-wing mainstream media in Britain waging an ideological war against such people and movements. As an example, a study of journalistic representations of Jeremy Corbyn found that in 89% of 812 analysed news stories, Corbyn's views were absent, distorted or challenged. Forty-three per cent of all stories ridiculed or personally attacked Corbyn. The study concludes that 'the degree of viciousness and antagonism with which the majority of the British newspapers have treated Corbyn is deemed to be highly problematic from a democratic perspective.'[56] Another study showed how anti-socialist ideology directed against Corbyn also spread on Twitter and was organised as a red scare 2.0.[57] 'In the analysed dataset, users for example argued that because of being left-wing, Corbyn is loony, an extremist and dangerous (compressed general ideology), is a friend of terrorists, radicals and dictators and thereby supports Britain's enemies (foreign policy discourse topic), wants to create a state-controlled economy that will result in poverty and deprivation for all (command economy-discourse topic), wants to create a totalitarian state like Stalin or Mao did (authoritarian and totalitarian politics discourse politics), and is an old, badly dressed, vegetarian, bike-riding loony-left hippie with a beard (culture and lifestyle discourse topic). The foreign policy, command economy, and lifestyle-discourse topics were also prominently featured in the right-wing media. User-generated ideology on Twitter in these cases is closely related to ideologies spread by the mass media. It copies the latter's contents by linking to articles, using certain headlines or biased phrases such as 'the Loony Left' and at the same time feeds these media by showing that there is an interest in and positive response to stories that scapegoat the Left.'[58]

But social media and society are not exclusive terrains of the right. There is always the potential for contestation. The same study showed that left-wing activists can challenge ideology by characterising those attacked in positive terms, using satire, humour, sarcasm, provide links and arguments showing the world's complexity and contradictions, argumentative dialectical reversals. Such strategies tend to be smart, complex, and dialectical.

### 3. Assessment

Table 6.2 summarises the discussion of the online propaganda model.

On the one hand it seems like the propaganda model is also relevant in the online world because we continue to live in a society shaped by class and domination. On the other hand, the model also needs to be adapted and extended because of particular features of digital capitalism and digital media.

Above we have discussed the role of algorithms that partly automate propaganda in the form of intransparent search and ranking algorithms as well as political blogs. Native advertising and branded content enhance the power of corporations and enable them to displace journalism's autonomy and to present product propaganda as editorial content. A further differentiation that must be taken into account is that in computer networks and on networked computers, the production, diffusion and consumption of information converges. Audiences become users and prosumers (productive consumers). This model is different from the broadcast model of communication. Power asymmetries are, however, not automatically sublated, but further complicated. Another impor-

| Dimension | Internet |
|---|---|
| Size, Ownership, Profit Orientation | Concentrated social media markets, concentrated ownership, intransparent and secret algorithms that determine the priorities of how results and news are presented |
| Advertising | Transnational corporations are able to confront users with targeted ads and content; Native online advertising and branded online content threaten news-media's-independence; The online advertising-user-spiral increases social media's power in advertising and as news media and advances monopoly tendencies in the online economy; On social media, users' digital labour produces a data commodity and is exploited by the platforms in order to sell targeted ad spaces |
| Sourcing | Traditional news organisations are powerful actors in online news; Online attention as commodity manipulates political communication; Corporations and entertainment dominate social media attention; Political bots distort the political public sphere |
| Flak, Mediated Lobbying | Bots and other tools for automated lobbying; Social media use by politicians, parties, movements; Online hate speech |
| Ideologies | Ideologies of the internet; Ideologies on the internet and user-generated ideologies; Algorithmic amplification of online ideologies |

**Table 6.2:** The Online Propaganda Model (PM).

tant aspect is that we should always think of potentials for resistance and study actual oppositional developments.

I find the PM a useful model for the analysis of power structures in media systems, as this chapter demonstrates. But we also need a further refinement and extension that brings us beyond the PM and takes critiques of capitalism, anti-democratic elements of state power, acceleration, etc. into account when analysing media systems. There is a range of topics, such as the exploitation of labour and surveillance, that relates to (digital) media that need to be critically analysed.[59] Wherever there are communications systems in capitalism, there are also workers. And a specific share of them is exploited in class relations. In the production of digital media, there is an international division of digital labour in which we find diverse workers, such as African slave-miners, Chinese hardware-assemblers working at Foxconn, highly paid and highly stressed software engineers, precarious clickworkers and call centre agents, online freelancers, precarious creative workers, social media user-workers, etc.[60] Edward Snowden unveiled the existence of a surveillance-industrial internet complex, through which secret services bulk-monitor users' online activities, which has resulted in concerns about the violation of basic rights. Social media are accelerated, high-speed media. Nobody can read all tweets posted about an important topic. Tweets and online information flow at such a speed that there is no time for real debate and controversy. Postings tend to be short, entertaining, and superficial. Online brevity provokes superficiality and the negation of the world's complexity. Online communication tends to take place in fragmented and isolated publics, filter bubbles, and echo chambers that lack constructive controversy.

All of these problems are not problems of propaganda but of power in general. We therefore need a model of power on social media. It needs to stress various dimensions, conflicts, and lines of potential struggle. For doing so, we also need a model of society. Society is the totality of communicative, social relations that take place in the context of dialectics of structure and agency. An understanding commonly used in sociology is that society and all social systems have three dimensions: the economy, politics, and culture. These are realms for the production of use-values (economy), collective decisions (politics), and meanings (culture). Any particular social system has an economic, a political and a cultural dimension. One of these dimensions may be dominant, which situates this social system in a particular subsystem of society. Table 6.3 shows the role of power structures in society in general and modern society in particular.

The internet and social media platforms are social systems. Power should therefore be analysed in the context of the economic, political and cultural dimensions. Modern society has a capitalist economy that is based on the accumulation of monetary capital. It is, however, according to Pierre Bourdieu, also based on the accumulation of political (influence) and cultural power (reputation).

| Dimension of society | Definition of power | Structures of power in modern society |
|---|---|---|
| Economy | Control of use-values and resources that are produced, distributed and consumed. | Monetary capital: Control of money and capital. |
| Politics | Influence on collective decisions that determine aspects of the lives of humans in certain communities and social systems. | Influence: Control of governments, bureaucratic state institutions, parliament, military, police, parties, lobby groups, civil society groups, etc. |
| Culture | Definition of moral values and meanings that shape what is considered as important, reputable and worthy in society. | Reputation: Control of structures that define moral values and meanings in society (e.g. universities, religious groups, intellectual circles, opinion-making groups, etc.). |

**Table 6.3:** Three forms of power.[61]

Accumulation of power is the defining feature of modern society that therefore not only has a capitalist economy but also is a capitalist society. Table 2 therefore also shows the forms that power take on in capitalist society.

Table 6.4 shows a theoretical model of power in digital capitalism.

As mentioned above, this model is based on a theoretical distinction between three realms of society: the economy, politics, and culture.[62] It is also grounded in the philosophical dialectic of the subject and the object that contains three dimensions: human subjects, inter-subjective processes, and objective structures/social systems. Power in class societies is contradictory. It is organised in the form of economic, political and cultural contradiction. Which pole is more powerful under particular conditions is not pre-determined. Those who control resources normally tend to have power advantages. Given that there are structural contradictions, there is always the potential for actual social struggles. These potentials are, however, not automatically realised.

Table 6.4 shows a power structure model for digital society that could also be more generalised for modern society as a whole, for class societies, etc. Herman and Chomsky's PM covers some aspects of the power structure model, especially those that focus on politics, economy, the system, and dominant subject groups.

This chapter has shown that the PM remains relevant for the critical study of the internet, social media, and Big Data. Given the dialectical and historical character of both communications and society, we need to think of subjects, processes, objects, contradictions, the economy, politics, and culture, as well as the interaction of these dimensions, when analysing power in class societies.

|  | Subjects | Processes | System |
|---|---|---|---|
| **Economy** | Digital labour (users) vs. digital capital | Exploitation, concentration, commodification vs. common ownership, self-management, commonification | Digital capitalism vs. digital socialism/ commonism |
| **Politics** | The Left online vs. the Right online | Political control, propaganda, hate speech, surveillance, algorithmisation of politics, war vs. self-determination, dialectical discourse, humanisation, peace | Surveillance-industrial internet complex vs. participatory democracy |
| **Culture** | Everyday users vs. online celebrities and influencers | Stratification of attention, acceleration, tabloidisation, spectacles, malrecognition vs. Equalisation, deceleration, critique, dialectisation of discourse, recognition | Disrespectful society vs. solidary society of mutual respect and aid |

**Table 6.4:** Power structures and power contradictions in digital capitalism.

## Notes and Bibliography

[1] Edward S. Herman and Noam Chomsky, *Manufacturing Consent: The Political Economy of the Mass Media* (London: Vintage, 1988).
[2] Ibid, p.2.
[3] Jürgen Habermas, *Between Facts and Norms. Contributions to a Discourse Theory of Law and Democracy* (Cambridge, MA: MIT Press), 377.
[4] See: Edward S. Herman (1996), 'The Propaganda Model,' *Monthly Review* 48 (3): 115–128.
[5] Joan Pedro (2011), 'The Propaganda Model in the Early 21st Century,' *International Journal of Communication* 5 : 1865–1926.
[6] Edward S. Herman, 'The Propaganda Model: A Retrospective,' *Journalism Studies* 1 (1) (2000), 101–112, 109.
[7] Ibid, p.122.
[8] Ibid, p.127.
[9] Ibid, p.109.
[10] Ibid, p.109.
[11] Data source: Alphabet, 2016 Proxy Statement.
[12] Data source: Facebook, Form DEF 14A for the period ending 20 June, 2016.
[13] Data source: netmarketshare.com, accessed on 15 September, 2016.

[14] PEW Research Center, 'The 2016 Presidential Campaign – a News Event That's Hard to Miss,' accessed 6 August, 2017, http://www.journalism.org/2016/02/04/the-2016-presidential-campaign-a-news-event-thats-hard-to-miss.
[15] Victor Luckerson, 'Here's How Facebook's News Feed Actually Works,' *Time Online*, 9 July, 2015.
[16] Christian Fuchs (2017), *Social Media: A Critical Introduction* (London: Sage) 2nd edition.
[17] Source: Ofcom, *International Communications Market Report 2015*. Available from: https://www.ofcom.org.uk, 26.
[18] Fuchs, *Social Media*.
[19] Edward S. Herman and Noam Chomsky, 'The Propaganda Model After 20 Years: Interview conducted by Andrew Mullen,' *Westminster Papers in Communication and Culture* 6 (2) (2009): 20.
[20] Herman and Chomsky, *Manufacturing Consent*, 17.
[21] Lars Furhoff (1973), Some Reflections on Newspaper Concentration. *Scandinavian Economic History* Review 21 (1): 1–27.
[22] http://www.sekkeistudio.com/blog/2015/08/who-are-adwords-biggest-ads-spenders/
[23] http://www.businessinsider.com/top-advertisers-on-facebook-2013-11?IR=T
[24] Dallas W. Smythe (1977), 'Communications: Blindspot of Western Marxism,' *Canadian Journal of Political and Social Theory* 1 (3): 1–27.
[25] Christian Fuchs (2015), *Culture and Economy in the Age of Social Media* (New York: Routledge); Christian Fuchs (2014), *Digital Labour and Karl Marx* (New York: Routledge).
[26] Colin Sparks (2007), 'Extending and Refining the Propaganda Model,' *Westminster Papers in Communication and Culture* 4 (2): 68–84, 81.
[27] Des Freedman (2009), '"Smooth Operator?" The Propaganda Model and Moments of Crisis,' *Westminster Papers in Communication and Culture* 6 (2): 59–72.
[28] Ibid, 71.
[29] Herman and Chomsky, *Manufacturing Consent*, xii.
[30] Manuel Castells (2009), *Communication Power* (Oxford: Oxford University Press).
[31] Fuchs, *Social Media*.
[32] Herman and Chomsky, 'The Propaganda Model After 20 Years': 12–22, 20.
[33] Data source: alexa.com, accessed on November 11, 2016.
[34] Fuchs, *Social Media*.
[35] Herman and Chomsky, 'The Propaganda Model after 20 Years', 20.
[36] Bence, Kollanyi, Philip N. Howard, and Samuel C. Woolley, 'Bots and Automation over Twitter during the Third U.S. Presidential Debate,' accessed 6 August 2017, http://politicalbots.org/wp-content/uploads/2016/10/Data-Memo-Third-Presidential-Debate.pdf
[37] Pedro, The Propaganda Model in the Early 21st Century, 1871.
[38] Herman and Chomsky, *Manufacturing Consent*, 26.

[39] Fuchs, *Social Media*.
[40] Christian Fuchs (2014), *OccupyMedia! The Occupy Movement and Social Media in Crisis Capitalism* (Winchester: Zero Books).
[41] Data source: twitter.com. Accessed on 12 November 2016.
[42] 'Facebook's failure: did fake news and polarized politics get Trump elected?' *The Guardian Online*, 10 November 2016.
[43] Anikó Félix (2015), '"Migrant Invasion" as a Trojan Horseshoe,' In *Trust Within Europe*, (Budapest: Political Capital), 63–79.
[44] Jacob Aasland Ravndal (2013), 'Anders Behring Breivik's Use of the Internet and Social Media,' *Journal EXIT-Deutschland* 1 (2): 172–185.
[45] Herman and Chomsky, The Propaganda Model after 20 Years, 14.
[46] Fuchs, *Culture and Economy in the Age of Social Media*.
[47] Herman and Chomsky, *Manufacturing Consent*, xiv.
[48] Ibid, 29.
[49] Ibid, 35.
[50] Ibid, 99.
[51] Ibid, 145.
[52] Ibid, 113.
[53] Fuchs, *Culture and Economy in the Age of Social Media*, chapter 3.
[54] https://www.theyworkforyou.com/debates/?id=2014-07-15a.704.0&s=iain+wright
[55] Christian Fuchs, 'Racism, Nationalism and Right-Wing Extremism Online: The Austrian Presidential Election 2016 on Facebook,' Momentum Quarterly – Zeitschrift für sozialen Fortschritt (Journal for Societal Progress) 5 (3) (2016): 172–196.
[56] Bart Cammaerts, Brooks DeCillia, João Carlos Magalhães, and César Jimenez-Martínez, (2016), *Journalistic Representations of Jeremy Corbyn in the British Press: From Watchdog to Attackdog* (London: LSE), 12.
[57] Christian Fuchs (2016), Red Scare 2.0: User-Generated Ideology in the Age of Jeremy Corbyn and Social Media. Journal of Language and Politics 15 (4): 369–398.
[58] Ibid, 393.
[59] Fuchs, *Social Media*.
[60] Christian Fuchs, 'Digital Labor and Imperialism,' *Monthly Review* 67 (8) (2016): 14–24.
[61] Source: Christian Fuchs, *Social Media*, chapter 2.
[62] Christian Fuchs (2008), *Internet and Society: Social Theory in the Information Age* (New York: Routledge); Christian Fuchs, *Social Media*.

CHAPTER 7

# System Security: A Missing Filter for the Propaganda Model?

Daniel Broudy and Miyume Tanji

## 7.1 Introduction

In the present post-9/11 dispensation, the world's so-called indispensable nation[1] has managed, to a great extent, to dispense with liberty in the interest of security.[2] As with the spread of neoliberal ideology, the spreading assault on civil liberties appears to be a global phenomenon. But, what can be said of societies and their systems of public awareness and mass surveillance that seek to reinforce and normalise the destruction of these cherished liberties? We hypothesise from our close studies of the public discourse that powerful forms of state and corporate propaganda play integral parts in the political theatre conditioning citizens to tolerate the revolting decomposing corpse of liberty. For insights on how this decay appears today we turn to a postulated model of propaganda to help us apprehend what it can tell us about resistance to this contemporary stagecraft.

While gaining currency as a research tool, the 'Propaganda Model' (PM hereafter) set out by Edward Herman and Noam Chomsky in *Manufacturing Consent: The Political Economy of the Mass Media* has, over the past three decades, helped throw a critical light on elite control and management of

How to cite this book chapter:
Broudy, D. and Tanji, M. 2018. System Security: A Missing Filter for the Propaganda Model? In: Pedro-Carañana, J., Broudy, D. and Klaehn, J. (eds.). *The Propaganda Model Today: Filtering Perception and Awareness*. Pp. 93–106. London: University of Westminster Press. DOI: https://doi.org/10.16997/book27.g. License: CC-BY-NC-ND 4.0

the public discourse. Since the book first appeared in 1988, leaders in post-industrial societies have successfully mobilised support through technological advances in cybernetic communications. Efforts to control public perception and awareness have also been greatly enhanced through mass media consolidation[3] and have, since 9/11, advanced to new levels of influence. In this chapter, we highlight the need for an additional filter in response to recent re-configurations of political and corporate power and emerging systems of control over information and public debate.

The original PM featured five conceptual 'filters' which have been useful in scholarship theorizing, exposing, and analysing the complex connections among society's dominant institutions and non-coercive methods used to propagandise citizens and to control public awareness.[4] As an effective filter both permits and impedes the flow of whatever materials seek to pass through it, they play a crucial role in the creation of clean fuel fit for an engine's efficient use. Filters screen harmful debris that might hamper the (re)production of power. The motors of heavy industry, for example, run as a result of these functions, so, from a maintainer's perspective, debris must be filtered out when it threatens to infect and compromise the overall system. Corporate media and ideological institutions that strategise and run the gathering, analysis, and dissemination of news information employ similar means of filtering out potentially dangerous debris in ideas, perspectives, and voices.

In an effort to explain mainstream media responses to voices such as Edward Snowden's and other 'leakers' over the past decade as well as revelations regarding National Security Agency (NSA) counter-intelligence activities, this chapter engages with the question of how the general public is 'driven from the arena of political debate'[5] and conditioned to support political elites promulgating policies claiming to be essential for state security and public safety. While these mechanisms of cultural conditioning comprise interconnected networks of print and digital media, they also represent and reflect interlocking government and corporate interests that span international boundaries. We suggest that 'state security' can now be read as code for 'system security', which is the protection of a global capitalist system through digital media control mechanisms. We, thus, wonder to what extent elite responses to 'security leaks' can explain the high value placed upon secrecy as a purported guarantee for system security and stability of the status quo. While contemporary media performance suggests that a System Security Filter (SSF hereafter) has emerged as a safeguard for this post-9/11 era of global capitalism, we propose that this filter be considered as a component of the PM's conceptual framework.

## 7.2 The Elite 'System'

As the SSF is meant to be a metaphorical filter, we detect a 'System' that utilises the SSF for its own interest. Systems are complex collections of interacting, interrelated, and interdependent parts (or people) forming a largely organised whole. Whereas horsepower generated from systems of internal combustion, for example, rely upon unique sets of pistons, cams, and interlocking gears and pulleys, political power may be generated from unique sets of interdependent persons interacting in an interlocking self-interested whole. News in the corporate media constitutes such pulleys and gears, interacting with other essential components that (re)generate the political power of wealthy individuals, larger industries and the state, which we call the elite 'System.'

While governments are more visible within the public sphere, Chomsky contends, the state is relatively invisible but more stable and comprised of institutions that routinely establish the actual conditions for public policy, including the media. *The state* constitutes the 'actual nexus of decision-making power … including investment and political decisions, setting the framework within which the public policy can be discussed and determined,' whereas *government* consists of 'whatever groups happen to control the political system, one component of the state system, at a particular moment.'[6]

In the United States, private interests appear to the electorate to occupy one or both political parties that have long dominated the public discourse.[7] Concerning the Republican system of governance, for example, Ian Haney López observes, that, 'They're giving over control of the regulatory state to the corporations, they say they want to shrink the Federal deficit, but in fact they're spending massive amounts of money either on tax cuts for the really rich or in big subsidies that go to corporations.'[8] The public's voice has been filtered out and replaced by the 'corporate managers [who] can in effect buy elections directly.'[9] Beyond American party politics, the System, beholden to the imperatives of transnational big business, assumes a global standing, next to the state and government. In its turn, mass media have, through the government's gift of deregulation, largely seized power over the public discourse to filter out dissenting views that might challenge or defy elite interests.

While the precise meanings of the term 'elite' are not so easy to pin down, Raymond Williams provides some background – observing that 'elite', from Old French, was used originally to describe someone elected but was, in time, extended from those formally chosen in the social process to those specially selected by God for some particular purpose. Today's associated meanings of the elite in society are wealth, power, position, authority, and control. Williams' final thought on the term is particularly relevant today: 'the forgotten etymological association between elite and elected has a certain wry interest.'[10]

Herman and Chomsky describe the System as a 'guided market system'[11] within which the guidance is 'provided by the government [the elected elite], the leaders of the corporate community, the top media owners and executives, and the assorted individuals and groups' who are assigned or allowed to assume positions that enable them to handle the levers of power. Globalization processes comprise part of the 'guided market system' in today's transnational political economy.

Reflecting in 1928 on the democratizing influence of the steam engine, the press, and public school to shift power from the aristocracy to the masses, Edward Bernays observed that even the bourgeoisie came to fear the emerging might of the public. As a response to this progressive downward diffusion of social and economic influence, the elite minority found an effective counterweight in prevailing techniques of mass persuasion made possible by modern psychoanalysis to better understand and manage (or manipulate) the public mind. 'Modern propaganda,' observed Bernays, 'is a consistent, enduring effort to create or shape events to influence the relations of the public to an enterprise, idea, or group.'[12] This socializing enterprise with its underlying aims from the early twentieth century persist in many contemporary capitalist democracies: manufacture, through mass media, public consent to political, corporate, and military strategies profiting the centres of elite power and wealth.

Critiquing the elite perspective on the market guided system, Chomsky distils some of the results of a 1975 Trilateral Commission study, aptly titled *The Crisis of Democracy*, that urged more 'moderation in Democracy'[13] to curb excesses in social freedoms exercised during America's 1960s protest movements. As regards the Commission's assessment of American democracy during this 'counter-cultural' period, Chomsky reinterprets and casts some of its central propositions in plain language: 'the general public must be reduced to its traditional apathy and obedience, and driven from the arena of political debate, if democracy is to survive.'[14]

Pure democracy, from the vantage point of the elite class, was/is thought to be an unwieldy and destructive force for achieving and maintaining civil order and control.[15] As witnessed through the 1960s, direct democratic action emboldened by a widespread belief in the power of utilitarian democracy[16] had come to profoundly alter institutionalised systems of racial and gender oppression. Indeed, 'shifts in public opinion dramatically [illustrate] how the vitality of democracy in the 1960s (as manifested in increased political participation) produced problems for the governability of democracy in the 1970s (as manifested in the decreased public confidence in government).'[17]

## 7.3  Managing Information

Standing at odds with these elite interests are recent citizen movements initiated by the likes of Edward Snowden, Chelsea Manning, and Julian Assange who have sought to expose and challenge privileged exploits and abuses of power. Their disruptions to official counter-intelligence policy have been called 'illegal' and read as unacceptable interpretations of patriotism. However illegal they may have been, it was also the structure of exploitation that was exposed – the System that exploits the public's faith that civic participation in democratic actions (voting, petitioning, etc.) can bend elite power to the will of the people.

The Snowden, Manning, and Assange cases have shown that enduring confidence in the effectiveness of American-styled democracy is a false assurance.

US government agents engaged in the work of gathering and analysing counter-intelligence data on American citizens must have construed Snowden's 2013 interview with Glenn Greenwald as a critical 'service disruption' to the System. A key indicator of this perception appeared in the propaganda disseminated by those in power that portrayed Snowden (and earlier Manning) as grave dangers to national security. As such, their reputations as patriotic citizens necessitated a kind of assassination. It was vital that the positive qualities they had enjoyed as servants of the state be 'filtered out' immediately in the interests of maintaining System Security.

With the publication of Bradley (now Chelsea) Manning's classified disclosures to WikiLeaks, a significant moment in history unfolded on 25 July 2010, 'the beginning,' notes Denver Nicks, 'of the information age exploding upon itself.'[18] Following the publication of 'Collateral Murder'[19] and other later eruptions of raw news about the wars in Iraq and Afghanistan and American diplomacy more broadly, P.J. Crowley, former Assistant Secretary of State for Public Affairs, observed that the leaks, 'literally touched on just about every relationship the United States [has] had with every other government around the world.'[20]

Acquitted on the charge of aiding the enemy, Manning revealed to the public rather alarming details long concealed concerning civilian casualties during the war as well as evidence already known to US authorities that the Maliki government was torturing its political opponents, and US officials did nothing to stop it. These revelations represent a significant shock to the System as concealed truths concerning system-wide abuses came to light. Indeed, despite Manning's prosecution, confinement, early clemency, and continued castigation,[21] the signals communicated in Executive Orders, and President Obama's own insistence on the value of rules and laws at the time, must have offered, at least, some hope to those in positions to do so to call public attention to state breaches of law.

> In no case shall information be classified ... in order to: conceal violations of law, inefficiency, or administrative error; prevent embarrassment to a person, organization, or agency ... or prevent or delay the release of information that does not require protection in the interest of the national security.[22]

Subsequent news stories featured a range of unambiguous declarations about Manning, his character, his motives, and the conjectured damage that his leaks had created. Right-wing commentators pronounced Manning guilty 'of treason' and that 'anything less than an execution [would be] too kind a penalty.'[23] According to Fox News' Bill O'Reilly, 'the Sleaze ball ... Julian Assange' who runs 'this despicable website' [where Manning's disclosures appeared] is 'bent on damaging America.'[24] Neither did the left-wing leaders hold back. President Obama proclaimed: 'We're a nation of laws. We don't individually make our own decisions about how laws operate,' and concluded, '[Manning] broke the law.'[25]

More recently, Edward Snowden's 9 June 2013 interview with *The Guardian*'s Glenn Greenwald posed yet another significant shock to the System, characteristic of the sort of debris routinely 'filtered out' of power structures. Snowden and the stories he had told posed an almost immediate danger to the established order by exposing to the public rather serious systemic impurities which, in turn, immediately made Snowden himself both politically and ideologically toxic.

Nevertheless, the very breadth and depth of today's counter-intelligence system and the conceptualization of it were scarcely fathomed by the broader populace, and this pervasive societal ignorance is indicative of hegemonic domination. As in the case of Manning, dominance is demonstrated in the methods used by agents of social power to silence any threats to the established order, such as character assassination, or literal assassination (i.e. 'I can't wait to write a defense of the drone strike that takes out Julian Assange,'[26] or 'Can't we just drone strike this guy?')[27]

Among the epithets used to describe Snowden, 'traitor,'[28] 'criminal,'[29] 'defector,'[30] and 'thief'[31] appear to have largely supplanted 'whistleblower,' 'leaker,' and 'dissident.' John Bolton, then Senior fellow at the American Enterprise Institute suggested lynching as he observed that Snowden, 'committed treason, he ought to be convicted of that, and then swing from a tall oak tree.'[32]

## 7.4 Controlling the Public Debate

Greenwald's interview with Snowden did more than verify what many Americans had already tacitly sensed about their own government in this post-PATRIOT Act era: the government routinely spies on its own citizens with impunity. Indeed, to those aware of the lessons of history, recent news of the NSA's PRISM[33] program was hardly surprising as the past half-century reveals a range of government efforts to tap into the lives of its citizens. Operation SHAMROCK (1945–1975), Project MINARET (1967–1973),[34] COINTELPRO (1956–1971),[35] Main Core (1980s-present),[36] STELLARWIND (2001–2011)[37] and ECHELON (1966-present)[38] all reveal, in part, the extent to which elite power in a 'free' society moves to assert with impunity its sweeping privileges.

With increased uses of personal electronic devices to communicate messages across the globe have come increased beliefs in the internet to equalise power between the private citizen and the corporate person. The public at large, thus, appears possessed by a mostly uncritical trust in its relative power and autonomy to access and direct the forces of digital communication in ways that temper traditional forms of elite control over discourse.

Yet, observes Edward Herman, there is 'no evidence to support this view,' that the opposite, in fact, could be argued. These new and more powerful technologies now 'permit media firms to shrink staff even as they achieve greater outputs, and they make possible global distribution systems that reduce the number of media entities.'[39] The digital nature of information and the near-real-time production of news stories disseminated in text, signs, symbols, and videos enable 'elite domination of [mass] media and the marginalization of dissidents'[40] with the temerity to alert the public to its hidden flaws.

Beyond 'corporate media consolidation'[41] in the private domain lay power consolidation and joint coordination in the public. In San Francisco, for example, Mark Klein, a telecommunications expert formerly with AT&T for over twenty-two years, testified in a class action suit filed in June 2006 that he was required as part of his job to maintain a 'splitter' that effectively shares all AT&T communications data traffic with the NSA. He also 'learned that other such [splitters] were being installed in other cities, including Seattle, San Jose, Los Angeles, and San Diego.'[42] Freedom rights advocates at the Electronic Frontier Foundation point out that, 'AT&T's deployment of NSA-controlled surveillance capability apparently involves considerably more locations than would be required to catch only international traffic.'[43] These sorts of coordination efforts have emerged from presidential decrees which, in recent years, are 'lawlessly bypassing Congress ... and gutting privacy protections.'[44]

In accordance with the 'Assignment of National Security and Emergency Preparedness Communications Functions' – an Executive Order defining justification for an Executive internet 'kill switch' – the System is also part of ' ... a joint industry-Government center ... capable of assisting in the initiation, coordination, restoration, and reconstitution of NS/EP communications services or facilities under all conditions of emerging threats, crisis, or emergency.'[45] The euphemistic title of this Order, whose enforcement is free from judicial review, reflects corresponding efforts in corporate media to enhance their dominance over the public's free speech rights.

In demonstrating on CBS's *Face the Nation* an inability (or unwillingness) to acknowledge already-existing abuses of power, Senator Dianne Feinstein obfuscated the NSA's activities, since Snowden's disclosures, by arguing that, '[she has] seen no abuse by these agencies, nor ... any claim ... made in any way shape or form that this (power) was abused.'[46] In referencing Glenn Greenwald's suggestion about why Snowden may have fled, Bob Schieffer, host of *Face the Nation*, couched his query in his own speculation about Snowden's motives: 'This (leak) seems to me to go beyond your basic whistle-blower case.'[47] Feinstein agreed and re-asserted her position that Snowden is not, 'a whistle-blower ... [that] he has taken an oath (of secrecy)' and that 'if [he] can't keep the oath, [he ought to] get out (of the NSA) and then do something about it in a legal way.'[48]

The ironies, absurd as they appear on the surface, are scarcely inescapable, as Senator Feinstein's calls for legal challenges come from the lawmaker herself who, at the same time, holds the position of Chair of the Senate Intelligence Committee. Within this medium of corporate discourse, the tight boundaries drawn around a discussion of Snowden's actions by two powerful public personalities, as well as the labels used to define Snowden himself, illustrate a level of hegemonic control over public debate. Viewers of *Face the Nation* witness an unfolding narrative restricted to a discursive framework of law within which legislative leaders are free to condemn anyone who questions or uncovers System abuses while, at the same time, absolving themselves of responsibility.

When asked to put into perspective and make sense of the present issues of intelligence breaches, Senator Feinstein responded that, 'What this is all about is the nation's security.'[49] The 'nation' referenced here is part of the larger global System, or world order. In the words of Herbert Schiller, the System is built upon and employs an informational infrastructure that 'produces meaning and awareness,' and has a strong hand in controlling the key definitions, 'images, and messages of the prevailing social order.'[50] The internet represents a key component of that infrastructure.

## 7.5 Protecting the System

Systems, as we have shown, are vulnerable to attack and, so, require powerful mechanisms of protection. Safeguarding today's System demands both the routine maintenance of compliant actors working within as well as accommodating media without, which can effectively educate the masses by reflecting the policies of established power.

Protections for this particular System dominating US political power and its interests in the globalised market economy today are peculiar to the present Information Age. Public acquiescence, central to maintaining social control, is reinforced more explicitly within the System where well-paid participants, such as Manning and Snowden, signal their willingness to comply (through signed non-disclosure agreements) with the demands of secrecy in the interest of maintaining System Security. Indeed, the language of the intelligence apparatus serves as an unequivocal reminder that security trumps all other concerns, legal or illegal.[51] In the domain of intelligence gathering, for example, those who work within this System understand and accept at least one guiding principle underlying the successful protection of sensitive information: one must have a 'need to know' in order to be 'read on' (i.e. gain access) to the information that one works with.[52]

As such, this aspect of the System is certainly not a democracy: that participants are not free to speak of its inner-workings but most forgo some of the rights of citizenship even as national intelligence-gathering practices plainly infringe upon the constitutional rights of the larger nation. The Manning and Snowden cases (and others that have preceded and will likely follow) illustrate a strange paradox: access to highly sensitive secrets confers a kind of power that can be self-destructive. When secrets conflict with ethics, the resulting cognitive dissonance can compromise notions of unquestioned obedience. Yet, the expectations to maintain unswerving compliance remain. Widespread societal submission to the dictates of the System can confer upon the public an abiding sense of security and peace of mind. It suggests, also, that all is well and that the elite, as usual, have things under control. This kind of necessary conformity to the status quo, Chomsky observes, is well reflected in the media we consume: 'The United States is unusual among the industrial democracies in the rigidity of the system of ideological control – "indoctrination" we might say – exercised through the mass media.'[53]

The filters of protection are generally comprised of privately owned, publicly traded, organizations oriented toward rational market-driven efficiencies and the processing of digital information – the concepts, ideas, and definitions that form the 'raw materials of news'[54] fit to print. One can observe the mechanisms of protection that sustain the System embedded in the doctrine of *arcanae imperii* (secrets of the empire). These are reflected in the words, signs, symbols, and actions of right-minded actors at work in various leading institutions. Sheldon Wolin commented on the latest processes of wiretapping, secret surveillance, and extreme interrogation (torture) as an apparent aim to 'extend the privileged secrecy of foreign policy to domestic affairs.'[55] Such activities bespeak a kind of paranoia on the part of elites obsessed with controlling leaks to the public and maintaining security classifications for official communications from the distant past so as to shape future readings of history.[56]

Access to the System is guarded by powerful telecommunications companies whose public slogans serve to reinforce the impression, however insincere, that meaningful relationships between consumer and producer are forged through 'free market' ideals. Operating with the full weight of corporate power to imbue 'free market' with unique stipulated definitions, companies such as Comcast boast, 'The Future of Awesome.' Verizon asks, 'Can you hear me now? Good.' AT&T reminds consumers, 'Your world. Delivered.' Yet, in light of recent counter-intelligence revelations, it is also worth inquiring, to whom in this 'free market' is our 'world' being delivered, and who exactly is 'hearing' what we say? And, yes, the future may appear 'awesome,' but from whose perspective? From the perspective of the citizen secure in his or her personal communications, answers to these questions appear rather grim. In clarifying how dark the clouds over public discourse are presently gathered, Robert McChesney observes in a 2014 interview that we no longer have:

> … privacy anymore and [large monopolistic corporations] use [our] information to sell to advisors. [...] They work closely with the government and the national security state and the military. They really walk hand-in-hand collecting this information, monitoring people in ways that by all democratic theory are inimical to a free society.[57]

McChesney's criticisms are verified by recent efforts in the US Congress to eradicate consumer privacy protections that, according to Glenn Greenwald,

'... free Internet service providers (ISPs) – primarily AT&T, Comcast and Verizon – from the Obama-era FCC regulations barring them from storing and selling their users' browsing histories without their consent.'[58] Backed by legions of lawyers campaigning in the corridors of political power for rules that profit their corporate employers, defences for the present System are also fortified by the public's own participation in social networking and internet commerce where all activities, habits, sentiments, and attitudes are secretly monitored. This contemporary reconfiguration of the 'free market' has seen a compelling downward trend in civil freedoms over the years.

## 7.6 Conclusion

As we have aimed to illustrate in the cases of Manning, Snowden, Assange, and others, the System grants the elite a virtual monopoly over the definition of the acceptable boundaries of public debate and control over the 'correct' interpretation of key terms and ideas. This is the power of the System today, to impose upon the general public the designs of corporate, political, and military power, to define dissenters and differences in opinion with the status quo as traitorous, and to consign to the fringe of the public discussion whistleblowers who expose wrongdoing in the interest of the public itself. In these times when the interests of the corporate and political elite have merged, the rights of corporate persons subvert the intrinsic value of individual citizen rights, and mass media have had a direct hand in painting unflattering portraits of figures who call public attention to abuses.

Today, despite the conviction (and clemency) of Manning, Jim Michaels observes that, 'the country faces threats from thousands of people with access to information and the ability to publish it instantly.'[59] Whereas corporate media performance today maintains a façade that a System Security Filter has emerged as a safeguard for this post-9/11 era of global capitalism, we propose that the SSF be considered for further discussion as a possible sixth filter for the PM. As the cases of Manning and Snowden show, the public discourse has become a well-managed elite enterprise featuring tight controls over dissenting views and private figures who risk their personal freedoms defending the Constitution against foreign and domestic assaults.

### Notes and Bibliography

[1] In his final official trip abroad, Barack Obama urged incoming president Trump to regard America as the 'indispensable nation'. For details of his final speech, visit https://www.ft.com/content/643f6c9c-af84-11e6-a37c-f4a01f1b0fa1.

² A summary of key details concerning surveillance and government overreach under the PATRIOT Act can be found at https://www.aclu.org/infographic/surveillance-under-patriot-act.
³ Ben Bagdikian (2004), *The New Media Monopoly,* Boston: Beacon Press, 16.
⁴ In rare instances of transparency, mainstream media personalities publicly reveal some of their underlying aims as news presenters. In responding to a perceived threat from President Trump and his habit of circumventing mass media filters to communicate directly to the public, Mika Brzezinski, MSNBC news anchor, observed that '...while unemployment and the economy worsens, [Trump] could have undermined the [corporate media] messaging so much that he c[ould] actually control exactly what people think. And that, that is our job.'
⁵ Noam Chomsky (2003), *Necessary Illusions: Though Control in Democratic Societies*, Anansi: Toronto, 3.
⁶ Noam Chomsky (1985), *Turning the Tide: US Intervention in Central America and the Struggle for Peace*. London, Pluto, 230; also see Jeffery Klaehn (2002), 'A Critical Review and Assessment of Herman and Chomsky's "Propaganda Model"', *European Journal of Communication*, 177.
⁷ In Japan, alternatively, nearly complete dominance over the public discourse has been maintained since the end of World War II by the Liberal Democratic Party, the de facto rulers of the postwar political economy.
⁸ Ian Haney-López (2014b), 'The Dog Whistle Politics of Race, Part II' Interview with Bill Moyers. *Moyers & Company*, Web. 10 March 2014.
⁹ Noam Chomsky (2010), 'The Corporate Takeover of U.S. Democracy', *In These Times*, 3 February 2010. Web. 2 March 2014.
¹⁰ Raymond Williams (1976), *Keywords: A Vocabulary of Culture and Society*, London: Fontana, 113.
¹¹ Edward Herman and Noam Chomsky (1988), *Manufacturing Consent: The Political Economy of the Mass Media.*, New York, Pantheon, xii.
¹² Edward Bernays, *Propaganda.* (2005 [1928]), New York, Ig Publishing, 52.
¹³ Michael Crozier, Samuel P. Huntington, and Jyoji Watanuki (1975). *The Crisis of Democracy: Report on the Governability of Democracies to the Trilateral Commission*, New York, New York University Press, 113.
¹⁴ Noam Chomsky (1989), *Necessary Illusions: Thought Control in Democratic Societies*, Boston, South End Press, 3.
¹⁵ It may be no coincidence that George H. W. Bush's calls for a 'new world order' during 1990 began taking shape during his work in the CIA as well as his involvement in the formation of the Trilateral Commission during the mid-1970s.
¹⁶ Utilitarian democracy: created to be practical and useful rather than attractive and vacuous. While the abstraction 'democracy' tends to hold positive connotations, practices of democratic principles in representative democracies, such as in the United States, are becoming increasingly anti-dem-

ocratic. Widespread public belief in democracy, generally, as a useful and practical way for the masses to engage in government affairs has not prevented elected representatives from acquiescing to their corporate donors. Direct forms of democratic action undertaken by the masses are increasingly seen as utilitarian and, thus, a threat to the representative order.

[17] Op cit., Crozier, 76.
[18] Denver Nicks (2012), *Private: Bradley Manning, Wikileaks, and the Biggest Exposure of Official Secrets in American History*. Chicago IL, Chicago Review Press, 191.
[19] 'Collateral Murder' is the title of a segment of leaked footage from Iraq displaying the killing of journalists covering the war. The title appears to be an attempt by Wikileaks to reverse the flow of Orwellian language (i.e. pre-emptive War is Peace) into the public discourse by using accurate descriptions for the action taken against journalists. It is also worth noting that the title (Collateral Murder) of the leaked segment itself made news because of its honesty, yet the English title can be found in Wikipedia under the innocuous search term 'July 12, 2007 Baghdad airstrike'. By its own admission, Wikipedia states that it, 'has been criticised for allegedly exhibiting systemic bias, presenting a mixture of 'truths, half-truths, and some falsehood', and, in controversial topics, being subject to manipulation and spin.' We let our readers decide whether the Wikipedia appearance of 'collateral murder' qualifies as manipulation. A version of the segment can be found here: https://www.youtube.com/watch?v=5rXPrfnU3G0
[20] P. J. Crowley (2009), Interview by Matthew Bell. *What Did Bradley Manning Disclose? PRI's The World*. Web. 21 August 2013.
[21] James Kirchick (2017), 'When transgender trumps treachery,' *New York Times*. 29 August. Web. 30 August 2017.
[22] Barack Obama, 'Classified National Security Information.' Executive Order 13526 of December 29, 2009. Section 1.7 1 March 2014.
[23] Mike Huckabee (2010), '101129 Huckabee at the Reagan Library.' *Maria Sanchez Show*, 20 November. Web. 3 March 2014.
[24] Bill O'Reilly (2010), 'There Are Traitors in America.' *The O'Reilly Factor*, 29 November. Web. 1 March 2014.
[25] Barack Obama (2011), 'Obama_Bradley.3GP' *Free Bradley Manning Protest*, 21 April. Web. 1 March 2014.
[26] According to Mediaite's Evan McMurray, *Time* magazine journalist Michael Grunwald tweeted Saturday night that he was thrilled for the imminent assassination of WikiLeaks founder Julian Assange, a tweet that was deleted just as quickly as it was condemned (18 August 2013).
[27] Hillary Clinton on Assange can be found at: https://twitter.com/wikileaks/status/782906224937410562
[28] John Bolton, Interview by Bill Hemmer. *Fox News*. 17 December 2013.
[29] Rick Perry, 'Snowden: U.S, 'setting fire to future of the Internet': NSA leaker chides companies for not protecting customers,' 10 March 2014, quoted in Mike Ward, *The Houston Chronicle*. Web.

30 Michael Hayden, 'Hayden Labels Snowden a "Defector," 11 August 2013, quoted in Emma Caitlin, *Politico*. Web.
31 Mike Rogers, 'House Intelligence Chairman Hints at Russian Help in Snowden Leaks,' 18 January 2014. *Meet the Press*. Web.
32 John Bolton, Interview by Bill Hemmer. *Fox News*. 17 December 2013.
33 Glenn Greenwald and MacAskill, 'NSA Prism program taps in to user data of Apple, Google and others.' *The Guardian*, 7 June 2013.
34 Ed Pilkington, 'Declassified NSA files show agency spied on Muhammad Ali and MLK.' *The Guardian*, 26 September 2013.
35 Branko Marcetic, 'The FBI's secret war.' *Jacobin*, 31 August 2016.
36 Tim Shorrock, 'Main Core: New Evidence Reveals Top Secret Government Database Used in Bush Spy Program,' *Democracy Now*, 25 July 2008.
37 Glenn Greenwald and Spencer Ackerman, 'NSA collected US email records in bulk for more than two years under Obama,' *The Guardian*, 27 June 2013.
38 Jane Perrone, 'The Echelon spy network,' *The Guardian*, 29 May 2001.
39 Edward Herman (2013), 'The Propaganda Model: A Retrospective.' *Against All Reason: Propaganda, Politics, Power*. 9 December. Web. 3 March 2014.
40 Edward Herman and Noam Chomsky, *Manufacturing Consent: The Political Economy of the Mass Media*, New York, Pantheon, 1988, 2.
41 B. Yu, 'Cable Monopoly's Gain is Community Media's Loss: Comcast/Time Warner Cable Merger Threatens Local Voices.' *Fairness & Accuracy In Reporting*. 1 April 2014. Web. 2 April 2014.
42 Detailed testimony of Klein can be found at: https://www.eff.org/files/filenode/att/Mark%20Klein%20Unredacted%20Decl-Including%20Exhibits.PDF
43 The full article may be found at: https://www.eff.org/files/filenode/att/presskit/ATT_onepager.pdf
44 Alex Newman, 'Obama Vows to Bypass Congress and Rule by Decree.' *The New American*, 15 January 2014. Web. 15 July 2014.
45 Further details of this Executive Order can be found at :http://www.whitehouse.gov/the-press-office/2012/07/06/executive-order-assignment-national-security-and-emergency-preparedness-
46 Dianne Feinstein, Interview by Bob Schieffer. 'Sen. Feinstein on Edward Snowden: "The Chase is On".' *Face the Nation*, CBS News. 23 June 2013. Web. 3 March 2014.
47 Bob Schieffer, Interview by Bob Schieffer. 'Sen. Feinstein on Edward Snowden: "The Chase is On".' *Face the Nation*. CBS News. 23 June 2013 Web. 3 March 2014.
48 Op cit., Feinstein.
49 Ibid.
50 Herbert I. Schiller (1999), 'U.S. as global overlord: Dumbing down, American-style,' *Le Monde Diplomatique*, August 1999.
51 *DHS Instruction Handbook 121-01-007: The Department of Homeland Security Personnel Suitability and Security Program*. June 2009. Accessed 24 May. Web

[52] U.S. Office of Personnel Management. Position Classification Standard for Security Administration Series, GS-0080. December 1987. Web. 24 May.
[53] Noam Chomsky (1988), *On Language*, New York, The New Press, 8.
[54] Herman and Chomsky (1988), *Manufacturing Consent*, 2.
[55] Sheldon Wolin (2008), *Democracy Inc.: Managed Democracy and the Specter of Inverted Totalitarianism*, Princeton, NJ: Princeton University Press, 133.
[56] Ibid.
[57] Robert McChesney (2013), 'Digital Disconnect: Robert McChesney on 'How Capitalism is Turning the Internet Against Democracy,' Interview with Amy Goodman and Juan González, *Democracy Now*. 5 April. Web. 4 March 2014.
[58] Glenn Greenwald (2017), 'To Serve AT&T and Comcast, Congressional GOP Votes to Destroy Online Privacy,' *The Intercept*, 29 July. Web. 29 March 2017.
[59] Jim Michaels, 'Manning Case Redefines Meaning of Traitor.' *USA Today*. Gannett, 30 July 2013. Web. 4 March 2014.

CHAPTER 8

# From #15M to *Podemos*: Updating the Propaganda Model for Explaining Political Change in Spain and the Role of Digital Media

Miguel Álvarez-Peralta

*Every system has its own vulnerabilities.*
Anonymous

### 8.1 Introduction

This chapter presents a contribution to the ongoing debates regarding the updating of the Propaganda Model for the twenty-first century. It will focus on the model's boundaries, those situations where it faces difficulties for apprehending some communication dynamics, like social media, countries with a particular political culture (like Spain) and contexts of crisis and instability (2008–2016).

These aspects have been noted as possible vulnerabilities of the model that require further exploration,[1] together with personal agency and strategies for social change, which I will also take into account. Herman and Chomsky

---

How to cite this book chapter:
Álvarez-Peralta, M. 2018. From #15M to *Podemos*: Updating the Propaganda Model for Explaining Political Change in Spain and the Role of Digital Media. In: Pedro-Carañana, J., Broudy, D. and Klaehn, J. (eds.). *The Propaganda Model Today: Filtering Perception and Awareness*. Pp. 107–124. London: University of Westminster Press. DOI: https://doi.org/10.16997/book27.h. License: CC-BY-NC-ND 4.0

observed that, 'it has to be evaluated on a case-by-case basis given the varying degrees and forms of penetration, and different cultural conditions'.[2] This chapter aims to open the debate on a meaningful case.

## 8.2 Discussing the Propaganda Model: Dead Ends and Hot Spots

Since the Propaganda Model (hereafter PM) was first formulated, media research has provided strong evidence of its validity[3] as a tool to explain the constrictions of news-making processes and the dominance of news framing that favour the interests of elites during periods of stability.

Most of the early criticism against the PM came from ideological positions which basically failed to acknowledge the importance of class division in the operation of the media system. The controversies between the PM's assumptions and the classical liberal view of the media (which conceptualises journalism as a 'free marketplace of information' or as a 'watchdog' that defends the interests of the people from power abuse by government and corporations) have already been thoroughly explored, and the arguments involved in such exchanges have been contested.[4]

Herman and Chomsky themselves have addressed in a satisfactory manner the main issues pointed by this kind of dismissive criticism.[5] They recognised that the PM is both simplistic and deterministic to some extent, as every model is. That's a common characteristic of clearly defined theoretical models in sociology and political science, because they need to remain applicable to a large range of different particular situations.[6] These arguments do not address the PM itself, but they pick on the use of simple theoretical models to schematise social interaction. Such discussions are doomed to a dead end as it happens in other fields, like economics or sociology. There aren't many reasons to expect any positive resolution for these debates, as the positions in dispute belong to different paradigms in the Kuhnian's sense.[7]

The second wave of criticism[8] was more fruitful. It accepted to engage with the fundamentals of the model, sharing a common ground that made fertile controversies possible. It produced the exchanges between Corner and Klaehn,[9] for example, or the stimulating criticism from Boyd-Barrett[10]–who suggested more emphasis on intentionality and a sixth filter regarding the direct buying-out of journalists – and Sparks[11] – who was interested in the application of the model in different international contexts, especially those involving difficulties for consensus between the elites. These exchanges helped to broaden the scope of the PM by pointing useful directions for future research.

The operation of the filters is considered contingent and variable within different contexts. The PM is an open prototypical clarification of media performance in modern capitalism, not a detailed, final or totalizing explanation of the process of news circulation:

> We don't claim that it explains everything and we are clear that *elite differences and local factors (including features of individual media institutions)*

can influence media outcomes. We argue that the model works well in many important cases, and we await the offering of one that is superior. But we also acknowledge that there remains lots of room for media studies that do not rest on the PM. This same room opens the way to criticizing the model for its failure to pursue those tracks and fill those spaces.[12]

These claims set the goal of describing PM's vulnerabilities in different concrete contexts, as a way to improve the model. Joan Pedro-Carañana[13] has highlighted this need for updating and expanding the model:

[The PM] could be enriched by relating it to an analysis of the specific logic of capital in the current socio historical process (…) by placing a greater focus on the specific social and market conditions and relations, on contradictions, on divisions and dysfunctions, on counter-forces, on moments of crisis, and on the gaps and the exceptions, all so as to better understand the existence of a real, if limited, plurality and dissent, and the possibility of change. (…) It is necessary to first consider the scope of the PM's applicability to the media of countries other than the United States (where Herman and Chomsky focused their analysis), to Internet media, and to media products other than news.[14]

Accepting these indications from Edward Herman and Pedro-Carañana, my framework focuses on *elite differences*, *local factors* and 'features of individual institutions', as aspects that explain interesting *exceptions* to the PM *on moments of crisis*, where 'counter-forces' take advantage of the *contradictions* of the media system to advance *the possibility of change*, specially through internet media and *products other than news*. We will consider those key aspects in a very different time-space context from the one where the PM was created: Spain, three decades later.

## 8.3 Contextual Limitations of the Model: Southern Europe, New Media and Situations of Crisis

Thirty years after the publication of *Manufacturing Consent*, some global dynamics of capitalism have changed, due to macroeconomic phenomena. The collapse of the Soviet Union and the neoliberal revolution pioneered by Thatcher and Reagan inaugurated a cycle of uni-polar geopolitics and global deregulation policies. The development of internet and low-cost computing fostered the financialization of the economy and the globalization of free-market ideology.

If anti-communism played a major role in the first PM, this fifth filter has had to be reformulated in the post-Cold War cycle, as 'convergence in the dominant ideology,'[15] the 'provision of a Face of Evil,'[16] 'pro-war dichotomies' against Islamic Fundamentalism[17] or the more abstract formulation 'Us/Them narratives.'[18] Today, we see how populism occasionally plays the role of the universal enemy of democracy. In any case, this filter has been blurred and broadened after the fall of the Iron Curtain.

But the liveliest debates about the PM today are those regarding internet. The arrival of digital social media during the past decade, like Facebook (after 2006) or Twitter (after 2010), is having an undeniable impact in the structure of global communication fluxes. The obsolescence of traditional business models of the press and broadcasting has been accelerated, and different survival strategies regarding ownership structure and profit sources are being tested.[19]

A third hot area within PM discussions concerns its applicability under different geopolitical and cultural contexts. In our case, the political system and culture in Spain differ strongly from the US. In the first democratic elections, for example, after a four decades-long military dictatorship, in 1977, the Communist Party got 20 seats out of 350 (and has maintained representation in Parliament until today, directly or through coalitions). The *Spanish Socialist Workers' Party* (PSOE), whose official ideology at the time was Marxism, was second with 118 seats and 29% of the vote. Altogether, self-proclaimed socialist forces reached 45% of the vote. Five years later, PSOE wan the elections (already as a social-democratic party) and its leader, Felipe González, was President of Spain for 14 years.

Those were the times when the Propaganda Model was being elaborated in a strongly different *zeitgeist*. According to the *Values and Worldviews Report 2013*, elaborated by the BBVA bank, the Spanish are still the people of Europe that feel less identified with 'capitalism' and have the most negative view of corporations and free-market economy.[20] These brief remarks give an idea of how national 'common sense' (Gramsci) depends on the history and international position of each nation.

Spanish political culture demands an adaptation of the PM's filters as the conditions for hegemony change. While anti-communism was indeed promoted by right-wing fractions of Spanish elites, it always coexisted with strategies that advocated political openness and the assimilation of critical discourses as part of the 'legitimate diversity,' that were much more efficient in creating stability and articulating functional narratives. They became hegemonic. This illustrates what Sparks[21] and Pedro-Carañana have already pointed out, 'the strength of the filters is not as great in regions such as Europe', due to their 'more open cultural and ideological context […], strong critical currents, the presence of leftist political parties with representation in government, […] which permit a wider range of news content. In general, there is greater diversity in countries with a tradition of social democracy than that found in the United States.'[22]

The presence of a strong public broadcast system, with national, regional and local channels (television, radio, and now also internet services), has also functioned as a counterbalance to corporate discourses and as a decent standard of independency, diversity and political openness in key moments (thanks to the pressure from renowned professionals and unions, among other factors). This also indicates the necessity of adapting the PM, as its second hypothesis restricts its application to countries where the media is 'under corporate rather than state control.'[23] But, the first private TV channels (Antena3, Canal+ and Tele5) arrived to Spain in 1989, after the publication of *Manufacturing Consent*. Until then, Spain only had public televisions, which is significant since 'the Propaganda Model is not applicable to public media outlets,'[24] or at least not entirely.

A final important divergence must be pointed out. Politics in Spain can, increasingly, be elucidated through postcolonial theoretical frames. During Franco's dictatorship, the cooperation of Eisenhower's government with the extreme-right regime was crucial for explaining its duration and the late subaltern integration of Spain in the European Union. Still today, the submission of domestic economic policies (even the Constitutional Reform) to the declared interests of the Paris-Berlin axis, corroborate Spain's vulnerability in the post-subprime crisis of economic reorganization.[25]

The relations of global powers with Spain have an increasingly colonialist profile, but PM does not work in the same way in the colony as in the metropole. There is a visible conflict of interests between global corporations and smaller national companies that still hold a great power of influence on domestic public opinion. This has an impact in the operation of the filters. While, in the case of the US, we can generally assume that the largest national corporations widely overlap with global ones and share common interests, this is not the case for Spain. Actually, in the south of Europe, though some corporations have also become transnational or are increasingly penetrated by foreign capitals, the strategy for many economic sectors and corporate associations, including cultural industries, relies on combining moderate internationalization with inland lobbying against their governments for protection. Lobbying here also means public criticism. They try to force the government to resist pressure from global digital giants such as telecommunication conglomerates or the so-called 'Over The Top' companies (like Netflix, Google, and Amazon) and favour domestic industries.

This dynamic led the Spanish right-wing neoliberal government of Mariano Rajoy, for example, to accept the requirements of the National Newspaper Editors Association (AEDE) and set a new toll for search engines that included their contents within search results. It was known as the 'Google Tax' (or 'AEDE canon'), and it made Google News abandon the country.[26] A similar phenomenon takes place when national private DTT broadcasts (cable and satellite TV have never been prominent in Spain) aggressively lobby on the ruling party so that it transfers or at least extends the specific taxes and obligations that affect them (to invest in Spanish films, co-fund state media, etc.) to their global competitors like YouTube, HBO or Netflix. Governments have to choose who to favour here, and whom dissatisfaction to bear with, but we cannot speak of elite consensus, in this case. This helps to explain the weak influence of some filters, and the hard criticism of some primetime TV shows against Government and transnationals. The impact of neocolonialist confrontation between elites and PM contextual validity deserves more attention.

Due to these conditions, along with the credibility crisis of Spanish journalism[27] and the mobilization of the so-called '*indignados*' or 15-M movement, there are reasons to think that the first hypothesis of the PM does not fully apply to Spanish context. According to the remarks made by Klaehn and Mullen:

The first hypothesis put forward by Herman and Chomsky is that, *where there is consensus amongst the corporate and political elite* on a particular issue, the media tend to reflect this. Herman asserts that 'where the elite are really concerned and unified, **and/or where ordinary citizens are not aware of their own stake in an issue or are immobilized** by effective propaganda, the media will serve elite interests uncompromisingly'. (…) 'Where the powerful are in disagreement, there will be a certain diversity of tactical judgements on how to attain generally shared aims, reflected in media debate' (Herman and Chomsky, 1988, p.xii). (…) The PM acknowledges dissent and makes no predications regarding the effectiveness of hegemonic control. [28]

In terms of the political culture, the last decade in Spain has been characterised as an erosion (and even *rupture*) of the 'Transition Consensus,'[29] the name given to the cultural climate that gave birth to the agreements and implicit redlines that allowed for the stable equilibrium of forces (dictatorship's apparatus, peripheral independentism, the monarchy, recently legalised parties and unions, etc.) frequently called as the *Regime of the 78*.

The 15-M movement exploded in 2011 and aggravated that erosion thanks to the combination of physical and digital mobilization. It soon reached a support of 81% of the population.[30] From the beginning, the internet was the second most-used source to get information about it (66.3%) after TV (77.58%), and it was first (82%) within young people under 24 years old. Preferred internet sources were the digital press (70.04%) and Facebook (51.45%). Twitter, which had just arrived in Spain, was the favourite source among youngest people.[31] It was in fact popularised by the social movement; they became attached to each other.

If we consider these data as indicators of 'ordinary citizens' being 'aware of their own stake' within the issue of the financial crisis, or at least 'not immobilized by propaganda,' then they demand a closer look at the PM in that context and after, how it worked differently (or possibly failed) as an explanation of media behaviour.

At the same time that the print press faced its reputation and profit crisis, new digital left-wing media were created reaching a considerable support and credibility (e.g. *eldiario.es*, *infoLibre*, *La Marea*, *Cuarto Poder* or *CTXT*, all of them created after 2011). Moreover, a new kind of high-impact progressive 'parajournalistic' TV magazines and talk-shows were breaking records of share on a daily basis, bringing pluralistic political debates to the primetime and late morning fringes.[32] That's the case with *El Intermedio, Salvados, La Sexta Noche, El Objetivo, Al Rojo Vivo, Las Mañanas de Cuatro*, all of them sharing some common characteristics: 1) they serve as a 'reserve' for moderators or guests with unprecedented critical opinions; 2) they use humour, political incorrectness, and other infotainment trends to get more audience; 3) they have created their own star-system of popular anchormen and anchorwomen that attract significant volumes of audience (and who have publicly resisted flak), which is the case of Jordi Évole,[33] Gran Wyoming, Ana Pastor, Antonio Maestre, Jesús Cintora, Ignacio Escolar, Antonio Ferreras, Jesús Maraña, etc.

The fourth and fifth filters do not seem to be working here. These became most prominent voices also in the digital press and Twitter. Pablo Iglesias himself, the leader of *Podemos* party, is a product of such a new wave of pluralistic political TV shows, where his fame was produced before jumping to electoral competition.[34] The vital importance of Star-System agency within the PM is strategic and deserves also further attention.

## 8.4 Digital Social Media: A New Playground for Information

As I have mentioned, there is a lively discussion regarding the need to adapt the PM to the internet age, particularly to digital multimedia newspapers, where entrance-barrier costs have dramatically decreased, and to online social networks (hereinafter OSN), where content production is mainly assumed by users who interact through the networks (*prosumers*). The observation that prosumers represent both the unpaid digital labour-force and the commodification of audiences[35] is essential but does not answer the questions about diversity of discourses, agency amplification or cultural effects. Unpaid labour already existed in the pre-Twitter age, since analogical audiences completed the commodification cycle of information contributing to its production and consuming the advertisements that surround it. Audiences were considered a commodity to be produced and sold to advertisers in traditional media, as well.[36] These are not innovations of social media, though they have escalated. In the case of user-generated content platforms, the direct role of prosumers in achieving capital gains is clearer, but the dependency of benefits on the ability of each digital environment to attract users and keep them connected is strong, as well, and plays a role on the PM revision.

The propagation of mobile devices has also had enormous impact on the way information is sold and consumed. A well-established corporate press faces a significant business-model crisis today because it has to share the income from advertising they used to manage on a national scale with several kinds of new digital competitors on a global scale. Digitalization also reduced newspaper sales as the new generations got used to receiving information for free, directly on their mobile devices, selected and commented by equals through their digital communities. OSNs are the main source of visits for online news sites and are, thus, more important than Google or their own homepages.[37]

These reading practices threaten editorial agenda-setting and priming strategies, as they change selection criteria and foster ironic and critical comment of the news being shared. That means a significant loss of control for corporate media. At the same time, they deepen the fragmentation of the public sphere into isolated regions (the so-called 'filter bubble,'[38] which should probably be incorporated into a new more abstract filter of the PM in order to address the impact of personal ecosystems within OSNs). Regardless of the questionable quality of the selection criteria on that news circulation processes, the result is a structural mutation on the information lifecycle, with consequences to be gradually revealed during the coming years.

When the PM saw the light, such alterations were hardly predictable or properly evaluable. Even for some cultural industries like books or records, things happened so fast that adapting to the new habitat was not always possible. Instability led to important bankruptcies. Financialization and concentration processes after the subprime crisis have not made it easier to overcome new phenomena like massive online file sharing, decreasing ads revenue, pay-walls failure, the so-called click-bait tendency, citizen-journalism, automated content creation, peer-to-peer economy, open source movements and many other new challenges coming into scene year after year. In the case of Spain, the press audience fell from 42.1% in 2008 to 26.5% in 2016.[39] The main newspaper, *El País*, dropped from selling 440.226 copies in 2003, to 115.402 in 2015, a decline of 73.8%.

The notion of 'filter' needs to be adjusted in order to apprehend these vicissitudes. Social media's role in today's communications cannot be dismissed as 'secondary' or 'marginal.' Keeping the PM unaltered would lead to a quick obsolescence of a model that has nonetheless proved its prognosis strengths in pre-Twitter times. Additionally, the PM revitalization needs to deal with a wider question: to what extent is public opinion based on *news* and *information*? It seems to be increasingly influenced by other kinds of emotional and spectacular communication, so it would be a mistake to disregard OSN because most of its contents are 'not political,' nor informational. For good or bad, cultural hegemony disputes seem to have less to do with *truth*, *facts* and *objectivity*, and more with emotions, feelings, self-storytelling and desires, as professional politicians know very well.[40]

### 8.5  Twitter: A Newborn News Lifecycle

Facebook became open to every adult with a valid email address only in 2006. In 2009, Herman and Chomsky were asked if alternative sources of information provided by the internet could render the PM 'increasingly marginal in its applicability.' They predicted the opposite (as "old media" have a growing place and advertising has become steadily more important [on the Web]'), but they left an open door to that eventuality: 'It is possible that this might happen.'[41]

By that time, Facebook was not much more than a new trend, a very promising start-up. Smartphones were just starting to take over our pockets and permanent attention, and the modern networks that allow fluid mobile navigation were only a project. The iPhone was elected invention of the year by *Time* magazine at the end of 2007, but still didn't support 3G networks. After that, Twitter gradually came onto the scene: the 'Trending Topics' list didn't exist in 2009, and users couldn't see pictures without leaving the platform until 2010. It did not reach its first hundred-million users until September 2011,[42] three years after Facebook.

In Spain, these developments arrived years later. The first Spanish version of Twitter came out in January 2010, one year after Facebook's Spanish version. It took a few years for OSNs to become mainstream and to be used by a substantial range of the population and deserve regular media attention. The first digitally-centred campaign was run by *Podemos* for European elections, in 2014, six years after Obama's first Big Data-driven campaign.

These remarks lead to a conclusion: the ongoing cultural and ideological impact of 'mass self-communication networks' (as Manuel Castells calls them) was impossible to estimate back in 1989 and hardly evaluable even in 2009. Even today, the long-term impact of social networking on information practices and consent-production is dubiously predictable. In an analysis devoted to 'rebooting' the PM for the new media, Goss concludes that the internet is being conscripted for authoritarian purposes.[43] This conclusion applies for the professional blogging activities he examines but specific analysis of OSN phenomena like the evolution of prosumers' informational practices remains pending.

While old media focused on content production, OSNs just needed to keep a growing number of users interacting and producing their own contents, instead. So, networks focused on carefully providing an addictive experience for prosumers, knowing that any false step (like excessive ads, or censorship, or too limited interactions) could mean an unexpected downfall (as happened to *Hi5*, *Tuenti*, *MySpace* or other big OSNs that did not survive). They do not create (nor fully control) contents, in any case, and this is a key difference.

Does this mean that Twitter or Facebook are committed to freedom of speech and ideological pluralism? Certainly not. The pluralism and diversity of the contents is just a side-effect of their business model. They are aware that repeated failures on interaction management, or simple lack of renewal, could mean quick obsolescence, an opportunity for rivals, or massive migrations to open-source rivals (as recently happened from *Whatsapp* to *Telegram* network). There are many social networks, some of them based on a peer-to-peer structure without central servers, which could profit from an eventual freezing of Facebook fever, like *N-1.cc, identi.ca, friendi.ca, OSSN, pump.io, Kune, GNU-Social, Diaspora\*, BuddyCloud*, etc.

The underlying question here is: why would big corporations like OSNs be helpful to grass-root criticism? As global warming and other environmental threats demonstrate (and history does, as well) global capitalism is not a perfectly stable system which is able to foresee and plan or carefully calculate and produce the conditions for its own sustainability. But, quite often, radical intellectuals depict it in that way, against the fundamentals of Critical Theory. Because of its subordination to the short-term logic of the competitiveness within unregulated markets, capitalism works much more like an out-of-control machine that can only focus on immediate maximization of profits and permanent competition regardless of distant-future consequences. It constantly digs its own grave in different ways.

Massive online social communication can also be regarded as an unexpected progressive externality of the evolution of digital capitalism (quite like the print was for pre-capitalist orders). From the Political Economy point of view, the outbreak of global real-time human cooperation, despite its contradictory procedures (or thanks to them), could also start to be regarded as a critical turning point. A milestone where 'the development of productive forces of society comes in conflict with the existing relations of production or – what is but a legal expression for the same thing – with the property relations within which they have operated hitherto. From forms of development of the productive forces these relations turn into their fetters. Then begins an epoch of social revolution.'[44]

## 8.6 Refining the PM: Beyond Cyber-pessimism and Cyber-euphoria

This last claim will of course be contested as unreasonably optimistic. But it can only be read as such if we consider *an epoch of revolution* as a necessarily positive event. It could also mean, as happened before in the history of capitalism after periods of economic instability, the advent of new kinds of war and authoritarian regimes. The current flourishing of xenophobic and chauvinistic populisms and new sorts of terrorism in western countries, the rise of 'governability issues' discourses and the escalation of military budgets worldwide do not seem to point in an optimistic direction. So, this perspective is not to be read as techno-euphoria, although it certainly diverges from the techno-pessimism that dominates debates about internet and the PM.

Against some predictions,[45] interactive media have served democratic ends, at least in Spain and other countries. Spontaneous coordination as seen in the 15-M Movement, the Arab Spring, the Kitchenware Revolution in Iceland, the Umbrella Revolution in China, or some left-wing electoral populist irruptions like those embodied by Pablo Iglesias, Jean Luc Mélenchon or Jeremy Corbyn, would have been categorically different without the existence of OSNs, if they had ever existed at all. They have made intense use of viralisation, crowdfunding, crowdsourcing, meme seeding and curation, gamification, online discussing and voting, mobile apps, etc.

There is growing evidence of massive interactive dynamics challenging mainstream framings, 'hacking' official agendas and conquering visibility for new subjects and issues that used to remain invisible, for example about the financial crisis and banking bailout in Spain.[46] Activists who moved from traditional to digital social media know this very well, as they are able to reach wider audiences. We observe that the internet is serving for social control in the long-term but also for democratic ends, occasionally, in the meantime. The internet opens a field for stable worldwide collaboration, as projects like Wikipedia, Linux,

Indymedia or eMule and Torrent networks have evidenced, among other experiences that do not fully meet commercial logics. Regarding the PM's filters, the fact that social media like Facebook or search engines like Google belong to huge private corporations with concentrated ownership must of course be acknowledged. They are totally dependent on ads revenue and operate through opaque algorithms that select what we read first and what appears in less visible positions or do not appears at all.[47] OSNs won't render the PM redundant, but they do need to satisfy new kind of requirements in order to maintain their dominant position.

### 8.7 'Old Media', Online Social Networks and the Propaganda Model

Opinion-driving campaigns on OSNs are being carried out by governments, but also by social organizations. At least in Spain, it is nowadays very strange not to have a critical political Trending Topic every day on Twitter. This is a situation which activists couldn't dream of in traditional media's landscape. Prosumers are not fired by the network due to advertisers or government's pressure as happened to journalists in traditional media. How could owners condition what I write on my Twitter account the way they did with my column on a newspaper or my local radio debate? Can they easily get my mouth shut, or could that generate what the net jargon calls a 'Streisand Effect' (increased circulation of the censored content) or 'Underdog Effect' (solidarity with the excessively punished or relegated)? It is clear that within OSNs the filters do not apply to content creation, but to content promotion. That is another key difference, as promotion also depends in prosumers' actions, not only opaque algorithms. Filters do not work like they did for professional journalism. They do not prevent mentions, answers, re-mediations and other exchanges between individuals, public institutions, journalists, corporate accounts, political parties, social movements, candidates, celebrities, well-known activists, scholars, advertisers, etc. This freedom of interaction creates possibilities that were unthinkable in traditional media's landscape.

Concluding that 'old media' have a growing place within OSNs would not be accurate. During the twentieth century, one-way media had almost total control on the visibility of their Star-System, including renowned anchormen. They also controlled the visibility of their audience's feedback. But in the OSNs they don't. Interaction between TV broadcasts and Twitter is constantly producing examples where an attempt at manipulation or a simple imprecision is immediately contested and generates a Trending Topic in seconds. Communication is not strictly unidirectional anymore. Moreover, Twitter produces its own Star-System: individuals that surpass the digital audience of news broadcasts and governments, with infinitely more engaged followers. As Pedro-Carañana[48] has pointed out the, internet constitute[s] a media model quite different from that of radio, newspapers, or television. Indeed, the internet is the platform on which non-corporate, participatory media outlets with critical perspectives and support for social change have been able to develop and grow. In this respect, there are different dynamics intrinsic to the way the internet operates that the PM does not consider.

## 8.8 Flak Against Twitter Stars? A Brief Review of the Spanish Twittersphere

In his critical review of Twitter as a new public sphere, Christian Fuchs considers the asymmetrical power of the visibility of personal accounts[49] concluding that celebrities from the entertainment business, particularly pop stars, dominate attention measured by number of followers. Politics is much less represented (…) Alternative political figures, such as political documentary producer Michael Moore, have far fewer followers, which is an expression of the asymmetrical political attention economy of capitalism that discriminates critical voices.

| Group | Twitter account | Social significance | .000 followers |
|---|---|---|---|
| Traditional newspapers | El País | Most important newspaper | 6.1M (52% fake) |
| | El Mundo | Newspaper with most-visited digital edition. | 2.84M |
| | 20minutos | Most read cost-free newspaper. | 1.28M |
| Politicians & political parties | Pablo Iglesias | Leader of Podemos (left-wing populist party) | 2.01M |
| | Mariano Rajoy | President of Spain. | 1.41M |
| | Alberto Garzón | Leader of PCE and the left coalition IU. | 777K |
| | Partido Popular | Ruling party. | 620K |
| Critical online newspapers & editors | Publico.es | Left-wing digital-only newspaper. | 812K |
| | Nacho Escolar | Editor of eldiario.es. | 724K |
| | Eldiario.es | Most read digital-only left wing newspaper | 722K |
| | Jesús Maraña | Editor of infoLibre.es. | 253K |

**Table 8.1:** Some politically significant accounts on Twitter (29 June 2017).

| Group | Twitter account | Social significance | .000 followers |
|---|---|---|---|
| Private TV Channels and Broadcasts | Antena3 | First private TV-channel created in Spain. | 1.29M |
| | Antena3 Noticias | Third most-watched news broadcast. | 1.58M |
| | La Sexta Noticias | Second most-watched news broadcast. | 981K |
| | El Intermedio | Critical 'parajournalistic' daily magazine. | 903K |
| | TeleCinco | Largest audience TV channel. | 830K |
| | Salvados | Audience-leading political documentaries | 696K |
| | Informativos T5 | Most-watched news broadcast. | 634K |
| Progressive TV star-system anchormen | Buenafuente | Critical ironical late-night show moderator. | 3.42M |
| | Jordi Évole | Producer of *Salvados* (political documentaries). | 3.02M |
| | Ana Pastor | Moderator of *El Objetivo* (critical journalism). | 1.91M |
| Others | EFE | National state-owned news agency. | 1.2M |
| | La SER | Audience-leader national radio station. | 1.09M |

**Table 8.1:** Continued.

He also notes that only 7% of the Trending Topics (TT) were 'political' in 2009, and politics has been even more marginal in the following years. This is not the case of Spanish TTs.[50] Accepting these quantitative criteria as an indicator of visibility, we can turn to Table 8.1 and check some Twitter audiences in Spain.

A Spanish alternative political documentary producer, Jordi Évole, who can undoubtedly claim the title *the Spanish Michael Moore*, amply surpasses the twitter-audience of every traditional media, politician, or TV broadcast.[51] The public face of the Communist Party, Alberto Garzón, has more followers than the ruling party and more than the most-watched TV news broadcast (*Informativos Telecinco*). The leader of the disrupting anti-liberal left-wing populist party, *Podemos*, who belongs to the Marxist school of thought as well,[52] surpasses the number of followers of most mainstream news media, parties, and politicians. If we look at the progressive 'born-digital' press, the audience gap with traditional media has been shortened in social networks. They reach similar digital audiences as the most watched television channels and news-broadcasts.

In this sense, it wouldn't be accurate to say that 'old media' have a growing place within OSNs, or that technologies such as the internet have been colonised by established media outlets. Of course, personalist individualism is a controversial trend to be observed on the web, but the fact is that PM does not cope in detail with the structure-agency dialectics regarding individuals that enter a profitmaking Star-System. It mostly disregards the role of personal agency within cultural industries, which is absolutely key in advancing social change.[53] In Twitter, the formation of a local or sectorial Star-System is less dependent on structural factors than it was in television or press, more open to outsiders with appealing discourses, and this multiplies personal agency of individuals.

## 8.9 Conclusion

Before the commercial boom of OSNs, Herman and Chomsky acknowledged four factors protecting the hegemony of traditional media in the internet age: (1) they are still dominant news providers; (2) they have pre-existing audiences and resources; (3) Internet operators are also dependent on advertising revenue; and (4) new media is oriented toward facilitating social connections, with politics secondary at best, with limited resources and outreach, and specialise in critical analysis rather than news-making.[54]

As we have seen, these 'protecting factors' are increasingly uncertain, at least in some contexts. Pre-existing audiences are not directly transferable to the social media, where the resources needed to publish have dramatically decreased. This has reduced the gap between traditional and new alternative media or individuals as news providers in the OSNs (see Table 8.1). In times of political instability, Twitter becomes a privileged arena for real-time information, widely used by journalists, politicians and activists. The hegemony of Spanish traditional national media has entered an impasse, and it is at stake in front of new global actors (like Google, Twitter or Facebook themselves as news providers) and new alternative media and individuals that maintain large online audiences. This dynamic may help to explain the fall of the two-party system in Spain after 2011, and the decline of the opinion-industry that supported them.

Therefore, the arguments that recommend maintaining the PM mainly unchanged within new media because old media have quickly dominated the new scene must be re-examined in the light of new evidence from different countries and political circumstances. The growing power of Twitter and Facebook as the biggest real-time self-fed databases of human interaction is undeniable, and it is clear that they are becoming the means for new sorts of social control through Big Data exploitation. But at the same time, in a contradictory manner as the very nature of capitalism, they only reach that power by maintaining an attractive arena for sufficiently free global real-time communication, which creates unpredictable externalities, interactional practices, and windows of opportunity for political change in episodes of instability, at least in peripheral countries.

## Notes and Bibliography

[1] John Corner (2003), 'The Model in Question: A Response to Klaehn on Herman and Chomsky,' *European Journal of Communication* 18, no. 3: 367–375; Colin Sparks (2007), 'Extending and Refining the Propaganda Model,' *Westminster Papers in Communication and Culture* 4, no. 2: 68–84; Joan Pedro-Carañana (2011), 'The Propaganda Model in the Early 21st Century (Part II),' *International Journal of Communication* 5: 1906–1926.

[2] Herman and Chomsky, interviewed by Andrew Mullen (2009), 'The Propaganda Model after 20 Years: Interview with Edward S. Herman and Noam Chomsky,' *Westminster Papers in Communication and Culture* 6, no. 2: 18.

[3] For an ample list of references see Jeffery Klaehn and Andrew Mullen (2010), 'The Propaganda Model and Sociology: Understanding the Media and Society,' *Synaesthesia: Communication Across Cultures* 1, no. 1: 13.

[4] Klaehn and Mullen (2010), 'The Propaganda Model and Sociology'; Andrew Mullen and Jeffery Klaehn, 'The Herman-Chomsky Propaganda Model: A Critical Approach to Analysing Mass Media Behaviour,' *Sociology Compass* 4, no. 4 (April): 215–29, DOI: https://doi.org/10.1111/j.1751-9020.2010.00275.x; Joan Pedro-Carañana (2011), 'The Propaganda Model in the Early 21st Century (Part I),' *International Journal of Communication* 5: 1865–1905.

[5] Edward S. Herman and Noam Chomsky (2004), 'Reply to Kurt and Gladys Engel Lang,' *Political Communication* 21, no. 1: 103–7, DOI: https://doi.org/10.1080/1058460049027334-1699.

[6] Mullen, 'The Propaganda Model after 20 Years,' 17.

[7] Thomas S. Kuhn (1996), *The Structure of Scientific Revolutions*, 3rd ed. (Chicago: University of Chicago Press).

[8] Mullen and Klaehn, 'The Herman-Chomsky Propaganda Model,' 219.

[9] Jeffery Klaehn (2003), 'Model Construction: Various Other Epistemological Concerns: A Reply to John Corner's Commentary on the Propaganda Model,' *European Journal of Communication* 18, no. 3: 377–383.

[10] Oliver Boyd-Barrett, (2004), 'Judith Miller, *The New York Times*, and the Propaganda Model' *Journalism Studies* 5, no. 4: 436–38, DOI: https://doi.org/10.1080/14616700412331296383.

[11] Sparks, 'Extending and Refining the Propaganda Model,' 72–73.

[12] E. S. Herman, interviewed by Jeffery Klaehn (2008), 'Media, Power and the Origins of the Propaganda Model: An Interview with Edward S. Herman.,' *Fifth Estate Online: The International Journal of Radical Mass Media Criticism*, emphasis added.

[13] Pedro-Carañana, 'The Propaganda Model in the Early 21st Century (Part II),' 1914.

[14] Ibid., 1907.

[15] Pedro-Carañana, 'The Propaganda Model in the Early 21st Century (Part I),' 1888.

[16] Herman and Chomsky, interviewed in Mullen, 'The Propaganda Model after 20 Years,' 14.

[17] Francisco Sierra Caballero (2006), 'Pensar el control informativo. Fundamentos y perspectivas del Modelo de Propaganda norteamericano.,' in *La Construcción del Consenso. Revisitando el Modelo de Propaganda de Noam Chomsky y Edward S. Herman.*, by Miguel Vázquez and Francisco Sierra Caballero, Comunicación. 4 (Madrid: Siranda), 18.

[18] Brian Michael Goss (2013), *Rebooting the Herman and Chomsky Propaganda Model in the Twenty-First Century*, New York: Peter Lang,, 101.

[19] Nuria Almirón and Ana I. Segovia (2012), 'Financialization, Economic Crisis, and Corporate Strategies in Top Media Companies: The Case of Grupo Prisa,' *International Journal of Communication* 6: 24; Miguel Álvarez-Peralta (2014), 'La crisis estructural del periodismo en España,' *El Viejo topo*, no. 322: 58–64.

[20] Press release by *BBVA Foundation* accessible at: https://www.fbbva.es/wp-content/uploads/2017/07/NdPpresentacioncrisiseconomica.pdf

[21] Sparks, 'Extending and Refining the Propaganda Model,' 70.

[22] Pedro-Carañana 'The Propaganda Model in the Early 21st Century (Part II),' 1909.

[23] Mullen, 'The Propaganda Model after 20 Years,' 13.

[24] Pedro-Carañana, 'The Propaganda Model in the Early 21st Century (Part II),' 1909.

[25] María Josefa Ridaura Martínez (2012), 'La Reforma del Artículo 135 de La Constitución Española: ¿Pueden los mercados quebrar el Consenso Constitucional?,' *Teoría y Realidad Constitucional*, no. 29: 242; Miguel Álvarez Peralta (2015), 'La Crisis En Portada: Representaciones de La Crisis Económica En La Prensa Española de Referencia (2008–2012)' Universidad Complutense de Madrid, 299.

[26] Europa Press, 'Google News shuts down today in Spain', *El Mundo*, 16 December, 2014, accessed 2 May 2, 2017, http://www.elmundo.es/tecnologia/2014/12/16/548f9448e2704eed688b458d.html

[27] Nic Newman (2015), *Reuters Institute Digital News Report 2015: Tracking the Future of News*, Oxford: Oxford-Reuters Institute for the Study of Journalism, 11, accessed 2 May 2017, https://reutersinstitute.politics.ox.ac.uk/sites/default/files/Reuters%20Institute%20Digital%20News%20Report%202015_Full%20Report.pdf

[28] Klaehn and Mullen, 'The Propaganda Model and Sociology,' 12, emphasis added.
[29] Íñigo Errejón and Chantal Mouffe (2015), *Construir pueblo: hegemonía y radicalización de la democracia*, 1. ed, Más madera 116 (Barcelona: Icaria), 18–22.
[30] Havas Media, 'Actitudes ante el Movimiento 15M/Acampadas.' (Havas Media Group, June 2011), 2. Actitudes ante el Movimiento 15M/Acampadas.' (Havas Media Group, June 2011), 2, accessed 2 May 2017, http://recursos.anuncios.com/files/428/77.pdf.
[31] Ibid, 9.
[32] S. Berrocal Gonzalo et al. (2014), 'La presencia del infoentretenimiento en los canales generalistas de la TDT española,' *Revista Latina de Comunicación Social*, no. 69: 85–103, DOI: https://doi.org/10.4185/RLCS-2014-1002.
[33] His program confronted public campaigns since the beginning, when big corporations like *Heineken*, *El Corte Inglés* or *Seguros Ocaso* retired advertising from it as a public protest. After that, the programme became a more frequent and audience leader in prime time, with critical reports about the banking bailout, financial sector opacity, media corruption, frauds in the biggest corporations, etc.
[34] Pablo Iglesias (2015), 'Understanding Podemos,' *New Left Review*, II, no. 93: 17, accessed 4 May 2017, https://newleftreview.org/II/93/pablo-iglesias-understanding-podemos.
[35] Christian Fuchs (2014) *Social Media: A Critical Introduction*. Los Angeles, CA: Sage, 63–66 & 103–20.
[36] Dallas Walker Smythe, *Dependency Road: Communications, Capitalism, Consciousness, and Canada* (Norwood, N.J: Ablex Pub. Corp, 1981), 22–51.
[37] 'Público' marca el millón de fans en Facebook y sigue siendo el diario más 'social' de Europa', *Publico.es*, June 29, 2015, accessed May 3, 2017, http://www.publico.es/economia/comunicacion/publico-marca-millon-fans-facebook.html
[38] Eli Pariser (2011), *The Filter Bubble: What the Internet Is Hiding from You*. New York: Penguin Press.
[39] AIMC (2017), 'Marco General de los medios en España 2017' (Asociación para la Investigación de los Medios de Comunicación), 46, accessed 15 July 2017, http://www.aimc.es/spip.php?action=acceder_document&arg=3245&cle=7ed4b7bc76b68dede4d8125e3526b2ea0a614af7&file=pdf%2Fmarco17.pdf.
[40] Iglesias, 'Understanding Podemos,' 16.
[41] Mullen, 'The Propaganda Model after 20 Years,' 20.
[42] J.P. Mangalindan (2011), 'Dick Costolo: Twitter has 100 million active users', 8 September, accessed 5 May 2017, http://fortune.com/2011/09/08/dick-costolo-twitter-has-100-million-active-users/.
[43] Goss, *Rebooting the Herman & Chomsky Propaganda Model in the Twenty-First Century*, 197.

44 Karl Marx (1859), 'Preface,' in *A Contribution to the Critique of Political Economy*, 1977 ed. Moscow, Progress Publishers.
45 Edward S. Herman (2000), 'The Propaganda Model: A Retrospective,' *Journalism Studies* 1, no. 1: 10.
46 Miguel Álvarez-Peralta, 'Hegemonías Discursivas En El Relato Transmediático de La Crisis: Narrativas Digitales vs Periodísticas,' *CIC Cuadernos de Información Y Comunicación* 19, no. 0 (30 April, 2014): 125–44, DOI: https://doi.org/10.5209/rev_CIYC.2014.v19.43907.
47 Fuchs, *Social Media*, 185–200.
48 Pedro-Carañana, 'The Propaganda Model in the Early 21st Century (Part II),' 1911.
49 Fuchs, *Social Media*, 190.
50 As I write these lines, last two day's TTs include: *#MeFaltan2000, #PodemosSerAlternativa, #JusticiaParaAltsasu, #CCOOsocial2017, #LasCloacasDeInterior, #LasCloacasCatalanas, #LDPabloIglesias, #CorrupcionARV, #RitaBarberá, #PlenoPozuelo, #StopDeportació, #PactodeEstado,* etc. (all of them political, mostly critical). Accessible online at http://www.trendinalia.com/twitter-trending-topics/spain/spain-170720.html.
51 The only (dubious) exception would be the main newspaper, *El País,* which is the most international Spanish reference and gets many of its followers from Latin-America. But it is known to have 52% fake followers (source: twitteraudit.com).
52 Iglesias, 'Understanding Podemos.'
53 Ibid., 16.
54 Mullen, 'The Propaganda Model after 20 Years,' 20.

CHAPTER 9

# Anti-Communism and the Mainstream Online Press in Spain: Criticism of Podemos as a Strategy of a Two-Party System in Crisis

Aurora Labio-Bernal

## 9.1 Introduction

The year 2016 will be remembered in Spain for a prolonged electoral crisis marked by the elections of December 2015, the repeat elections in June of the following year and the looming threat of a third call to the ballot box, which ultimately did not materialise. The inability to form a government after the first vote was due to the absence of a majority for either of the two traditional major parties as a result of the rise of other political forces, such as the Ciudadanos and Podemos parties. Both these groups emerged as alternatives to the two dominant parties, seizing a place of their own on the traditional ideological spectrum: Ciudadanos drawing votes on the right; and Podemos turning into the voice of many voters on the left. It is important to bear in mind that

---

How to cite this book chapter:
Labio-Bernal, A. 2018. Anti-Communism and the Mainstream Online Press in Spain: Criticism of Podemos as a Strategy of a Two-Party System in Crisis. In: Pedro-Carañana, J., Broudy, D. and Klaehn, J. (eds.). *The Propaganda Model Today: Filtering Perception and Awareness*. Pp. 125–141. London: University of Westminster Press. DOI: https://doi.org/10.16997/book27.i. License: CC-BY-NC-ND 4.0

Podemos was born in the context of the 15-M protest movement and the public discontent with the austerity policies of recent years. Established as a party in January 2014, just three months later it took five seats in the European elections and won 69 in the national elections of 2015. In the repeat elections in June 2016, Podemos formed a coalition with Izquierda Unida, winning 71 seats.

The rise of Podemos, along with the fragmentation of the Spanish political spectrum into different ideological forces, has precipitated a crisis for the 'governmental monopoly'[1] maintained by the two major parties, the *Partido Popular* (People's Party, or PP) and the *Partido Socialista Obrero Español* (Socialist Party, or PSOE). These special circumstances in the political life of the country have led mainstream newspapers to adopt positions in defence of the establishment, while taking a critical line with Podemos based on its classification as a radical leftist and/or ideologically communist political party. In light of this situation, I believe it particularly interesting to apply the concept of the fifth filter in Herman and Chomsky's[2] propaganda model to the case of the online editions of the main Spanish newspapers. Despite the view that 'anti-communism' could be deemed a somewhat outdated notion[3] since the fall of the Berlin Wall, this idea has taken on a certain relevance to the media agenda today and demonstrates the contemporary validity of the propaganda model.[4] Although Herman himself has acknowledged[5] that they added free market ideology to the fifth filter in the 2002 edition, he also asserted that the concept of anti-communism as a value of the establishment continued intact. On the other hand, some authors speak of the 'prevailing ideology'[6] to expand the framework to include superstructural aspects that represent a dissident voice in media messages. Although I agree with this view, I argue and will demonstrate in this paper that anti-communism has seen a powerful re-emergence in Western countries due to the crisis of traditional parties and the threat to the status quo.

Thus, in Spain the association of Podemos with the regimes of Venezuela, Bolivia, or Cuba has been a common strategy in the speeches of different political leaders as a way of attacking the new force, but also in the news stories and editorial opinions of Spain's major newspapers. The vocabulary which, explicitly or implicitly, revives communism as the enemy of the Western democratic order has flooded the pages of the newspapers. The origin of this behaviour in news publications is rooted in the relationship with the other filters listed by Herman and Chomsky, as the two-party system currently in crisis bears a close relationship with the ownership interests of the media corporations and their connections to the political and business elite.

## 9.2 Anti-communism Revived in the Neoliberal Era

When considering how Herman and Chomsky's propaganda model may be revised and/or updated, it is always more interesting to try to avoid repeating previous studies and offer a perspective that takes recent events into account as much as possible. Although it is obvious that we cannot compartmentalise the filters identified by the two authors to describe the propaganda strategies of the establishment, I have decided here to focus on one of them in particular, anti-communism, applying it to the current political reality in Spain and the rise of a new party, Podemos, a leftist movement that has burst onto the political landscape as an alternative to the traditional parties.

As a premise for this study, I argue that Herman and Chomsky's Propaganda Model continues to be perfectly valid for analysing the ideology of the media, broadening the scope of application to contexts outside of the United States. I concur with other authors[7] who argue that with the increasing complexity of the media industry and the intensification of capitalist ideals in the new neoliberal era, the Propaganda Model reveals the mutual support the different filters provide one another as the means whereby the establishment continues to control society through the manufacturing of consent.[8]

According to this line of argument, it follows that the dominant ideology operating as a superstructure of the system would repress or even silence any dissenting voice. But to understand how discourses are created, it is essential to analyse the communicative structure at global and national levels. In this respect, it is interesting to note that the context of corporate oligopoly, despite the crises that the big media groups have been suffering in recent years,[9] continues to be one of the basic features of the media industry. Ownership of the media thus remains in the hands of the same elite that share connections with the political and financial powers. As suggested in a recent study by various authors in the anthology *Global Media Giants*:

> By ascribing to a relational definition of power, we argued that economic, political, and cultural power are all woven into the fabric of media power precisely because media corporations are situated within these spheres, but they also have the ability to influence these spheres in different ways.[10]

It is important to remember that for Herman and Chomsky the ideology of anti-communism was the fifth filter of the Propaganda Model of the Western system. It is obvious that this issue was much more palpable during the existence of the Soviet Union and the first years after the Cuban Revolution; however, anti-communism has regained relevance on the media agenda today due to the new use that the political classes themselves have been making of it. During the US elections, Donald Trump described Bernie Sanders, one of the Democratic candidates for the White House, as a 'communist'.[11] The shadow of the radical left was also invoked by Tony Blair when he referred to Jeremy Corbyn, the leader of Britain's Labour Party, as a 'populist politician' of the left, and a 'dangerous experiment' that represented 'a big challenge for the [political] centre'.[12] Meanwhile, in the French elections of 2017, the conservative newspaper *Le Figaro* described the leftist candidate Jean-Luc Mélechon as the French Hugo Chávez.[13] For several days the campaign headlines continued to depict the French politician as the defender of the 'Bolivarian regime'[14] or as the 'apostle of the revolutionary dictators'.[15]

These examples make it clear that any effort to push the boundaries of socialism is quickly identified by the establishment as communism, an approach which, according to Herman and Chomsky, constitutes the creation of an enemy to the order, as will be demonstrated in the analysis of the sample chosen for this paper. But first, it would be timely here to offer a description of the genesis of Podemos as an alternative party emerging in the context of a profound economic, political and social crisis in Spain.

## 9.3 Birth of Podemos in the Two-Party Context

In February 2017, the journalist Pablo Pombo published an article in the digital newspaper *El Confidencial* with the headline 'Podemos becomes the Communist Party 2.0'.[16] It was not the first time that this term was used to describe the movement that arose out of the 15-M protests; a few months earlier, José Carlos Díez in *El País* published an article with the title 'Populism: Communism 2.0'.[17] In both cases, the reporters dismissed Podemos as the political heirs to the Communist Party of Spain and promulgators of old and outdated policies. Such references were nothing new in the media's treatment of Podemos and its leaders, despite the fact that Pablo Iglesias himself has denied any political identification with communism on repeated occasions.

The insistence of the Spanish media on linking Podemos to communism has from the outset taken a biased view of the party as being against the established order. In this respect, the idea of the 'communist peril' represented by Podemos has been accompanied by another term: populism. Indeed, this word was chosen as the word of the year in Spain by the Fundación del Español Urgente (Foundation of Emerging Spanish), whose coordinator, Javier Lascuráin, described it as applying to 'politicians of all ideologies but with the same trait of making an emotional appeal to the public and offering simple solutions to complex problems'.[18] Podemos would thus be depicted in the media as a movement that is both communist and populist, definitions that conveyed a markedly negative image to society.

To understand this portrayal of Podemos by the mainstream media, we need to examine what the birth of the party has represented, and what its platform and ideology have been. Emmanuel Rodríguez López[19] has studied the civic-political trajectory from the protest movements of the *'indignados'* in May 2011, also known as 15-M, to the creation of Podemos, in January 2014. It seems undeniable that the birth of the party led by Pablo Iglesias was the necessary culmination of the public discontent in the period of economic crisis, welfare cutbacks and sharply rising unemployment.[20] The ultimate idea of not trusting the institutions of the State or the traditional parties to turn the situation around was summed up perfectly in the declaration *'no nos representan'* ('they don't represent us') chanted by the crowds at all the demonstrations. As Rodríguez López suggests:

15-M and the wave of movements that followed it seemed to have been based on a political critique that went further than the traditional (leftist) criticism of the 'regime'. Unlike such criticism, which viewed the inadequacies of Spanish democracy as the result of the continued presence of certain underlying elements of Francoism (from the political class and the judiciary to state terrorism and the 'governing style'), the new criticism viewed the parties of the left as major players in the political regime.[21]

Out of these demonstrations, 15-M would develop its own network organization through meetings, the so-called citizens' circles or discussion groups, online mobilization and horizontal decision-making. Citizens became activists, but without adopting specific symbols or ideologies, other than their outrage over the problems related to issues such as public housing, healthcare and education or the lack of jobs for young people. This empowerment of the citizenry needed to be channelled, and in this respect organizations like *Democracia Real Ya* played an important role; however, it was necessary to establish a political party to move from civil protest to political struggle. This would be the task taken up by Podemos as of January 2014.

The creation of a new political force to run in the European elections of May 2014 was proposed only a few days earlier with the presentation of the *Manifiesto Mover Ficha. Convertir la indignación en cambio político* ('Make a Move: Turning Outrage into Political Change'). As Rodríguez López explains, the project was led by Pablo Iglesias, who in only two days obtained the 50,000 signatures needed to endorse the initiative. José Ignacio Torreblanca[22] has studied the profile of Podemos voters to draw some rather interesting conclusions. Torreblanca suggests that Podemos has captured the votes of abstainers and generally apathetic citizens all over Spain. He also supports the view that they are votes of discontent, from the moment the party obtained higher percentages in poorer neighbourhoods and regions hardest hit by the crisis. With respect to age, it appears that Podemos has won support from every generation, although it has been more successful with voters under thirty. In relation to academic level, Podemos voters tend to be among the most highly educated. In ideological terms, Pablo Iglesias' party has seized votes from the parties on the left: Izquierda Unida and the Socialist Party (PSOE), although it has also captured the attention of voters in the center. Geographically, Podemos has been more successful in cities than in small towns, and, although it has voters all over Spanish territory, its biggest support is located in Madrid, Asturias, Aragón, and the Balearic and Canary Islands.

## 9.4 Analysis of the Sample

For this study, I have developed a content analysis that I will apply using a series of categories for the period running from the birth of Podemos in January 2014 to the Spanish general elections in June 2016. The categories will be applied to the online versions of two major newspapers in Spain: *El País* and *ABC*, two papers representative of the two-party political system. Furthermore, these two periodicals are owned by two large media corporations, Prisa and Vocento respectively, both connected to the national and international corporate and financial apparatus. In the case of the owner of *El País*, the company Prisa, its stakeholders include the British investment fund Amber Capital, as well as Caixa Bank, Telefónica and Banco Santander. A block of shares is also in the hands of the Polanco family, which in turn is associated with organizations such as the Trilateral Commission, where we find another prominent family in the media world, the Ybarra family. The Ybarras are related to the owner of the other newspaper under study, *ABC*, in the hands of Vocento. One of its members, Emilio Ybarra, along with his brother Santiago, controls Vocento and is a member of the Trilateral Commission, which also includes figures such as Ana Patricia Botín, Chairwoman of Banco Santander Central Hispano. Meanwhile, another family with a presence in Vocento, the Bergareches, have an influence that extends to the oil giant Cepsa and the infrastructure and services operator Ferrovial, as Santiago Bergareche has held or currently holds various executive posts in all these companies.

The above information is provided to place the media outlets under study here in their political and corporate context, in order to understand that their message is directly related to the interests of the group to which they belong and the system of which they form a part. The analysis of news stories published in *El País* and *ABC* about Podemos is thus connected to the corporate structure of Prisa and Vocento as companies present in the framework of the market economy. Anti-communism therefore operates as a variable to convey a negative image of Podemos to the public. The corpus of the sample is made up of 150 news articles (70 from *ABC* and 80 from *El País*) from the period indicated above retrieved by means of key word searches in the digital archives of both newspapers. These key words constitute the references for the following categories of my content analysis:

- Podemos and Venezuela. As will be shown, both newspapers have repeatedly linked the party to the government of Hugo Chávez and Nicolás Maduro to raise doubts about the democratic nature of Podemos and its leaders. The variables in this category include repeated references to alleged illegal financing of Podemos by the Venezuelan government (the legal proceedings for which have been dismissed by the Spanish courts as many as seven times)[23], as well as the identification of Pablo Iglesias or Juan Carlos Monedero with a regime described as a dictatorship and a violator of human rights.
- Podemos and its relationship with countries with governments of the so-called 'radical left'. Principally, a connection would be made with Cuba, and in so doing, with communism. But this would also extend to other nations and leaders like Evo Morales in Bolivia, Rafael Correa in Ecuador, and Alexis Tsipras in Greece.
- Podemos and countries considered to form part of the 'axis of evil'. The term was of course coined by George W. Bush in 2002 to refer to enemy states of

the West. Specifically, it referred to Iraq, Iran and North Korea. For the case that concerns us here, the main link made is with Iran.
- Podemos, explicit communism and populism. In this category, I will analyse the terminology used to identify Podemos directly with the communist party, or with Marxism or any of its derivatives, including anti-establishment characteristics. Directly associated with this and as a means of attempting to discredit the new political movement, there are constant references to Podemos being a 'populist' party. In this respect, I adopt the approach of Vicenç Navarro, who considers that the 'term "populism" has no scientific value and is used as an insult by the Spanish and European establishments to define any movement they deem a threat or that does not have their approval.'[24] The negative references to Podemos and its supposedly populist character are frequent in the newspapers studied.

Having defined the categories and variables, I will next offer a qualitative analysis with certain quantitative data. Firstly, it is important to note that most of the news articles that link Podemos to communism are based on the party's relationship with the government of Venezuela. In the case of *ABC*, 60% of the samples studied contained news on this topic, while in the case of *El País* it was a little higher, at 62.5%. The main content of these articles is related to the idea that Venezuela is a communist-style dictatorship and that its leaders, both Hugo Chávez previously and Nicolás Maduro today, are tyrants who wield power on their own. This relationship is made by the media sources studied either through the repetition of statements by other political leaders or through the disclosure of documents that allegedly demonstrate financial ties between the Venezuelan government and Podemos. Some examples of this strategy can even be found in the headlines, such as one in *ABC* on 23 June 2016: 'Rajoy responds to Iglesias: 'Spain is not Venezuela.' The PP leader assesses the statements of the Podemos leader on the security of the voting process.'[25] Another of the fundamental issues associated with the long shadow cast by the Venezuelan government over Podemos has to do with the financial backing which it allegedly received in the Chávez era. The misinformation began with the publication of headlines like the one appearing in *ABC* on 25 February 2015: 'Venezuelan Government and CEPS accused of illegal financing of Podemos.'[26] The theory of the newspaper has always been that Podemos was financed by consultancy services provided by the Centre for Political and Social Studies (CEPS, for its initials in Spanish) prior to the existence of Podemos, but in which some of its future leaders participated, including Pablo Iglesias himself, Iñigo Errejón, and Juan Carlo Monedero. It is not a case of false information, but of information taken out of context and a lack of evidence. There were payments for these services that met all legal requirements, and it was never demonstrated that they were used to finance the party. In fact, *ABC* itself recognised that it was Venezuela's main opposition party that had made the accusation of '*alleged* illegal financing' of Podemos.

*El País* took a similar line, repeating the story of the payment of Podemos leaders by the Venezuelan government. Although it did not directly claim that this was a case of illegal financing, it did adopt the same theory as *ABC*. Some of the news articles published in *El País*, such as an article on 17 June 2014, ran with headlines like 'Foundation related to Podemos charged Chávez 3.7 million euros over 10 years,'[27] or attempted to establish a direct connection with one of the founders of Podemos, such as the story on March 1, 2015, stating that '*El Nacional* links Monedero to payments of 3.2 million euros. The Venezuelan newspaper claims that the co-founder of Podemos took payments from a *Chavista* think tank of which he was a director.'[28] Days prior to the elections of June 2016, *El País* brought up the topic once again with a news story with the headline: 'Venezuelan Assembly investigates financing of Podemos by *Chavismo*.'[29]

The negative impact of the media allegations of the financing of Podemos by Venezuela was intensified with the alleged involvement of another country: Iran. As mentioned above, this country is one of the nations classified as enemies of the West within the 'axis of evil'. The validity of the anti-communist filter, adapted to the current era through the 'us versus them' binary,[30] is reinforced with the inclusion of Iran as one of the supporters and financiers of Podemos. Both *ABC* and *El País* would corroborate this link in their news stories and opinion pieces to characterise Podemos' leaders as heretics against the system. The difference between the two media sources in relation to the Podemos-Iran connection lies in the focus of attention in each case. In the case of *ABC*, the focus is placed on the money received by Pablo Iglesias from Tehran for his work as a presenter on the program *Fort Apache* for the Madrid-based Iranian network HispanTV.[31] According to *ABC*, this network was sponsored by 'the Iranian government in the final years of the presidency of the Islamist conservative Mahmoud Ahmadinejad to influence Spain and other Spanish-speaking countries.' The article also claims that this alleged financing is being investigated by the Economic and Fiscal Crime Unit of the National Police. This story from January 2016 would continue to be cited in the months that followed, with *ABC* directly asserting that the birth of Podemos had been 'sponsored'[32] by Venezuela and Iran, with captions like 'Chavistas and Ayatollahs have contributed more than 6 million euros to the growth of the party.'

In the case of *El País*, the presence of Iran takes more of a political focus in an effort to demonstrate that its link to Podemos is an attempt to undermine the foundations of democracy in Spain. In this case, the newspaper uses opinion columns to promulgate this theory, like the article penned by Ángel Mas in February 2016, in which he warns of Iran's interest 'in destabilizing a Western democracy in the heart of Europe.'[33] He goes on to argue that:

> [...] the party that has benefited from the support of a regime like that does not even feel the need to conceal it from voters, who in any mature democracy would run screaming from the possibility of being associated with such a brutal theocracy.

Equally critical of Pablo Iglesias is Ignacio Martín Blanco, for whom:

> [...] it is abominable to listen to someone who aspires to be your nation's prime minister, or at least deputy prime minister, acknowledging unashamedly that he has collaborated with a theocratic regime that stones women and homosexuals, with the sole objective of destabilizing our country from within.[34]

Martín Blanco takes an even stronger tone when he asserts that:

> [...] instead of accepting the rules of the democratic game, Iglesias expresses his determination to take drastic measures, with no consideration whatsoever for political pluralism, and to join forces with Iran and Venezuela against their common adversary, which is none other than constitutional Spain regardless of whether it is governed by the PP or the PSOE.

Beyond the question of financing, the idea that Podemos is a force working against the democratic order due to its proximity to radical ideologies also appears in relation to other countries of Latin America and other European leaders who have offered alternatives to the prevailing two-party system. Specifically, it is also common to read of connections between Pablo Iglesias or other members of Podemos and leaders like Evo Morales, as asserted in October 2014, when *ABC* published a news story that cites the Bolivian president as suggesting that 'Spain should be the door for Bolivia to enter Europe,' which can be achieved 'with brothers like Pablo Iglesias.' It should be highlighted that, although apparently a news article reporting the statements of Evo Morales, the interest lies in the fact that the Bolivian president himself is a dissident force according to the power structures and the media establishment. The researcher Manuel Rodríguez Illana has published a study on this, based on his doctoral dissertation, in which he concludes that *ABC* is the Spanish newspaper that is most hostile in its treatment of news on Evo Morales, to such an extent that he could be classified as a 'devil of the media'.[35] This theory seems to be supported by an analysis of an interview published by this newspaper with the Bolivian colonel Germán Cardona, with the headline 'Germán Cardona: The Bolivian and Venezuelan military exports cocaine on official planes.'[36] The interview, which attempts to uncover a cocaine trafficking network, contains two moments that reflect the negative treatment of the Bolivian president and the contaminating effect of this bias on Podemos. When Cardona is asked whether Evo Morales is involved in cocaine trafficking, the colonel replies: 'I cannot accuse him directly, but Evo is the maximum leader of the coca growers and everything that happens in the Chapare, in the crop regions and cocaine production goes through him.' The second and more disturbing moment in the interview occurs when Cardona is asked about the possible entry of cocaine by drug cartels using political influences. Cardona answers:

The cartel wants the Podemos party to take over the Government of Spain so that they can open a door for direct entry of cocaine into Europe. My sources tell me, 'Colonel, the MAS (*Movimiento Al Socialismo*, Evo Morales' party) is going to have its president in Spain; we have a party now; Evo is financing brother Pablo (Iglesias), he has been to the Chapare, our brother president brought him here.' I asked whether money was given to Pablo Iglesias and they told me no, that it is given 'to an organization in Spain'. My informant assures me that Evo Morales says that with the 'MAS' party (Podemos), we are going to get our products directly into Spain, that 'brother Pablo has said so' (Evo Morales had received Pablo Iglesias in Santa Cruz the previous September). I asked whether they were going to take advantage of this legal trade to get cocaine in and he told me 'possibly'.

This serious accusation by the newspaper *ABC* has its political parallel in the praise which, according to other writers for the newspaper, the leaders of Podemos heap on countries like Cuba. Thus we have the words of Mayte Alcarazen in June 2014, discussing Juan Carlos Monedero, one of the founders of Podemos:

Knowing that Mr Monedero considers that the repression, the execution of dissidents and the lack of the most basic elements of democracy in Cuba are, as he revealed yesterday, 'situations that need to improve', I have reached a conclusion. Cuba is the model.[37]

Also following this line of argument is Isabel San Sebastián, who in April 2016, only a few weeks before the elections, asserted:

Podemos is not a typical democratic force, comparable to the PSOE or even to Izquierda Unida. It does not defend ideological positions compatible with pluralism. It does not even take the trouble to conceal its true nature by raising its voice to condemn the unrelenting persecution suffered by the opposition in Venezuela or Cuba.[38]

Also included in this Bolivarian axis of evil is Ecuador. Thus, as if it were a criminal act, in December 2015 *ABC* featured the headline: 'One of Iglesias' deputies worked for eight years for Correa'. In the body of the article we find references to the similarities between the Ecuadorean president and Pablo Iglesias, after which the newspaper chose to insert the following:

The political leader Diego Ordóñez (center-right) commented to ABC that 'Podemos' alliance with the Bolivarian regimes is parasitic and the impact is felt by Venezuelan and Ecuadorean citizens, who suffer the loss of their civil liberties and impoverishment due to the populist recipes that have already proven to be pernicious in the handling of the Greek crisis.'

This manifestly hostile attitude toward Podemos and its leaders by linking it to socialist Latin American countries appears to be somewhat more moderate in the case of *El País*, although the association of the party with communist principles is still present. One example of this is a column written by Enrique Collado Pérez entitled: 'Castro and Iglesias: Starting Over', with the subheading: 'Podemos isn't proposing anything new. 60 years later it offers a clear parallel with the postulates of Castro's Cuba.'[39] It is true that the identification of Podemos with the Cuban regime is made mostly by its columnists, as also demonstrated by a piece penned in May 2015 by Ernesto Ekaizer in response to the departure of Juan Carlos Monedero from the party, in which he suggests: 'Monedero's letter oozes nostalgia. It gives the impression that Monedero identifies with Ernesto Che Guevara when he left Fidel Castro's Cuba.'[40] The suggestion of alignment with Cuba and other countries within the socialist orbit even leads some reporters, such as Paulina Gamus, to speculate on what would happen if a party like Podemos, which she describes as a 'Tyrannosaurus', were to come to power:

> The essential ingredient for the victory of a Tyrannosaurus is resentment. Those seeking to achieve it must foment rage, envy and a desire for revenge against the politicians, who are responsible for the fact that you, them and I have a hard life. When the Tyrannosaurus comes to power, it doesn't empower anybody except itself and its clique. In its speeches it had already announced, without many noticing, that a break with democracy was needed. It thus proceeds to destroy the institutions that guarantee civil rights and freedoms, and applies the same economic recipes that sank Cuba, that have sunk Argentina time and again, and that are now sinking Venezuela in the deepest pit of the most shameful misery. [41]

The apocalyptic tone taken with Podemos goes to its furthest extreme in discussions of the danger it poses to the established order when it is also linked to two other issues: populism and radical leftism, or directly to communism. Clear examples of this linkage can be found in both newspapers. Thus, in an article announcing the publication of the book *El engaño populista* (*The Populist Deception*) by Gloria Álvarez and Axel Kaiser, in May 2016 *ABC* published the headline: 'A Podemos government would be catastrophic.'[42] A few days earlier, the newspaper had already begun promoting the book and criticizing Podemos when it published an article under the headline 'The five pillars of communist populism', which includes quotes from the aforementioned authors like this one:

> The Bolivarian movement sweeping through Latin America does not belong to the leftist tradition, say Kaiser and Álvarez; it is pure populism. The leader of Podemos, like the presidents whom he has taken as his model, 'has deliberately fostered a great deception, which is the promise of wellbeing for all with ideas and political projects whose only outcome would be the destruction of any chance of progress and freedom for the people.'[43]

According to *ABC,* in addition to Latin American populism, there is another European model, embodied in the figure of Alexis Tsipras in Greece and of Beppe Grillo in Italy. These are examples of leftist populists, but the break with the two-party system also appears, according to *ABC,* on the right in Marine Le Pen in France, and Nigel Farage in the United Kingdom. On this same spectrum of so-called populism, *ABC* decides to include all these leaders, thereby engaging in an ideological simplification typical of the commercial logic of the mainstream media. This is reinforced with the help of certain opinion pieces in the paper, such as one written by Ramón Pérez Maura, who talks directly of the 'communists' of Podemos in the following way:

> The tension we have seen this week between the Iglesias and Errejón factions in Podemos brings to mind the old days of the Russian Social Democratic Workers' Party, which in the early twentieth century faced up against Lenin's Bolsheviks and Yuli Martov's Mensheviks.[44]

On other occasions, however, it is the paper's news stories themselves that speak boldly of communism in their references to the new party. A few days prior to the elections of 2016, *ABC* ran the headline: 'This is how Podemos is camouflaging its communist plan.'[45] And in the body of the article, the conservative journalist identified this as 'taking power, putting communism into practice and establishing a new "constitutional process" that will topple the current constitutional system.'

*El País* also uses its columnists to make the same comparison and association between populism, Marxism and post-Marxism, as can be seen in a column by Héctor E. Schamis, who argues: 'The so-called "populism" of this century in the end is profoundly authoritarian, resulting in a kind of Stalinist restoration.'[46] Other authors, like Antonio Elorza, decide that it is better to link the 'populism' of Podemos with the idea of 'anti-systems' intended to 'dismantle a fragile democratic State.'[47] But without doubt the most explicit example in *El País* in this sense is the previously mentioned article titled 'Populism: Communism 2.0', by José Carlos Díez, who asserts that:

> In Europe, populism is unfeasible within the democratic and legal framework of the EU. Syriza tried it and ended up rescuing the banks and applying tough cutbacks like Rajoy's in 2012. In Spain, Podemos and its partners will not even be able to attempt it, holding only around 80 out of 350 seats. Their municipal leaders are already paying the debt they promised not to pay, the austerity continues, the youth are still angry and the same poverty is still there.[48]

All of the above constitutes a few examples of the constant criticism that the two biggest newspapers in Spain make of Podemos in the context of the rise of this new party. This study aims to offer an exploration of the biased and decontextualised treatment of news stories related to Podemos and its leaders at a moment of clear crisis in the two-party system. This criticism has been based on the use of the fifth filter in Herman and Chomsky's propaganda model, in what I consider to be an updated version of that model. While perhaps during the 1990s, the fall of the Berlin Wall made it hard to see any signs that anti-communism would continue to form part of the apparatus of the establishment, the economic and financial crisis of the last few years, which has provoked a public reaction and mobilization in various regions of the world (including Spain) has given rise to new parties like Podemos, and this emergence of new ideological forces that have broken up the usual alternation of power between progressives and conservatives has represented a disruption of the established order. In this situation, traditional politicians and mainstream media, integrated in the power structures, have revived the anti-communism filter as a propaganda method. In the next section, I will set out the main conclusions of this study, which will need to be expanded on in future years as the Spanish political context evolves.

## 9.5 Conclusion

The rise of Podemos as a new political force in the context of two-party dominance has constituted an unprecedented development in the recent history of Spanish democracy. The traditional power structures, heirs to Francoism albeit updated in the context of globalization, have thus felt threatened (at least in the early days of Podemos' existence) by this new party. As a result, the other political parties and the mainstream media (both their paper and digital editions) have identified it as a new 'enemy' which they have been quick to label as radical leftist, thus making new use of the 'anti-communism' filter as a means of averting the dangers posed to the established order. Although it is true that 'anti-communism' does not operate like it did in the past,[49] it is nevertheless clear that the binary of good guys and bad guys, of us versus them, continues to work effectively. Moreover, in the case that concerns us here, I have demonstrated that the identification of 'them', the 'enemy', or the 'bad guy' is closely associated with the resurgence of a possible communist threat.

To make this negative impact clear, two of Spain's biggest newspapers, *El País* and *ABC*, have published news stories and opinion pieces that associate Podemos with other 'devils of the media', to quote Ramón Reig.[50] The study presented here shows that there has been a clear media manipulation in an effort to demonise Pablo Iglesias' party, to which end various techniques have been used. One of these has involved the prioritization of content, as demonstrated by the ongoing importance given to the alleged financing of Podemos by Venezuela. In this case, furthermore, certain important pieces of information have been purposefully omitted, resulting in the decontextualization of the facts. Despite the fact that no court has been able to confirm such financing and that every legal action filed has been dismissed due to a lack of evidence, the two newspapers have repeated the story, in many cases using sources from the Venezuelan opposition and casting doubt on the words of Podemos' leaders. The contamination of the information has been further supported by opinions published in both media sources that have given columnists free reign to classify the members of Podemos as populists and radicals. The negative bias is also evident in the choice of sources, with priority given to actors who are manifestly against the new political party. Furthermore, the anti-Podemos slant has also been demonstrated by the choice of preconceived ideas in the collective imagination associated with the axis of evil (Iran or the Bolivarian states of Latin America) to develop this superstructural identification.

As noted above, this analysis is only a first approach to the treatment of Podemos by the Spanish, mainstream, online media. The fundamental purpose of this study has been to confirm what seemed to me to be a scientific intuition that Podemos was not being accepted by the media system because it is viewed as a threat to the latter's survival, as was communism during the Cold War. It is clear that the new Left apparently represented by Podemos has been turned into an enemy to attack for the power structures in which the media, politicians and corporations all appear to share the same interests.

## Notes and Bibliography

[1] Emmy Eklundh (2016). 'El soberano fantasmático: Las implicaciones políticas de la apropiación de Laclau por parte de Podemos', *Relaciones Internacionales*, no. 31: 111.

[2] Edward S. Herman and Noam Chomsky (2002), *Manufacturing Consent: The Political Economy of the Mass Media*. New York: Pantheon Books, 29–31.

[3] Brian McNair (2003), 'From Control to Chaos: Towards a New Sociology of Journalism', *Media, Culture & Society*, Vol. 25: 547–555 and Antonio Pineda Cachero (2001), 'El Modelo de Propaganda de Noam Chomsky: Medios Mainstream y Control del Pensamiento', *Ámbitos*, no 6: 191–210.

[4] Brian Michael Goss (2013), *Rebooting the Herman & Chomsky Propaganda Model in the Twenty-First Century*, New York, Peter Lang; Joan Pedro (2011), 'The Propaganda Model in the Early 21st Century', *International Journal of Communication*, Vol. 5: 1906–1926; Andrew Mullen (2010), 'Twenty Years On: The Second-Order Prediction of the Herman-Chomsky Propaganda Model, *Media, Culture & Society*, Vol. 32 (4): 673–690; Francisco Sierra Caballero (2006), 'Pensar el control informativo. Fundamentos y perspectivas del modelo de propaganda norteamericano', en *La construcción del consenso. Revisitando el modelo de propaganda de Noam Chomsky y Edward S. Herman*, eds. Miguel Vázquez and Francisco Sierra. Madrid: Siranda Editorial, 13–38.

[5] See interview at http://www.cubadebate.cu/opinion/2013/02/12/esta-claro-que-el-poder-economico-dicta-las-politicas-de-los-medios-de-comunicacion/#.WSHTJ0vZVXk

[6] Joan Pedro (2009), 'Evaluación crítica del modelo de propaganda de Herman y Chomsky', *Revista Latina de Comunicación social*, n° 64 Available at http://www.revistalatinacs.org/09/art/19_818_35_ULEPICC_02/Joan_Pedro.html; Michael Albert (2014), *Vida más allá del capitalismo*. Barcelona: Icaria Editorial.

[7] Mullen, 'Twenty Years On: The Second-Order Prediction of the Herman-Chomsky Propaganda Model'; Pedro, 'The Propaganda Model in the Early 21st Century'; Goss, *Rebooting the Herman & Chomsky Propaganda Model*.

[8] Sierra Caballero, 'Pensar el control informativo. Fundamentos y perspectivas del modelo de propaganda norteamericano', 25.

[9] Aurora Labio-Bernal (2015), 'From Phone Hacking to the Splitting of Businesses in Times of Corporate Crisis: The Case of News Corporation', *Global Media Journal*, Vol. 13 (24), 2015. Available at http://www.globalmediajournal.com/open-access/from-phone-hacking-to-the-splitting-of-businesses-in-times-of-corporate-crisis-the-case-of-news-corporation.php?aid=55028

[10] Benjamin Birkinbine, Rodrigo Gómez and Janet Wasko (2016), eds, *Global Media Giants*, New York: Routledge, 482.

[11] http://www.washingtontimes.com/news/2015/oct/14/donald-trump-bernie-sanders-communist/

[12] https://www.theguardian.com/politics/2016/may/28/tony-blair-corbyn-government-dangerous-experiment

[13] https://dominiquelesparre.files.wordpress.com/2017/04/catalog-cover-large-png.jpg

[14] http://www.lefigaro.fr/elections/presidentielles/2017/04/14/35003-20170414ARTFIG00168-alliance-bolivarienne-le-camp-melenchon-tente-d-eteindre-la-polemique.php

[15] http://www.lefigaro.fr/elections/presidentielles/2017/04/11/35003-20170411ARTFIG00264-melenchon-l-apotre-des-dictateurs-revolutionnaires-sud-americains.php

[16] 'Podemos se convierte en el Partido Comunista 2.0', http://blogs.elconfidencial.com/espana/cronicas-desde-el-frente-viral/2017-02-13/podemos-se-convierte-en-el-partido-comunista-2-0_1330511/

[17] 'Populismo: comunismo 2.0', http://economia.elpais.com/economia/2016/06/23/actualidad/1466711391_937233.html

[18] https://elpais.com/cultura/2016/12/30/actualidad/1483092782_433550.html

[19] Emmanuel Rodríguez López (2016), *La políticas en el ocaso de la clase media. El ciclo 15M-Podemos*. Madrid: Traficantes de sueños.

[20] Aurora Labio-Bernal and Antonio Pineda Cachero (2016), 'Leftward Shift, Media Change? Ideology and Politics in Spanish Online-Only Newspapers After the 15-M Movement', *International Journal of Communication*. Vol. 10: 2661–2682.

[21] Rodríguez López, *La política en el ocaso de la clase media. El ciclo 15M-Podemos*, 53.
[22] José Ignacio Torreblanca (2015), *Asaltar los cielos. Podemos o la política después de la crisis*, Barcelona: Ed. Debate, 38–39.
[23] https://www.infolibre.es/noticias/politica/2016/07/15/la_justicia_archiva_por_septima_vez_una_accion_penal_contra_podemos_sus_dirigentes_52566_1012.html
[24] Vicenç Navarro (2013), '¿Qué es populismo?', Available at http://www.vnavarro.org/?p=10013
[25] 'Rajoy responde a Iglesias: «España no es Venezuela. El líder del PP valora las declaraciones del líder de Podemos sobre la seguridad de las votaciones.' Pablo Iglesias' doubts about the elections to be held in Spain arose in the context of a previous controversy involving the Minister of the Interior, Jorge Fernández Díaz, related to tapped phone calls that revealed that investigations were being conducted into independent leaders in Spain. For further information, see: http://www.eldiario.es/politica/Pablo-Iglesias-votaciones-Fernandez-Diaz_0_529847670.html
[26] 'Denuncian al Gobierno venezolano y a CEPS por financiación ilegal de Podemos.' http://www.abc.es/espana/20150225/abci-venezuela-financiacion-podemos-201502252210.html
[27] 'La fundación relacionada con Podemos cobró 3,7 millones de Chávez en 10 años.' https://politica.elpais.com/politica/2014/06/17/actualidad/1403039351_862188.html
[28] 'El Nacional' vincula a Monedero con el cobro de 3,2 millones. El diario venezolano afirma que el cofundador de Podemos cobró de un 'think tank' chavista del que fue directivo.' https://politica.elpais.com/politica/2015/03/01/actualidad/1425237452_690891.html
[29] 'La Asamblea de Venezuela investiga la financiación de Podemos por el chavismo' https://politica.elpais.com/politica/2016/06/16/actualidad/1466113124_463561.html
[30] Goss, *Rebooting the Herman & Chomsky Propaganda Model in the Twenty-First Century*, 6.
[31] http://www.abc.es/espana/abci-pablo-iglesias-cobrado-93000-euros-iran-entre-2013-y-2015-201601140057_noticia.html
[32] http://www.abc.es/espana/abci-iran-y-venezuela-patrocinaron-nacimiento-podemos-201603180503_noticia.html
[33] https://elpais.com/elpais/2016/02/12/opinion/1455304545_909230.html
[34] https://elpais.com/elpais/2016/03/15/opinion/1458059076_469460.html
[35] Manuel Rodríguez Illana (2014), *Factores estructurales y coyunturales en el mensaje periodístico: la llegada al poder de Evo Morales en ABC, El Mundo y El País*. Buenos Aires: OETEC-CLICET, 2014. Available at http://www.oetec.org/informes/evomorales210114.pdf
[36] 'Germán Cardona: «Militares bolivianos y venezolanos exportan cocaína en aviones oficiales»' http://www.abc.es/internacional/20150521/abci-entrevista-coronel-boliviano-droga-201505202123.html

[37] http://www.abc.es/lasfirmasdeabc/20140613/abci-viva-monedero-201406121818.html
[38] http://www.abc.es/opinion/abci-podemos-heredar-201604081729_noticia.html
[39] 'Castro e Iglesias: comenzar de nuevo. Podemos no propone nada nuevo. 60 años después presenta un claro paralelismo con los postulados de la Cuba castrista.' https://elpais.com/elpais/2015/03/27/opinion/1427485079_782081.html
[40] https://politica.elpais.com/politica/2015/05/01/analitica/1430507872_143050.html
[41] https://internacional.elpais.com/internacional/2014/06/20/actualidad/1403223088_840640.html
[42] 'Un gobierno de Podemos sería catastrófico.' http://www.abc.es/espana/abci-gobierno-podemos-seria-catastrofico-para-espana-201605301839_noticia.html
[43] 'Los cinco pilares del populismo comunista.' http://www.abc.es/espana/abci-cinco-pilares-populismo-comunista-201605160318_noticia.html
[44] http://www.abc.es/opinion/abci-bolcheviques-y-mencheviques-podemos-201603121943_noticia.html
[45] 'Así camufla Podemos su plan comunista.' http://www.abc.es/espana/abci-camufla-podemos-plan-comunista-201606050301_noticia.html
[46] https://elpais.com/elpais/2014/10/04/opinion/1412446363_765944.html
[47] https://politica.elpais.com/politica/2016/10/14/actualidad/1476465202_109323.html
[48] https://economia.elpais.com/economia/2016/06/23/actualidad/1466711391_937233.html
[49] Goss, *Rebooting the Herman & Chomsky Propaganda Model*, 143.
[50] Ramón Reig (2004), *Dioses y Diablos mediáticos*, Barcelona: Urano, 2004.

# PART III

# Screen Entertainment and Broadcast Media

CHAPTER 10

# A Screen Entertainment Propaganda Model

Matthew Alford

How useful is Edward Herman and Noam Chomsky's Propaganda Model (PM) for analysing the entertainment media? I have previously established that the PM is an essential tool for analysing cinema[1] and that the objections raised to such an enterprise are insubstantial.[2] Both Herman and Chomsky have indicated that they consider the model to be more widely applicable but that the entertainment media is beyond their immediate fields of interest.[3] This article applies the PM to both the cinema industry and to network television, as a means by which we can assess the model's utility more widely in contemporary America.

The PM hypothesises that the US media 'mobilise support for the special interests that dominate state and private activity'[4] and that media representations of the US' role in the world can be explained through five contributory factors or 'filters,' which 'cleanse' information from the real world to leave only the 'residue' which is acceptable to established power systems.[5] The filters are as follows: 'size, ownership and profit orientation' (first filter); 'the advertising license to do business' (second filter); the need for the media to use power-

---

**How to cite this book chapter:**
Alford, M. 2018. A Screen Entertainment Propaganda Model. In: Pedro-Carañana, J., Broudy, D. and Klaehn, J. (eds.). *The Propaganda Model Today: Filtering Perception and Awareness*. Pp. 145–158. London: University of Westminster Press. DOI: https://doi.org/10.16997/book27.j. License: CC-BY-NC-ND 4.0

ful organisations in 'sourcing' information (third filter); the ability of powerful organisations to issue flak (fourth filter), and a dominant ideology of a superior, benevolent 'us' in the West versus a backward 'them' overseas (fifth filter).

The residue never goes beyond certain 'bounds of acceptability',[6] including the idea that the US is a 'terrorist' state,[7] 'rogue' state,[8] or 'failed' state.[9] In turn, the US and its media consciously or unconsciously classify all populations as 'worthy' (the US and its allies) and 'unworthy' (everyone else – the 'unpeople' to borrow Mark Curtis' term[10]).[11] America's image of itself, in short, is rendered benevolent and, even, exceptionalist.

## 10.1 A Screen Entertainment Propaganda Model: Predictive Capabilities

To test their hypothesis, Herman and Chomsky examine the news residue carefully to see if any remaining elements challenge fundamental assumptions about established power systems, particularly the US treatment of 'official enemies' overseas. They find very little. What does remain – the 'residue' – we can further categorise into five distinct areas:

1. That which has little or no political relevance, and, in terms of the political world, is merely distraction;
2. That which is overtly supportive of establishment goals;
3. That which initially appears to criticise the political system but, on closer reading, provides it with fundamental support;
4. That which does genuinely challenge Western power systems but is explicitly marginalised by the media mechanisms;
5. That which does genuinely break through the filtration system, which invariably occurs for irregular reasons and/ or with serious caveats.

I will now address each of these five elements of the residue and also establish how they relate to a screen PM, specifically how well they can predict output. This is followed by a discussion of the limitations of the model in this context.

**(i) That which has little or no political relevance, and, in terms of the political world, is merely distraction.**
Herman and Chomsky point to astrology, crossword puzzles, sports, and the 'funnies' in newspapers that serve only to entertain the public and provide no relevant information to the real world. As Chomsky explains:

> This is an oversimplification, but for the eighty per cent [of the population] or whatever they are, the main thing is to divert them. To get them to watch National Football League. And to worry about 'Mother with Child with Six Heads,' or whatever you pick up on the supermarket stands and

so on. Or look at astrology. Or get involved in fundamentalist stuff or something or other. Just get them away. Get them away from things that matter. And for that it's important to reduce their capacity to think.[12]

Similarly, large quantities of film and television relates in little or no way to the US' role in the world. Shows like *X-Factor* and films like *Sharknado* do not tell us much, at least not directly, about American politics, whilst some shows like *Who Wants to Marry a Multi-Millionaire?* may even be construed as actively damaging broader socio-cultural advances such as feminism.

**(ii) That which is overtly supportive of establishment goals, particularly the treatment of official enemies.**
Herman and Chomsky take it for granted that there is a strong strain of thinking on the right that reflexively supports the core planks of establishment thinking, specifically the benevolence of the US system and its right to utilise force at its sole discretion. This plank of the media is 'crazy' and may be equated to fascism.[13]

Similarly, film and television is replete with products that follow this line. In fact, we know that the CIA, Pentagon and White House explicitly support a long line of political products. My latest research with Tom Secker, drawing on Freedom of Information Act requests, demonstrates that this has consisted of over 800 Hollywood films, over one thousand TV shows along with hundreds more supported by the CIA, NSA, White House, and State Department.[14] We know now that the state is far more involved in entertainment, with scant acknowledgement or open documentation, than scholarship has ever been able to demonstrate previously and its ability to control narratives is similarly remarkable.

Many more products are commonly accepted as supporting establishment narratives, but without explicit production assistance, from *Rambo* to *Taken*.

**(iii) That which initially appears to criticise the political system but, on closer reading, provides it with fundamental support.**
The above two categories are relatively uncontroversial. It is widely accepted that the media is 'dumbed down' and even Ben Shapiro, a prominent media researcher who bemoans what he sees as pervasive left-wing messages in entertainment culture, admits that there is a body of right-wing products including the TV series *24*.[15] The remaining three categories are more controversial.

Herman and Chomsky examine examples of where the media is commonly assumed to have challenged the state, as with the coverage of the Watergate break-in or the Vietnam War (2002). As key parts of their critique in these cases, respectively, they point to: the media supporting the Democrat desire to oust President Richard Nixon over comparatively minor domestic crimes, and it ignoring the aggression by the US against South Vietnam.

Similarly, with screen entertainment, we can try to identify output that genuinely challenges established power systems. Here are some prominent examples of products from the past thirty years that have been labelled as very challenging to Western political structures but which, at their core, are embedded with messages that actually support these narratives. I give two examples here, one from cinema (*Munich*) and one from television (*West Wing*) although to this list we might add *Avatar*, *Hotel Rwanda*, *Three Kings*, *Thirteen Days*, *Amistad*, *Homeland* and *Newsroom*, amongst others, many of which I have discussed in detail elsewhere.[16]

*Munich* (2005) was condemned by various Israeli groups as being opposed to Israeli policy. It was boycotted by the Zionist Organisation of America (ZOA) and mainstream media outlets emphasised its even-handedness. In a single article, uncited elsewhere, director Steven Spielberg said explicitly: 'I agree with [Israeli Prime Minister] Golda Meir's response [to the 1972 terrorist attack at the Munich Olympics].'[17] A year after the release of the film, his foundation, The Righteous Persons Foundation donated $1m to Israel during the US-backed invasion of Lebanon in 2006.[18] The most celebrated 'anti-war scene'[19] is a two-and-a-half minute exchange between an Arab and an Israeli, but a close textual reading shows that this merely points out that the Palestinian struggle is both futile and immoral.[20] The film elsewhere contrasts the emotional struggle felt by the civilised Israelis compared with the callousness of the Arabs. The film is, therefore, an apologia for the state of Israel, the 'worthy' victim, and, by extension, its closest ally, the United States.

*The West Wing* (1999–2006) was dubbed by right-wing critics as 'The Left Wing'.[21] In fact, the series depicts the White House team as well-meaning, competent, and idealistic. According to one of its stars, Rob Lowe, who spoke to President Bill Clinton in 2000, the White House staff was 'obsessed with the show' and Clinton himself was reported as thinking it was 'renewing people's faith in public service'.[22] *The West Wing* bromide worked for the Bush administration too – just after 9/11, the series' creator Aaron Sorkin rushed through production a special episode about a massive terrorist threat to America entitled 'Isaac and Ishmael.' 'I'm going to blow them [the Jihadists] off the face of the earth with the fury of God's thunder,' says the President, in rhetoric more audacious than that of even the real-world incumbent, despite it being spoken by Hollywood's leading anti-war liberal, Martin Sheen. In series two, the anti-globalization movement is cut down in a stylish and impassioned speech by a White House official that concludes: '… Free trade stops wars! And we figure out a way to fix the rest. One world, one peace.' The two central theoretical underpinnings of US foreign policy, neoliberalism and neo-conservativism, are thereby endorsed with a flourish.

**(iv) That which does genuinely challenge Western power systems but are explicitly marginalised by the media mechanisms.**

Herman and Chomsky also find examples of news reports that are buried, barely publicised. For example, the isolated news reports that the Bush administration was deliberately avoiding a diplomatic solution to Iraq's invasion of Kuwait in 1990.[23] Or Arthur Schlesinger's op-ed on the eve of the Iraq War that it was the US that today lived in infamy.[24] Herman and Chomsky routinely emphasise the rarity of such articles.

A number of comparable cases of screen entertainment products do indeed similarly present genuinely challenging narratives, just like those rare exceptions Herman and Chomsky point to in the news, but which are similarly given remarkably limited distribution, in line with the first and fourth filters of the PM. Of course, in some cases it might simply be that the products did not resonate with the public and therefore had no box office successes. Prominent cases of these include *Canadian Bacon* (1995) (investment $11m, box office $178,000, Rotten Tomatoes 14%), *They Live* (1988) (investment $3m, box office $13m, Rotten Tomatoes 83%), *Redacted* (2007) (investment $5m, box office $782,000, Rotten Tomatoes 43%) and *War, Inc* (2008) (investment $10m, box office $1,296,184, Rotten Tomatoes 29%).

In some of cases, we know of targeted campaigns to shut the films down for political reasons. In the cases of NewsCorps' *Bulworth* (1998) and Disney's *Fahrenheit 9/11*, the distributors ultimately impeded the release of their own films for political reasons.[25]

In several cases on television, we know that the hardest hitting material was also either suppressed or edited by its own distributors for political reasons.

Elaine Briere[26] struggled to get her film *Bitter Paradise: The Sell-Out of East Timor* (1997) to CBC. This was not for lack of quality or opportunities but rather because the film challenged the interests of CBC. The film had won the prestigious Hot Docs award for best political documentary, which usually results in screenings on CBC. Briere commented:

> I offered first window to the CBC but it was tossed around like a hot potato between three of their current documentary programs. It was lawyered, something that rarely happens with the CBC. The CBC wanted several important changes including deleting the part about Pierre Trudeau, our then Prime Minister, meeting with [Indonesian dictator] Suharto several months before the Indonesian invasion of East Timor, taking out the part about Canadian oil and mining companies investing in Indonesia, and at one point even replacing me as a narrator, saying I was too subjective and not journalistic enough. *Bitter Paradise* never at any point claimed to be journalistic, but was a point-of-view documentary, an accepted genre of the day.[27]

Eventually, Briere saw no alternative but to work with a different distributor – TV Ontario – but she writes about the film's ongoing problems:

> *Bitter Paradise* was screened only once [on TV Ontario] in a strand called *A View from Here* when I got a call from the then head of TVO, Rudy Buttingol. He said that INCO, Canada's giant multinational nickel

mining company based in Sudbury, Ontario, with large mining operations in Sulawesi, Indonesia, wanted the film off the air or they would sue TVO. (there was a short section on INCO's operations in Indonesia in the film.) INCO, at the time, was TVO's second largest corporate donor. Rudy told me not to go to the media and that they would handle it. I heard nothing back from TVO and the film never aired again. Normally it would have had four screenings on *A View from Here*.[28]

A similar pattern of events affected the cases of *Lumumba* and *Strip Search*.[29] Even on *The Daily Show*, seemingly a law unto itself, host Jon Stewart was forced to apologise publicly after calling President Harry Truman a 'war criminal' for dropping atomic bombs on Hiroshima and Nagasaki.[30]

**(v) That which does genuinely break through the filtration system, which invariably occurs for irregular reasons and/ or with serious caveats.**
There does remain a small but significant quality of productions that have made it through the filtration system and with a reasonable level of studio backing (over $10m), without seeming to have been subject to the usual filters, most famously as follows:

*JFK* (1991); *Malcolm X* (1992); *Heaven and Earth* (1993); *Nixon* (1995); *Wag the Dog* (1997); *Starship Troopers* (1997); *Lord of War* (2005); *Syriana* (2005); *V for Vendetta* (2006); *Rendition* (2007); *Green Zone* (2009); *Fair Game* (2011); *The Bourne Identity* series (2002-); *Kill the Messenger* (2014); *Selma* (2014). In television, the list includes *Roots* (1977) and Oliver Stone's *Untold History of the United States* (2012).

Each film is at least loosely based on true stories about American systems of domination and sympathetically highlights 'unworthy' victims. Their existence points to a still flickering flame of permissible oppositional discourse. It is important, however, not to overstate the importance of these products in terms of the challenge they present to the PM. This is where Herman agrees that the model only offers 'a broad framework of analysis that requires modification depending on many local and special factors, and may be entirely inapplicable in some cases.' In line with the model, some of the films reflect dissensus amongst the elites, as with *Rendition* (rendition and torture) and *Malcolm X* and *Selma* (minority rights). In the case of *Heaven and Earth* (the Vietnam War), *Green Zone* and *Fair Game* (the Iraq War), in particular, it is worth bearing in mind that these products came many years too late to influence the political debates with which they are primarily concerned. Other films on the list might be better placed in the second category, in that although they may be critical of some aspects of the US system, they are very supportive of it in other ways – the clearest cases being *JFK* and *Nixon*, which assault the system but glorify a bygone era dominated by the Kennedy family.

## 10.2 Analytical Limitations

There are four limitations to the screen PM: (i) the relative difficulty in measuring results; (ii) the non-specificity of the filter metaphor; (iii) the vagueness of the fifth filter, (iv) the apparent weakness of the first four filters.

I shall explain each in turn.

**(i) The relative difficulty in measuring results.**
Reading entertainment products using Herman and Chomsky's theoretical framework does not sit well in cultural studies, and with some justification. Herman and Chomsky are particularly interested in the representation of victims, perpetrators, heroes and villains but if we are to identify these quite limited representations in cinema, we would miss many subtle differences between films. For example, we would be unable to distinguish between a macho militaristic action-thriller like *Executive Decision* (1996), and a macho militaristic action-comedy like *True Lies* (1994). Both these films had very similar plots (Islamic terrorists threaten the US government with nuclear weapons) but they are very different products in terms of what they offer audiences, in respect of genre, but also in terms of gender, race, imagery, and so on. Because the PM does not accommodate such perspectives, its reading of any cultural product is liable to be caustic and lacking in subtly. The point is well summarised by a review of this author's book *Reel Power: Hollywood Cinema and American Supremacy* (2010) that sympathetically applied the PM to cinema: '[it] renders much that film studies has tried to do over the last fifty years ... as effectively wasted effort.'[31]

In defence of the model, Chomsky himself points to some 'paired examples' in cinema, in some very unusual forays into the field. He notes that in the early 1950s the establishment heaped extensive praise onto *On the Waterfront* (1954) whilst *Salt of the Earth* (1954) was subjected to the most extraordinary attacks by the FBI and other official organisations. Both films are now regarded as classics but their differing experiences at the time appear to come down to the fact that the former was anti-Union and the latter was pro-Union[32] Chomsky drew a similar comparison between the box office record-breaker *American Sniper* (2014), with the civil rights drama *Selma* (2014).[33] For his part, Herman stresses that a focus on micro-issues of language, text interpreting and gender and ethnic identity is 'politically safe and holds forth the possibility of endless deconstruction of small points in a growing framework of jargon,'[34] which implies that being overly concerned with genre, gender, race, and imagery is a distraction from the fundamentals.

However, neither Herman nor Chomsky can refute the limitation entirely. Stuart Hall[35] contends that textual meaning cannot be finally 'fixed' because the same image can carry several different meanings and, in the words of Philip Davies and Brian Neve 'a reading' is precisely what the word implies – 'not a revealed truth.'[36] Of course, certain aspects of an entertainment product can be observed with very broad, if not an absolute, consensus. For example, we can usually agree on the general phenotypes for each character – 'good guy,' 'bad guy,' hero, villain, victim, and so on. Nevertheless, whilst Herman and Chomsky can readily demonstrate bias in the US news media by examining quantity of coverage in paired examples, for example when they contrast the shocking lack of coverage on the Indonesian invasion of East Timor with coverage of Pol Pot's killing fields in Cambodia,'[37] comparably elegant results are not as easy to establish in screen entertainment.

As Robert Kolker argues, the formal conventions of Hollywood film tend to 'downplay or deny the ways in which it supports, reinforces and even sometimes subverts the major cultural, political and social attitudes that surround and penetrate it.'[38] In contrast, news media convey their messages in more straightforward terms. For example, Robert Ray (1985) argues that 'problem pictures critique large social issues but ultimately have happy endings that resolve those problems.'[39] Richard Dyer concurs and illustrates with a popular example: in the second and third *Rambo* movies (1985 and 1987), the protagonist John Rambo is 'doing the job… that the United States government should be doing. Thus, he repeatedly upholds basic American values against the actuality of America.'[40]

Decoding screen entertainment becomes even less accurate when we consider the value of wholly metaphorical readings. For example, Alan Nadal (1997) claims that the Disney cartoon *Aladdin* (1992) is a 'metaphor for American culture,' 'a critique of the Muslim Middle east,' and 'asserts the immense destructive potential of a nuclear armed Middle East.'[41] Whilst there is a case to be made for such a reading, there are, of course, no direct references within Aladdin to nuclear weapons, US power, or contemporary Middle Eastern politics and so the case remains mired in the ambiguities of a post-Structuralist reading.

In turn, this ambiguity about interpretation opens up the debate about the PM's evasion of audience effects. Herman and Chomsky rightly insist that the model is one of 'performance' not 'effects'[42] and Klaehn neatly states that '[t]o criticise the model for failing to scrutinise that which it was not designed to explore, investigate or assess is perhaps analogous to condemning a book for failing to provide surround sound.'[43] However, in light of the difficulties in agreeing how to read an entertainment product, it is arguably more important to establish which products need to be read. If *Aladdin* has a significant political impact on audiences (which we do not know, since audience studies of cinematic effects are scarce), this suggests it should be analysed. If we do not know whether it did or did not, then it makes deciding on a sample for analysis much harder and more subjective.

### (ii) The non-specificity of the filter metaphor.
John Corner argues that the notion of a filtration model is 'ambitious,' considering that the PM is 'in essence a broad checklist of downflow tendencies.'[44] Chomsky essentially agreed when he told me there's no algorithm for judging relative importance [of each filter] abstractly. It varies from case to case. Simi-

larly, Oliver Boyd-Barrett accepts the premises of the PM but complains that it does not 'identify methodologies for determining the relative weight of independent filters in different contexts.'[45] This somewhat detracts from the beauty of the metaphor and, so, understandably, Corner concludes that he is more comfortable with Herman's later description of the PM as a 'first approximation.'[46]

Klaehn contests this by posing a rhetorical question: 'How vague are the concepts of "alienation" and "reification" (conflict theory) or "systems" and 'collective conscience" (structural functionalism)?' Arguably very. Should the PM be held to a higher standard than other models within the social sciences? If yes, why? Is it because it challenges power and can be understood and utilised without the need for intermediaries?' The answers to Klaehn's questions are obvious but it is nevertheless important to identify the extent to which the PM can predict and explain, rather than just settling on it as being eminently serviceable, as Thompson (2009) also opines when he applies the PM to financial media reporting.[47]

Oliver Boyd-Barrett argues that the PM privileges structural factors and 'eschews or marginalizes intentionality.'[48] He recommends greater attention to journalistic departures from, rather than routine conformity with, the preferences of official sources, and further study of journalistic fears of flak from editors, the right-wing media, and government officials. Boyd-Barrett also suggests a sixth filter: the 'buying out' of individual journalists or their media by intelligence agencies, other government bodies and/or special interest groups. Disputing Chomsky's stance on 'conspiracy theory,' Boyd-Barrett points to the 1970s US Senate investigations and the 'irrefutable evidence of wide-scale, covert CIA penetration of media – by definition, an illustration of conspiracy' at work.[49] As such, it might be more appropriate to have some of the purifying work of the filters assisted by needles injecting additional fluids to generate that resultant residue. Klaehn[50] responds that the PM does not 'make predictions concerning agency and/or subjectivity' but rather 'highlights the fact that awareness, perception and understandings are typically constrained and informed by structures of discourse.'[51] Again, Klaehn is right to defend the integrity of the model but nevertheless I maintain it is important to highlight where its limits lie.

### (iii) The vagueness of the fifth filter.
The fifth filter is egregious because it does not specify a powerful entity like advertisers, the government or corporations that filter material. Rather, it is just what Herman and Chomsky call a 'cultural milieu,'[52] which is hard to reconcile within the filtration system. Klaehn disagrees, saying that:

> Analytically, the fifth filter is extremely useful and applicable to a range of case studies. It may play out in different ways at different times, contingent upon specific time/place contexts, and is extremely broad (as are many other concepts within the social sciences, such as hegemony and/ or patriarchy, for instance). That the fifth filter is so generalised makes it

relatable to a range of social phenomenon, and creates space for the PM to be utilised in a variety of social scientific research.[53]

A less charitable term for 'generalised' though is 'vague.' If, indeed, it is necessary, it seems at least to warrant being given a single, fixed and neutral phrase such as 'tribe mentality,' since the present formulations provided by Herman and Chomsky emphasise a range of a priori leftist bug-bears: dominant ideology, anti-Other, anti-communism, and pro-free market.

**(iv) The apparent relative weakness of the first four filters.**
As the videogames industry shows, even if we quite dramatically reduce the concentration of US ownership, output remains comparably de-radicalised. Whereas the Hollywood majors own at least three quarters of the movie market, US gaming companies own just a third of the videogame market and are very much challenged by Japan and Europe in an industry that has global successes from numerous countries. Yet there remains a substantial contingent of gaming products that are highly militaristic and nationalistic, and very little could be described as opposing US exceptionalism.[54]

The importance – or otherwise – of advertising can also be identified by examining the output of Home Box Office (HBO), which relies on subscription rather than any advertising revenue. HBO has produced shows that appeal more to anti-authoritarian sensibilities, such as *The Daily Show* (1996-), *South Park* (1997-), and *Game of Thrones* (2011-). Yet none of these productions could be identified as agitating for radical political change.

David Edwards of Media Lens, argues that the attempt to isolate the filters is essentially an impossible task:

> HBO might be protected from the impact of direct advertising but it's immersed in a media, cultural, political and economic system that isn't protected. Its workers, managers, stars, viewers and critics are all products of that advertiser-dependent culture, so that culture impacts HBO indirectly that way. Everyone is responding to HBO from inside an advert-drenched and conditioned culture.[55]

The point is well made but it only adds to the case that the filtration metaphor in any Screen Entertainment PM must be non-specific and that the first and second filters do not function with the efficiency Herman and Chomsky imply, even whilst they do contribute to the 'strong tendency' for narratives that support US power.

None of this is to say that the PM is inaccurate – each filter applies to the screen entertainment industry overall. It just means that it is not good at measuring or predicting when each filter applies with regards to screen media beyond the news. These are the 'special factors ... that will modify its applicability'[56] to which Herman refers, that add to the overall sense that a Screen

Entertainment Propaganda Model is of less direct use than the original formulation for news and that even the original PM cannot be defended uncritically.

## 10.3 Conclusions

The PM rightly characterises elite news media as keeping political debate within tightly controlled boundaries and therefore as ranging between not challenging established power systems to directly supporting them. When we apply the PM across screen media, in predictive terms it suffers from the same limitations as with news and is also harder to test because theorists are understandably more liable to disagree about interpretations of entertainment texts. Its explanatory capabilities are also weaker, since although each filter can be important, screen products so infrequently challenge organised power that the fourth filter is rarely activated, although some evidence suggests it does become important in exceptional cases when the other filters fail. The second filter – advertising, is significant, but even when its role is significantly reduced, as with HBO, the impact on the ideology of output is not decisive. The first filter – ownership, is important but shows like *TV Nation* indicate that the system is prepared to allow some forms of dissent and the greater reduction in US ownership in video-gaming points to the limits of its importance. Recent evidence has suggested that the third filter, sourcing, is considerably more important than scholarship has hitherto accepted, with government entities directly affecting the politics of many thousands of entertainment products, although even here it is typically hard to say exactly how much influence such forces are actually able to exert, or the extent to which similar or identical products would be made regardless.

Of course, if all existing forms of media ownership, funding and sources were revolutionised, the outputs would be very different, akin to a 'PBS-plus' model, but for this to have a decisive impact on the way it represents the interplay between heroes, villains and victims, rather than just tonal changes – the kind of differences exhibited between HBO and Fox, or the BBC and Disney – these kinds of changes would need to be total rather than incremental. We are left with a model that remains a clear framework for predicting and highlighting the ideological constraints and regressive characteristics of wider cultural output but one which relies on a loose 'catch-all' final filter to account for the unmeasurable impacts of the first four factors.

## Notes and Bibliography

[1] Matthew Alford (2009), 'A Propaganda Model for Hollywood', *Westminster Papers for Communication and Culture*, Vol. 6 (2); Alford, Matthew (2010), *Reel Power: Hollywood Cinema and American Supremacy*, London, Pluto Press.

[2] Matthew Alford (2011), 'Why not a Propaganda Model for Hollywood?' In: Hammond, Philip, ed. *Screens of Terror*. Arima.
[3] Noam Chomsky (2004), Personal email to Matthew Alford, 28 May; Edward Herman (2007), Conversation with author, Windsor University Conference, Canada, 20 Years of the Propaganda Model, 15th–17 May.
[4] Edward Herman and Noam Chomsky (2002), *Manufacturing Consent: The Political Economy of the Mass Media*, New York: Pantheon Books, p. lix.
[5] Ibid, p. lx.
[6] Noam Chomsky (1989), *Necessary Illusions: Thought Control in Democratic Societies*, New York: South End Press, p. 45.
[7] Noam Chomsky (2003), *Understanding Power: The Indispensable Chomsky*, New York Vintage, p. 258.
[8] Noam Chomsky (2000), *Rogue States: The Rule of Force in World Affair*, New York, South End Press.
[9] Noam Chomsky (2007), *Failed States: The Abuse of Power and the Assault on Democracy*, New York, Penguin.
[10] Mark Curtis (2004) *Unpeople: Britain's Secret Human Rights Abuses*, New York, Vintage.
[11] Herman and Chomsky (2002), p. 37–86.
[12] Noam Chomsky (2012), Excerpts from 'Manufacturing Consent: Noam Chomsky' interviewed by various interviewers, 1992 https://chomsky.info/1992____02/ (29 March 2017).
[13] Noam Chomsky (2009), Noam Chomsky Compares Right-Wing Media to Nazi Germany, https://www.youtube.com/watch?v=6MHEuudJ-o0 (29 March 2017).
[14] Matthew Alford and Tom Secker (2017), *National Security Cinema: The Shocking New Evidence of Government Control over Hollywood*, Drum Roll Books.
[15] Ben Shapiro (2011), *Primetime Propaganda: The True Hollywood Story of How the Left Took Over Your TV*, New York, Broadside Books.
[16] Matthew Alford (2010), *Reel Power: Hollywood Cinema and American Supremacy*, London: Pluto Press; Matthew Alford and Tom Secker (2017) *National Security Cinema*.
[17] Roger Ebert(2006), 'I Knew I Would Lose Friends Over This Film', Sunday Telegraph, News Review and Comment, 1January, p. 14–15.
[18] http://usatoday30.usatoday.com/life/people/2006-08-09-spielberg-donation_x.htm
[19] Walter Reich (2006), 'Something's Missing in Spielberg's Munich', *Washington Post*, 1 January, http://www.washingtonpost.com/wpdyn/content/article/2005/12/30/AR2005123001581.html (19 September 2014).
[20] Alford (2010), *Reel Power*.
[21] Naomi Pfefferman (2001), 'The Left "Wing"', *Jewish Journal*, 11 October.
[22] Chris Lehmann (2001), The Feel-Good Presidency, *The Atlantic Monthly*, Vol. 287, No. 3; pp. 93–96, 1 March.

23 Noam Chomsky (1991), Gulf War Pullout Noam Chomsky, Z Magazine, February, 1991 https://chomsky.info/199102__/ (29 March 2017).
24 Arthur Schlesinger Jnr (2003), 'Good Foreign Policy a Casualty of War', *Los Angeles Times*, http://articles.latimes.com/2003/mar/23/news/war-opschlesinger23 (19 September 2014).
25 Peter Swirski (2005), 'Bulworth and the New American Left', *The Journal of American Culture*, Vol. 28, Issue 3, pp. 293–301, September; Jim Rutenberg (2004), 'Disney Is Blocking Distribution of Film That Criticizes Bush', *New York Times*, 15 May.
26 Elaine Brière (2014), email to author, 17 February.
27 Ibid.
28 Ibid.
29 Alford (2010), *Reel Power*; Alford and Secker, Tom (2017) *National Security Cinema*.
30 Greg Mitchell (2013), 'When Jon Stewart Apologized—for Calling Harry Truman a "War Criminal"'; 8 August, *The Nation*, http://www.thenation.com/blog/175672/when-jon-stewart-apologized-calling-harry-truman-war-criminal (19 September 2014).
31 Stafford, Roy (2010), Book Review: The Case for Global Film, 15 October, http://itpworld.wordpress.com/2010/10/15/reel-power-hollywood-cinema-and-american-supremacy/ (19 September 2014).
32 Noam Chomsky, John Schoeffel and R. Mitchell, eds (2002), *Understanding Power: The Indispensible Chomsky*, New York: The New Press.
33 Sarah Gray (2015), 'Noam Chomsky discusses terrifying "American Sniper" mentality', Salon Magazine, 26 January http://www.salon.com/2015/01/26/noam_chomsky_on_the_terrifying_american_sniper_mentality/ (27 January 2015).
34 Edward S. Herman (1996b), 'Postmodernism Triumphs', *Z Magazine*, January, p.16.
35 Stuart Hall (1993), 'Encoding, Decoding', in Simon During (ed.), *The Cultural Studies Reader*, London, Routledge, p. 283.
36 Philip Davies and Brian Neve, eds., (1981), *Cinema, Politics and Society In America*, Manchester: Manchester University Press, p. 3.
37 Herman and Chomsky (2002) *Manufacturing Consent*, p. xxi.
38 Robert Kolker (2000), *A Cinema of Loneliness: Penn, Stone, Kubrick, Scorsese, Spielberg, Altman* (Third Edition). New York: Oxford University Press, p. 11.
39 Robert Ray(1985), *A Certain Tendency of the Hollywood Cinema, 1930–1980*, Princeton, NJ, Princeton University Press, p. 147.
40 Richard Dyer, *White*, New York, Routledge, 1997, p. 159–60.
41 Alan Nadal (1997), 'A Whole New (Disney) World Order: Aladdin, Atomic Power, and the Muslim Middle East', in Matthew Berstein and Gaylyn Studlar (eds), *Visions of the East: Orientalism in Film*, Newark, Rutgers University Press, p. 187.

42. Herman and Chomsky (2002), *Manufacturing Consent* p. xii.
43. Jeffery Klaehn (2003b), 'Behind the Invisible Curtain of Scholarly Criticism: Revisiting the Propaganda Model,' *Journalism Studies*, Vol. 4(3), p. 362.
44. John Corner (2003), 'Debate: The Model in Question: A Response to Klaehn on Herman and Chomsky', *European Journal of Communication*, 2003, Vol. 18(3), pp. 367–375.
45. Noam Chomsky (2006), Email to author, Sun 10 December.
46. Edward S. Herman (2000) 'The Propaganda Model: A Retrospective', *Journalism Studies* 1(1): 101–12, available at http://www.humannature.com/reason/01/herman.html. Accessed 10 April 2009: 107.
47. Peter Thompson (2009), Market Manipulation? Applying the Propaganda Model to Financial Media Reporting, *Westminster Papers for Communication and Culture*, Vol. 6(2), p. 75.
48. Oliver Boyd-Barrett (2004), 'Judith Miller, *The New York Times*, and the Propaganda Model', *Journalism Studies*, 5(4), 435–449. Retrieved from http://ics.leeds.ac.uk/papers/pmt/exhibits/2658/boydbarret.pdf.
49. Ibid, p.436.
50. Jeffery Klaehn (2003a), 'Model Construction, Various Other Epistemological Concerns: A Reply to John Corner's Commentary on the Propaganda Model,' *European Journal of Communication*, 2003, Vol. 18(3), p. 379.
51. Ibid.
52. Herman and Chomsky (2002) *Manufacturing Consent*, p. 29.
53. Jeffery Klaehn (2009), 'The Propaganda Model: Theoretical and Methodological Considerations', *Westminster Papers in Communication and Culture*, Vol. 6(2), pp. 43–58.
54. Robin Andersen and Marin Kurti (2009), 'From America's Army to Call of Duty: Doing Battle with the Military Entertainment Complex', *Democratic Communiqué 23*, No. 1, Spring.
55. David Edwards (2014), email to author, 11 June.
56. Jeffery Klaehn (2008) 'Media, Power and the Origins of the Propaganda Model: An Interview with Edward S. Herman', *Fifth-Estate-Online – International Journal of Radical Mass Media Criticism*, December.

CHAPTER 11

# American Television: Manufacturing Consumerism

Tabe Bergman

## 11.1 Introduction

Television plays a central, highly *visible* role in American society as well as across the globe. It is little wonder then that scores of scholars have examined television in all its facets and from a wide range of perspectives. Equally unsurprising, the conclusions have been diverse. Despite the flood of scholarship, as far as the author can tell, devising a critical model of the political economy of American television has not been a focus, although critical political economists, and scholars often cited by them, have of course studied popular culture and television. This chapter, then, provides a critical political-economic model of American television. It introduces a Propaganda Model for American Television (PMTV) by adapting the five filters of Herman and Chomsky's Propaganda Model (PM) to the American television industry and programming.

---

**How to cite this book chapter:**
Bergman, T. 2018. American Television: Manufacturing Consumerism. In: Pedro-Carañana, J., Broudy, D. and Klaehn, J. (eds.). *The Propaganda Model Today: Filtering Perception and Awareness.* Pp. 159–172. London: University of Westminster Press. DOI: https://doi.org/10.16997/book27.k. License: CC-BY-NC-ND 4.0

## 11.2 A Propaganda Model for American Television (PMTV)

### 11.2.1 Filter One: Private Ownership and Pro-business Regulation

Not just television news but all programming is ultimately the product of a few corporations. Setting up a television station requires a large amount of capital, which severely limits who can do so. The freedom to influence American culture by broadcasting television thus belongs to the happy few who own and run the handful of corporations that dominate the American market and, thus, the public mind. Additionally, they control many other media holdings, including radio stations, magazines, film studios, cable channels, and so on.[1] Often they bundle their forces in joint ventures. Virtually everyone else is effectively barred from entering the market, though on occasion an independent production breaks into the mainstream.

The television corporations belong to even larger conglomerates. For instance, NBC is owned by telecom giant Comcast and by the Walt Disney Company. The people who own and manage these corporations and conglomerates are wealthy and have definite domestic and foreign policy interests, which they often successfully promote in Washington DC through an army of lobbyists. They often have connections at the highest levels. For instance, Disney's CEO advised President Donald Trump.[2]

Unlike with print journalism, the Federal Communications Commission (FCC) has the legal right and duty to regulate US broadcasting in the public interest. The constitutional freedom of the press clause has no bearing on fictional shows and other non-news programming. The FCC prohibits cursing and what it considers excessive nudity, especially during the day and primetime. More to the point, the FCC holds the authority to distribute and revoke broadcast licenses, and to prevent excessive market concentration by setting limits on cross-ownership and the market share that any one entity is allowed to control.

Potentially, then, the special legal status of broadcasting allows the FCC to take action to ensure that programming serves the interests of the population. Public broadcaster PBS is an underfunded, largely unsuccessful attempt to do just that. The central problem is that the FCC has been effectively co-opted by the media industries it purports to regulate, as illustrated by the revolving door between them. Many FCC commissioners and staffers have gone on to work for media corporations, while many employees of media corporations have accepted positions at the FCC.[3]

Unsurprisingly, the television industry usually, though not always, gets its way in Washington DC.[4] For instance, the deregulation of the television industry in the 1990s was a boon to corporations, causing 'all the small [production] businesses [to fall] apart as big TV corporations moved production in-house so that they could sell texts on through infinite other territories and media.'[5] In short, federal regulation provides crucial support to the television industry in its never-ending quest for more and more profit. The policy-making process has been captured and co-opted by big business, showing the tight and mutually reinforcing connections between capital and the state in American society. Hence private ownership and regulation make up the first filter together.

### 11.2.2 Filter Two: Advertising

Advertising is the lifeblood of American television. About a quarter of total broadcast time consists of commercials.[6] Television additionally features covert advertising, known as product placements. With programming, corporations first amass and then sell audiences to other corporations, the advertisers. The audience thinks of itself as a mass of consumers, but from the perspective of media owners it is the product. If shows prove unable to attract a sizeable, preferably affluent audience – and thus the interest of advertisers – they run a high risk of getting cancelled. From a program's inception particular attention is therefore paid to creating narratives that support the 'buying mood.' Advertisers, big businesses for the most part, generally do not appreciate complicated, socially-engaged programming, especially the kind critical of capitalism.[7] In short, the needs and demands of advertisers are central to understanding what's on. Television is 'an effective corporate instrument, whose sole purpose – as its executives will tell you – is to sell you to the advertisers.'[8]

It has been like this since the very beginning. In the early years, advertisers even produced the shows themselves, and this still happens on occasion.[9] The demands of advertising of course influence programming. This is why programs often play up, or at least do not damp, the many supposed joys of consumption. For instance, as Mark Crispin Miller explains, advertisers prefer programming to avoid 'dark suggestiveness':

> For advertisers are obsessed not just with selling their own specific images but also with universalizing the whole hermetic ambience for selling itself – the pseudo-festive, mildly jolting, ultimately tranquilizing atmosphere of TV and its bright epiphenomena, the theme park and the shopping mall.[10]

In this age of advertising glut, television sometimes consciously provokes to garner attention, for instance by showing gay people kiss. Reality shows are some of the main culprits:

> TV execs believe that the more they bait advocacy groups like NOW, the NAACP, and GLAAD, the more controversy a show will generate. Offensiveness = hype = increased eyeballs for advertisers and cash for networks, making outrageous bigotry less a by-product of reality TV than its blueprint.[11]

In short, both in the past and the present, per the second filter, advertisers supply networks with a de facto licence which permits the networks to remain in show *business*. Or not.

### 11.2.3 Filter Three: The Rules and Conventions of Production

The following discussion of a number of American television's conventions and rules of production intends not to be comprehensive, but merely indicative of how the production process primarily serves the needs of advertisers and the television industry, rarely the interests of citizens. First, it should be noted that the production process is, to a large extent, top down. Making television has always been typified by the 'characteristic modes of production' and the hierarchical 'organization of industrial corporations.'[12] For instance, that shining symbol of American entertainment, Walt Disney, introduced a highly compartmentalised, factory-like process for producing animations.[13] Industry deregulation in the 1990s strengthened management's hold on production. From then on, 'The people who made the creative decisions about everything from storylines to wallpaper were overridden again and again by men in suits who lacked relevant expertise.'[14] In short, and with exceptions, television's creative intelligentsia are totally free to produce what they like – as long as their bosses like what they produce.

'Common sense' notions as to what constitutes gripping television guide the production process. One of these is that rapid movement works well on the screen. Enter acts of violence, car and other chases, and special effects. The violence is almost always person-on-person and committed for personal motives, including the virtually ubiquitous revenge. Never mind that taking revenge plays a distinctly minor role in motivating people's behaviour in the actual world. The crux to understanding television is realizing that it resembles more of a fun house mirror than an ordinary one. Television thrives when the focus is on individuals, with plenty of opportunity for close-ups conveying stark emotions. Shots are kept short, not to say ultra-short, as the act of changing shots and thereby the viewer's perspective is a tested way of keeping eyeballs glued to the screen. It's simple physiology. Too much information, on the other hand, confuses the screen. In short, commercial television focuses on depicting individuals and providing compelling images, with the result that the content tends to be superficial and more about conveying emotions than explicating ideas.

Much more than print journalism, making television is a long, collective undertaking. The vision of the screenwriter, the true creative, often gets diluted by the subsequent persons that revise the original work with an eye on the bottom line. The original work gets 'mainstreamed': made more palatable for the market. The short length of shows, which in part is a result of the need to reserve time for commercials, together with their highly formulaic structure, probably limit the ability to tell non-stereotypical stories. Sitcoms, for instance, are only about 22 minutes long and adhere to a rigid, almost minute-by-minute structure.[15]

Like corporate journalists, then, the individuals working in television production are highly restricted in their creativity. They need to honour the common conventions and rules of production, which are enforced by management with the bottom line in mind. On occasion, the process produces (or rather allows) enlightening or subversive programming. A tiny number of writers and actors has reached such an exalted status that they can push through projects that normally would not stand a chance. Yet most of the time, the production process serves the interests of owners and advertisers. In short, the business of television strongly prefers the profitable predictability of business as usual.

### 11.2.4 Filter Four: Overt and Covert Influence

Aside from media corporations themselves, and regulators and advertisers, many other organizations and institutions are profoundly concerned with, and try to influence, television content. Congressional hearings on supposed communist subversion in Hollywood right after World War II sent a chill through the entertainment industry by making suspect anything that smacked of progressivism. All through the Cold War, state agencies influenced television and movies, often with the active cooperation of the networks. The CIA has a long and successful history of influencing, behind the scenes, its image in movies and television shows.[16] Right after the 9/11 terrorist attacks, executives from Hollywood and the major television networks met with a top advisor of President George W. Bush. The goal of the meeting reportedly was 'to discuss how the entertainment industry could cooperate in the war on terrorism and to begin setting up a structure to make it happen.'[17]

It is no different today, as files released by the Department of Defense show:

> The sheer scale of the Army and the Air Force's involvement in TV shows, particularly reality TV shows, is the most remarkable thing about these files. 'American Idol,' 'The X-Factor,' 'Masterchef,' 'Cupcake Wars,' numerous Oprah Winfrey shows, 'Ice Road Truckers,' 'Battlefield Priests,' 'America's Got Talent,' 'Hawaii Five-O,' lots of BBC, History Channel and National Geographic documentaries, 'War Dogs,' 'Big Kitchens' — the list is almost endless.[18]

State agencies, thus, frequently enlist the entertainment industry, including television, in information campaigns, which are likely to be all the more effective for not easily being identifiable as such.

In addition, various kinds of pressure groups on both the left and the right organise campaigns to influence content. The conservative Parents Television Council mounted so many successful campaigns against broadcasters that the

*New York Times* once dubbed it a 'superstar in the culture wars'. The Council was responsible for 'record-setting fines against media giants like CBS' as punishment for programming that supposedly crossed the line, for instance as to profanities or nudity.[19] Yet, in the final analysis, broadcasters probably care more about displaying shapely bottoms to pad bottom lines than catering to the sensibilities of cultural conservatives, or anyone else for that matter. In the aftermath of the financial crisis of 2008 a media expert remarked on the difficulty for the Parents Television Council 'to stir up indignation about cultural issues at a time of economic woe.'[20] Additionally, compared to the state and big corporations, the resources at the disposal of pressure groups are paltry. They are likely to lose out, in the end, to the needs of capital.

### 11.2.5 Filter Five: Neoliberalism as a Control Mechanism

Neoliberalism is America's dominant ideology. It is a worldview that includes the core belief that private interests can do just about anything better than the state. With its opposition to social welfare programs, unions, public education, and idolization of the individual and 'free markets,' neoliberalism serves the interests of economic elites, including media owners. Just like 'anti-communism' during the Cold War, the ideology called neoliberalism

> helps mobilise the populace against an enemy, and because the concept is fuzzy it can be used against anybody advocating policies that threaten property interests or support accommodation with [left-wing] states and radicalism. It therefore helps fragment the left and labour movements and serves as a political control mechanism.[21]

The people involved in creating programming will, to some extent, be believers in American society's dominant myths taught in school and by the media. And many people working in the television industry, especially the higher-ups, will have 'fully internalised' neoliberal values.[22] Dissenters will encounter opposition in a myriad of subtle or overt ways. It is, thus, logical to expect programming to reflect neoliberal biases.

Indeed, neoliberalism pervades much television content. The iconic *Oprah Winfrey Show*, with its incessant refrain of self-reliance and self-help, is a shining example.[23] Many reality shows, including *The Apprentice* starring the future American president, mirror the neoliberal vision of society. The few at the top advise, criticise and disdain. From Olympian heights, they pronounce harsh verdicts on the countless aspirants, who desperately compete among each other in the vain hope of one day reaching an exalted position themselves. Cooperation often ends up with deceit, which teaches a valuable lesson. In the quest for fame and fortune that is every American's Reagan-given right, if not duty, no one can be trusted. We are all lone individuals trying to make it big in the only way society affords. Cooking competitions mirror the worker's precarious position in a neoliberal economy by depicting cooking as a 'strictly regimented, highly individuated, labour hierarchy within an economic circuit.'[24] Extreme makeover shows often promulgate individual solutions to problems, like obesity, that have an inescapable social dimension.

Dramas also often affirm neoliberal articles of faith. They bubble over with depictions of physical or emotional blackmail, violence, manipulation, and assertions of authority. Time and again the moral of the story appears to be that individuals simply pursue their own self-interest, which is necessarily distinct from and in opposition to everybody else's. The popular crime series *CSI*, for instance, 'promises a form of governance that appeals to a post-9/11 society in which mitigating factors of social life are rendered irrelevant. On *CSI*, the state has or will fail the citizen, but science cannot.'[25] The hospital series *House*, with its recurring mantra that 'Everybody lies,' also portrays other people as necessarily hostile and selfish, and preaches a belief in science. Much content, thus, primes viewers to think in neoliberal terms, before, during and after which advertisers tickle status anxiety, generously providing the instant 'scratch' of consumerism.

The PM highlights what was not chosen as fit for print. So it is instructive to consider not just what American television is, but also what it is not. For only then the ideological limits that its 'invisible' political economy imposes on content become clearly discernible. Television is hardly concerned with the plight of the dozens of millions of poor people in the US. It is not anti-capitalist, anti-corporate or even merely critical of capitalism. It hardly criticises US foreign policy or the many wars the US has been involved in; in fact, it has often cheered the armed forces on. It rarely portrays unions or other social organizations in a positive light. It can hardly be deemed democratic, because it rarely portrays citizens successfully coming together to improve their lives.

## 11.3 Additional Thoughts on a PMTV

### 11.3.1 Television as Technology

The PM identifies factors that influence information across media, but a PMTV models a medium. Thus, the influence of the technology of television needs to be considered. In the author's view, the medium influences the content. As earlier noted, television makers know that rapid movements on the screen make for more gripping television than static 'talking heads.' So, it is unsurprising that programming has greatly sped up over the years. Quite a few contemporary viewers will find it hard to watch old movies, because of their leisurely pace. The question is whether the technology or commercialism is the driving force, or rather, to which extent each can be considered responsible. In the author's opinion, where technology ends and capitalism begins, is impossible to tell. The issue appears intractable beyond the observation that television's technological characteristics *to some extent* influence content. Technology's influence is subsumed in the PMTV's third filter, for technology's assumed characteristics help shape the rules and conventions of production.

### 11.3.2 The Uses of Television

Apart from content and technology, other features of the phenomenon of television broadly conceived also promote inimical values and behaviours. For instance, the widespread association of television with the home might reinforce in people a view of society as nothing but separate individuals with competing interests. There is, of course, nothing inevitable in the widespread practice of watching TV at home alone, although capitalism certainly has had a hand in stimulating the idea that the good life constitutes owning one's own home, car, lawnmower, television, and so on. These days, mobile television affords watching in many places, but the smallness of the screen still favours watching alone. On the other hand, social media do stimulate sharing content and interaction. To be clear, the ways people use television are not part of a PMTV.

### 11.3.3 Methodology: Comparing the PM and PMTV

Compared with the original model, a PMTV has a notable methodological weakness. After describing the political economy of the news media, Herman and Chomsky prove in detail that the biases one would expect the American news to exhibit can indeed be found. First, they identify 'paired examples,' for instance two sets of atrocities of similar scale occurring at about the same time, the main difference being that one is committed by Washington or with its complicity, and the other by an enemy state. Then, they document that the news media treat these two similar series of events very differently. When Washington is implicated in crimes, coverage is sparse and condemnation mild at best, whereas when official enemies are the culprits, coverage is plentiful and condemning. Unfortunately, such a sophisticated method is unavailable for a PMTV. Herman and Chomsky disprove much of the mainstream media's coverage with facts from more reliable and independent sources, but because fiction cannot be proven factually right or wrong, the same cannot be done for American television as a whole. As to evidence, then, the PM is more convincing than a PMTV. Yet, an added value of a PMTV is that it contextualises the PM. A PMTV provides a critical evaluation of the programming that surrounds, arguably overwhelms, television news. A PMTV, thus, helps explain the media environment in which the PM is embedded.

### 11.3.4 Strength: Comparing the PM and PMTV

The PMTV's filters perhaps function as even more potent censorship mechanisms than the PM's. The PMTV's first, second and third filters – ownership and regulation, advertising, and the production rules and conventions – are unrestrained by professional journalism's norm of a separation between management and editors. In other words, because pandering to advertisers is simply an integral part of television's business model, it might be that a PMTV is stronger than the PM. The same goes for the fourth filter, overt and covert influence on the television industry. Among television producers one might expect less reticence to cooperate openly or behind the scenes with state agencies than among journalists. One might also expect the former to be more amenable to influence by other organizations, unless the supreme right to make money is challenged.

As to the fifth filter, both television's creators and journalists have a reputation for liberal politics. Beyond that observation, we can only speculate as to the relative strength of the respective fifth filters. One might argue for instance that, compared to the news, dramas contain more opportunities for and actual instances of fundamental criticisms of society. For the driving force behind drama is conflict. The need for stark conflict opens the door for perspectives that challenge received wisdom. Yet, even if this point has merit, it remains doubtful that fictionalised criticism leads to a more socially engaged audience. Perhaps its consumption often has the opposite effect, amounting to just another form of escapism through catharsis.

### 11.3.5 American Television: Aim and Effects

There can be no dispute as to what American television aims for. Those in charge have clearly explained. The goal is to sell people's attention to large corporations that promote buying stuff, experiences, and services. Corporate television, thus, attempts to manufacture consumerism. Draping itself in the flag, especially during times of war and other crises, television routinely links consumerism with patriotism. Corporate television happily relayed President George W. Bush's admonition in the aftermath of the 9/11 attacks that Americans continue shopping, to show the terrorists that they were not cowed. Consumerism, of course, does not serve the public's interests. In fact, much empirical evidence shows that it damages people's mental and physical health.[26]

Corporate television provides an additional crucial service to elites by inundating people with depoliticizing entertainment. It is the Great Distraction Machine. As one of the foremost thinkers on propaganda, Jacques Ellul, noted in the late 1980s:

> Today the greatest threat is that propaganda is seeking not to attract people, but to weaken their interest in society. I am astonished by the enormous number of TV game shows, football games, computer games.

They encourage people to play: 'Let yourselves be entertained, amuse yourselves, do not concern yourselves with politics, it's not worth the trouble.'[27]

This second service, too, is rendered not without premeditation. As the late founder of the Mexican network Televisa frankly proclaimed: 'Mexico is a country of a modest, very fucked class, which will never stop being fucked. Television has the obligation to bring diversion to these people and remove them from their sad reality and difficult future.'[28]

How effective is American television in stimulating consumerism and depoliticizing citizens? Like the original PM, a PMTV is not an effects model. It remains silent on the extent to which American television succeeds. Indeed, empirically establishing media effects is tricky. On the individual level, effects are mediated by a myriad of factors, including gender, religion, education, age, and so on. Even after thousands of studies much uncertainty and controversy remain.[29] Nonetheless, Americans clearly live in a depoliticised, consumerist society. To imagine American television washing its hands in innocence of all that does not seem right at all. An American businessman once famously complained that, 'Half my advertising is wasted, I just don't know which half.'[30] Usually, this statement is trotted out to illustrate the *difficulty* of influencing people with media or establishing media effects. But, if one half of the money spent on advertising is wasted, then the other half is not. The statement, thus, simultaneously points out a truth that probably all media influencers have discovered: the media do in fact influence people.

## 11.4  Addressing Objections to a PMTV

Some will reject a PMTV. Here, five anticipated objections are discussed. One, a PMTV is only a general model, a first approximation, for understanding American television. A PMTV surveys the television industry and captures the thrust of the programming, but recognises that social reality is endlessly complicated and that exceptions exist. To point to examples of anti-neoliberal content on American television, for instance, thus constitutes an unconvincing argument for dismissing the model.

Two, advancing a PMTV is not meant to imply that people who enjoy watching television, including the author, are therefore stupid or inferior. People can love American television – wholly but more likely in part – while at the same time cultivating a critical distance as to its overall social function. Three, some will object to the word 'propaganda,' with its connotations of conscious duplicity. But the word means not to suggest that the television industry is populated with conscious propagandists, although some owners and producers will knowingly act as propagandists some of the time. The term is still apt because it is often defined, including here, as exerting influence that serves special interests as opposed to the public interest.[31]

Four, a PMTV does not contend that American television serves a conservative agenda on cultural matters. Television has, in fact, become more progressive on a range of issues, for instance playing a role in promoting the social acceptance of gay relationships, however problematic the portrayals often remain. A PMTV does contend that on issues that directly affect the interests of elites, for instance the economy, television remains a steadfast supporter of the status quo.

Five, some will assert that recent changes in society, including the rise of the internet and streaming services, undermine a PMTV. Certainly, much has changed since the broadcast era. In this digital age, viewers can enjoy an ample array of quality shows and have more control over when and where they watch. No wonder that some have talked of television's New Golden Age. But as a late media columnist for the *New York Times* recognised, there is a dark side: 'Television's golden age is also a gilded cage, an always-on ecosystem of immense riches that leaves me feeling less like the master of my own universe, and more as if I am surrounded.'[32] Indeed, in an age of climate change, with progressive change possibly necessary for survival, the recent flood of quality programming poses a peculiar problem. Depoliticizing programming so enjoyable that many people, including hard-to-please viewers like professional media columnists, simply cannot resist, constitutes bad news for the prospects of change instigated by an engaged citizenry.

The rapid permutations taking place in the television industry perhaps affect the efficacy of a PMTV because, for instance, consumers can now easily block advertising. Yet, apart from a PMTV not being an effects model, the changes hardly threaten the television industry or its dominance, and therefore also do not threaten the analytical viability of a PMTV. Streaming services like Hulu are growing rapidly but are still dwarfed by traditional delivery channels.[33] Networks and cable channels supply the bulk of the offerings on streaming services. Leading streaming service Netflix is itself a publicly-traded global enterprise. It has dispensed with commercials, but other streaming services, including Hulu, which are owned by traditional television powerhouses, in part depend on them.

The television industry, thus, remains a highly concentrated, corporate undertaking buttressed by pro-business regulation. It remains firmly in elite hands. Although the relative importance of advertising as a revenue source is on the decline, it remains crucially important. Programming is still a commodity.[34] The television industry is still influenced by a myriad of powerful organizations, including state intelligence agencies, and they promote neoliberal ideology. Viewers do currently enjoy more convenient access to television and more control over how to consume it. Although liberating in a way, these innovations also deepen television's reach into the everyday fabric of people's lives. Once upon a time, we could run away from the television set. These days, who runs without a smart phone? Television also remains profitable and popular, although perhaps not all is well on the horizon.[35] In 2014, the average

American over fifteen years old watched almost three hours of television per day.[36] Baseball is often referred to as America's national pastime, but would it not be more accurate to grant watching television that honour? How, after all, do most Americans watch their games?

## 11.5 Conclusion

The internet is turning out to be mostly a faux threat to the television industry. Compared to the 1990s, when many observers were sanguine about the democratic potential of the internet, elites have made great strides in incorporating the internet in existing power structures. Intrusive surveillance practices are shifting much of the power early internet users once had to comment and organise back to elites. Commercialism runs rampant online. Google and Facebook depend on advertisers too. A mutually beneficial synergy has developed between the television industry and the internet giants, including Google, which owns advertising-supported YouTube. The website has become an additional treasured outlet for mainstream channels.[37]

In other words, it is unlikely that the mere availability of certain technologies will upend a PMTV as long as the five filters, especially the first two, remain in place. Hope, such as there is, lies with the coming together of people who realise the need for change, and who will employ the available technologies not for tuning out the crucial issues of the day by tuning into American television, but for raising critical awareness and organizing resistance.

## Notes and Bibliography

[1] Free Press, Who Owns the Media? Accessed 19 February 19, http://www.freepress.net/ownership/chart.

[2] Peter Bradshaw, Hollywood Isn't 100% Anti-Trump. Isn't It Time For Some Internal Dissent? *The Guardian*, 1 February 2017, accessed February 9, 2017, https://www.theguardian.com/commentisfree/2017/feb/01/hollywood-trump-academy-award-protest-speeches.

[3] Michael Hiltzik (2014), Comcast deploys its army of revolving-door lobbyists against the FCC, *LA Times*, 27 May accessed 15 April 2017, http://www.latimes.com/business/hiltzik/la-fi-mh-comcast-deploys-20140527-column.html.

[4] Andrew Calabrese and Colleen Mihal (2011), The Public-Private Dichotomy in Media Policy, in *The Handbook of Political Economy of Communications*, ed. Janet Wasko, Graham Murdock and Helena Sousa (Chichester: Wiley-Blackwell).

[5] Toby Miller (2010), *Television Studies: The Basics*, New York: Routledge, 2010, Kindle edition, 66.

[6] Joe Flint (2014), TV Networks Load Up on Commercials, *LA Times*, 12 May accessed 18 February 2017, http://www.latimes.com/entertainment/envelope/cotown/la-et-ct-nielsen-advertising-study-20140510-story.html.
[7] Edward S. Herman and Noam Chomsky (1988), *Manufacturing Consent: The Political Economy of the Mass Media*, New York: Pantheon Books, 17.
[8] Mark Crispin Miller (1988) *Boxed In: The Culture of TV*, Evanston IL, Northwestern University Press, 24.
[9] Erik Barnouw (2004) *The Sponsor: Notes on a Modern Potentate*, New Brunswick, NJ, Transaction Publishers; Jennifer L. Pozner (2010), *Reality Bites Back: The Troubling Truth about Guilty Pleasure TV.* Berkeley CA: Seal Press, 2010, 15.
[10] Mark Crispin Miller (1990), 'Hollywood: The Ad', *The Atlantic*, April, accessed 9 February 2017, https://www.theatlantic.com/magazine/archive/1990/04/hollywood-the-ad/305005/.
[11] Pozner (2010), *Reality Bites Back*, 12.
[12] Nicholas Garnham cited in Miller, *Television Studies*, 112.
[13] Eric Schlosser (2012), *Fast Food Nation: The Dark Side of the All-American Meal* Boston MA, Houghton Mifflin Harcourt, 36.
[14] Miller (2010), *Television Studies*, 66.
[15] Noah Charney (2014), Cracking the Sitcom Code, *The Atlantic*, 28 December, accessed 9 February 2017, http://www.theatlantic.com/entertainment/archive/2014/12/cracking-the-sitcom-code/384068/.
[16] Tricia Jenkins (2013), *The CIA in Hollywood: How the Agency Shapes Film and Television*, Austin, TX: University of Texas Press.
[17] Rick Lyman (2001), Hollywood Discusses Role in War Effort, *New York Times*, 12 November, accessed 9 February 2017, http://www.nytimes.com/2001/11/12/politics/12HOLL.html.
[18] Tom Secker (2015), Biggest Ever FOIA Release from Pentagon Entertainment Liaison Offices, 12 July, accessed 9 February 2017, http://www.spyculture.com/biggest-ever-foia-release-from-pentagon-entertainment-liaison-office/#documents.
[19] Brooks Barnes (2010), TV Watchdog Group Is on the Defensive, *New York Times*, 24 October accessed 9 February 2017, http://www.nytimes.com/2010/10/25/business/media/25watchdog.html.
[20] Cited in Barnes (2010), TV Watchdog Group.
[21] Herman and Chomsky, *Manufacturing Consent* (1988), 29.
[22] Ibid.
[23] Janice Peck (2008) *Age of Oprah: Cultural Icon for the Neoliberal Era*, London, Routledge.
[24] Tasha Oren (2013), On the Line: Format, Cooking and Competition as Television Values, *Critical Studies in Television*, Vol. 8, No. 2, 30.
[25] Michele Byers (2010), 'Neoliberal Dexter?' in *Investigating Cutting Edge Television*, ed. Douglas L. Howard, New York, I.B. Tauris, 144.

26. Tim Kasser (2002), *The High Price of Materialism*, Cambridge, Bradford Book/MIT Press.
27. Cited in Randal Marlin (2013), *Propaganda and the Ethics of Persuasion* - Second Edition (Peterborough: Broadview Press, Kindle edition, location 838.
28. Cited in Robert W. McChesney (2001), Global Media, Neoliberalism, and Imperialism, *Monthly Review* 52(10), accessed 9 February 2017, https://monthlyreview.org/2001/03/01/global-media-neoliberalism-and-imperialism/.
29. Sonia Livingstone (1996), 'On the Continuing Problem of Media Effects Research', in *Mass Media and Society*, 2nd Edition, ed. James Curran and Michael Gurevitch, London: Edward Arnold.
30. *Ad Age*, John Wanamaker, accessed November 3, 2016, http://adage.com/article/special-report-the-advertising-century/john-wanamaker/140185/.
31. J. Michael Sproule (1994), *Channels of Propaganda*. Bloomington IN, EDINFO Press and ERIC Clearinghouse on Reading, 3. Accessed 3 November 2016, http://files.eric.ed.gov/fulltext/ED372461.pdf.
32. David Carr (2014), Barely Keeping Up in TV's New Golden Age, *New York Times*, 9 March, accessed 9 February 2017, http://www.nytimes.com/2014/03/10/business/media/fenced-in-by-televisions-excess-of-excellence.html?_r=2.
33. Nathan McAlone (2016), Services Like Netflix and Hulu Are Growing Much Faster Than Cable, *Business Insider*, 11 April. Accessed 8 February 2017, http://www.businessinsider.com/growth-of-streaming-services-outpacing-traditional-cable-2016-4.
34. Dwayne Winseck (2011), The Political Economies of Media: The Transformation of the Global Media Industries, p.34 in *The Political Economies of Media: The Transformation of the Global Media Industries* ed. Dwyane Winseck and Dal Yong Jin, London, Blomsbury.
35. Ibid; McAlone (2016), 'Services like Netflix'; Sam Thielman, Netflix and Ill: Is the Golden Age of TV Coming to an End?' *The Guardian*, 16 October 2016 accessed 8 February 2017, https://www.theguardian.com/media/2016/oct/16/is-golden-age-tv-over-netflix-shows-cable-television.
36. Bureau of Labor Statistics, American Time Use Survey Summary, 24 June 2016, accessed 9 February 2017, http://www.bls.gov/news.release/atus.nr0.htm.
37. Miller (2010), *Television Studies*, 15; also Winseck, *The Political Economies of Media*, 35.

CHAPTER 12

# The Sport of Shafting Fans and Taxpayers: An Application of the Propaganda Model to the Coverage of Professional Athletes and Team Owners

Barry Pollick

This paper applies Herman and Chomsky's Propaganda Model (hereafter called the 'PM') to the media's coverage of sports team owners vs. professional athletes, hypothesizing that the media will use more negative terms (e.g., 'greedy') to describe the *athletes* than to describe the *owners*. This hypothesis reflects the predictions of the PM, which posits that the dominant classes will tend to receive favourable coverage while workers' interests will tend to be excluded from the debate. While it is true that professional athletes are typically privileged workers with high salaries and influential public profiles, the main role they are expected to perform is to generate massive profits for team owners, sponsors, and TV networks by providing non-controversial entertainment. Furthermore, these athletes may suffer serious injuries such as ACL tears or even brain trauma, which may eventually lead to arthritis or chronic traumatic

---

How to cite this book chapter:
Pollick, B. 2018. The Sport of Shafting Fans and Taxpayers: An Application of the Propaganda Model to the Coverage of Professional Athletes and Team Owners. In: Pedro-Carañana, J., Broudy, D. and Klaehn, J. (eds.). *The Propaganda Model Today: Filtering Perception and Awareness*. Pp. 173–190. London: University of Westminster Press. DOI: https://doi.org/10.16997/book27.l. License: CC-BY-NC-ND 4.0

encephalitis (CTE) respectively. As former NFL player and present Noam Chomsky enthusiast John Moffitt put it, in explaining why he abruptly gave up the fame and fortune of pro football, 'I think it's really madness to risk your body, risk your well-being and risk your happiness for money. He added, 'Once you tear away the illusions of it, it's hard work. And it's dangerous work. And you're away from your family.... It's very tough on families'—sentiments that would characterise any number of professional sports.[1]

## 12.1 Summary of Empirical Studies Using the PM

There has been ample empirical evidence for the PM with respect to the coverage of such issues as the North America Free Trade Agreement, anti-globalization protests, the environment, regulation of the chemical industry, US foreign policy, union-management skirmishes, etc. from studies in the US, UK, Canada, Australia, and Spain.[2] Yet this author could find no test of the PM vis-á-vis sports coverage. Since Chomsky argues that critical theorists should consider a wide range of cultural artefacts, not restricting themselves to elite subjects,[3] it would be useful to content-analyse the coverage of professional athletes vs. that of sports team owners to determine *quantitatively* the extent of the hegemonic biases predicted in the PM. Such a content analysis may enable sports enthusiasts to recognise and resist manipulative coverage. As Kellner puts it,

> Cultural studies shows how media culture articulates the dominant values [and] political ideologies ...of our era and provides tools that enable us to read and interpret our culture critically, empowering us to resist media manipulation, increase our freedom and individuality, and strive for alternative cultures and political change.[4]

To achieve that end, this paper will conduct a key word analysis of the media's coverage of professional athletes vs. that of team owners in major US sports, with a particular focus on what is widely viewed as America's national sport, NFL football.[5] Specifically, the paper will analyse coverage by both the elite *New York Times*, which represents what Herman and Chomsky call the 'agenda-setting' elite press that determine what issues and events are deemed newsworthy by the lower-level media and establish the parameters within which debate and interpretation can occur[6] and Google.com, which represents a more universal source of sports news that includes newspapers, magazines, blogs, etc. If Herman and Chomsky's claims are true—that the media frame issues in a way that favours elite interests—we should find that players are rarely described in positive terms (as, say, generous), whereas team owners, by contrast, are rarely described in negative terms (as, say, greedy or lazy or overpaid).

## 12.2 Context of the Study

Ironically, while Herman and Chomsky point out that it is taboo for media organizations, as corporate entities that depend on other corporate entities (advertisers), to mention socialism in a positive light,[7] one type of socialism seems to receive a free pass: that which benefits powerful interests. Namely, major cities across America have socialised the profits of multi-millionaire sports team owners at the expense of those cities' taxpayers. Indeed, owners of teams in the four largest sports leagues (the NFL, MLB, the NBA, and the NHL) received nearly $20 billion in taxpayer subsidies for new arenas from 1990 to 2011, even though 'urban planners and economists have argued that building facilities for private sports teams is a massive waste of public money.'[8] Yet Easterbrooke notes that this economic injustice has earned little coverage by the media—local or national—whereas the free agencies of Robinson Cano (in baseball), Lebron James and Carmelo Anthony (in basketball) and Terrell Suggs (in football) have received considerable coverage[9] (e.g., James has been a free agent for just two days, yet a Google search on June 26, 2014, yielded 3,670,000 'hits'), much of it negative—focusing on how overpaid the players are.[10]

What's more, whereas team owners have been demanding socialised profits, free agent players are merely exercising their free-market right to play for the highest bidder, after 5–7 years of being required to play for the team that drafted them—in violation of free-market principles and, arguably, anti-trust laws. In light of such ironies, were Herman and Chomsky's PM to be *inaccurate*, we would expect to see professional athletes covered in a fairly sympathetic light—given that they were compelled to play for a team not of their choosing for many years (via a draft)—and sports team owners covered in a more critical manner, given that their tax-payer-subsidised profits would seem to be the sort of scandal that a vigilant press, dedicated to acting as the public's watchdog, as Thomas Jefferson advocated, would pounce on. On the other hand, if the PM is accurate, we would expect to see neutral or favourable coverage for team owners and more negative coverage for professional athletes. For, to paraphrase the two scholars, hegemonic ideas favouring powerful elites are internalised by beat journalists and presented to news consumers as 'common sense.'[11]

## 12.3 Methods Section

To test the prevalence of various stigmatizing terms describing athletes vs. those describing team owners in both the internet at large and America's so-called 'paper of record,' the *New York Times*, I typed such terms as *spoiled athlete*, *spoiled owner*, etc. into the search engines of Google, as well as that of the *Times'* site, which searches issues of the *Times* all the way back to the first edition in 1851. I chose to pair the *Times*, a so-called 'liberal' paper, with Google.

com because the latter gives a more macro-oriented perspective, including blogs, the professional news media, and fan posts. Thus, in using Google, I'm implying a broader definition of media, which is what one encounters when one accesses Google.com as so many do each day.

Due to the imprecision of Google searches as a methodological tool, however, the study also includes quantitative dimensions, checking websites to see what they actually say and whether they are commercial outlets or fan blogs. This added check is important because, as Pedro notes, Google search results are not website neutral:

> A review of specialised literature suggests that . . . the selection and ordering of the results respond to hierarchical criteria which tend to favour sites belonging to established, dominant institutions, at the expense of new and less well-established sites, and thus for innovation and diversity.[12]

Key words and phrases examined by the study include 'greedy athletes' and 'greedy team owners'; 'spoiled athlete' and 'spoiled team owner'; 'selfish athlete' and 'selfish owner'; 'unmotivated professional athletes' and 'unmotivated team owners'; and "*inflated salaries*,' players' vs. '*inflated salaries*' owners. Pedro, however, notes that the order of the keywords affects the search results, with the first words carrying more weight than later terms, so this study uses various permutations of keyword phrases (e.g., '*lazy owner*' team; '*lazy owner*' sports team; etc.).[13]

## 12.4 Financial Information on the *New York Times* and Google.com

The *New York Times* has a market capitalization of $2.35 billion, as of 3 July 2014.[14] It also owns 40 per cent of a paper company and in recent years has owned nine television stations, the *Boston Globe*, Boston.com, 16 other daily newspapers, and more than 50 web sites, including About.com, an online digital information provider, according to *NewYorkTimes.com*.[15] As a multi-billion-dollar enterprise, the *Times* shares common interests with such dominant institutional sectors as the banks (from which the *Times* acquires loans) and other major corporations (from which the *Times* seeks its large-dollar advertising revenue) and thus would be expected to view issues such as union-management skirmishes through a corporate-friendly prism. Google, by contrast, is worth roughly 350 billion dollars, as of 2013.[16] Celebritynetworth.net adds that Google is an 'international corporation' based in the US that offers internet services and products, such as advertising techniques, cloud computing, and internet searches.[17] Note, then, that Google, not even 20 years old, is worth more than one hundred times what the 'Gray Lady,' as the 163-year-old *New York Times* is nicknamed, is worth—for precisely the reasons that Herman identifies in updating the filters: that the ascendance of the internet and the corresponding decline of the newspaper industry has meant that newspapers are ever more dependent on senior beat sources and corporate public relations departments and less able to deploy investigative reporters that may, for example, run an exposé on the trend toward government subsidization of sports stadiums and other incentives given to prevent team owners from moving their teams.[18]

Below, I've listed the results of the key-word analysis, bold-facing key findings. A brief discussion of the results follows each table.

One trend stands out in Table 12.1: Terms disparaging NFL players' salaries or just athletes' salaries drew vastly more hits than terms disparaging team owners' salaries. For example, the phrase *inflated athletes' salaries* (not in quotes) drew 567,000 hits and the term *inflated NFL salaries* drew over 423,000 hits. (A random check of 30 of the hits indicated that all referred to players' salaries, none to the earnings by owners.) By contrast, the phrase *'inflated salaries'* owners drew just 16,000 hits and perhaps 85 per cent of them referred to players' salaries. This discrepancy seems to underscore Herman and Chomsky's point that the common-sense view, expressed via the internet, reflects the interests of hegemonic forces, such as the extremely affluent team owners.

It should be acknowledged, however, that *'inflated sports ticket prices'* drew 12 million hits but fans may not hold team owners directly responsible for such inflation; in fact, it is just as likely that they would blame players' inflated salaries, since owners' team related earnings do not appear much on the web,

| Google.com, 1/6/2014 | No. of 'hits' |
|---|---|
| Inflated athletes' salaries | 567,000 |
| Inflated sports ticket prices | 12,000,000 (but at least half refer to 'ticket scalping' in Europe |
| Inflated NFL salaries | 423,000 |
| Inflated NFL ticket prices | 837,000 |
| 'inflated NFL salaries' | 53 (but all refer to players' salaries) |
| 'inflated NFL players' salaries' | 0 |
| 'Inflated NFL owners' salaries' | 0 |
| 'NFL owners' inflated salaries' | 0 |
| 'Inflated salaries' players | 20,100 |
| 'Inflated salaries' owners | **16,000** (but perhaps 80% of the hits refer to players' salaries) |

**Table 12.1:** Keyword search on Google.com Focusing on 'Inflated' and 'Salaries'.

| Google.com 6 January 2014 | |
|---|---|
| Overpriced NFL tickets | 131,000 |
| 'overpriced NFL tickets' | 8590 |
| Overpriced NFL players | 46,000 |
| 'Overpriced NFL players' | 2 |
| Overpriced professional athletes | 29,900 |
| Overpriced NFL (athletes OR players) | 131,000 |
| 'Overpaid NFL players' | **9670** |
| 'Overpaid NFL owners' | **4** (and 3 of the 4 are from fans' blogs/web-pages; only 1 is from a media organization) |
| 'Overrated NFL players' | **46,400** |
| 'Overrated NFL owners' | 1 (a blog-post from a fan) |
| 'Lazy professional athletes' | 703 |
| 'Lazy professional athlete' | 85 |
| 'Lazy athletes' | 5460 (but many don't refer to professional athletes) |
| 'Lazy athlete' | 450 (likewise, many don't refer to professionals) |
| 'Lazy owner' sports teams | 894 |
| 'Lazy NFL owner' | 0 |
| 'Unmotivated NFL owner' | 0 |
| 'Lazy owner' team | 28,200 (but the vast majority seem to refer to fantasy football or baseball owners; motorboat owners; or dog-owners. An examination of the first 20 hits showed that just one of them referred to an NFL team owner: the Philadelphia Eagles owner. And this is a fan's blog post speculating that the Eagles' owner might be lazy or might not. |
| 'Unmotivated professional athletes' | **963** |
| 'Unmotivated professional athlete' | 35 |
| 'Unmotivated owner' | 829 (but I didn't see any hits related to sports team owners) |
| 'Unmotivated owners' sports teams | 41 (but none refer to sports team owners) |
| 'Unmotivated owner' sports teams | 7 (only two refer to sports team owners) |

**Table 12.2:** Keyword Search on Google.com Using '*Overpriced*,' '*Lazy*,' and '*Unmotivated*'.

relative to players' earnings. Nor does the media tend to provide much analysis of owners' influence on pricing, further insulating them from the fans' ire.

Sample quote: 'Sports fans hate nothing more than lazy, unmotivated athletes. By that standard, Albert Haynesworth...'[19]

Note the stark contrast between the number of hits for *'overpaid NFL players'* (9,670 hits) and that for *'overpaid NFL owners'* (4—and just one came from a media organization). So, as Herman points out in a different context, the issue of inflated salaries is framed in terms favourable to elites—despite a massive increase in NFL owners' income relative to players' in recent years.[20] Specifically, over the past ten years, the NFL TV contract, which is paid to the owners, has more than doubled in value,[21] as has NFL parking prices,[22] and ticket prices have risen over 50 per cent.[23] By contrast, NFL players' salaries have only risen 40% during those 10 years and most of that money is unguaranteed.[24] What is more, there seems to be hardly any recognition that team owners and high level management receive handsome salaries. NFL Commissioner Roger Goodell, for example, earned $29.5 million in 2011, according to Bleacherreport.com—even though the NFL is classified as a non-profit organization and thus can secure public funds for building stadiums and tax subsidies for the land on which the stadium is built, so that the public is effectively subsidizing much of Goodell's considerable salary.[25]

In addition, ticket and parking price hikes affect the fans more directly than players' salaries do, since the team owners can offset higher player salaries by reducing their own salaries. Finally, the trope of the overpaid NFL athlete, which appears to be perpetuated by the media and fans alike on Google, belies four facts: (a) that NFL players make 30 to 70 per cent less than their counterparts in professional basketball and baseball and, unlike the latter two, tend to have unguaranteed contracts;[26] (b) that they also make far less than each of the 32 NFL owners (17 of whom are billionaires), whose teams have an average worth of over a billion dollars[27] and tend to be family-owned, so that many of the owners, like those that inherit newspapers, have not needed to work for a salary;[28] (c) that the players 'play' a sport so violent that the league recently settled a class action lawsuit involving thousands of players who retired with debilitating brain injuries apparently due to the many concussions they suffered while playing professional football; (d) that the players are considerably underpaid for the first five to seven years of their career due to a draft that artificially deflates salaries.[29]

It is also interesting to note that 'overrated NFL players' [46,400 hits] and 'unmotivated professional athlete/athletes' [998 hits] receive vastly more hits than 'overrated owners' [just one hit—from a fan's blog post] and 'unmotivated owners' sports teams' [only 2 of the 48 'hits' for "unmotivated owners' sports teams' refers to sports team owners]. While it is true that some players may not live up to their athletic potential, they did manage to reach the elite league in their given sport, which means they are among the top 600 players in the entire country (if one is referring to the NBA) or 1,200 players in the country (if one is referring to the NFL). Conversely, while some owners made their own fortunes, many of them inherited their wealth (e.g., the current Rooney ownership in Pittsburgh, Jimmy Haslam in Cleveland; Mike Brown in Cincinnati) and thus may be considered both 'overrated' (in that their financial power is not correlated with how hard they worked for it) and unmotivated (in that they have little incentive to work hard). Finally, many owners do not invest their team revenue in acquiring expensive free agents, preferring to pocket the revenue—yet another sign of a lack of motivation.

Note the vast gap between *spoiled athletes* or *spoiled players* [about 40,000 hits altogether] and *spoiled team owners* [about 820 hits]—a gap even more pronounced *vis-á-vis* NFL owners and players. Yet it is the players who must stay in shape, practice almost daily during a gruelling season (162 games in baseball, 82 in the NBA and 16 in the NFL, plus four pre-season games) in which they are away from their families for long periods, and endure relatively short professional athletic careers that which can end suddenly, due to injury or nonrenewal of contract; conversely, the owners cannot be cut or fired—except under extremely unusual circumstances (as San Diego Clippers owner Donald Sterling discovered), generally remain team owners for

| Google.com, 11 January 2014 | |
|---|---|
| 'spoiled athlete' | **34,800** |
| 'spoiled owner' | **2,860** (but virtually none concern sports team owners) |
| 'spoiled team owner' | **8** |
| 'spoiled owner' team | 809 |
| 'spoiled player' team | 3,470 |
| 'spoiled player' | 6,230 |
| 'spoiled NFL player' | **1,290** |
| 'spoiled NFL owner' | 3 (including a blog spot from a fan) |
| 'greedy owner*' sports team | 101,000 |
| 'greedy player*' | 103,000 |
| 'greedy player*' sports team | 2,450 |
| 'greedy athlete*' | 67,400 |
| 'greedy athlete' sports team | 15,100 |
| 'greedy professional athletes' | 3,470 |
| 'greedy professional athlete' | 943 |

**Table 12.3:** Keyword Search on Google.com Using 'Spoiled' and 'Greedy'.

many years (e.g., the Rooney family in Pittsburgh has owned the Steelers for over 50 years), and can hire *others* to manage and travel with the team, while they may remain home with their families. This public misperception of players being more spoiled than owners may stem from the fact that the public identifies with the players, most of whom come from working or middle-class backgrounds, but accept as 'the natural order' that team owners are fabulously wealthy. Herman and Chomsky note that such a 'common sense' perspective—akin to the public's disdain for affirmative action that benefits historically underrepresented classes while feeling neutral about the legacy affirmative action that benefits the children of elites—serves the interests of hegemonic groups.[30]

Now that the keyword search of Google.com has been performed, the study will search for keywords from NYT.com.

Note that 'lazy player' significantly outnumbers 'lazy team owner,' in that only two of the latter refer to a sports owner—and this is the same article listed twice. By contrast, 'lazy player' or 'lazy players' appears a total of 18 times. This

| 8 January 2014, NewYorkTimes.com | |
|---|---|
| 'Unmotivated professional athlete' | 0 |
| 'Unmotivated professional athletes' | 0 |
| 'Unmotivated athletes' | 0 |
| 'Unmotivated owners' sports teams | 0 |
| 'Unmotivated owner' sports teams | 0 |
| 'Unmotivated owner' | 0 |
| 'Lazy athletes' | 0 |
| 'Lazy athlete' | 0 |
| 'Lazy players' | 7 |
| 'Lazy player' | 11 |
| 'Lazy owner' | 0 |
| 'Lazy owners' | 7 (none refer to sports owners) |
| 'Lazy team owner' | 3 (One refers to fantasy football owners; another refers to the 'Princess Vampire' fan site; the third refers to Michigan's 'Dash for Cash,' which involves small-time race cars, not multi-millionaire team owners) |
| 'Lazy NFL owner' | 0 |
| 'Unmotivated NFL owner' | 0 |

**Table 12.4:** Keyword Search on NYT.com Using 'Lazy' and 'Unmotivated'.

is ironic in light of the inherited wealth of many sports franchise owners, particularly NFL owners, vs. players who, in reaching the top 500–1,000 or so in a sport played by millions, most likely polished their skills for thousands of hours even as children, so that they were good enough to make the pros by their late teens (in basketball and baseball) or early twenties.[31] By contrast, even owners who did work hard to earn their vast fortunes do not have to work particularly hard as team owners; they generally hire general managers, team presidents,

| | |
|---|---|
| 'Spoiled athlete' | 14 |
| 'Spoiled player' | 4 |
| 'Spoiled player' team | 3 |
| 'Spoiled owner' team | 0 |
| 'Spoiled owner' | 0 |
| 'Spoiled team owner' | 0 |
| 'Spoiled NFL owner' | 0 |
| 'Spoiled NFL player' | 584 |
| 'Spoiled NFL athlete' | 0 |
| 'Selfish player' | 105 |
| 'Selfish owner' | 5 (but none are about sports—e.g., dog owners are discussed) |
| 'Egotistical athlete' | 1 |
| 'Egotistical owner' | 1 |
| 'Egotistical player' | 4 |
| 'Ungrateful owner' | 1 |
| 'Ungrateful player' | 2 |
| 'rich player' | 8 |
| 'rich athlete' | 17 (16 are related to sports) |
| 'rich owner' | 90 (over 2/3 are not related to sports owners) |
| 'overpaid athlete' | 19 |
| 'overpaid player' | 10 |
| 'overpaid owner' | 0 |
| Inflated NFL salaries | 125 (but at least one sides with the players, noting that the owners were accused of inflating salaries and capping contracts) |
| 'Inflated salary' player | 10 (2 are used as metaphors—e.g., a stockbroker is deemed 'a player') |

**Table 12.5:** Search on NYT.com Using 'Spoiled,' 'Egotistical,' 'Lazy' etc., 11 January 2014.

| | |
|---|---|
| 'Inflated salary' owner | 30 (but none are related to sports team owners—in fact, 5 are related to players' salaries) |
| Inflated NFL owners' salaries | 55 (but most concern inflated players' salaries. In fact, when the limiter '-players' was added to the search, no results appeared.) |
| Inflated NFL owners' salaries –players | 0 |
| 'undeserving player' | 3 |
| 'undeserving owner' | 0 |
| 'greedy athletes' | 10 |
| 'greedy athlete' | 1 |
| 'greedy professional athlete' | 0 |
| 'greedy professional athletes' | 0 |
| 'greedy owner' team | 6 |
| 'greedy owners' team | 38 |
| 'greedy owner' sports | 13 |
| 'greedy owners' sports | 61 |
| 'generous player' | 4 (only one is related to sports players) |
| 'generous athlete' | 3 |
| 'generous owner' | 42 (only 13 are related to sports owners) |

**Table 12.5:** Continued.

coaches, etc. to do the work for them. Finally, it is ironic because owners tend to receive hundreds of millions of dollars in subsidies from cities desperate to keep a given team from moving to another city.[32]

Sample quote: 'I think the vast majority of players in the N.F.L. have guns,' former Giants ... He's just one more spoiled egocentric prima donna who is being ...'

As Table 12.5 shows, the *New York Times* uses the phrases 'overpaid athlete' and 'overpaid player' a total of 29 times but never uses the phrase 'overpaid owner.'[33] On the other hand, the *Times* does use the phrase 'rich owner' 90 times vs. 'rich player' or 'rich athlete' a total of 25 times, but only about 20 of the 90 are related to sports owners. The search term *inflated NFL salaries* appeared 125 instances in the *Times*, whereas the *Times* much more rarely referred to the inflated salaries of owners. On the other hand, the *Times* did refer to the term 'greedy owners' and 'greedy owners' sports about six times as frequently as 'greedy athletes' but they referred to the quoted term 'generous owner' four times as often as 'generous player' or 'generous athlete'.

Why then aren't *New York Times* and other professional writers pointing out how *underpaid* professional athletes are relative to the owners that drafted them? Herman and Chomsky's third filter—involving journalists' sourcing and beats—offers a plausible explanation for this discrepancy. To understand how, consider that sports writers routinely rely on the teams they cover to provide press releases, press conferences, interviews with the press secretary of a given team, etc. Indeed, every NFL team has a public relations office that facilitates the sports beat of the press in the given city. By contrast, the NFL players, or the players of any league, for that matter, have only one union headquarters and no union offices in given cities. Furthermore, if a beat reporter starts asking players about the issues mentioned above (e.g., the draft), that reporter can be denied access to the team's players and press conferences, and thus be rendered unable to perform his/her job as a beat writer, a privileged position that pays a healthy salary and affords him/her access to superstar athletes and a pass to all of the team's games.

Another reason might be more subtle. Journalists, like fans, don't identify with owners the way they do with professional athletes, many of whom suddenly ascended from impoverished backgrounds (especially in the NBA) to earn annual pay checks the average American won't accumulate in a lifetime, often despite having little education, poor articulation skills, and gang-like attire. By contrast, journalists and fans generally see owners like Jerry Jones wearing a dark business suit, articulating their thoughts well, and avoiding the kinds of reckless behaviour that seems to plague so many young athletes. What is more, as Gramsci's interpreter notes, fans and journalists alike tend to grow up in a city where a family like the Rooneys (in Pittsburgh) or the Hunts (in Kansas City) have owned the team for generations, so that this ownership dynasty becomes internalised as our common sense idea of how things ought to be, just as it doesn't strike us as undemocratic that presidents predominantly come from the upper middle and upper classes and attended Ivy League schools.[34] Moreover, since sports journalists interact with corporate elites far more so than fans do, they may gradually take on the hegemonic perspectives of those elites, seeing a player like Alex Rodriguez as vastly overpaid but not noticing that 'A-Rod' was denied his true market value until eight years into his career or that the league itself is a monopoly. In taking on such perspectives, journalists are acting in accordance with Herman and Chomsky's fifth filter: they are reinforcing the dominant ideology that social inequality, as exemplified by the monopolistic practices of billionaire owners, is beyond questioning or even examining.[35]

## 12.5 Conclusion

Following Herman's call for using the PM to understand how the mainstream US media works, this paper has tried to sensitise readers to the subtle ways in which media discourses on sports strive to legitimate an increasingly unequal economic system by characterizing professional athletes in largely negative terms and sports team owners in relatively more favourable terms.[36] Specifically, the quantitative analysis found that stigmatizing terms such as 'spoiled', 'greedy', 'unmotivated', 'overrated', 'egotistical', 'overpaid', 'rich', and 'lazy' are used far more often to disparage professional athletes, particularly NFL players, than to describe team owners; by contrast, the benevolent term 'generous' is used far more often to describe team owners than to describe players. This finding holds not only for a Google search of the internet in general but even for reporting in the august and ostensibly 'liberal' *New York Times*. In fact, ironically, the *New York Times* was even slightly more favourable to NFL team owners than Google.com was—at least in characterizing players, but not owners, as spoiled. Whereas Google.com had 1,290 hits for '*spoiled NFL player*' vs. 3 for '*spoiled NFL owner*,' (a ratio of about 400 to 1), the *Times* had 594 hits for '*spoiled NFL player*' vs. none for '*spoiled NFL owner*'. And whereas Google had 3470 hits for '*spoiled player*' team vs. 809 for '*spoiled owner*' team (a 4 to 1 ratio), the Grey Lady had 3 hits for '*spoiled player*' team and 0 hits for '*spoiled owner*' team.

That even *Times* journalists display this hegemonic bias reinforces the micro-level theory of media sociologists such as Tuchman and the Langs that reporters over time tend to reflect the views of their senior beat sources (in this case, team management/ownership, which has a public relations department, instead of the players, who, although having a union, lack a centralised public relations office, in the city in which they play), who would naturally see themselves as generous and the players whose salaries they hope to hold down as greedy. Yet the findings also reflect what Mullen and Klaehn call the more macro-level perspective of the PM, which focuses on power and social class, theorizing that constraints inherent in the social system—such as the dearth of labour reporters vs. the proliferation of business journalists—incline journalists to internalise as common sense ideas and language that favour the powerful.[37] What is more, the findings show a correlation between the biased, hegemonic sports coverage in an elite, well-respected publication, the *Times*, and the biased, hegemonic sports coverage on Google.com, which includes online versions of news publications (e.g., *USA Today*), public comments posted on those sites, and *personal* blogs or websites. Thus, we can posit that the team-owner-friendly perspective of prestigious papers like the *Times*, America's so-called 'paper of record,' may influence the perspective of both less prestigious publications/ websites and news consumers that post comments online.[38]

Finally, as Klaehn notes about the PM in general, the findings in this study do not imply that journalists are *consciously* favouring team owners over professional athletes but merely that 'awareness, perception and understandings are typically constrained and informed by structures of discourse.'[39] Yet paradoxically, Herman argues that this more subtle bias enhances the media's propaganda effects *all the more,* as the public presumably attaches more credence to the 'objective reporting' of papers like the *Times* than it does to explicitly ideological sources like Rush Limbaugh.[40] Thus, as Herman argues, it is incumbent on researchers to use the PM to show how the mainstream media frame issues and events and 'allow debate only within the parameters of the elite perspectives. . . . When ordinary citizens are not aware of their own stake in an issue or are immobilised by effective propaganda, the media will serve elite interests uncompromisingly.[41] And as Kellner adds, it is incumbent on researchers using the PM to focus not only on 'serious issues' but on low-brow subjects like sports, in order to show how voices and struggles are 'omitted from mainstream views,' thus preserving the existing power structure.[42] For by becoming more aware of this double standard in media coverage, sports fans can more easily resist such hegemonic values and begin to challenge the increasingly undemocratic system that has given rise to them.

## Notes and Bibliography

[1] Associated Press (2013), 'John Moffitt Was Unhappy, Quits NFL', *ESPN.com*, 8 November http://www.espn.com/nfl/story/_/id/9935642/john-moffitt-denver-broncos-quits-walks-away-1m. (Accessed 29 May 2017).

[2] Edward S. Herman, *The Myth of the Liberal Media* (1999), New York: Peter Lang Publishing, 231–252; Noam Chomsky (2002). *The New Military Humanism: Lessons from Kosovo*, Monroe ME, Common Courage Press; Edward Herman and Noam Chomsky, *Manufacturing Consent: The Political Economy of the Mass Media*, 2nd ed. (New York: Pantheon Books); Eric Herring and Piers Robinson (2003), 'Too Polemical or Too Political? Chomsky on the Study of the News Media and US Foreign Policy', *Review of International Studies*, 29, no. 4, 553–568; Robert Babe (2005), 'Newspaper Discourses on Environment', in *Filtering the News: Essays on Herman and Chomsky's Propaganda Model*, ed. Jeffery Klaehn (London: Black Rose Books); Oliver Boyd-Barrett (2004), 'Judith Miller and the *New York Times* and the Propaganda Model', *Journalism Studies*, 5, no. 4: 435–449; James Winter and Jeffery Klaehn (2005), 'The Propaganda Model Under Protest', in *Filtering the News: Essays on Herman and Chomsky's Propaganda Model*, ed. Jeffery Klaehn (London: Black Rose Books); Peter Phillips (2010), 'Left Progressive Media Inside the Propaganda Model', Projectcensored.org, 2 May. Accessed 4 July 2014. http://www.projectcensored.org/left-progressive-media-inside-the-propaganda-model/; John Robertson (2008), 'It Looks Like There's No Alternative: UK TV News Coverage of the 2008 Budget and the Propaganda Model', *Fifth Estate Online*, accessed 29 May 2014; John Robertson and E. McLaughlin (2013), 'Still Bad News? UK TV Coverage of Industrial Action in 2010', *Fifth Estate Online*, accessed 4 July 2014, http://www.fifth-estate-online.co.uk/wp-content/uploads/2013/10/J.-Robertson-paper1.pdf; Daniel Broudy (2009), 'The Propaganda of Patriotism and Color', *Synaesthesia*, 5, no. 1, 2–19; Michael Baker (2007),

'Conform or Reform? Social Movements and the Mass Media', *Fifth Estate Online, International Journal of Radical Mass Media Criticism*, 1 February. http://www.fifth-estate-online.co.uk/?p=50, accessed 4 July 2014; Francisco Sierra and Miguel Vasquez (2006), ed., *La construcción del consenso. Revisitando el modelo de propaganda de Noam Chomsky y Edward S. Herman* [*The Construction of Consensus. Revisiting the Propaganda Model of Noam Chomsky and Edward S. Herman*], Madrid, Siranda, quoted in Joan Pedro (2011), 'The Propaganda Model in the Early 21st Century Part II', *International Journal of Communication,* 5: 1906–1926.

[3] Mark Achbar and Peter Witonick (1992), *Manufacturing Consent: Noam Chomsky and the Media* (Zeitgeist Video, 1992), Documentary, 167 min., http://topdocumentaryfilms.com/manufacturing-consent-noam-chomsky-and-the-media/ (Accessed 1 July 2014).

[4] Douglas Kellner, Cultural Studies, 'Multiculturalism, and Media Culture', (nd) accessed 1 July 2014. http://pages.gseis.ucla.edu/faculty/papers/SAGEcs.htm.

[5] For example, the NFL's annual revenue is now about $10 billion a year, $7 billion from its TV contract alone. Brent Schrotenboer, 'NFL Takes Aim at $25 Billion a Year.' *USA Today.* 5 February 2014. http://www.usatoday.com/story/sports/nfl/super/2014/01/30/super-bowl-nfl-revenue-denver-broncos-seattle-seahawks/5061197/ (Accessed 1 July 2014). NFL teams earn, on average, $286 million annually, vs. $152 million dollars annually for NBA teams and $236 million dollars for Major League baseball teams and $88 million dollars for NHL teams, according to Businessinsider.com. Chart: NFL and MLB Teams Top Premier League Teams When It Comes to Making Money. 14 May 2014. http://www.businessinsider.com/chart-nfl-mlb-premier-league-revenue-2014-5 (accessed 1 July 2014).

[6] Herman and Chomsky, *Manufacturing Consent: The Political Economy of the Mass Media,* 1–2.

[7] Ibid; Edward Herman (2000), 'The Propaganda Model: A Retrospective,' *Journalism Studies,* 1, no. 1, 101-112.

[8] Neil Demause (2011), 'Why Do Mayors Love Sports Stadiums?' *The Nation,* 27 July 2011. http://www.thenation.com/article/162400/why-do-mayors-love-sports-stadiums (accessed 29 January 2014).

[9] Gregg Easterbrook (2013), 'How the NFL Fleeces Taxpayers', *The Atlantic,* 18 September. http://www.theatlantic.com/magazine/archive/2013/10/how-the-nfl-fleeces-taxpayers/309448/ (accessed 8 January 2014).

[10] Here is an illustration of the vituperative coverage of free agent athletes. Several leading football analysts confirmed Wednesday that most NFL teams are just one or two ridiculously overpriced free agent signings away from a Super Bowl victory. Giving out a bloated contract to an aging pass rusher or promising a ton of guaranteed money to a declining wide receiver with a history of injuries is all it takes to push a franchise over the top, said ESPN NFL analyst Bill Polian, adding that even the worst team in the league

would become an instant contender for the Lombardi Trophy by wasting most of their salary cap on a couple of unproven or overhyped defenders (http://www.therichest.com/sports/10-of-the-most-overpaid-athletes-in-sports/10/). Note that the reporter made no attempt to interview a player or union rep but only the ESPN analyst, who was the former general manager of the Indianapolis Colts football team and thus is not unbiased on the issue of free agent players.

11. Herman and Chomsky, *Manufacturing Consent: The Political Economy of the Mass Media*, 2.
12. Joan Pedro, 'A collection of samples for research in Google: Design and application of a sample selection method. Results and problems of research.' *GMJ: Mediterranean Edition*. 2012; 7 no.1: 29–40, accessed 18 June 2017, http://globalmedia.emu.edu.tr/images/stories/ALL_ARTICLES/2012/Spring/4._Joan_Pedro.pdf
13. Pedro, 'A collection of samples for research in Google: Design and application of a sample selection method. Results and problems of research.'
14. 'The New York Times Company,' Google Finance, accessed 3 July 2014, http://www.google.com/finance?cid=407690
15. 'The New York Times Company: Company: Business Units', The New York Times Company. Accessed July 3, 2014. http://investors.nytco.com/investors/stock-and-debt-information/default.aspx
16. 'Google's Net Worth -- How Much Is Google Worth?', accessed 4 July 2014, http://www.theirnetworth.com/Businesses/Google/.
17. Ibid.
18. Herman, 'The Propaganda Model: A Retrospective,' 3.
19. David Whitley (2011), 'It Doesn't Take Much Effort to Dislike Albert Haynesworth,' SportingNews.com, 9 November) accessed 4 July 2014. http://www.sportingnews.com/nfl/story/2011-11-09/it-doesnt-take-much-effort-to-find-albert-hayesworth-unlikable
20. Herman, 'The Propaganda Model: A Retrospective,' 3.
21. Daniel Kaplan (2013), 'Can the NFL get to $25 billion?' SportsBusinessDaily.com, last modified 28 January, http://m.sportsbusinessdaily.com/Journal/Issues/2013/01/28/In-Depth/NFL-revenue.aspx.
22. Melanie Hicken (2013), 'The high cost of being a football fan,' CNN.com, last modified September 7, 2013, http://money.cnn.com/2013/09/07/pf/football-prices/index.html
23. Easterbrook, 'How the NFL Fleeces Taxpayers.'
24. Ibid.
25. Alex Dunlap (2013), 'How Much Money Do NFL Front Office Executives Make? Last modified 15 May, http://bleacherreport.com/articles/1638485-how-much-money-do-nfl-front-office-execs-make Dunlap notes that these 'non-profit' organizations 'make money hand over fist' by designating themselves as non-profit organizations and thus receiving the aforementioned public subsidies.

26 Joe Dorish, 'Average Salaries in the NBA, NFL, MLB, and NHL,' Yahoo.com, last modified 12 November 2011, http://sports.yahoo.com/nba/news?slug=ycn-10423863; 'Are NHL Players Overpaid?' Stats Professor, last modified 29 November 2012, http://www.statsprofessor.org/2012_11_01_archive.html. Stats Professor points out that the 2011-2012 NFL contract is worth nearly twice as much as those of the NBA, MLB, and NHL combined.
27 Kaplan, 'Can the NFL Get to $25 Billion?', 3.
28 Easterbrook, 'How the NFL Fleeces Taxpayers.'
29 That journalists have internalised this anti-free-market idea so utterly can be seen in this analogy: suppose that press owners proposed a draft of aspiring journalists, so that these journalists could only negotiate and work for one company for the first seven years of their career and, if they couldn't reach a contract with that employer, would have to leave journalism. Would journalists view such a situation from management's perspective?
30 Herman and Chomsky, *Manufacturing Consent*, 1–2.
31 Malcolm Gladwell (2008), *Outliers: The Story of Success* (New York: Little, Brown and Co).
32 Easterbrook, 'How the NFL Fleeces Taxpayers.'
33 One interesting exception to this rule of deferential treatment toward sports team owners is the following letter to the editor of the *New York Times*, published in 1981: 'To the Sports Editor: Many feel that the grossly inflated salaries paid to professional athletes are justified because sports fans are paying the tab by purchasing tickets. This appealing and seemingly logical free enterprise rationalization is wrong. We live in an economically complex society. The fans who attend games are not the only ones paying for the astronomical salaries. Many professional athletes have refined the skills that command high salaries at public expense while attending public universities on athletic scholarships. Most professional teams play in stadia built and, in some cases, maintained with tax dollars. Because the owners do not have to provide their place of business, they can pay higher salaries. For tax purposes, owners are able to depreciate the value of their players and charge the expenses of their sports holdings against the earnings of their other business enterprises. Thus, they are able to reduce significantly their tax liability. Many high-priced season tickets are held by other businesses and are charged as business expenses for tax purposes. One man's tax deduction is another man's tax. When the rich avoid taxes, the rest of us pay higher taxes. A large portion of the astronomical salaries are financed with television revenue. The demand for increased television revenue to pay the ever-increasing salaries results in higher prices to consumers for the products advertised on television. The owners of professional teams are counting on increased revenue from cable television to pay the huge deferred salaries of their athletes. You can bet that this will drive up the future cost of cable service. There are other, more subtle ways in which society pays for the huge salaries of sports stars. The salaries fuel the fires

of inflation. The salaries cruelly lead our youth, especially our inner-city youth, to believe that sports are the only way to financial success in our society. All Americans, including those with no interest in sports, are paying directly or indirectly for the obscene salaries paid to some professional athletes. CARL OLSON.' But note that this insightful critique of team owners as well as players was written not by a Times reporter or op-ed writer but a fan. Note also that it was written in 1981, well before the ascendance of spectator sports to meteoric heights, in terms of TV contracts, player salaries, etc. Carl Olsen (1981). 'Mailbox; Inflated Salaries For Pro Athletes Are a Public Tax,' *New York Times*, 1 March 1981, accessed 4 July 2014. http://www.nytimes.com/1981/03/01/sports/mailbox-inflated-salaries-for-pro-athletes-are-a-public-tax.html

[34] Gwyn A Williams (1960), 'The Concept of Egemonia in the Thought of Antonio Gramsci.' *Journal of the History of Ideas*, Vol 20 no. 4, 586-599.

[35] Herman and Chomsky, *Manufacturing Consent*, 2.

[36] Herman, 'The Propaganda Model: A Retrospective,' 3; Kellner, 'Cultural Studies, Multiculturalism, and Media Culture,' 4.

[37] Mullen and Klaehn, 'The Herman-Chomsky Propaganda Model: A Critical Approach to Analysing Mass Media Behaviour.'

[38] True, the causal relationship can just as easily be reversed—the *Times* reporters may be influenced by the public discourse on the internet. Most likely, there is a discursive relationship between *Times* articles and internet postings: each influences and is influenced by the other.

[39] Jeffery Klaehn (2003), 'Model Construction: Various Other Epistemological Concerns: A Reply to John Corner's Commentary on the Propaganda Model.' *European Journal of Communication* 18: 377–383.

[40] Herman, 'The Propaganda Model: A Retrospective,' 5.

[41] Ibid, 5.

[42] Kellner, 'Cultural Studies, Multiculturalism, and Media Culture,' 4.

PART IV

# Case Studies on Media and Power: The Interplay Between National and Global Elites

CHAPTER 13

# The 2008 Financial Crisis, the Great Recession and Austerity in Britain: Analysing Media Coverage Using the Herman-Chomsky Propaganda Model

Andrew Mullen

## 13.1 Introduction

The Propaganda Model (PM) developed by Edward Herman and Noam Chomsky – articulated in *Manufacturing Consent* in 1988 and Chomsky's *Necessary Illusions: Thought Control* in 1989 – falls clearly within the critical political economy tradition of mass media and communication research. Initially formulated to explain the performance of the mass media in the United States (US), its advocates and critics have long debated the relevance of the PM in countries with diverging media systems.[1] This chapter investigates the utility of the PM in Britain and how it can explain media coverage of the 2008 financial crisis and the Great Recession and austerity that followed.

---

**How to cite this book chapter:**
Mullen, A. 2018. The 2008 Financial Crisis, the Great Recession and Austerity in Britain: Analysing Media Coverage Using the Herman-Chomsky Propaganda Model. In: Pedro-Carañana, J., Broudy, D. and Klaehn, J. (eds.). *The Propaganda Model Today: Filtering Perception and Awareness*. Pp. 193–221. London: University of Westminster Press. DOI: https://doi.org/10.16997/book27.m. License: CC-BY-NC-ND 4.0

It begins with a brief overview of how the economic and political elite in Britain responded to the 2008 financial crisis (i.e. bailout), the ensuing recession (i.e. stimulus), and the consequent deterioration of the public finances (i.e. austerity). The second section presents original empirical data regarding mass media coverage of these events. It considers how mass media treated the idea of a wealth tax as a radical alternative to austerity. The third section applies the PM to such media coverage and suggests it is, indeed, relevant and applicable in Britain.[2]

### 13.1.1 Sampling and Methods

The chapter draws upon two sets of data from newspaper articles and television programmes. A Nexis database search was conducted using the terms 'cuts' or 'recession' and 'crisis' or 'financial crisis'. The search focused on eight periods between 2008 and 2010, each of four weeks in duration, wherein significant events occurred. These included: (1) the bailout of the financial system (24 September to 21 October 2008); (2) the New Labour Government's stimulus package (10 November to 7 December 2008); (3) the Conservative Party Leader's 'age of austerity' speech (12 April to 9 May 2009); and (4) the party conference season (13 September to 10 October 2009). They also included (5) the Treasury Select Committee's report on the 2008 financial crisis (13 November to 10 December 2009); (6) the 2010 General Election (15 April to 12 May 2010); (7) the Conservative-Liberal Democrat Coalition Government's Emergency Budget (8 June to 5 July 2010); and (8) the Coalition Government's Comprehensive Spending Review (8 November to 5 December 2010).

A sample of 1,586 articles was generated which encompassed news reports, commentary, editorials, and letters. It included 596 articles from *The Guardian* and *Observer* and 993 articles from the *Daily* and *Sunday Telegraph*. The *Guardian* and *Observer* represented the left while the *Daily* and *Sunday Telegraph* represented the right. These broadsheets demarcate the respective ends of the mainstream political spectrum in the mass media. A sample of 47 television programmes – produced by the British Broadcasting Corporation (BBC), the commercial Independent Television (ITV) network, Channel 4 and Channel 5 – broadcast between 2008 and 2015 on subjects related to the 2008 financial crisis, the Great Recession and austerity were recorded. These included several episodes of current affairs series such as the BBC's *Panorama* and Channel 4's *Dispatches*, commissioned programmes and live television debates.

Following the methodological approach pioneered by the Glasgow Media Group over three decades ago,[3] analysis of newspaper articles and television programmes focused on identifying (a) the primary sources used; (b) the main issues discussed plus those that were absent; (c) the quantity of text devoted to the main issues; and (d) the key discourses constructed. The comparative nature of the analysis enabled two secondary propositions to be tested. Firstly, coverage in *The Guardian* and *Observer*, which are ostensibly progressive newspapers, should reflect a broader and more oppositional (i.e., anti-austerity) range of voices, issues, and discourses. Secondly, the regulatory duties of Britain's broadcasters to ensure balanced reporting, due accuracy and due impartiality – which do not pertain to Britain's newspapers – should result in more critical and diverse coverage.

## 13.2 The 2008 Financial Crisis, the Great Recession and Austerity in Britain

The 2008 financial crisis and the Great Recession and austerity that followed had a significant economic, political, and social impact on Britain as a private sector debt crisis was converted, both discursively and policy-wise, into a sovereign (i.e., public sector) debt crisis.[4] In October 2008, with the financial system reportedly on the brink of collapse, the New Labour Government spent £500 billion on a bailout of the financial system and nationalised some of Britain's biggest financial institutions at a cost of £850 billion. It spent a further £200 billion in 2008 and 2009 on an economic stimulus package designed to mitigate the Great Recession. Although such action helped prevent economic calamity, it resulted in a marked deterioration of public finances. Sensing an opportunity to restore the neoliberal order after the New Labour Government's brief flirtation with Keynesianism, in April 2009 the Conservative Party argued that Britain was 'living beyond its means' and insisted that restoring the public finances would require significant public spending cuts and an 'age of austerity'.[5]

The Conservatives successfully transformed the discursive and ideological terrain; the three main political parties contested the 2010 General Election pledging to eliminate the budget deficit and reduce the level of national public debt. The Conservative-Liberal Democrat Coalition Government, formed in May 2010, introduced substantial public spending cuts and a programme of privatization with the support of the corporate sector and a network of right-wing pressure groups and think tanks. Having initially opposed such measures, from June 2011 the Labour Party embraced much of the Coalition Government's agenda in the form of its policy of 'austerity-lite'.[6] Some opposition appeared during this period, however. Certain political parties rejected austerity, while left-wing pressure groups, think tanks, and the student and trade union movements helped to organise demonstrations, engaged in strike action and promoted alternatives to public spending cuts (see Table 13.1).

| Supporters of Austerity | Opponents of Austerity |
|---|---|
| 1. Conservative Party<br>2. Labour Party (until 2015)<br>3. Liberal Democrats<br>4. United Kingdom Independence Party<br>5. Corporate sector (e.g. British Chambers of Commerce; Confederation of British Industry; Federation of Small Businesses; Institute of Directors)<br>6. British State (e.g. Treasury)<br>7. Right-wing think tanks (e.g. Adam Smith Institute, Institute of Economic Affairs)<br>8. Right-wing pressure groups (e.g., Taxpayers' Alliance) | 9. Green Party<br>10. Plaid Cymru<br>11. Scottish National Party<br>12. Trades Union Congress and wider trade union movement<br>13. Left-wing think tanks (e.g. Institute for Public Policy Research)<br>14. Left-wing pressure groups (e.g. People's Assembly Against Austerity, UK Uncut) |

**Table 13.1:** Position of Key Economic and Political Organizations on Austerity.

Nevertheless, the twin objectives of tackling the budget deficit and reducing the level of national public debt, via swingeing public spending cuts rather than substantial revenue-raising, became the 'new normal' in a classic example of what Naomi Klein termed the 'shock doctrine'.[7] In short, Britain's economic and political elite, having utilised taxpayers' money to rescue the financial system and stimulate the economy, cynically embraced austerity in yet another attempt to reconfigure the state to further their commercial interests and boost their political power.

### 13.3 Mass Media Coverage in Britain

#### 13.3.1 Newspaper Coverage

One of the most important aspects of any media analysis is to establish who gets to speak. In other words, which individuals and organizations constitute the primary sources of news and information used by editors and journalists when they construct their articles? These primary sources, which are often viewed as credible, have the power to set the agenda and to frame the parameters of debate. The primary sources used in the *Guardian/Observer* and *Telegraph* articles between 2008 and 2010 are shown in Table 13.2.

The *Guardian/Observer* and *Telegraph* articles exhibited similar sourcing patterns. Members of the New Labour and Coalition governments, their official oppositions and their spokespeople constituted the primary source in 28% of *Guardian/Observer* articles and 22% of *Telegraph* articles. Other prominent sources included corporations (14.4 and 30% respectively); the financial sector (5.2 and 12% respectively); and the Bank of England and other financial regulators (3.2 and 5.4% respectively). By contrast,

| Primary Source | Guardian/Observer Number of articles (% of all Guardian/Observer articles) | Daily/Sunday Telegraph Number of articles (% of all Telegraph articles) |
|---|---|---|
| Corporate representative | 86 (14.4%) | 228 (30) |
| Foreign government representative | 50 (8.4) | 94 (9.5) |
| Prime Minister | 34 (5.7) | 73 (7.4) |
| Government Department spokesperson | 64 (10.7) | 70 (7) |
| British bank representative | 12 (2) | 63 (6.3) |
| Foreign bank representative | 18 (3) | 52 (5.2) |
| Bank of England | 16 (2.7) | 41 (4.1) |
| Cabinet Minister/spokesperson | 32 (5.4) | 30 (3) |
| Chancellor of the Exchequer | 17 (2.9) | 28 (2.8) |
| Economist | 10 (1.7) | 27 (2.7) |
| Non-governmental organization (NGO) representative | 17 (2.9) | 22 (2.2) |
| Conservative politician | 11 (1.8) | 19 (1.9) |
| European Union representative | 3 (0.5) | 17 (1.7) |
| Former politicians | 9 (1.5) | 17 (1.7) |
| Scottish and Welsh politicians | 4 (0.7) | 17 (1.7) |
| Public sector representative | 21 (3.5) | 16 (1.6) |
| Celebrity | 8 (1.3) | 15 (1.5) |
| Member of the public | 23 (3.9) | 14 (1.4) |
| Financial regulator | 3 (0.5) | 13 (1.3) |
| International Monetary Fund representative | 14 (2.3) | 13 (1.3) |
| Leader of the Opposition | 7 (1.2) | 12 (1.2) |
| Media organization | 12 (2) | 10 (1) |
| Transnational organization | 4 (0.7) | 10 (1) |
| Trade union representative | 13 (2.2) | 8 (0.8) |
| Think tank representative | 5 (0.8) | 7 (0.7) |
| European Central Bank | 2 (0.3) | 7 (0.7) |

**Table 13.2:** Primary Sources Used in Coverage of 2008 Financial Crisis, the Great Recession and Austerity in the *Guardian/Observer* and the *Daily/Sunday Telegraph* (2008-2010).

| Primary Source | Guardian/Observer  Number of articles (% of all Guardian/Observer articles) | Daily/Sunday Telegraph  Number of articles (% of all Telegraph articles) |
|---|---|---|
| Charity representative | 12 (2) | 6 (0.6) |
| Banking sector lobbyist | 1 (0.2) | 5 (0.5) |
| Shadow Chancellor/Minister/Spokesperson | 8 (1.3) | 4 (0.4) |
| Labour politician | 7 (1.2) | 4 (0.4) |
| Academic | 20 (3.4) | 4 (0.4) |
| Liberal Democrat politician | 2 (0.3) | 2 (0.2) |
| Religious leader | 2 (0.3) | 2 (0.2) |
| Royal Family | 1 (0.2) | 2 (0.2) |
| Deputy Prime Minister | 5 (0.8) | 1 (0.1) |
| Green politician | 0 | 1 (0.1) |
| Organization for Economic Cooperation and Development representative | 1 (0.2) | 1 (0.1) |
| World Bank representative | 2 (0.3) | 0 |
| Anti-cuts activists | 5 (0.8) | 0 |

**Table 13.2:** Continued.

members of the public constituted the primary source in only 3.9% of *Guardian/Observer* articles and 1.4% of *Telegraph* articles. Other relatively neglected sources included the public sector (3.5 and 1.6% respectively); trade unions (2.2 and 0.8% respectively); and anti-cuts activists (0.8 and 0% respectively). Put simply, the corporate elite and their political allies who caused the 2008 financial crisis and the subsequent Great Recession, and who systematically profited from these events, were dominant in terms of sourcing. Meanwhile, the voices of the victims of austerity (i.e. members of the public and public sector), or those arguing for alternatives (i.e. anti-cuts activists and trade unions), were marginalised. Some notable sourcing differences, however, appeared. The *Telegraph* articles were twice as likely to prioritise the voices of corporations and the financial sector, while the *Guardian/Observer* articles were twice as likely to feature oppositional voices (i.e. members of the public, the public sector and trade unions) – albeit in a small number of cases.

The main issues discussed in the *Guardian/Observer* and *Telegraph* articles between 2008 and 2010 are set out in Table 13.3.

| Main Issue | Guardian/Observer<br>Number of articles<br>(% of all Guardian/<br>Observer articles)<br>Number of words in sum | Daily/Sunday Telegraph<br>Number of articles<br>(% of all Telegraph<br>articles)<br>Number of words in sum |
|---|---|---|
| Trade (impact of crisis/cuts/recession on) | 72 articles (12.1%)<br>42,726 words | 153 (15.4)<br>63,214 |
| Stocks and shares (impact on) | 19 (3.2)<br>9,956 | 101 (10.2)<br>59,622 |
| Bailout (details of) | 37 (6.2)<br>21,901 | 98 (9.9)<br>62,252 |
| Party politics (influence of/impact on) | 52 (8.7)<br>38,188 | 82 (8.3)<br>47,330 |
| Spending cuts (Government Departments) | 56 (9.4)<br>8,958 | 61 (6.1)<br>25,141 |
| Human cost (of crisis/cuts/recession) | 66 (11)<br>43,967 | 54 (5.4)<br>29,037 |
| Interest rates/inflation (impact on) | 7 (1.2)<br>3,742 | 46 (4.6)<br>17,810 |
| Financial system (failure of) | 13 (2.2)<br>7,079 | 44 (4.4)<br>23,740 |
| Property market (impact on) | 5 (0.8)<br>2,196 | 34 (3.4)<br>16,989 |
| Failing banks | 7 (1.2)<br>4,025 | 27 (2.7)<br>15,631 |
| Private sector redundancies | 18 (3)<br>7,335 | 23 (2.3)<br>6,053 |
| Financial cost (of bailout/cuts/recession) | 11 (1.8)<br>5,379 | 23 (2.3)<br>11,353 |
| Employment (impact on) | 15 (2.5)<br>8.025 | 19 (1.9)<br>7,988 |
| Taxes (changes to) | 8 (1.4)<br>4,141 | 17 (1.7)<br>8,710 |
| Regulators (failure of) | 4 (0.7)<br>3,308 | 17 (1.7)<br>11,349 |
| Eurozone (impact of/on) | 3 (0.5)<br>2,620 | 14 (1.4)<br>11,145 |

**Table 13.3:** Main Issues Discussed in Coverage of the 2008 Financial Crisis, the Great Recession and Austerity in the *Guardian/Observer* and the *Daily/Sunday Telegraph* (2008-2010).

| Main Issue | Guardian/Observer — Number of articles (% of all Guardian/Observer articles) Number of words in sum | Daily/Sunday Telegraph — Number of articles (% of all Telegraph articles) Number of words in sum |
| --- | --- | --- |
| Government spending (impact on) | 18 (3) 8,958 | 11 (1.1) 6,991 |
| Activist state (return of) | 4 (0.7) 2,886 | 11 (1.1) 8,372 |
| International relations (impact on) | 9 (1.5) 7,793 | 11 (1.1) 5,096 |
| Profligate public spending (as cause) | 11 (1.8) 6,576 | 10 (1) 3,745 |
| Demonstrations/protests (against austerity) | 55 (9.2) 30,441 | 9 (0.9) 4,613 |
| Systemic causes (of economic crisis) | 8 (1.3) 5,821 | 9 (0.9) 6,546 |
| Government-backed guarantee schemes | 1 (0.2) 658 | 9 (0.9) 3,744 |
| Public sector redundancies | 8 (1.3) 3,829 | 9 (0.9) 3,373 |
| Welfare benefit cuts | 16 (2.7) 7,014 | 8 (0.8) 5,112 |
| Greedy bankers (as cause of economic crisis) | 2 (0.3) 700 | 8 (0.8) 3,494 |
| Individuals responsible (for economic crisis) | 2 (0.3) 1,219 | 7 (0.7) 4,470 |
| Neoliberalism (claimed demise of) | 1 (0.2) 435 | 7 (0.7) 5,242 |
| Public sector pay cuts | 10 (1.6) 4,633 | 7 (0.7) 2,314 |
| Green policies (impact on) | 6 (1) 4,393 | 6 (0.6) 2,744 |
| Regulatory changes (claimed need for/proposed) | 1 (0.2) 657 | 6 (0.6) 2,410 |
| Tax rises (in general) | 4 (0.7) 2,344 | 6 (0.6) 2,176 |
| Other failing financial institutions (i.e. other than banks) | 1 (0.2) 1,757 | 6 (0.6) 2,435 |

**Table 13.3:** Continued.

| Main Issue | Guardian/Observer | Daily/Sunday Telegraph |
|---|---|---|
| | Number of articles (% of all Guardian/Observer articles) Number of words in sum | Number of articles (% of all Telegraph articles) Number of words in sum |
| Government social programmes (impact on e.g. Sure Start) | 7 (1.2) 3,863 | 6 (0.6) 2,435 |
| Strike action | 1 (0.2) 272 | 5 (0.5) 1,135 |
| Education system (impact on) | 11 (1.8) 9,051 | 5 (0.5) 1,628 |
| Arrests/criminal charges (lack of) | 0 | 3 (0.3) 1,526 |
| Nationalization of banks | 1 (0.2) 600 | 3 (0.3) 2,190 |
| Economic models/theories (failure of) | 0 | 2 (0.2) 1,175 |
| Increased taxes on the rich | 1 (0.2) 717 | 2 (0.2) 684 |
| Pension system reforms (e.g. closure of final salary schemes) | 2 (0.3) 483 | 2 (0.2) 1,408 |
| Local government spending cuts | 3 (0.5) 1,045 | 2 (0.2) 413 |
| Misunderstanding of financial risk | 0 | 2 (0.2) 2,296 |
| Tackling tax avoidance and tax evasion | 1 (0.2) 412 | 1 (0.1) 803 |
| Quantitative Easing | 2 (0.3) 2,027 | 1 (0.1) 799 |
| Housing Benefit cuts | 6 (1) 2,937 | 1 (0.1) 411 |
| Reduced working hours/rise of part-time working | 1 (0.2) 631 | 1 (0.1) 268 |
| Credit rating agencies (complicity of) | 0 | 1 (0.1) 283 |
| Sub-prime housing market (as cause of economic crisis) | 2 (0.3) 1,427 | 1 (0.1) 819 |
| Abolition of quangos | 2 (0.3) 1,004 | 1 (0.1) |

**Table 13.3:** Continued.

| Main Issue | Guardian/Observer | Daily/Sunday Telegraph |
|---|---|---|
| | Number of articles (% of all Guardian/Observer articles) Number of words in sum | Number of articles (% of all Telegraph articles) Number of words in sum |
| Big Society | 3 (0.5) 2,865 | 0 |
| End of inflation-indexed welfare benefits | 2 (0.3) 2,089 | 0 |
| Privatization of public services | 1 (0.2) 1,046 | 0 |
| Wealth tax | 0 | 0 |
| Land tax | 0 | 0 |
| Tax on bankers' bonuses | 0 | 0 |
| Tax on financial institutions | 0 | 0 |

**Table 13.3:** Continued.

Both the *Guardian/Observer* and *Telegraph* articles downplayed the causes of the 2008 financial crisis and the Great Recession. Only 4.5% of *Guardian/Observer* articles and 5% of *Telegraph* articles explored the role of greedy and reckless bankers; the complicity of the credit rating agencies; sub-prime mortgages; flawed economic models; 'high public spending'; regulatory failure; and systemic factors (i.e. capitalism). Significantly, the demonstrably false charge of 'profligacy' by the New Labour Government was twice as likely to be cited in the *Guardian/Observer* articles, while only the *Telegraph* articles attended to the lack of criminal prosecutions against bankers, politicians, and/or regulators. A significant number of *Guardian/Observer* and *Telegraph* articles detailed the bailout of the financial system and stressed the consequences of this for the public finances (8% and 12.2% respectively). Only 0.3% of *Guardian/Observer* articles and 0.3% of *Telegraph* articles, however, mentioned higher taxes levied on the rich and the efforts to tackle tax avoidance and tax evasion by corporations and wealthy individuals. Moreover, no consideration was given to the various ways in which substantial revenues might have been generated, as alternatives to spending cuts, in either the *Guardian/Observer* or the *Telegraph* articles. Attention to radical measures such as a banker bonus tax, a financial transactions tax, a land tax and a wealth tax[8] – which could have helped to avoid austerity and a prolonged recession – were conspicuously absent.

Some notable thematic differences, however, emerged. The *Guardian/Observer* articles focused more on the human and social impact of the Great Recession and austerity while the *Telegraph* articles tended to concentrate on the macroeconomic aspects of the 2008 financial crisis and the Great Recession. More specifically, and manifest in both the number of articles and the volume of text on these issues, 40.1% of *Guardian/Observer* articles, but only 21% of *Telegraph* articles, discussed the loss of public services, public sector pay cuts and pension changes, public and private sector redundancies, and welfare benefit cuts. Meanwhile, 33.6% of *Telegraph* articles, but only 17.3% of *Guardian/Observer* articles, assessed the implications for inflation, interest rates, property prices, stocks and shares, and trade. Furthermore, there were proportionately ten times as many articles in the *Guardian/Observer* about the protests against austerity.

Key discourses constructed in the *Guardian/Observer* and *Telegraph* articles between 2008 and 2010 appear in Table 13.4.

| **Key Discourse** | ***Guardian/Observer*** Number of articles (% of all *Guardian/Observer* articles) | ***Daily/Sunday Telegraph*** Number of articles (% of all *Telegraph* articles) |
|---|---|---|
| Economic crisis inherited from actions of Labour Government | 9 (1.5%) | 53 (5.3) |
| Public spending cuts necessary/unavoidable | 10 (1.7) | 22 (2.2) |
| Inaction will lead to financial ruin | 5 (0.8) | 21 (2.1) |
| Protests against the cuts | 66 (11) | 17 (1.7) |
| Bailout of banks necessary/unavoidable | 6 (1) | 12 (1.2) |
| Strikes against the cuts | 6 (1) | 8 (0.8) |
| Tax rises necessary/unavoidable | 3 (0.5) | 8 (0.8) |
| Public spending cuts risk a double-dip recession | 8 (1.3) | 4 (0.4) |
| Cuts will hurt the poorest most | 36 (6) | 4 (0.4) |
| Cuts are too fast and too deep | 11 (1.8) | 3 (0.3) |
| Cuts made in a way that is fair and progressive | 0 | 2 (0.2) |
| Britain is bankrupt | 1 (0.2) | 2 (0.2) |
| Cuts will affect women more than men | 11 (1.8) | 1 (0.1) |
| Cuts will affect young people more than the general population | 1 (0.2) | 1 (0.1) |

**Table 13.4:** Key Discourses Constructed in Coverage of the 2008 Financial Crisis, the Great Recession and Austerity in the *Guardian/Observer* and the *Daily/Sunday Telegraph* (2008-2010).

Both the *Guardian/Observer* and *Telegraph* articles indulged the elite discourses that the New Labour Government 'crashed the economy' and that public spending cuts were 'necessary' and 'unavoidable' (3.2% and 7.5 % respectively). Notable discursive differences, however, appeared. Reflecting their partisanship, the Coalition Government's discursive claim that the 2008 financial crisis was caused by the New Labour Government was reflected in 5.3% of *Telegraph* articles but only 1.5% of *Guardian/Observer* articles. Paradoxically, given that the *Telegraph* purportedly supports 'free markets', the *Telegraph* featured twice as many articles endorsing the discourse that a state rescue of the financial system was essential to avoid ruin (2.1% compared to 0.8% in the *Guardian/Observer*). Furthermore, the latter were more likely to entertain oppositional discourses than the former. Specifically, 21.3% of *Guardian/Observer* articles, but only 3.7% of *Telegraph* articles, focused on protests against public spending cuts, public sector strikes, risk of a 'double-dip' recession, and the regressive nature of austerity (i.e. that it disproportionately impacts the poorest, women and young people).

Data presented above regarding sourcing, issues, and discourses are similar to findings of other studies.[9]

*Television Coverage*
Details of the 47 programmes on subjects related to the 2008 financial crisis, the Great Recession and austerity broadcast between 2008 and 2015 – highlighting the primary sources – are shown in Table 13.5.

The most quoted sources in these programmes, with 29 appearances, were current or former members of the Coalition and New Labour governments, previous Conservative administrations, and their official oppositions. Other prominent sources included bankers (15 appearances); backbench politicians (13); corporate executives (12); journalists (12); and academics (10). Middle-ranking sources included economists (7); members of the public – excluding participants in the live debates (7); foreign finance ministers (6); right-wing think tanks (6); tax justice campaigners (5); and welfare recipients (5). Relatively neglected sources included religious representatives (4); the Treasury (4); the Bank of England (3); anti-cuts activists (3); the House of Commons Public Accounts Committee (3); left-wing pressure groups (3); right-wing pressure groups (3); the poor (3); left-wing think tanks (3); public sector workers (2); regulators (2); and the super-rich (2). One celebrity appeared, as did a trade unionist. While a direct comparison is not possible, sourcing patterns in these programmes are strikingly similar to those in newsprint; in short, the corporate elite and their political allies dominated while oppositional voices were marginalised.

Categorizing the 47 programmes by their subject matter, 14 focused on how and why the 2008 financial crisis occurred. Others highlighted public spending cuts and the state of the public finances (11 programmes);

| Broadcast Date | Programme | Primary Sources |
|---|---|---|
| March 2008 | BBC 'Super-Rich: The Greed Game' | Philip Beresford (compiler of *Sunday Times* Rich List) |
| January 2009 | BBC 'The City Uncovered' | Various bankers |
| February 2009 | BBC *Panorama* 'Tax Me If You Can' | Tax Justice Network; Treasury |
| March 2009 | Channel 4 *Dispatches* 'How They Squander Our Billions' | House of Commons Public Accounts Committee; Taxpayers' Alliance; various politicians |
| June 2009 | Channel 4 *Dispatches* 'Crash Gordon: The Inside Story of the Financial Crisis' | Gordon Brown (Prime Minister); Alistair Darling (Chancellor); George Osborne (Shadow Chancellor); other politicians; Bank of England; Treasury; bankers; civil servants; economists; foreign finance ministers |
| September 2009 | BBC 'The Love of Money: The Banking Crisis One Year On' | Gordon Brown (Prime Minister); Alistair Darling (Chancellor); Tim Geithner (US Treasury); Alan Greenspan (US Federal Reserve); Mervyn King (Bank of England); Robert Reich (economic advisor to US President Barack Obama); foreign finance ministers |
| September 2009 | BBC *Panorama* 'Banks Behaving Badly?' | Peter Mandelson (Business Secretary); Richard Murphy (offshore tax specialist); Treasury |
| June 2010 | Channel 4 *Dispatches* 'Crash' | Various bankers |
| June 2010 | Channel 4 *Dispatches* 'How to Save £100 Billion – Live' | Andrew Haldenby (Reform); Neil O'Brien (Policy Exchange); Bridget Rosewell (former Treasury advisor); Dr Karol Sikora (Doctors for Reform); Robin Hood Campaign |

**Table 13.5:** Synopses of Television Programmes on the 2008 Financial Crisis, the Great Recession and Austerity (2008-2015).

| Broadcast Date | Programme | Primary Sources |
|---|---|---|
| September 2010 | BBC *Look North* 'Spending Review – The *Look North* Debate' | Public sector workers |
| October 2010 | Channel 4 *Dispatches* 'How the Rich Beat the Taxman' | Danny Alexander (Chief Secretary to the Treasury); Chris Bryant (Shadow Cabinet Minister); David Cameron (Prime Minister); Philip Green (businessperson); Philip Hammond (Secretary of State for Transport); Tax Justice Network |
| November 2010 | Channel 4 'Britain's Trillion Pounds Horror' | Brendan Barber (Trades Union Congress); James Bartholomew (author of *The Welfare State We're In*); Alistair Darling (former Labour Chancellor); Nigel Lawson (former Conservative Chancellor); various politicians |
| March 2011 | BBC *Panorama* 'The Big Squeeze' | Ros Altmann (pensions expert); Nicola Horlick (businessperson); Mick McAteer (Financial Inclusion Centre); members of the public |
| March 2011 | ITV 'Charities in Crisis' | David Cameron (Prime Minister); several Cabinet Ministers; representatives of charities |
| March 2011 | Channel 4 *Dispatches* 'Selling Off Britain – Live Debate' | Antony Beever (historian); Kevin Cahill (author of *Who Owns Britain*); Katie Clarke (Labour politician); Tim Cross (British Army); Edwina Curry (former Conservative minister); Allister Heath (City AM); Afua Hirsch (*Guardian* journalist); Maxwell Hutchinson (architect); Michael Kitson (economist); Jonny Irwin (property developer); Peter Roberts (Drivers' Alliance); Ralph Silva (banker); Zoe Williams (*Guardian* journalist); Quentin Wilson (motoring journalist) |
| October 2011 | BBC 'The Future of Welfare' | Centre for Social Justice; welfare claimants |

**Table 13.5:** Continued.

| Broadcast Date | Programme | Primary Sources |
|---|---|---|
| November 2011 | BBC 'Your Money and How They Spend It' | Ken Clarke (former Conservative minister); Alistair Darling (former Labour chancellor); Alan Johnson (Labour politician); Boris Johnson (London Mayor); Norman Lamont (former Conservative chancellor); David Laws (former Liberal Democrat minister); Nigel Lawson (former Conservative chancellor); Peter Mandelson (former Labour minister); Alex Salmond (Scottish First Minister); Peter Stringfellow (businessperson); Tax Research UK; anti-cuts campaigners; members of the public |
| November 2011 | BBC *Panorama* 'Britain on the Fiddle' | Jim Gee (PKF Littlejohn Forensic and Counter-Fraud Services) |
| November 2011 | BBC 'When Bankers Were Good' | Giles Fraser (former canon of St Paul's Cathedral); Jacob Rothschild (banker); Jonathan Sacks (Chief Rabbi); Adair Turner (Financial Services Authority); Andrew Wilson (historian) |
| November 2011 | BBC *Panorama* 'Who's Getting Rich on Your Money?' | House of Commons Public Accounts Committee; Mark Hellowell (author of report on Private Finance 2); David Metter (chief executive of Innisfree) |
| May 2012 | BBC *Panorama* 'The Truth About Tax' | House of Commons Public Accounts Committee; Revenues and Customs; Treasury |
| July 2012 | BBC *Panorama* 'Britain on the Brink: Back to the 1970s?' | Academics; bankers; members of the public; Joseph Rowntree Foundation; Stewart Lansley (author of *The Cost of Inequality*) |
| October 2012 | Channel 4 *Dispatches* 'Secrets of Your Bosses' Pay' | Various chief executive officers; members of the public; Will Hutton (economist); various politicians |

**Table 13.5:** Continued.

| Broadcast Date | Programme | Primary Sources |
|---|---|---|
| November 2012 | BBC<br>'The Year the Town Hall Shrank' | David Cameron (Prime Minister); local councillors; members of the public |
| November 2012 | BBC<br>*Panorama*<br>'Undercover: How to Dodge Tax' | Corporate service providers |
| March 2013 | ITV<br>*Tonight*<br>'Breadline Britain' | George Osborne (Chancellor); Department for Work and Pensions; Barnado's; Resolution Foundation; poor people |
| May 2013 | BBC<br>*Money Programme*<br>'Bankers' | Andrew Bailey (Bank of England); Gillian Tett (*Financial Times* journalist); Jean-Claude Trichet (European Central Bank); Jonathan Welby (Archbishop of Cantebury); Martin Wheatley (Financial Services Authority); various bankers |
| February 2014 | Channel 5<br>'The Big Benefits Row – Live' | Steve Chalke (Reverend); Terry Christian (broadcaster); Edwina Currie (former Conservative minister); Sam Delaney (journalist); White Dee (star of *Benefits Street*); Katy Hopkins (celebrity); Ken Livingstone (former London Mayor); Jack Monroe (anti-poverty campaigner) |
| February 2014 | Channel 4<br>'Benefits Britain – Live Debate' | John Bird (founder of *Big Issue*); White Dee (star of *Benefits Street*); Douglas Murray (Henry Jackson Society); journalists (Mehdi Hasan and Owen Jones from the *Guardian/Huffington Post* and Allison Pearson from the *Daily Telegraph*); various politicians |
| April 2014 | BBC<br>*Panorama*<br>'Don't Cap my Benefits' | Various politicians; welfare claimants |
| June 2014 | Channel 4<br>*Dispatches*<br>'Breadline Kids' | Members of the public; civil servants; various politicians |

**Table 13.5:** Continued.

| Broadcast Date | Programme | Primary Sources |
|---|---|---|
| October 2014 | Channel 4 *Dispatches* 'Benefit Britain: Universal Credit' | Iain Duncan Smith (Conservative Secretary of State for Work and Pensions); Child Poverty Action Group; welfare claimants |
| November 2014 | Channel 4 'How Rich Are You?' | Ryan Bourne (Institute of Economic Affairs); Owen Jones (*Guardian* journalist); Stewart Lansley (author of *The Cost of Inequality*); Paul Mason (economist); Faiza Shaheen (New Economics Foundation); poor people; wealthy people |
| November 2014 | Channel 4 *Dispatches* 'How the Rich Get Richer' | Iain Duncan Smith (Conservative Secretary of State for Work and Pensions) |
| January 2015 | BBC 'The Super-Rich and Us' | Ha-Joon Chang (economist); David Graeber (anthropologist and author of *Debt*); Chrystia Freeland (author of *Plutocrats*); Thomas Piketty (economist); High Pay Centre; various politicians; wealthy people |
| January 2015 | Channel 4 *Dispatches* 'Low Pay Britain' | Undercover reporters; members of the public; whistleblowers; corporations; employment agencies |

**Table 13.5:** Continued.

inequality and poverty (11); welfare reform (6); tax avoidance and tax evasion (4); and the Private Finance Initiative (1). Two distinct periods are discernible. Between January 2009 and June 2010, *before* the Coalition Government came to power, ten television programmes focused on explaining the 2008 financial crisis and the Great Recession that followed. Encompassing 'The City Uncovered' (BBC), 'Crash Gordon' (Channel 4 *Dispatches*), 'The Love of Money' (BBC), 'Banks Behaving Badly' (BBC *Panorama*) and 'Crash' (Channel 4 *Dispatches*), these broadcasts were highly critical of the financial sector. The causes of the 2008 financial crisis were clearly identified (i.e. de-regulation, financialization, flawed economic models, and risk-taking) as were the culprits (i.e. greedy bankers, inept regulators and complicit politicians) and the consequences (i.e. the state of the public finances). By contrast, only one programme – 'How They Squander Our Billions' (Channel 4 *Dispatches*) – implied that 'high public spending' was responsible for the budget deficit and public debt 'problems'.

From June 2010, *following* the formation of the Coalition Government, a marked shift in the nature of television coverage appeared. Two Channel 4 *Dispatches* live debates, 'How to Save £100 billion' and 'Selling Off Britain', set the tone for explicitly embracing the Coalition Government's austerity and privatization agendas. While the former debate considered some revenue-raising proposals (i.e. a financial transactions tax, user charges, and increasing VAT), the onus was clearly on public spending cuts. Radical proposals, such as levying a wealth tax, were conspicuously absent during both debates. It is significant, however, that despite attempts by the presenters and other contributors to frame the proposed public spending cuts and privatizations as 'necessary' and 'unavoidable', most audience members, plus online participants at home, rejected these options when given the chance to vote.

Three other programmes – 'Britain's Trillion Pound Horror' (Channel 4) and 'Your Money and How They Spend It' (BBC) – enthusiastically endorsed the case for substantial public spending cuts and, thus, bolstered the Coalition Government's austerity discourse. Unlike the ones broadcast in 2008 and 2009, these programmes failed to link the state of the public finances with the costs of the bailout, the stimulus, and the Great Recession. In short, since zero historical context was provided, viewers were led to believe that public finances were 'out of control' due to the 'profligacy' of successive governments. Another five programmes – 'Spending Review' (BBC *Look North*), 'Charities in Crisis' (ITV) and 'When the Town Hall Shrank' (BBC) – considered the impact of public spending cuts on local services. One further programme about the 2008 financial crisis aired during this period. 'When Bankers Were Good' (BBC) contrasted public perceptions in 2011 (i.e. bankers as greedy and reckless) with historical perceptions (i.e. bankers as philanthropists) and questioned whether the financial sector could ever redeem itself.

Of the eleven television programmes focusing on inequality and poverty in Britain, ten were broadcast during the Coalition Government's term in office. 'The Big Squeeze' (BBC *Panorama*); 'Britain on the Brink' (BBC *Panorama*); 'Secrets of Your Bosses' Pay' (Channel 4 *Dispatches*); 'Breadline Britain' (ITV *Tonight*); 'Breadline Kids' (Channel 4 *Dispatches*); 'How Rich Are You?' (Channel 4); 'How the Rich Get Richer' (Channel 4 *Dispatches*); 'The Super-Rich and Us' (BBC); and 'Low Pay Britain' (Channel 4 *Dispatches*) explicitly linked growing inequality and rising poverty in Britain with the 2008 financial crisis, the Great Recession, and austerity. Significantly, 'The Super-Rich and Us' – arguably the most critical and incisive programme during this period – was unique in actively exploring the radical option of levying a wealth tax as an alternative to austerity. The oddity – 'Super-Rich' (BBC) – predated, but presciently foretold, the 2008 financial crisis.

Six programmes covering welfare aired during this period, and all linked debates about reform with either the state of the public finances or austerity. 'The Future of Welfare' (BBC); 'Britain on the Fiddle' (BBC *Panorama*), and two live debates – 'The Big Benefits Row' (Channel 4) and 'Benefits Britain' (Channel 5) – explicitly endorsed the claim that welfare reform was 'necessary' because of the 'crisis' in the public finances. By contrast, 'Don't Cap My Benefits' (BBC *Panorama*) and 'Benefits Britain: Universal Credit' (Channel 4 *Dispatches*) were much more sympathetic to the plight of welfare recipients in the context of the Great Recession and austerity.

The four programmes on tax avoidance and tax evasion – 'Tax Me If You Can' (BBC *Panorama*); 'How the Rich Beat the Taxman' (Channel 4 *Dispatches*); 'The Truth About Tax' (BBC *Panorama*); and 'Undercover: How to Dodge Tax' (BBC *Panorama*) – were highly critical of such activities. The first three explicitly connected losses of tax revenues from corporations and wealthy individuals to the state of public finances; explained that such taxes could offset the need for austerity; and criticised the Coalition Government's discourse that 'we are all in this together'.

One programme – 'Who's Getting Rich on Your Money?' (BBC *Panorama*) – was highly critical of the Private Finance Initiative (PFI). It cast the scheme as providing poor value for money and questioned why the Conservatives, having opposed PFI in opposition, had participated in the Coalition Government's expansion of the scheme. Although not the main subject of the broadcast, 'How They Squander Our Billions' (Channel 4 *Dispatches*) was also highly critical of PFI. Both broadcasts pointed out that, if the Conservatives were so opposed to leaving future generations with large amounts of public debt – the party's main justification for austerity – then why persist with PFI which does just that and which is more costly than state financing alone?

### 13.3.2 A Wealth Tax as a Radical Alternative to Austerity: The Media Response

As noted, zero articles analysed attended to the radical idea of levying a wealth tax as an alternative to austerity. To gain a more accurate picture of newspaper coverage of this issue, a supplementary search of 'wealth tax' in the Nexis and *Financial Times* databases was conducted for the period between 24 September 2008 and 5 December 2010 consecutively. This generated a sample of 113 articles – including news reports, commentary, editorials, and letters – across eleven national dailies (see Table 13.6).

Exposing a clear ideological divide, 20 articles about levying a wealth tax appeared in the *Guardian/Observer* during this period, with 15 positive and 5 negative, while the *Telegraph* featured 12, with 10 negative and 2 positive. In short, this more comprehensive analysis reveals that the wealth tax idea was, indeed, a neglected one. While the positive articles endorsed a wealth tax as an alternative to public spending cuts and a manifestation of social justice, the negative articles included several advising readers how and where they could invest their money and *avoid* wealth taxes. Other articles rejected the wealth tax on principle, portraying it as a form of theft, and attacked Labour and Liberal Democrat politicians for contemplating the idea. From a broader perspective, all of Britain's newspapers except the *Morning Star*, the socialist daily read

|  | Morning Star | Guardian/ Observer | Independent/ Independent on Sunday | Mirror | Daily Express/ Sunday Express | Financial Times | Daily Mail/ Mail on Sunday | Sun | Daily Telegraph/ Sunday Telegraph | Times/Sunday Times |
|---|---|---|---|---|---|---|---|---|---|---|
| Negative about a wealth tax | 0 | 5 | 5 | 0 | 7 | 5 | 7 | 2 | 10 | 17 |
| Positive about a wealth tax | 28 | 15 | 3 | 1 | 1 | 0 | 0 | 0 | 2 | 5 |

**Table 13.6:** Coverage of the Wealth Tax Idea in British Newspapers (2008-2010).

by around 10,000 people, marginalised the wealth tax idea. Nevertheless, it received more attention in the broadsheets (i.e. the *Financial Times, Guardian/Observer, Independent, Telegraph* and *Times*), read by approximately 2.4 million mainly middle class and wealthy people, compared to the tabloids (i.e. the *Mirror* and *Sun*) and mid-market newspapers (i.e. the *Express* and *Mail*) read by approximately 7 million mainly working class people.[10] Furthermore, it received more support in left-liberal newspapers (i.e. the *Guardian/Observer, Independent* and *Mirror*) compared to right-wing ones (i.e. the *Express, Financial Times, Mail, Sun, Telegraph* and *Times*).

As noted, only one programme in the sample attended to the wealth tax proposal. It is worth considering, at this point, how the ostensibly impartial BBC treated the proposal developed by Greg Philo from the Glasgow Media Group. Philo penned an article in *The Guardian* in August 2010 suggesting that a one-off tax of 20% levied on the wealthiest 10% of Britons would raise enough revenue to pay off the national public debt, clear the budget deficit and, thus, obviate the need for austerity. Philo had commissioned YouGov to conduct a survey which found that 74% of respondents – with majorities across all age groups, classes and genders – supported the wealth tax idea. Philo then toured the BBC studios to promote his proposal.[11] The reaction of the presenters and guests is instructive. In short, the wealth tax idea, popular with the public, was treated with barely disguised contempt. The principal strategy adopted by the BBC and the other broadcasters in the sample was simply to ignore the wealth tax idea. When it did receive attention, as in these four BBC shows, the tactic employed seems to have been one of ridicule and dismissal.

### 13.4 Applying the Herman-Chomsky Propaganda Model

The PM advances three hypotheses, identifies five operative filters, and employs a comparative methodological approach.[12]

### 13.4.1 Hypothesis 1: Elite Consensus and Media Compliance

The economic and political elite in Britain actively supported austerity – evident in the manifestos of the three main political parties during the 2010 General Election, the Coalition Government's budget deficit-reduction plan pursued from 2010 and the 'austerity-lite' variant promoted by Labour in opposition from 2011. The elite consensus persisted until the election of Jeremy Corbyn as Labour Party Leader in 2015 on an anti-austerity platform.

Politicians, corporations, and the financial sector (i.e. the economic and political elite) constituted the dominant sources in the sampled coverage of the 2008 financial crisis, the Great Recession, and austerity. Such a privileged position enabled these interests to set the agenda and frame the parameters of debates about these events. The actual causes of the 2008 financial crisis and the Great Recession – the nefarious activities of the financial sector and inherent contradictions of capitalism – received little attention in the sampled media coverage. This clearly suited the economic and political elite who were responsible. Allied to this, there was very little scrutiny of the lack of criminal prosecutions against bankers, politicians and/or regulators in the sampled media coverage. This also suited the economic and political elite who would have been liable. Blaming the New Labour Government's supposed 'profligacy' for the 2008 financial crisis and the Great Recession, plus more general complaints about 'high public spending' in Britain, gained some traction in the sampled coverage. Aided by the near silence of the Labour Party on its handling of the 2008 financial crisis and subsequent economic downturn when in government – more specifically the bailout, the stimulus and the implications these had for the public finances – this discourse served the interests of the economic and political elite in their quest to 'shrink the state'. The budget deficit and level of national public sector debt were portrayed as 'problems', either explicitly or implicitly, in much of the sampled coverage. This helped to reinforce the austerity discourse fashioned by the elite. Attention focused on the expenditure rather than the revenue-raising side of the public finances debate in much of the sampled coverage. For the elite, public spending cuts, which predominantly affect the masses, are clearly preferable to higher taxes and determined efforts to tackle tax avoidance and tax evasion, as these threaten elite wealth. Allied to this in the sampled coverage was little debate about levying a wealth tax. Such a tax would clearly not serve the pecuniary interests of most members of the economic and political elite.

The evidence supports Herman and Chomsky's first hypothesis that an elite consensus will create media compliance. The elite consensus in Britain regarding the appropriate response to the 2008 financial crisis and the Great Recession (i.e. bailout and stimulus), the apportioning of blame for these events (i.e. 'high public spending'), the preferred solution (i.e. austerity), and the unacceptability of alternatives (e.g. the wealth tax idea) was, significantly degree, reflected in the sampled coverage.

The results were far from uniform, however. The *Guardian/Observer* articles included more oppositional voices, issues, and discourses than the *Telegraph* articles. The differences are manifest in the more frequent use of members of the public, the public sector and trade unions as primary sources; greater attention to the human and social impact of the Great Recession and austerity, plus the protests against public spending cuts; and the questioning of the Coalition Government's discursive claims. Similarly, the television programmes entertained a more diverse and challenging set of issues and discourses than the newspaper articles. The differences are manifest in the pre-2010 tendency to blame bankers for the 2008 financial crisis and the Great Recession, and the post-2010 focus on rising inequality and poverty, plus tax avoidance and tax evasion by corporations and wealthy individuals.

Such differences seemingly confirm the author's secondary propositions, but with two important caveats. Firstly, the differences are slight: most *Guardian/Observer* articles and a majority of the programmes reproduced the elite consensus. Secondly, the relative neglect of radical alternatives to austerity (e.g. the wealth tax idea) by the *Guardian/Observer* and public service broadcasters, such as the BBC, bolsters the argument advanced by Chomsky and others about the role of left-liberal media.[13] By marginalizing certain issues and policy options, and/or treating them with contempt, the left-liberal media serve a dual purpose: they establish and defend the boundaries of thinkable thought and, thus, reinforce the status quo. By ignoring and/or ridiculing the wealth tax idea, the *Guardian/Observer* and the BBC helped cast it 'beyond the pale' as 'unthinkable'. By giving the idea at least some attention, however, they also reinforced the 'necessary illusion' of a lively media debate about the issue. Furthermore, by concentrating on the expenditure rather than the revenue-raising side of the public finances debate – albeit with more sympathetic coverage of the human and social impact of spending cuts – the *Guardian/Observer* and the BBC contributed to the misimpression that 'there is no alternative' to austerity. In the supposed absence of 'viable' sources of revenue, the discursive claims of the elite became 'common sense' and the debate logically shifted focused on where, when, and how the 'necessary' and 'unavoidable' public spending cuts should be executed (e.g. Labour's 'austerity-lite', the Channel 4 live studio debates, etc.).

### 13.4.2 Hypothesis 2: The Five Filters

The first filter identified by Herman and Chomsky is the *size, ownership and profit orientation of the mass media* and the associated contention that bias derives, partly, from ownership. Media ownership in Britain, like in the US, has long been highly concentrated.[14] In 2015, eight companies owned Britain's national newspapers with a readership of approximately 63 million people. The Telegraph Media Group owns the *Daily* and *Sunday Telegraph*. These same companies also monopolised the online news market. Five companies controlled 75% of Britain's regional and local newspapers. Five companies dominated cable and television broadcasting, with Viacom International owning Channel 5, while two companies enjoyed a 40% share of the radio market. Many of these companies are interlocked (i.e. common directorships and stock holdings) and own shares in non-media companies. Others, such as News Corp UK, are foreign-owned.[15] The Scott Trust oversees the Guardian Media Group that publishes *The Guardian* and the *Observer*. Lauded for pioneering a 'unique form of media ownership', the Scott Trust claims that 'editorial interests' at the *Guardian* and *Observer*, unlike other newspapers, 'remain free of commercial pressures' because 'profits are reinvested in journalism and do not benefit a proprietor or shareholders'.[16] Nevertheless, these newspapers operate on a commercial basis (i.e. the advertising-based business model), while the Guardian Media Group is 'thoroughly embedded within corporate networks and depends on corporate advertisers for 75% of its revenues'.[17] The state-owned BBC is subject to non-commercial forms of control. The government appoints the BBC board of governors and the director general, while the license fee regime, which is reviewed every ten years, grants the government a considerable amount of leverage as renewal is usually preceded by lively debates about bias and value for money, plus complaints of market dominance. The BBC is also subject to commercial pressures. Since the 1980s, successive governments have encouraged the marketization of both the BBC's structure and activities. Meanwhile, the state-owned Channel 4, which operates on a commercial basis, is frequently threatened with privatization. In short, although not privately owned, these media are subject to the corporate ethos, plus, in the case of the BBC and Channel 4, direct state power.[18]

The owners and managers of the media companies in Britain, in common with the corporate sector more generally, had an obvious commercial interest in the state rescue of the financial system (i.e. the bailout) and the prevention of a Great Depression-style recession (i.e. the stimulus). Put simply, their continued profitability depended on such state intervention. As an example, in December 2008 the Confederation of British Industry (CBI) – with a membership that includes media companies such as the BT Group – urged the New Labour Government to follow the US lead and bail out Britain's car industry.[19] Furthermore, there was a clear commercial and ideological rationale for supporting the austerity-driven reconfiguration of the state. Commercially, a smaller public sector potentially means a bigger private sector and more profit-making opportunities for non-media companies partly-owned by the media companies. Ideologically, it was not in the interests of the media companies, nor the corporate sector more generally, to accept the *permanent* return of an activist state which, under a progressive administration, might boost the regulation of the media industry and/or levy higher taxes on businesses and their owners. The logical choice was to resurrect neoliberalism via austerity. As an example, the chief executive of News Corp, Rupert Murdoch, delivered a lecture in October 2010 honouring the late Conservative Prime Minister, Margaret Thatcher, in which he endorsed the Coalition Government's budget deficit-reduction plan. Furthermore, acknowledging that 'the financial crisis was a shock to the system', Murdoch insisted that, 'while the effects linger, it must not be used as an excuse by governments to roll back economic freedom'.[20]

The second filter identified by Herman and Chomsky is the *advertising license to do business*. Endorsing the historical observation that advertisers 'acquired a de facto licensing authority since, without their support, newspapers cease to be economically viable',[21] they claimed that the preferences of advertisers constitute another source of bias, in three senses. Firstly, advertisers discriminate against working class media on commercial grounds. Secondly, advertisers shun left-wing media on ideological grounds, and thirdly, advertisers prefer those media forms that do not interfere with the 'buying mood'.

The 2008 financial crisis and the risk of a Great Depression-style recession clearly imperilled the 'buying mood' as well as the continued profitability of the advertising industry. Advertisers, thus, joined the corporate sector more generally in welcoming the state's efforts to avoid economic calamity. As an example, the chief executive of the British-based multinational advertising agency WPP, Martin Sorrell, commenting in April 2009 on the state of the British advertising market, expressed the hope that 'the fiscal stimulus we have seen in this country must have some effect'.[22] Furthermore, advertisers supported austerity. With the government spending nearly £208 million on advertising in 2009, making it the biggest player,[23] sections of the advertising industry obviously suffered following the implementation of government department, and other, public spending cuts. The opportunity to transform the state and the economy, however, eclipsed such financial losses. Sorrell, for example, backed the Coalition Government and its austerity agenda: 'the Coalition Government's economic policy has a lot going for it' because 'they have done the tough stuff and they are dealing with the deficit.' Indeed, 'for the first time in a long time you can feel bullish about the UK in the medium term'.[24] Furthermore, having published a report in 2013 claiming that the advertising industry contributed £100 billion a year to the British economy, the Advertising Association called for 'government and regulators to get out of the way'. Seeking to exploit the Coalition Government's deregulation agenda, Gavin Patterson from BT Group told the annual summit of the Advertising Association in February 2013 that the sector 'needed to be set free from overregulation to make an even greater contribution to economic growth'.[25]

The third filter identified by Herman and Chomsky is the *sourcing of news*. They insisted that the provision of regular and reliable sources of information by governments and corporations draws media into a symbiotic relationship that results in another source of bias. These sources also benefit from the general perception that they are credible and objective.

The sampled coverage of the 2008 financial crisis, the Great Recession, and austerity found that governments and corporations did, indeed, constitute the primary sources of news. Such privileged positions enabled these sources to set the agenda (i.e. the unquestioning acceptance of the need for the bailout in 2008, the stimulus in 2008 and 2009 and, from 2010, austerity). It also enabled these entities to frame the parameters of the debate about public finances (i.e. the 'necessity' of public spending cuts and the 'implausibility' of alternatives on the revenue-raising side such as a wealth tax). A prime example of the importance and role of sourcing is the observed transformation in 2010 of the sampled television coverage. In short, when the government changed from New Labour to the Coalition so did much of the coverage.

The fourth filter identified by Herman and Chomsky is the role of *flak and the enforcers*. They observed that the ability to attack the media for its coverage, and to elicit a change in its behaviour, is a potent weapon and, thus, another source of bias. One particularly effective method is the corporate funding of right-wing monitoring organizations designed to attack the media – such as Accuracy in Media, the Center for Media and Public Affairs, and the Media Institute in the US – which attempt to enforce media compliance with elite interests.

Examples of flak deployed as enforcers appeared as the Coalition Government attempted to ensure media compliance with their preferred reporting of austerity. The BBC has long been a target of the Conservative Party and other right-wing forces for its supposed 'left-liberal bias'.[26] Osborne attacked the BBC in December 2014 for its 'hyperbolic coverage' of the Coalition Government's public spending cuts and future plans to 'shrink the state'. Osborne also took the opportunity to complain about the BBC's earlier reporting of his budget deficit-reduction plan in 2010.[27] Tesco's 2008 libel suit against *The Guardian* over an article critical of the company's tax affairs is another example of the effectiveness of flak. Facing possible bankruptcy from the suit if it lost, *The Guardian* withdrew the article. This sordid affair had a 'chilling effect' on journalists at *The Guardian*, and the media more generally, according to then editor Alan Rusbridger.[28] Tax avoidance and tax evasion by corporations and wealthy individuals are issues of significant public interest. They also deprive Her Majesty's Revenue and Customs of substantial sums of money. The risk of legal action against the media by corporations and the wealthy individuals, however, helps to explain, in part, their reluctance to investigate these issues.

The fifth filter identified by Herman and Chomsky is *anti-communism as a control mechanism*. In an updated edition of *Manufacturing Consent* (2002), Herman and Chomsky acknowledged that the end of the Cold War had weakened the ideology of anti-communism. In its place, they suggested that the ideology of the 'miracle of the market' performs a similar dichotomization function.

Although the Cold War ended decades ago, anti-communism arguably has a residual functional utility for the economic and political elite in Britain – manifest, for example, in the right-wing newspaper coverage of Ed Miliband, and his successor Jeremy Corbyn, as Leader of the Labour Party.[29] The 2008 financial crisis and the Great Recession exposed the fragility of neoliberalism. Britain's elite temporarily abandoned their rhetorical faith in markets and hypocritically advocated a state bailout of the financial system. Furthermore, in a brief flirtation with Keynesianism, they also used the state to stimulate the economy. *Objectively*, such interventions reveal one of the fundamental contradictions of capitalism: that it periodically needs rescuing from itself by the state. *Subjectively*, however, such facts barely registered in the sampled media coverage. Instead, much of the reporting, particularly post-2010, was re-infused with the revitalised neoliberal claim that 'the state is the problem'.

Such evidence supports the second Herman and Chomsky hypothesis that the interplay of key structural forces (i.e. the five filters) shapes media coverage. Furthermore, their political economy analytical framework provides a more sophisticated understanding and explanation of media coverage of austerity than the other studies to date.

## 13.5 Conclusion

The Herman-Chomsky PM challenges the pluralist view of how the media system operates (i.e. the claims that it is independent, features diverse perspectives, serves as a guardian of the public interest and acts as a watchdog on the exercise of power) and provides an alternative analytical framework for understanding and explaining media performance. A truly pluralist media, which reflected and represented the interests of the masses, rather than just the elite, would have educated and warned audiences about the nefarious activities of the financial sector.

Following the 2008 financial crisis, it would have campaigned for prosecutions and an end to banker bonuses. It would have called for the fundamental reform of the financial system so that it served the public good and the needs of the real (i.e. productive) economy. It would have exposed the self-destructive contradictions of capitalism and the hypocrisy of those who preach the virtues of 'free markets' while turning to the state for help when market failures invariably strike. It would demand concerted action to tackle inequality, poverty, unemployment, tax avoidance, and tax evasion. Regarding the public finances debate, it would have informed audiences about the historic and invaluable role of debt in the economy,[30] while defending the public realm and the public services upon which we all rely. It would have emphatically rejected the option of austerity, as regressive and self-defeating, and would have stressed the need to raise additional government revenue (e.g. levying a wealth tax) in any attempt to 'balance the books'. The sampled coverage, however, found little or no evidence of such perspectives.

Instead, coverage largely reflected the interests and outlook of the elite. This is also true of the coverage in the putatively left-wing *Guardian/ Observer* and the regulated broadcasters, with important implications for the debates about the role of the left-liberal media and media regulation. The

PM, with its political economy focus, provides an alternative and arguably more robust analytical framework for understanding and explaining such media performance.

## Notes and Bibliography

[1] See Andrew Mullen and Jeffery Klaehn (2010), 'The Herman-Chomsky Propaganda Model: A Critical Approach to Analysing Mass Media Behaviour', *Sociology Compass*, 4:4, pp.215–229.

[2] See Andrew Mullen (2010), 'Bringing Power Back'. In: The Herman-Chomsky Propaganda Model, 1988–2008' in Jeffery Klaehn (ed.) *The Political Economy of Media and Power*, Oxford, Peter Lang.

[3] See www.glasgowmediagroup.org.

[4] See Richard Seymour (2014), *Against Austerity*, London: Pluto Press.

[5] David Cameron, 'The Age of Austerity', Speech at Conservative Spring Conference, 26 April 2009.

[6] John McDonnell (2013), 'Ed Miliband's austerity-lite is already out of date', *Guardian*, 7 June.

[7] Naomi Klein (2017), *No is Not Enough: Defeating the New Shock Politics*, London, Allen Lane, p.2.

[8] See Prem Sikka (2008), 'Rebalancing the Books', *Guardian*, 24 November; John Harris (2009), 'Introduce a Wealth Tax', *Guardian*, 17 March; Greg Philo (2010), 'Deficit crisis: Let's Really Be in it Together', *Guardian*, 13 August; Prem Sikka (2010), 'The Ultra-Rich Could Solve this Financial Crisis', *Guardian*, 1 December 2010; Kenneth Rogoff (2013), 'The Moral Case for a One-off Wealth Tax is Compelling' *Guardian*, 5 November; Kenneth Scheve and David Stasavage (2016), *Taxing the Rich: A History of Fiscal Fairness in the United States and Europe*, Oxford, Princeton University Press.

[9] See Justin Pritchard (2009), 'United Kingdom: The Politics of Government Survival' in Paul 't Hart and Karen Tindall (eds.), *Framing the Global Economic Downturn: Crisis Rhetoric and the Politics of Recessions*, Canberra, Australian National University E Press, 2009; Mike Berry (2012), 'The *Today* Programme and the Banking Crisis', *Journalism*, 14:2 (2012), pp. 253–270; Steve Schifferes (2012), 'Downloading Disaster: BBC News Online Coverage of the Global Financial Crisis', *Journalism*, 14:2, pp. 228–252; Mike Berry (2015), 'The UK Press and the Deficit Debate', *Sociology*, 50:3, pp. 542–559; Keith Butterick (2015), *Complacency and Collusion: A Critical Introduction to Business and Financial Journalism*, London, Pluto Press; Steve Schifferes and Sophie Knowles (2015), 'The British Media and the 'First Crisis of Globalization' in Steve Schifferes and Richard Roberts (eds.), *The Media and Financial Crises: Comparative and Historical Perspectives*, London, Routledge, 2015; Luke Temple (2015), 'Neo-liberalism, Austerity and the UK Media', Brief No.18, Sheffield: Political Economy Research

Institute, 2015; Mike Berry (2016), 'No Alternative to Austerity: How BBC Broadcast News Reported the Deficit Debate', *Media, Culture and Society*, 38: 6, pp. 844–863.

[10] See Audit Bureau of Circulations figures from December 2008; readership data available via the National Readership Survey (www.nrs.co.uk).

[11] For details of the proposal, the survey results and links to the YouTube clips of these interviews see www.glasgowmediagroup.org/the-wealth-tax.

[12] See Andrew Mullen (2010), 'Twenty Years On: The Second-order Prediction of the Herman-Chomsky Propaganda Model', *Media, Culture and Society*, 32:4, pp. 673–690.

[13] See Chapter 3 of Chomsky's *Necessary Illusions*. Also see David Edwards and David Cromwell (2006), *Guardians of Power: The Myth of the Liberal Media*, London, Pluto Press, 2006; David Edwards and David Cromwell (2009), *Newspeak in the 21st Century*, London, Pluto Press; Tom Mills (2016), *The BBC: Myth of a Public Service*, London, Verso, 2016.

[14] See James Curran and Jean Seaton (1981), *Power Without Responsibility: The Press and Broadcasting in Britain*, London, Fontana.

[15] See Media Reform Coalition (2014), *Media Ownership Reform: A Case for Action*, London, Media Reform Coalition; Media Reform Coalition (2015), *Who Owns the UK Media?* London, Media Reform Coalition.

[16] See http://www.theguardian.com/the-scott-trust/2015/jul/26/the-scott-trust.

[17] David Edwards and David Cromwell (2009), *Newspeak in the 21st Century*, London, Pluto Press, p. 208.

[18] See Alex Doherty (2005), 'Propaganda and the BBC', ZNet, 7 February; Tom Mills (2016), *The BBC: Myth of a Public Service*, London, Verso.

[19] See Angela Balakrishnan (2010), 'CBI urges government to follow US lead with bail-out', *Guardian*, 20 December.

[20] Quoted in Michael Holden (2010), 'Rupert Murdoch Backs Britain's Austerity Measures', Reuters, 21 October.

[21] Curran and Seaton, *Power Without Responsibility*, p.41.

[22] Quoted in 'WPP Chief Upbeat on UK Ad Performance', *Evening Standard*, 28 April 2009.

[23] Cited in James Kirkup (2010), 'Government becomes Britain's biggest advertiser', *Daily Telegraph*, 30 March.

[24] Quoted in Richard Blackden (2010), 'WPP's Sir Martin Sorrell says UK austerity programme is 'the envy of Washington', *Daily Telegraph*, 19 December.

[25] Cited in Noelle McElhatton (2013), 'UK Ad Industry to Government: Set us Free of Red Tape', *AdWeek*, 1 February.

[26] See Tom Mills (2016), *The BBC: Myth of a Public Service*, London, Verso, – Chap 4.

[27] See Tara Conlan (2014), 'BBC Defends 'Hyperbolic Coverage' of Cuts after Chancellor's Criticism', *Guardian*, 4 December.

[28] See Alan Rusbridger (2009), 'A Chill on 'The Guardian', *New York Review of Books*, 15 January.
[29] See Ivor Gaber (2015), 'The "Othering" of "Red Ed"', or how the *Daily Mail* 'Framed' the British Labour Leader', 10 March 2015, British Politics and Policy Blog, London School of Economics and Political Science; Bart Cammaerts et al (2016). *Journalistic Representations of Jeremy Corbyn in the British Press: From Watchdog to Attackdog*, London, London School of Economic and Political Science.
[30] See, for example, David Graeber, *Debt: The First 5,000 Years* (2011), New York, Melville House Publishing.

CHAPTER 14

# Corporate-Market Power and Ideological Domination: The Propaganda Model after 30 Years – Relevance and Further Application

Florian Zollmann

## 14.1 Introduction

The Herman-Chomsky Propaganda Model (henceforth PM) is confirmed by a large body of scholarship.[1] Already thirty years ago, when *Manufacturing Consent: The Political Economy of the Mass Media* was initially published authors of a range of scholarly studies produced findings in agreement with the main predictions of the PM.[2] In spite of that, the PM has been marginalized by Western scholarship.[3] The emergence of the internet and the new digital media environment (henceforth NME) have contributed towards further weakening the cogency of PM and related approaches. The decentralized structure of the NME as well as novel applications such as Web 2.0 allow for multi-dimensional flows of information thus potentially rendering gatekeeping models obsolete. As a consequence, a new wave of claims about novel and nearly unprecedented

---

How to cite this book chapter:
Zollmann, F. 2018. Corporate-Market Power and Ideological Domination: The Propaganda Model after 30 Years – Relevance and Further Application. In: Pedro-Carañana, J., Broudy, D. and Klaehn, J. (eds.). *The Propaganda Model Today: Filtering Perception and Awareness*. Pp. 223–236. London: University of Westminster Press. DOI: https://doi.org/10.16997/book27.n. License: CC-BY-NC-ND 4.0

media freedoms has emerged in academia.[4] The arguments of the so-called internet celebrants, who mirror the postulations of the liberal school of thought in media and Communication Studies, have been somewhat mitigated by scholars who have been pointing to the flaws of what constitutes outright technicism.[5]

Notwithstanding, contemporary scholarship far too often lacks a structural critique of the corporate media system and its continued role as a dominant institution that serves state-corporate elite interests. In fact, much contemporary scholarship is concerned with applied research based on quantitative research designs at the expense of investigating broader societal issues.[6] This is striking because next to a digital revolution we are currently witnessing an era of almost unprecedented inequality, consolidation of power, militarization, serial Western wars, secret interventions, and retail-terrorist blowbacks as well as nuclear, and climate disasters.[7] McChesney, in fact, argues that society needs 'engaged communication scholarship from a broad range of traditions and employing a diverse set of methodologies to address the issues before us.'[8] A PM approach, which is underpinned by an epistemology aimed at challenging the co-optation of the media by powerful forces in society, should certainly factor well in what we conclude to be significant scholarly debates. Robertson even suggests the PM would still 'be of enormous value as a tool for direct criticism of complicit mainstream media by both elite academics and a much wider population of citizens.'[9]

The aim of this two-part-essay is to further consolidate the relevance and applicability of the PM in the internet age as well as to point to areas that promise its fruitful application. More specifically, part one of the essay will highlight the continued significance of corporate-market constraints as major news 'filters.' Part two will address the issue of ideology, arguing that 'humanitarianism' has become a major reference point to justify Western militarism. The concluding section will outline a set of broad research areas for scholars interested in applying PM.

## 14.2 Corporate-Market Constraints: Still the Engine of Media Deception

The technological architecture of the NME enables one-to-many and many-to-many flows of communication on a hitherto unprecedented scale. The World Wide Web, as a major service of the internet, allows for a multitude of applications that can be utilized in different ways to distribute information. Digitalization has eliminated spectrum scarcity entry barriers so that any individual or organization can set up web-applications to distribute information or otherwise communicate with people on local, national and international levels. With current technology, textual, audial, or visual information can easily be uploaded on a website and instantly be distributed across the globe. Furthermore, mobile phones and cameras accelerate the rapid exchange of information about world events. Hence, during the 1990s and subsequently, a dominant school of thought about the internet emerged that highlighted these virtues of digital technology.[10] Scholars, politicians, journalists, and public experts claimed that the internet would lead towards democratization, media freedom and empowerment potentially enabling a true Habermasian public sphere.[11] But as McChesney has highlighted, much of the scholarship and commentary about the internet had 'a single, deep, and often fatal flaw that severely compromises the value of their work' which constituted their 'ignorance about really existing capitalism and an underappreciation of how capitalism dominates social life.'[12] The so-called internet celebrants have overemphasized the technological potential of the internet, thereby neglecting to interrogate how digital technology had been shaped by economic power.[13]

McChesney's critique echoed important postulations that had been evoked in earlier epochs when shifts in media technology occurred. In 1973, Murdock and Golding cautioned 'against the euphoria which often accompanies discussion of [...] new media technologies.'[14] While speaking to developments in broadcasting, most notably innovations such as cable, cassette and satellite technology, Murdock and Golding pointed to an important fact:

> In each of the media there is an increasingly apparent opposition between the social potentialities for redifferentiation and the trends towards economic concentration. New techniques permitting greater control by the consumer, greater fragmentation and localization, and cheaper production are quickly being enveloped in the same economic structure [...].[15]

Murdock and Golding advanced the political economy perspective of the media suggesting that how media technology may evolve is crucially linked to wider societal structures and processes. Applying this framework, scholars have pointed to the fact that the technological potential of the internet had not been realized at the beginning of the twentieth century.[16] In agreement with the postulation by Murdock and Golding, scholars have highlighted how the evolving internet technology has been shaped by economic structure. Most notably, and despite major technological changes, the institutional environment that constituted the old mass media system has remained intact.[17] Due to the 'privatization' of important web-infrastructure during the 1990s, corporations became the major driving forces of the internet.[18] Furthermore, most internet transactions and applications became regulated via markets that have developed in a highly oligopolistic fashion - a well-known phenomenon in the media industries. Online market concentration was facilitated by network effects because, unlike in traditional media markets, the value of an online application increases relative to the amount of its users.[19] Furthermore, companies created artificial market entry barriers through conglomeration, the setting and patenting of technological standards as well as copyright legislation.[20] Corporate-market control has locked the internet by way of monopoly. Wu summarised the state of the developments as follows: 'There is strong reason to believe that there is nothing new under the sun, that the great universal network is as disposed to monopoly as its predecessors.'[21]

The underbelly of corporate online concentration constitutes advertising, which has effectively honeycombed the internet. Major online markets for social media, search engines, internet access and e-commerce are underwritten by targeted advertising based on surveillance. Since the 'privatization' of the internet, the advertising industry has shaped media policy enabling the use of cookies and other user tracking technology.[22] Today, major online firms including Facebook and Google, the leading companies in terms of users and revenues, use business models that rest on the exploitation of online user data for advertising purposes. Fuchs explained how this system operates with reference to Facebook:

> Surveillance on Facebook is surveillance of prosumers, who dynamically and permanently create and share user-generated content, browse profiles and data, interact with others, join, create, and build communities, and co-create information. The corporate web platform operators and their third-party advertising clients continuously monitor and record personal data and online activities; they store, merge and analyse collected data. This allows them to create detailed user profiles and to know about the personal interests and online behaviour of the users. Facebook sells its prosumers as a commodity to advertising clients. Money is exchanged for the access to user data that allows economic surveillance of the users.[23]

In the same fashion, Google, which has a portfolio of services including online search, e-mail, maps, video (YouTube) and operating systems (Android), amongst others, constitutes 'a vast network for the collection and mining of personal data.'[24] It is estimated that 90 per cent of Google's revenues stem from selling online adverts. Moreover, Google accounts for one third of the spending of global advertising.[25] As Fuchs further commented:

> Google generates and stores data about the usage of these services in order to enable targeted advertising. It sells these data to the advertising clients, who then provide advertisements that are targeted to the activities, searches, contents and interests of the users of Google services.[26]

Next to Google and Facebook, a multitude of other companies engage in similar activities. Turow described these practices as 'one of history's most massive efforts in stealth marketing.'[27] Online advertising, of course, poses serious questions about the nature and implications of surveillance. Furthermore, these developments demonstrate that the internet is geared towards the interests of the corporate and advertising industries. As McChesney observed: 'In most internet areas where profits can be generated, private interests have been able to convert beachheads into monopoly fortresses and generate endless profits. [...] Today, the internet as a social medium and information system is the domain of a handful of colossal firms.'[28]

The issues outlined above directly translate into the applicability of the first and second institutional 'filters' theorized by PM: the media's concentration in ownership size and audience markets as well as advertising dependency.[29] The performance of novel online applications is, thus, likely biased towards the interests that underwrite them. Hence, in 1998, Google founders Larry Page and Sergey Brin cautioned against advertising sponsorship: 'We expect that advertising funded search engines will be inherently biased towards the advertisers and away from the needs of consumers.'[30] Years later, when Google had already started to use advertising, some of its competitors had alleged that Google's searches might weight their results for the benefit of its commercial offerings thus undermining choice.[31] Similarly, at a US Senate hearing in 2011, Senator Herb Kohl asked: 'Is it possible for Google to be both an unbiased search engine and at the same time own a vast portfolio of Web-based products and services?'[32] Much more research is needed to answer questions about how corporate-market power and advertising funding might specifically impact online searches, networking, and other novel web-applications. For scholars utilizing the PM, this significant research gap, in fact, opens up new areas beyond the usually applied studies of news media content. Moreover, this section has so far revealed that the online environment is constrained by corporate power in the same fashion as theorized by PM.

This is similarly true for the realm of news, which has been the primary concern of studies using PM. The internet has not facilitated major changes in terms of corporate news media performance. It is well documented that contemporary off- and online news media sectors are heavily consolidated and commercialized.[33] Digital technology allows for the establishment of novel online offerings. This technically enables the production and distribution of news and could foster diversity in sources and opinions. Yet, at this point in time, a myriad of novel information websites and blogs are confined to niche spaces on the web - virtually invisible to larger publics.[34] In contrast, the traditional news media brands are still the dominant forces in the online world.[35] Markets for online news are heavily concentrated in terms of audiences. A major study by Hindman found that 'online audience concentration equals or exceeds that found in most traditional media.'[36]

It is true that consumption is becoming more fragmented as people increasingly use social media, mobile applications as well as aggregators based on algorithmic content selection to access news. Yet, these trends have not changed the fact that a handful of news brands remain dominant.[37] People may access news via social media and other applications. However, the news content that users actually consume stems from a small set of news brands. Accordingly, the 2016 *Digital News Report* of the Reuters Institute for the Study of Journalism found 'that even in the era of social media and atomised media, news organisations and traditional news brands still matter enormously' and 'most of the content consumed still comes from newspaper groups, broadcasters, or digital born brands that have invested in original content.'[38] While there are some novel, so-called online-only news organisations such as the *Huffington Post* or *Buzz-Feed*, research suggests that the top news brands in terms of audiences are large corporations. For instance, a report by the Media Reform Coalition found that in the UK, five companies accounted for 80 per cent of newspaper consumption including online, mobile readers and offline. In terms of local news, the report found that six giant conglomerates shared 80 per cent of all outlets while more than 50 other publishers allotted the remaining 20 per cent of titles. Similarly, the broadcasting sector in the UK was heavily consolidated with big US companies like Rupert Murdoch's 21st Century Fox empire, Liberty Global and Viacom International encroaching the market.[39] The authors of the report for the Media Reform Coalition drew the following conclusion:

> We believe that concentration within news and information markets in particular has reached endemic levels in the UK and that we urgently need effective remedies. This kind of concentration creates conditions in which wealthy individuals and organisations can amass huge political and economic power and distort the media landscape to suit their interests and personal views. Urgent reform is needed in order both to address high levels of concentration in particular media markets and to protect against further concentration in others.[40]

The current state of the media system thus suggests applicability of the analytical categories of the PM, which place importance on how corporate control and consolidation as well as market pressures determine news choices. As Herman explained, the PM's

> crucial structural factors derive from the fact that the dominant media are firmly embedded in the market system. They are profit-seeking businesses, owned by very wealthy people (or other companies); and they are funded largely by advertisers who are also profit-seeking entities, and who want their advertisements to appear in a supportive selling environment.[41]

Hence, as Herman further pointed out, these structural factors should be seen as 'the only possible root of the systematic patterns of media behaviour and performance.'[42]

Given the preceding outline of validity of the PM's structural foundations, the following section explores the continued relevance of ideology and discusses issues that are important in terms of resultant news media content bias. The chapter concludes by briefly outlining potential topics for further study.

## 14.3 Ideological Domination: Humanitarianism, Atrocities Management and Elite Utility of Suffering

Much scholarship applying the PM has focused on how military adventures, wars, and foreign policy issues have been reported in the news. Ideology has been an important concept in this research area: firstly, ideology has been used to explain why certain events and issues are able to permeate news filtering processes as opposed to others – as outlined by the fifth 'filter' of PM. Secondly, PM researchers have argued that media content patterns tend to be aligned with specific elite interests. As a result, corporate media content is regarded as necessarily ideological. Of course, both issues are connected: ideological assumptions can pass through the news gates if they are congruent with dominant ideology (the fifth 'filter') and consequently manifest as ideological media content. The section below thus further explores the continued relevance of as well as crucial shifts in contemporary ideology.

Traditionally, scholars have been concerned with how 'anti-communism' has served as an important ideological tool to legitimize policies in favour of state-corporate elites.[43] For example, 'anti-communism,' also coined as the ideology of the 'Cold War' or the 'Soviet threat,' was used as a reference point to justify US military interventions after World War II.[44] Since the end of the Cold War in 1991, 'anti-Soviet' ideology has become less important as a schema to legitimise foreign policy adventures.[45] According to Shalom: 'With the collapse of the Soviet threat, US officials have had to work overtime to concoct new alibis to disguise US foreign policy.'[46]

Research has established that governments have employed a range of devices to explain, justify, and rationalise overt and/or covert military interventions in the affairs of sovereign states.[47] Hence, old and new ideological narratives used to justify interventionist foreign policy agendas have been elaborated in the circles of state-corporate power. They include ideologies such as 'free-market democracy,' the 'war on terror,' the 'war on drugs,' 'basic Western benevolence,' and 'humanitarianism.'[48]

In terms of military intervention, 'humanitarianism,' applied as a highly selective interventionist ideology to shame countries unwilling to integrate into the 'Washington Consensus,' has obtained particular prominence since 1991.[49] 'Humanitarianism' played a major role in policy and news media discussions about potential or actual intervention in Somalia (1992), Rwanda (1994), Bosnia (1995), Kosovo (1999), Darfur (2003–2017), Libya (2011), and Syria (2012–2018).[50] 'Humanitarianism' was also evoked, in conjunction with other ideological devices, to legitimise the 2001 invasion of Afghanistan and the 2003 Iraq War.[51] It should be noted that 'humanitarianism' as an ideology can transport valid reasoning about human rights violations and how they should be addressed to alleviate human suffering. On the other hand, PM scholars have been concerned with how 'humanitarianism' has been instrumentalized to serve a narrow militarist agenda whose ultimate goal is not to stop human rights violations but to impose Western designs on other nations. Some examples of this will be further explored below.

An under-researched sub-set of 'humanitarianism' constitutes what this author defines as atrocity-shaming. In his early work on propaganda during World War I, Lasswell found that one goal of propaganda was 'to mobilise hatred against the enemy'.[52] According to Lasswell, this involved representing an oppositional country 'as a menacing, murderous aggressor'.[53] Such propaganda depicted the enemy in contrast to the noble aims of the home state and was used to legitimize the war effort to the public in the home country.[54]

Atrocity-shaming had also been the topic of early work by Chomsky and Herman who looked at how human rights violations conducted by so-called 'enemy' states of the West were designated to the status of nefarious bloodbaths.[55] Nefarious bloodbaths were highlighted in Western policy and human rights circles and consequently received significant news media attention. During the process of atrocity-shaming, designated perpetrator countries faced serious repercussions like criminal proceedings, sanctions, and regime-change interventions.[56] According to Chomsky and Herman, nefarious bloodbaths served 'an extremely important public relations function in mobilizing support for US military intervention'.[57] Chomsky and Herman's research demonstrates how countries have been shamed selectively if this served Western strategic interests. So-called 'allied' states of the West have largely remained exempt from public campaigns of shaming even if they conducted similar or greater human rights violations than 'enemy' states.[58]

Moreover, shaming has led to intervention even in cases when evidence for atrocities was hardly conclusive and the identity of perpetrators far from clear. For instance, NATO used the so-called 1999 Račak massacre in Kosovo as a pretext for intervention in the Former Republic of Yugoslavia, although facts suggested that the dead could have been killed in battle.[59] In fact, during the Yugoslav Wars, fought roughly between 1991–1999, selective atrocity-shaming took place in a range of theatres. Studies suggest that the Western news media, policy and human rights systems have mainly focused on Serbian villainy when assessing these conflicts.[60] Thus, atrocities conducted by the Serbs against Bosnians, like the Srebrenica massacre, have received significant media attention and were framed as genocide.[61] On the other hand, the major news media have failed to interrogate the preceding violence in the Srebrenica vicinity, conducted by Bosnian paramilitary forces against the Serbs.[62] Similarly, what arguably constituted one of the largest ethnic cleansings during the Yugoslav Wars, the purge of the Serbs of the Krajina (in the Republic of Croatia), has largely been ignored in the West.[63] In these latter cases of violence against the Serbs, the genocide label has not been applied in the West. This dichotomised framing of victims of violence has served Western policy objectives of establishing fragmented and estranged client states in the Balkans. In contrast, a more objective treatment of atrocities committed by all sides in the conflict could arguably have better contributed towards conflict resolution and reconciliation.[64]

Atrocity-shaming as an ideology to demonise an opponent has achieved its peak performance during the 2011 military intervention in Libya. The alleged 2011 Benghazi crackdown on protestors in Libya was used as a justification for NATO intervention against the regime of Muammar Gaddafi on the basis of the Responsibility to Protect (R2P) doctrine. It turned out, however, that the Benghazi 'massacre' was manufactured.[65] Careful analysis of the documentary record demonstrates that Gaddafi's forces had not used force indiscriminately against protestors.[66]

Similarly, in the present war in Syria, atrocities have been instrumentalised to justify proxy- and big power intervention.[67] In the Syrian theatre, a range of atrocities has been linked to the Syrian government and its forces. In many of these cases, however, responsibility for crimes could hardly be established because independent verification has not been possible. Furthermore, evidence suggested that the Syrian 'opposition' aimed at inciting foreign intervention by way of manufacturing bloodbaths.[68] Yet, contested atrocities like the Houla, Ghouta, or Khan Sheikhoun incidents have been used to justify regime-change agendas in Syria.[69]

The violence of preceding wars such as in Yugoslavia was evoked as an example to call for preventive 'humanitarian' interventions. But how likely is it that Western military force is going to mitigate violence? In both Libya and Syria, Western intervention has had significant repercussions: Kuperman estimated that, 'NATO intervention magnified the death toll in Libya by about seven to ten times.'[70] Moreover, Libyan society fragmented along sectarian lines. At the same time, public health and security collapsed, sending bursts of refugees towards Europe.[71] In Syria, proxy-intervention sparked high-intensity conflict and prolonged a deadly stalemate between the Syrian Army and 'opposition' forces.[72] Additionally, violent conflict fostered the disintegration of the Syrian nation state. Taken together, intervention in Libya and Syria destabilised the Middle East and fostered the rise of ISIS as well as the massive refugee crisis of 2014/2015.[73] As a PM would predict, these violent repercussions have largely been ignored by the news media in terms of relegating Western responsibility. Yet, the Balkanisation of the Middle East was well in line with US- and EU policy interests of establishing a set of weak and obedient vassal states. 'Humanitarian' ideology was crucial in facilitating these outcomes.[74]

## 14.4 Conclusion

This chapter discusses the continued relevance of PM in terms of three of its news 'filters': corporate-market power, advertising dependency, and ideology. Moreover, the chapter further provides indicative evidence that major conflicts since the end of the Cold War have been reported in the same dichotomous fashion that a PM would predict. Significantly, 'humanitarianism' has been applied as an ideological device during highly selective campaigns of shaming that led to military intervention. This suggests a shift from Cold War to 'humanitarian' ideology. Of course, the presented examples only constitute a first approximation and much more research is needed to solidify the extent to which the PM remains relevant in the internet era. The following list provides some of the research areas that may be utilized for further study:

1. Assessing the impact of corporate-market constraints and advertising funding on the performance of online applications such as online search, networking, news, blogging, etc...
2. Providing a comprehensive empirical overview of PM's 'filters' in relation to traditional as well as online news sectors.
3. Investigating potential changes and refinements to PM's 'filters' under consideration of increased political and interest-group pressure levelled against the free flow of information (e.g. suppression of whistle blowers, campaign against Wikileaks, etc.).
4. Investigating the vast PR and propaganda industries that currently use the internet to disseminate targeted 'information.'
5. Studying off- and online reporting of high- and low-intensity conflicts such as in Libya, Syria, Egypt, Yemen, Ukraine or Bahrain, the refugee crisis, as well as domestic political, economic and social issues in consideration of PM's predictions.

## Notes and Bibliography

[1] For an overview of some of this literature see Florian Zollmann (2009), 'Is It Either or? Professional Ideology Vs. Corporate-Media Constraints,' *Westminster Papers in Communication and Culture*, 6: 97–118. See also Joan Pedro (2011), 'The Propaganda Model in the Early 21st Century Part I and Part II,' *International Journal of Communication*, 5: 1865–1926.

[2] For an overview of some of the early studies that support the PM see Noam Chomsky (1989), *Necessary Illusions: Thought Control in Democratic Societies* (London: Pluto Press), Appendix 1 as well as chapter 1 note 23.

[3] Ibid, 153ff; see also Eric Herring and Piers Robinson (2003), 'Too Polemical or too Critical? Chomsky on the Study of the News Media and US Foreign Policy,' *Review of International Studies* 29: 553–568 and Andrew Mullen (2010), 'Twenty Years On: the Second-Order Prediction of the Herman-Chomsky Propaganda Model,' *Media, Culture & Society* 32(4): 673–690.

[4] For an overview of this debate see Robert W. McChesney (2013), *Digital Disconnect: How Capitalism Is Turning the Internet Against Democracy* New York:, the New Press, 5–8.

[5] See Robert G. Picard (2015), 'The Humanisation of Media? Social Media and the Reformation of Communication,' *Communication Research and*

*Practice* 1: 35. See particularly McChesney, *Digital Disconnect*. McChesney also refers to the so-called internet celebrants mentioned above. For further context see also footnote 13.

[6] See Robert W. McChesney (2007), *Communication Revolution: Critical Junctures and the Future of Media*, New York, The New Press, pp.6–7.

[7] See Florian Zollmann (2015), 'Nineteen Eighty-Four in 2014: Power, Politics and Surveillance in Western Democracies,' in *George Orwell Now!*, ed. Richard Lance Keeble, New York, Peter Lang, pp.31–47.

[8] McChesney, *Communication Revolution*, 7–8.

[9] John W. Robertson (2010), 'The Propaganda Model in 2011: Stronger Yet Still Neglected in UK Higher Education?' *Synaesthesia Communication Across Cultures* 1(2010): 32.

[10] McChesney, *Digital Disconnect*, 12.

[11] See McChesney, Ibid, 5.

[12] McChesney, Ibid, 13.

[13] McChesney uses the term celebrants for this school of thought. McChesney draws from Robin Mansell who initially assessed the internet literature in terms of celebrants and sceptics. See *Digital Disconnect*, 4ff.

[14] Graham Murdock and Peter Golding (1973), 'For a Political Economy of Mass Communications,' *The Socialist Register* 10: 230–231.

[15] Murdock and Golding, 'For a Political Economy,' 230.

[16] See McChesney, *Digital Disconnect*, 4–5. See also Robert G. Picard (2012), 'The Humanisation of Media' and James Curran (2012), 'Reinterpreting the Internet,' in *Misunderstanding the Internet*, James Curran, Natalie Fenton, and Des Freedman (eds.), London, Routledge, pp.3–33.

[17] The material and arguments provided in this section rest on McChesney, *Digital Disconnect*.

[18] Ibid, 104.

[19] Ibid, 132.

[20] Ibid, 132–134.

[21] Tim Wu (2010), *The Master Switch: The Rise and Fall of Information Empires*, London, Atlantic Books, p.18.

[22] See McChesney, *Digital Disconnect*, 146–148.

[23] Christian Fuchs (2014), *Social Media: A Critical Introduction*, London, Sage, p.169.

[24] Michael Wignall (2014), 'Google: What It Is, Why You Should Avoid It and How,' *Ethical Consumer* September/October, 26.

[25] Ibid, 26.

[26] Fuchs, *Social Media*, 131.

[27] Cited in McChesney, *Digital Disconnect*, 149.

[28] Ibid, 131, 137.

[29] See Edward S. Herman and Noam Chomsky (2008), *Manufacturing Consent: The Political Economy of the Mass Media*, 3rd edn. (London: The Bodley Head).

[30] Cited in McChesney, *Digital Disconnect*, 102.

31. Wignall, 'Google,' 26.
32. Ibid, 26.
33. See Florian Zollmann (2015), 'The Relevance of the Herman-Chomsky Propaganda Model in the 21$^{st}$ Century New Media Environment,' in *News from Somewhere: A Reader in Communication & Challenges to Globalization*, Daniel Broudy, Jeffery Klaehn and James Winter (eds.), Eugene, OR, Wayzgoose Press, pp.143–161.
34. See Matthew Hindman (2009), *The Myth of Digital Democracy*, (Princeton, NJ: Princeton University Press).
35. See James Curran (2012), 'Reinterpreting the Internet,' in *Misunderstanding the Internet*, James Curran, Natalie Fenton and Des Freedman eds., London: Routledge, pp.3–33. See also the discussion in Zollmann, 'Relevance of the Herman-Chomsky Propaganda Model.'
36. Hindman, *Myth of Digital Democracy*, 17.
37. For a study suggesting the increasing use of social media and mobile applications to access the news see Nic Newman with Richard Fletcher, David A. L. Levy and Rasmus Kleis Nielsen (2016), *Reuters Institute Digital News Report 2016* (Oxford: University of Oxford).
38. Ibid, 26.
39. For the report and the data outlined above see Media Reform Coalition, *Who Owns the UK Media*, 3, 11. Available online at: http://www.mediareform.org.uk/wp-content/uploads/2015/10/Who_owns_the_UK_media-report_plus_appendix1.pdf (accessed 29 June 2017).
40. Ibid, 3.
41. Edward S. Herman (2000), 'The Propaganda Model: A Retrospective,' *Journalism Studies* 1(1): 102.
42. Ibid, 101.
43. Zollmann, 'Is It Either or?,' 99.
44. See Daniel C. Hallin (1989), *The 'Uncensored War': The Media and Vietnam* (Berkeley and Los Angeles, CA: University of California Press), Stephen Rosskamm Shalom (1993), *Imperial Alibis: Rationalizing Intervention After the Cold War* (Boston, MA: South End Press) and William Blum (2004), *Killing Hope: US Military & CIA Interventions since World War II*, 2nd edn. (London: Zed Books).
45. Robert M. Entman (2004), *Projections of Power: Framing News, Public Opinion, and U.S. Foreign Policy* (Chicago, IL: University of Chicago Press).
46. Shalom, *Imperial Alibis*, 3.
47. Ibid.
48. See Herman, 'The Propaganda Model'; Piers Robinson (2004), 'Researching US Media–State Relations and Twenty-First Century Wars,' in *Reporting War: Journalism in Wartime*, Stuart Allan and Barbie Zelizer eds. (2004), London and New York, Routledge, pp.96–112; Matt Kennard (2015), *The Racket: A Rogue Reporter vs. The Masters of the Universe* (London: Zed Books); Mark Curtis (2003), *Web of Deceit: Britain's Real Role in the World* (London: Vintage)

and Philip Hammond (2007), *Framing Post-Cold War Conflicts: the Media and International Intervention* (Manchester: Manchester University Press).
[49] See Noam Chomsky (2012), *A New Generation Draws the Line: Humanitarian Intervention and the 'Responsibility to Protect' Today* (Boulder, CO: Paradigm Publishers).
[50] See Ibid; Hammond, *Framing Post-Cold War Conflicts*; Philip Hammond and Edward S. Herman eds., (2000) *Degraded Capability: the Media and the Kosovo Crisis* (London: Pluto Press); Edward S. Herman and David Peterson (2007), 'The Dismantling of Yugoslavia,' *Monthly Review*, 59. Available at http://monthlyreview.org/2007/10/01/the-dismantling-of-yugoslavia (Accessed 12 July 2017); Edward S. Herman and David Peterson (2010), *The Politics of Genocide* (New York: Monthly Review Press); Piers Robinson (2000), 'Research Note: the News Media and Intervention: Triggering the Use of Air Power During Humanitarian Crises,' *European Journal of Communication*, 15: 405–414 and Piers Robinson et al. (2010), *Pockets of Resistance: British News Media, War and Theory in the 2003 Invasion of Iraq* (Manchester: Manchester University Press).
[51] See Noam Chomsky (2003), *Hybris: Die Endgültige Sicherung der Globalen Vormachtstellung der USA* (Hamburg: Europa Verlag).
[52] Harold D. Lasswell (1971 [1927]), *Propaganda Technique in World War I* Cambridge, MA., M.I.T. Press, p.195.
[53] Ibid
[54] Ibid.
[55] Noam Chomsky and Edward S. Herman (1979), *The Washington Connection and Third World Fascism: the Political Economy of Human Rights: Volume I*, Nottingham: Spokesman, p.97.
[56] See Florian Zollmann (2017), *Media, Propaganda and the Politics of Intervention* (New York: Peter Lang).
[57] See Chomsky and Herman, *The Washington Connection*, 97.
[58] See Herman and Peterson, *Politics of Genocide* and Zollmann, *Politics of Intervention*.
[59] See Herman and Peterson, *Politics of Genocide*, Michael Mande (2005)l, *Pax Pentagon: wie die USA der Welt den Krieg als Frieden Verkauft* (Frankfurt am Main: Zweitausendeins) and Zollmann, *Politics of Intervention*.
[60] For an overview see Herman and Peterson, 'Dismantling of Yugoslavia.' See also Peter Brock (2005), *Media Cleansing: Dirty Reporting: Journalism and Tragedy in Yugoslavia*, 2nd edn.(Los Angeles, CA: Graphics Management Press).
[61] See Herman and Peterson, *Politics of Genocide*, 47–48.
[62] For the Srebrenica context see Lewis Mackenzie (2005), 'The Real Story Behind Srebrenica,' *The Globe and Mail*, 14 July: Available at: https://www.theglobeandmail.com/opinion/the-real-story-behind-srebrenica/article737584/ (accessed on 12 July 2017).
[63] See Herman and Peterson, *Politics of Genocide*, 81ff.

[64] See Denis Dzidic (2015), 'Distored Remembrance Culture 'Traps Bosnia in Past,"' *Balkan Transitional Justice*, 12 October: Available at: http://www.balkaninsight.com/en/article/distorted-remembrance-culture-traps-bosnia-in-past--10-09-2015 (Accessed 17 July 2017).
[65] Zollmann, *Politics of Intervention*.
[66] See Alan J. Kuperman (2013), 'A Model Humanitarian Intervention? Reassessing NATO's Libya Campaign,' *International Security*, 38: 105–136.
[67] See Zollmann, *Politics of Intervention*.
[68] See Tim Anderson (2016), *The Dirty War on Syria: Washington, Regime Change and Resistance* (Montréal: Global Research Publishers).
[69] For a discussion of some of these cases see Anderson, *Dirty War on Syria*. See also Florian Zollmann (2017), 'Giftgas in Syrien,' *Publik-Forum Extra Leben*, Juni: 30–31.
[70] Kuperman, 'A Model Humanitarian Intervention?', 123.
[71] See Florian Zollmann (2015), 'Tormenting Libya,' *teleSUR*, 6 August: Available at: http://www.telesurtv.net/english/opinion/Tormenting-Libya-20150806-0031.html (Accessed 9 February 2017).
[72] See Diana Johnstone (2016), 'Destroying Syria: A Joint Criminal Enterprise,' *Counterpunch*, 4 October: Available at: http://www.counterpunch.org/2016/10/04/overthrowing-the-syrian-government-a-joint-criminal-enterprise/ (Accessed 9 February 2017).
[73] See Florian Zollmann (2015), 'Refugees and the Crime Against Peace,' *teleSUR*, 25 September. Available at: http://www.telesurtv.net/english/opinion/Refugees-and-the-Crime-Against-Peace-20150913-0024.html (Accessed 9 February 2017).
[74] See Zollmann, *Politics of Intervention*.

CHAPTER 15

# Imperialism and Hegemonic Information in Latin America: The Media Coup in Venezuela vs. the Criminalization of Protest in Mexico

Francisco Sierra Caballero

## 15.1 Introduction

A systematic study and institutional analysis of the current performance of Latin American media groups based on the propaganda model illustrates how the mass media operate as effective transmitters of messages designed on the basis of strategic information manipulation criteria to mold, predict and control the public behaviour of the middle classes and popular sectors towards a colonial and imperialist logic, as evidenced by the recent media coups in the region.

If we take a look at the forms of ideological closure of public discourse and the voices capable of making themselves heard in the media sphere, the data reveal a steady and ruthless representation of the interests and criteria of the elites in newspaper accounts of vital issues for the countries of the South, which

---

How to cite this book chapter:
Sierra Caballero, F. 2018. Imperialism and Hegemonic Information in Latin America: The Media Coup in Venezuela vs. The Criminalization of Protest in Mexico. In: Pedro-Carañana, J., Broudy, D. and Klaehn, J. (eds.). *The Propaganda Model Today: Filtering Perception and Awareness*. Pp. 237–248. London: University of Westminster Press. DOI: https://doi.org/10.16997/book27.o. License: CC-BY-NC-ND 4.0

for decades have been under the hegemonic control of foreign cultural industries and subject to the imposition of the policy of the free flow of information.[1] Moreover, it has become clear how, after the long neoliberal night, there have been substantial changes in the foundations and problems of the structure of information, as well as in the economic functions of the media and cultural industries, especially regarding the neocolonial role that hegemonic information from the North plays in the contemporary capitalist crisis in which the countries of the subcontinent are currently immersed.

The governments of progress in the region introduced into the public debate observable historical contradictions created by the imbalance in the dominant structure of information against the right of access, popular communication and, of course, the rights of professionals, citizens and civil society as a whole. In the following pages, two illustrative cases of the social logic of journalistic mediation in Latin America are analysed: Venezuela and Mexico. These case studies illustrate the repetition of history as a farce through the systematic contribution of information dependence and the violation of human rights, as has occurred before in US imperial projects such as Operation Condor.

The publication in 1988 of the first edition of Edward S. Herman and Noam Chomsky's book, *Manufacturing Consent: The Political Economy of the Mass Media* coincided in the USA with the end of the 'Reagan era' (1981–1989), a period marked by political conservatism and a foreign policy of interventionism to which nobody remained indifferent, whose influence on Latin America would be decisive in episodes such as the dirty war in Nicaragua. It was in this context that Herman and Chomsky carried out a detailed investigation of the internal workings of the US media industry, its patterns of conduct, the motives behind the production of messages and their social function: the production of consent around a series of values destined to maintain the status quo at the time, both inside and outside the borders of the USA.

To illustrate the relevance of such a theoretical-methodological contribution, we will try to reveal the logic behind, and critical perspectives on, the basis and validity of the propaganda model and its application to recent newsworthy events in the region. The task is none other than to assess theoretical contributions by criticizing news mediation, on the basis of a structural analysis of the study context of the two cases discussed below. The comparative analysis shows that elite interests are strictly defended by mainstream media in both cases, resulting in the systematic support of elite actors who violate human rights combined with aggressive attacks on the social and political forces that are considered enemies.

## 15.2 The Permanent War Against Venezuela

Bearing in mind the distinctive features of the real structure of information in practically all the countries of the region, the state of siege under which the Bolivarian revolution has been placed can be regarded as a revealing example of the validity of the propaganda model for the purposes described here. Since Hugo Chávez became President of Venezuela, the private media, national and international alike, have subjected the country to continual and systematic harassment, thus contributing to the construction of a distorted picture of the democratic processes in the Republic of Venezuela, even to the extreme of justifying the failed coup d'état in 2002.[2]

The North American 'peace operations' have, nonetheless, gone unnoticed by the populace. As a matter of fact, in the public space audiences do not have access to any other type of narrative than the vilification of the revolutionary leaders. To such an extent that the coordination and lobbying activities of those representing the hegemonic geopolitical interests remain hidden from the public eye, by deliberate omission on the part of the mainstream media, while they contribute, without constraints, to control and repress the emergence of popular protest movements, if not to destabilize expressly unfavorable or unreliable governments, as is the case of the so-called 'unrestricted warfare' waged by the Pentagon against Venezuela.

Thus, the self-styled 'independent media' such as *El País* implemented an information policy to legitimize the planned coup and the destabilizing pro-insurgency captained from Washington by expert conspirators like Otto Reich, a former collaborator of Ronald Reagan and a leading expert in counter-insurgency and low-intensity operations such as those orchestrated in Central America against Nicaragua. The in-depth study of Fernando Casado illustrates analytically to what extent this process of psychological war relies on the committed work of the so-called 'anti-journalists.' A hundred qualitative interviews with Spanish-speaking journalists, both European and Latin American, from leading newspapers including *Clarín* (Argentina), *El Tiempo* (Colombia), *El País* (Spain) and *El Comercio* (Ecuador), revealed the existence of a deliberate propaganda campaign launched by the major media corporations against the Chávez government as part of a covert operation to counter the revolutionary process. In this coverage, several techniques have been employed to step up the media siege and propaganda war in which the country is currently immersed:

1. *The caricaturing of Presidents Chávez and Maduro.* The sensationalist representation of both heads of state has tended to waver between the ridiculous and the grotesque, both being criminalized by their antagonists, according to the Nixon hypothesis, as 'dangerous, mad criminals.' Be that as it may, at any rate it is possible to confirm a hugely negative and distorted portrayal of both presidents in the national and international media, which has gradually permeated public opinion to such a degree as to justify a possible intervention in 'defence of democracy.'

2. *Disinformation and psychological warfare.* The production of false news, from non-existent conflicts on the Colombian border, to putative shortage crises, through set-ups involving cases of corruption and ties with drug

trafficking, has aimed to destabilize the Bolivarian government and isolate it on the international stage. In short, 'information about Venezuela is usually spectacular and sensationalist; anecdotes turn into the focus of the news; important political figures as President Chávez are trivialized, emphasizing witty remarks rather than significant decisions which have benefited millions of people'.[3]

3. *Campaigns against the lack of freedom of expression and democracy.* The opposition and the international press have promoted continuous propaganda campaigns, describing the Chávez government as a dictatorship because of the purported absence of liberties, a term that has been repeatedly dismissed by the Carter Foundation, the Organization of American States (OAS) itself, the Union of South American Nations (UNASUR) and the European Union (EU), among other multilateral agencies.

4. *The spreading of rumors and the dearth of news on social networks.* Together with the clichés and the distorted picture of the country due to the continuous disinformation in the mainstream media, social networks have been used to reinforce this prevailing image by circulating all kinds of canards about the leaders of the Venezuelan government or their allies, even, as has occurred during the elections in Spain, to invoke the alleged danger of a Venezuelan-type drift in other countries whose progressive parties aspire to government.

5. *The bias and imbalance in the sources and the use of ideologically focused language on a lexicological and semantic level.* Furthermore, news about the country has been continually manipulated as regards the use of sources and semiotic operations, repeatedly employed with the clear purpose of propaganda. Thus, for example, the mainstream international media only cite sources reflecting the stance of the USA and its opposition allies, without giving voice to the Venezuelan government, except to reinforce a priori the bias in news coverage or to ridicule its representatives in a conspicuous fashion. By the same token, when reference is made to the democratically elected government of the country it is regularly referred to as a regime, which conjures up images of authoritarian systems such as that of the ex-USSR in the eyes of public opinion. This bias is applied across the board to North Korea, Ecuador, Nicaragua and Bolivia, and functions, in tandem with other semiotic strategies, to construct a view contrary to the revolutionary process.

Consequently, the media war against Venezuela 'is translated into a continuous deformation and manipulation of information, produced serving destabilizing agendas against Bolivarian Revolution', which systematically violates the right of readers and audience to receive truthful information'.[4]

It has always been held that, in war, as in times of peace, the first victim is the truth, but in the case of Venezuela the media have never, now or before, intended to shed light on the murky, coup-mongering web of interests opposing the Bolivarian revolutionary process. What is of real interest in the case, however, is that the major disinformation campaigns orchestrated in favor of covert operations before the coup d'état were not a success, in spite of the fact that they managed to snare many intellectuals, journalists and media companies, who believed the manipulated version of the facts purposefully fabricated by the Cisneros Group and the psychological warfare advisors sent by the USA for that purpose, in their discursive plot and strategy of persuasion.

The situation of the Bolivarian Republic, described by the Pentagon 'as a battle cry of communists and socialists' in the heart of South America, recalls in this sense the plan designed to topple the government of Salvador Allende in 1973: media smear campaigns, rumors and intense disinformation; the mobilization of the elites; unfounded accusations against the person of the President; an army divided; the economic blockade promoted by the employers' association; the flight of capital; an attempted coup; and considerable international pressure. In this respect, the tragic events of September 1973 in Chile should be recalled, because not by chance Charles Shapiro, one of the actors also responsible for operations in Trinidad and Tobago and an advocate of the terror campaigns in Central America (Nicaragua and El Salvador), occupied the post of US Ambassador to Venezuela in order to implement a destabilizing pro-insurgency program against the Bolivarian government.

As in the case of the operation against the Popular Unity (UP) government in Chile, the counter-revolutionary operation in Venezuela has focused on four lines of strategic action bolstered by the activities of the media:

1. Economic destabilization (as in Chile, the gains in welfare and economic equality, a result of the reallocation and exploitation of the country's oil resources, have been attacked by means of an active campaign based on the flight of capital and lockouts against the government's policy of redistribution).
2. Political-social destabilization (the economic and political establishment have attempted to present as a civil war what is none other than an active operation of psychological warfare and mobilization by means of reports with eye-catching headlines revolving around corruption, which have since proved to be unfounded).
3. Destabilization of the National Armed Forces (the protests of sectors of the army have been associated with the manoeuvring of the USA to garner support against Chávez and Maduro, inciting prominent military officers to implement a strategy of harassment and destabilization of the government).
4. Civil disobedience (after the failure of the coup d'état, minority groups of the population, overrepresented in the country's oligopolistic media, painted a picture of ungovernability, which has had a strong impact on public opinion, with *garimpas* and continual sabotages, such as those instigated by Leopoldo López).

Thus, media conglomerates such as PRISA have presented as a 'civil rebellion' what is none other than a mobilization organized by the corporate/media/military bloc in favor of US interests. The outcome of these covert operations is unpredictable and, if this symbolic escalation of violence continues, it could lead to an authentic class confrontation. We have outlined this as a working hypothesis in previous studies. The problem with the spiral of dissembling and silencing dirty wars like this is that it is highly likely that it will lead to upheavals and disruptions, multiple disturbances and wars, in the growing escalation of exploitation and indiscriminate violence of this fearsome product of military engineering in Latin America, as is currently the case in Mexico.

### 15.3 Mexico: From Chiapas to Ayotzinapa

The second case study is a counter-factual example that confirms the propaganda model as regards the distinctions made by the press between worthy victims (opponents such as Leopoldo López in Venezuela or the pro-coup movement of the Brazilian extreme right against Dilma Rousseff) and unworthy victims (indigenous communities, students and peasants in the case of Mexico). The distortion of news, as in the case of Ayotzinapa and, prior to this, the Zapatista insurgency, perfectly illustrates the institutional working model of the media oligopoly governing the country, whose maximum expression lies in the tendency to criminalize protests and collective mobilization, whether in Mexico's poorest states (Oaxaca, Guerrero, Veracruz) or, as has been recently observed, on the occasion of the demonstrations against the *gasolinazo*.[5] In this regard, the information blackout is, in these and other cases, striking indeed, as has been shown in studies conducted by the Technological Institute of Monterrey.

A content analysis of the coverage of the country's main news programs, which constitute the primary and practically exclusive source of information for Mexicans, reveals conspicuous inequalities. Thus, 'the public figures receiving most coverage belong to the Federal Government and, to a lesser extent, the legislative power and the State Government. By the same token and given that it is the ruling party, the Institutional Revolutionary Party (PRI) receives the lion's share in comparison with other political institutions. It is no wonder then that the main issues addressed in the news have been the economy, security and politics, since they are precisely the topics included on the agenda of these political figures'.[6] As a dominant pattern, this agenda tends to be marked by Televisa, characterized by the systematic concealment or stigmatization of the social actors taking part in the protests. 'The amount of time dedicated to social actors highlights the huge imbalance in their coverage, inasmuch as, whereas there is a vast amount of information about their political counterparts, those people concerned with social issues are relegated to the third, or even the fourth news slot. This difference in the coverage of the different actors within the social system denotes a lack of diversity in Mexican television content, a state of affairs that was reconfirmed when applying the Gini Index (GI) (IG= 0.58)."[7]

This logic has also been confirmed empirically in the case of the Zapatista uprising in Chiapas, the massacres of Acteal and the mobilizations in Oaxaca on the occasion of the teachers' strike. So, for instance, 'after analyzing the news broadcast by Televisa on 25 November 2006 following a huge demonstration, the researcher Margarita Zires concluded that, by means of its narrative logic and interpretation of reality, the news program represented the members of the APPO as *provocative vandals* even *criminals* and the federal security forces as the *legitimate forces of law and order*.'[8]

In the last few years, social breakdown and increased repression throughout Mexico due to the deepening of the economic crisis have favored, as a result, a polarization between the reality of the process of militarization and indiscriminate violence on the part of the elites and state apparatuses and reality according to the news programs and mainstream press. The contradiction between the dominant version in the media and the reality experienced by the majority of the population has consequently led to a crisis of trust in the Channel of the Stars (Televisa) and the quest for a greater control over information, with the resulting concealment and legitimization of state terrorism that has been unleashed against civil organizations, opposition parties and cooperatives and popular movements opposing the counter-insurgency policy of the Stalinist development model that President Peña Nieto currently represents. Notwithstanding the crisis of confidence in the state and its ideological apparatus, the influence of the media duopoly still prevails. This has been possible thanks to a high level of concentration throughout the country's history, under the sway of a small clique including the Azcárraga family. 'In Mexico, Televisa (with three national channels) monopolises 66% of 465 concessions, has 52% audience share and channels 70% of commercial screen advertising. TV Azteca has 28% of concessions, 21% of the audience and 25% of advertising. Together they account for 90% of the television audience.'[9]

The history of Mexican television has been characterized by the symbiotic relationship and alliance with the political-economic and media powers, thus constituting an authentic duopoly in which the vast majority of the population depends on a limited information framework:

> The concentration of the mass media industry in only two institutions has been one of the most criticised aspects of the Mexican political system, above all due to the impact that television has had on the democratic life of the country for many years now. However, despite the fact that Mexican population trust their national news, the concentration of television market could be working against them, in particular offering a biased view of reality as has been pointed out by some authors, who consider that, in the previously described conditions, media cannot strengthen democracy [...] The concentration characterizing Mexican

television is a factor that, in one way or another, has influenced the news content accessed by the majority of the country's inhabitants, and the media policies that are ultimately implemented will have an impact on the vision that viewers have of national reality. The partiality with which information is treated is one of the most questionable aspects since it contravenes the principle of diversity through which an attempt is made to describe reality in all its complexity.'[10]

Therefore, the regular reports released by bodies such as Amnesty International denouncing the systematic violation of human rights in states like Oaxaca and Guerrero, and in Chiapas itself, have not been covered in the mainstream media, which have only mentioned military sources or, failing that, high-level decision-makers of the Secretariats of National Defense and of the Interior, due to their continued structural dependence on the Party-State. The multitude of cases and individual complaints – which would make any journalistic investigation a simple matter – have been habitually relegated to the fringe networks of some community-based, counter-information networks and to a few – albeit important – independent media such as *La Jornada* or *Proceso*, amid the clamorous and critical situation of human rights in the country which even affects media professionals themselves. Threats, impunity and the persecution of journalists are nowadays the norm in a country living under a permanent state of emergency:

'In Mexico, threats, violence and persecution against information professionals are a daily constant and an effective tool to silence those who write about corruption or organised crime. According to several national and international organizations, Mexico has become one of the most dangerous countries in the world to exercise journalism profession.'[11] However, the international press has warned against the lack of freedom of expression in countries that have advocated for national communication policies for democratizing the digital radio spectrum. The book recently edited by Professor Bernardo Díaz Nosty, coordinator of the UNESCO Chair of Communication of Malaga University, underscores such contradictions.[12]

A careful reading of its report on and diagnosis of the situation of journalists in the region ought to lead us to other conclusions very different from those that the official mouthpieces of the 'free press' would have us reach; though we should not expect the guardians of freedom to try to denounce the violation of human rights in pro-coup processes such as those experienced in the region. Rather, making the most of the leading role of institutions such as the OEA, this has been a systematic pattern or logic with the blessing of the major oligopolistic media groups.

Returning to the case of Mexico, the operability of the propaganda model is more than evident. Since the beginning of Peña Nieto's six-year term, the Mexican government, far from meeting the social demands of the population, has attempted to conceal the most serious cases of corruption in alliance with Televisa, while diverting state resources to the country's main media monopoly.

Moreover, since the beginning of Peña Nieto's term in office government policy has been characterized by a substantial increase in militarization, a remarkable strengthening of the systems of law and order, an increase in counter-insurgency measures, the harassment of social leaders and human rights advocates, and systematic attacks against the main nascent opposition party MORENA and its leader Andrés Manuel López Obrador.

As shown by a content analysis of the main news programs of Televisa and TV Azteca, there is a clear predominance of the public agenda of the government authorities, fostered as sources in the media overrepresentation to which the television duopoly has led. 'Of these, the Federal Government emerges as the principal actor in journalistic reports, since 37% use some of its members as their main information source. The legislative power and the State Government trail far behind with 17% and 14%, respectively. In addition, the political origins of the people appearing in the content analysed also reinforces this situation. So it is that 72.2% are members of the Institutional Revolutionary Party and barely 7% belong to the Democratic Revolution Party. This absence of diversity of opinions is underlined when the corresponding Gini Index is applied, whose result points to a clear deficiency of equity in content (0.58 in the case of political actors and 0.80 for political parties)'.[13]

Meanwhile, the political-military action of the government remains concealed from public opinion, following the prescribed guidelines of low-intensity warfare in order to terrorize the peasant population immersed in a widespread climate of general insecurity and repression, unprecedented in the history of Mexico, regarded today by some as a failed state.[14] As a parody of the film *The Perfect Dictatorship*, the routine production of the mass media tends to focus the attention of audiences on other matters, supposedly of greater interest. Thus, for example, in 2012 the monopolistic company Televisa undeniably played a leading role as the stage for constructing the figure of the PRI candidate. Peña Nieto and the country's main television company sealed an alliance that still holds, albeit with some discrepancies. The 2014 massacre of young *normalistas* in Ayotzinapa was undoubtedly a hard blow for the image of the President: public opinion associated the lack of justice with his inaction. But, in essence, the limited coverage avoided drawing parallels between the causes and the terror policy implemented by the state against subaltern sectors.

Faithfully following the non-explicit manuals in use on counter-insurgency, the Mexican army, whose operations receive the benefit of the advice of the Pentagon and special operations units of the CIA, is proceeding in this way with the destruction and systematic harassment of civil populations, while any revealing knowledge of this rationale of creative devastation or destruction is discredited as an invention, typical of conspiracy theories, despite the evidence displayed, the continuities of the modus operandi of the *country's dominant media* and the authentic ideological apparatuses of the process of accumulation endured by the country's population, even to the extent of procedures infringing upon the right to life.

## 15.4 Conclusion

As Michel Collon has written:

> '[...] so at first the Cold War media portrayed a systematically exaggerated apocalyptic 'Soviet threat' (as has been shown in recent American studies), to justify the huge US military build-up. This was followed by the 'yellow peril' and in turn by Iraq and its 'four global armies': currently, the threat to the West comes from the Third World as a whole'.[15]

The threat to US hegemony posed by the processes of autonomy and regional unity taking place in Latin America, has been responded to with the expected denigration and criminalization of the progressive forces.

The process of concentration of media ownership has made globalization work in the interest of political and economic elites both in the US and Latin America. The capacity of governments, leaded by the United States, to direct media misinformation campaigns with the support of large corporations has naturally lead to an underreporting of the crimes committed by elite actors, who actually became the main sources of information. Attacks on alternative media and movements promoting change have gone together with a campaign of fear to demonise political and social change. As during Reagan's era, the scarecrow of communism, together with discourses on national security, has provided the ideological basis to defend elite interests and attack those who are labelled as enemies.

In Venezuela, the coup and destabilizing actions put into action by an alliance between the US government, the national political opposition, economic elites and media companies has resulted in a ferocious attack on the democratic leaders and the Bolivarian process, while the leaders promoting violence and coups d'état are enthroned as democratic heroes in the tradition of Dr King and presented as victims of totalitarianism. In contrast, the voice of indigenous communities, students and peasants who suffer from structural and direct violence in Mexico are systematically excluded from the public sphere, thus being rendered *unworthy* victims, as the priority of the oligopolistic media has been to side with the interests of the right-wing and violent forces that receive fundamental support from the US government. These two case studies confirm for Latin America the powerful influence of the filters identified by Herman and Chomsky and supports a key hypothesis of the propaganda model that the mainstream media will follow double-standards when informing about 'us' and 'our allies' as compared to 'them,' 'the enemies.' The reason for the difference in treatment is the same one: the structural interconnection between the media, governments and economic powers that impose its will over the peoples of Latin America, who nevertheless continue to resist and engage in processes of social and political transformation.

## Notes and Bibliography

[1] Rocío Orlando (2012), *Medios privados y nuevos gobiernos en Ecuador y Argentina*. (Quito: FLACSO).
[2] Francisco Sierra (2016), *Golpes mediáticos. Teoría y análisis de casos en América Latina* (Quito: CIESPAL), 181–202.
[3] Fernando Casado (2015), *Antiperiodistas. Confesiones de las agresiones mediáticas contra Venezuela* (Madrid: Ediciones Akal), 19.
[4] Ibid, 212 [author's translation].
[5] The rise in the price of petrol that led to a series of protests.
[6] Francisco Javier Martínez Garza, Rubén Arnoldo González Macías and Oscar Miranda Villanueva (2015), 'Actores políticos y sociales de los telediarios. Una tarea pendiente de las televisoras mexicanas', *Revista Latina de Comunicación Social*, 70, 750 [author's translation].
[7] Ibid, 759.
[8] Guiomar Rovira (2013), 'Activismo mediático y criminalización de la protesta: medios y movimientos sociales en México.' *Convergencia* 61 (January-April), 50 [author's translation].
[9] Ibid, 39.
[10] Martínez Garza et al., op.cit., 752 [author's translation].
[11] Amaia Arribas (2016), 'Ser o no ser periodista en México.' *Infoamérica* 10, 39.
[12] Bernardo Díaz Nosty (ed.), *Periodismo muerto* (2016) Temas de Hoy, México.
[13] Martínez Garza et al, op.cit., 760.
[14] Martínez Garza et al, op.cit., 760.
[15] Collon (1999): 378.

CHAPTER 16

# 'Dynamic' Obama Lectures 'Bumbling' Castro on Race Relations in Cuba, While Wilfully Blind to Black Lives Matter Movement in the US[1]

James Winter

### 16.1 Introduction

A small and select but expanding group of scholars and investigators have exposed some of the historical biases, inaccuracies, and distortions in corporate media. The most well known of these is an American, Noam Chomsky, who has opposed and exposed the corporate-government-media-military nexus since the Vietnam War in the 1960s.[2]

Chomsky has been joined in more recent years by authors such as William Blum, a former US State Department employee who has uncovered CIA 'adventures' around the globe.[3] Somewhat similar work has been done by former *New York Times* bureau chief Stephen Kinzer, who documented the US government's role in overthrowing leaders in countries ranging from Hawaii

---

How to cite this book chapter:
Winter, J. 2018. 'Dynamic' Obama Lectures 'Bumbling' Castro on Race Relations in Cuba, While Wilfully Blind to Black Lives Matter Movement in the US. In: Pedro-Carañana, J., Broudy, D. and Klaehn, J. (eds.). *The Propaganda Model Today: Filtering Perception and Awareness*. Pp. 249–262. London: University of Westminster Press. DOI: https://doi.org/10.16997/book27.p. License: CC-BY-NC-ND 4.0

and the Philippines, late in the twentieth century, to Iran in the 1950s and more recently Panama, Afghanistan, and Iraq.[4]

Canadian journalist Naomi Klein has taken a different tack: focusing on how the unfettered free-market capitalism envisioned by Milton Friedman and his followers has exported violence and subservience around the world in the form of disaster economics.[5]

British academic Matthew Alford has exposed how Hollywood 'entertainment' films actually support the US national security state and the use of American violence overseas.[6]

It is within this broader body of knowledge that the current study may be located. The portrayal of Cuba in the Western press since the 1959 Revolution has bordered on the ridiculous to anyone who has visited there and talked to the Cuban people. However, as Americans have generally been prohibited by law from visiting Cuba, they normally do not have first-hand experience to compare to corporate media depictions. As a consequence, the demonisation of Cuba and the Castro brothers has been among the most successful propaganda campaigns in the world over the past sixty years.

In March, 2016, then-US president Barack Obama paid a visit to Cuba. This chapter studies press coverage of that trip. The study compares the clichés of Cuba in press coverage to academic studies of Cuban realities, from pre-revolutionary days in the 1950s, to the present day.

Ironically, a media criticism show covered the clichés reported on the Obama trip, but failed to detect the significant clichés, only the superficial, such as how Cuba and the US are 'a mere 90 miles, but worlds apart,' and how Cuba is 'frozen in time,' with 'crumbling buildings,' and 'vintage cars,' along with 'cigars and music,' elements admittedly present in much of the coverage.[7] But the program failed to unearth the deeper and more significant clichés in coverage, which we will attempt to do here.

One standard cliché in coverage is that the Castro brothers have led a long, communist, one-party dictatorship, with Fidel at the helm for 42 years, and Raúl for the past nine years. To North American thinking, it is inconceivable that there are elections in Cuba, under a one-party regime. Another part of this is that while Fidel's predecessor Batista was not the best leader, Cuba flourished under him, relative to what has happened since.[8]

In the 1950s, under the dictator Fulgencio Batista, Cuba was a playground for the US Mafia, as documented in books by T.J. English and Enrique Cirules. Mob leaders such as Meyer Lansky and Lucky Luciano owned Havana's biggest luxury hotels and casinos. The 'Pearl of the Antilles,' as Cuba was known, was the Mob's playground, with gambling, fabulous entertainment, international celebrities, sex, sun, and sand.

The Mobsters had always dreamed of controlling their own country, free from police and government interference. Thanks to Batista's cooperation, in return for Mob payments in the millions of dollars, the Mafia effectively ran the country, with military and police enforcers, from the 1930s until the Revolution in 1959.

The resulting role for Cubans was one of prostitution, repression, collaboration, and servitude. According to Aviva Chomsky there were 'two Cubas' in the 1950s, the 1.5 million jobless or rural poor who survived mostly on rice, a few beans and sugar water. At the other end were the 900,000 wealthiest Cubans who controlled 43 per cent of the country's income. In between, another 3.5 million struggled to make ends meet.[9]

One need only look to some of the reportage at the time. An AP story in the *Globe and Mail* said, 'The rebels hated legalized gambling because it made Cubans poorer, rich US racketeers richer, and added millions to Batista's vast fortune. That fortune has been estimated at $200,000,000 safely stowed in foreign banks.'[10]

As with other periods of reportage such as during the trip to Cuba by former US president Jimmy Carter in 2002,[11] the media coverage of Obama's trip was an opportunity to trot out well-worn clichés about Cuba and the Castro brothers, revealing the corporate media's deep-seated ideological biases. For example, Patrick Luciani of the Atlantic Institute for Market Studies, writing in the *Financial Post*, noted that:

'Canadians are saying, 'Let's get down there before Americans ruin the place.' Too late; the ruin began with the 1959 revolution.'

Luciani praised Cuban life under Batista and belittled current Cuban accomplishments, for example in education, by saying, 'One has to ask what education means in a country that has little to read and what remains is filtered through Marxist ideology.'

The press coverage of Obama's visit provided absolutely no indication of what Noam Chomsky has identified as the real reason for the embargo against Cuba: the pro-capitalist 'rotten apple' or virus theory. That is, if Cuba is allowed to flourish on its own, unimpeded, then the 'virus' of socialism could spread to other Central American countries, as indeed it finally has done in the past decade or so. This assessment by Chomsky may be readily seen as part of his and Edward Herman's Propaganda Model of news media, relating to a number of the five filters, such as media ownership and profit orientation, the reliance on advertising and pursuant promotion of capitalism, and the anti-communism or ideology filter, which opposes nationalism anywhere other than the US.

## 16.2 It's All About Obama

In the Canadian and US press, Obama's visit to Cuba was—well—all about Obama. He was portrayed as a young 54-year-old man of mixed blood and 'fluid, lanky, youthful movement,' who visited Cuba with his beautiful wife and daughters. Whereas Calvin Coolidge had taken three days to arrive on a battleship in 1928, Superman Obama remarked, 'It only took me three hours'.

Obama marvelled at the significance of his trip, which he said enabled him to 'engage directly with the Cuban people,' forge 'new agreements and commercial deals,' and 'build new ties between our two peoples.' Also, he would be able to 'lay out my vision for a future that's brighter than our past.'[12]

The *New York Times* wrote, 'All around the city on Sunday, Mr. Obama's name could be heard.' The spectators who watched Obama's arrival were awe-struck, professing they never thought they'd live to see this. Others shouted greetings and his name and 'USA.' and 'We like you,' as his entourage passed on the street. A 17-year-old was quoted as saying 'he had given her generation hope.' Obama 'has long been admired by Cubans, first as a candidate, then as a president,' we learned. When he announced restored relations with Cuba on 17 December 2014, 'that date is now recited often as a new national starting point, joining other historic dates, like July 26, 1953,' when Fidel attacked the Moncada barracks and started the Revolution.[13]

Obama lectured Cubans about the extent of their racism, ironically, given the past and current state of race relations in the US. 'We want our engagement to help lift up Cubans who are of African descent,' he said. The *New York Times* noted solemnly, 'It was also an unusually direct engagement with race, a critical and unresolved issue in Cuban society that the revolution was supposed to have erased.'[14]

During a joint news briefing with Raúl Castro, Obama winked at the camera and took 'a mini victory lap afterward.' Obama smoothly handled the press questions, while the allegedly-bumbling and haughty 84-year-old Castro stumbled, with his 'stiff military bearing.'

A *New York Times* article headlined, 'Along With Obama, the 21$^{st}$ Century Visited Cuba,' stated that 'The 30 years between Mr. Obama, 54, and Mr. Castro, 84, help explain the vast gulf that separates the two leaders, on vivid display last week...'[15]

The article pointed to the lack of reliable internet access, oblivious to the role played in this by the US embargo. 'The iconic image was Castro getting all huffy about some pretty anodyne critiques of the human rights situation in Cuba...The gestalt of the visit for Obama was very much "I know you're on your way out, and I'm going to speak to the Cuban population about what the future looks like after you",' the paper quoted a political science professor as saying, seemingly unaware of the fact that it is Obama who was a lame duck, not Castro.

*The International New York Times* began its article dismissively. 'The thing about dictators is they don't have to answer any stinking questions from the press. We call it undemocratic; they call it job security,'[16] their reporter wrote.

After the first question to Raúl Castro about political prisoners, the reporter wrote, 'You could watch in real time as Mr. Castro came to terms with the idea that this was actually happening. He stammered and got himself into a muddle over how this whole news conference deal works, anyway. Was the question directed at him? It was only with prompting from President Obama that he finally answered Mr. [Jim] Acosta, though by demanding a list proving that any such prisoners even existed. (Happy to help you out with that, Sir.)'[17]

Almost all of the coverage portrayed Castro's request as a joke, as above. An exception was one article in *The Globe and Mail*, which stated: 'Cuba released dozens of prisoners as part of its deal to normalize relations with the United

States, and in a recent report, Amnesty International did not name any current prisoners of conscience in Cuba.'[18] The other media implied that Castro's request was outlandish: their presupposition was that everyone *knows* Cuba has political prisoners.

It's only when you go to a transcript of the session on *Granma*, that you learn how Raúl Castro answered questions. Instead of the bumbling fool portrayed in the press, we find his thoughtful analysis of the Cuban meaning of 'Human Rights,' and how it relates to other countries.

Raúl Castro: 'Give me the list of political prisoners right now to be released. Just mention a list. What political prisoners? Give me a name or names. Or once this meeting is over, you can give me a list of prisoners and if we have those political prisoners, they will be released before tonight. Next question.'

Jim Acosta (CNN): 'Donald Trump or Hillary Clinton, President Castro?'

Raúl Castro: 'Well, I still cannot vote in the United States (Laughter).'

Afterwards, another question was directed to Raúl Castro.

Andrea Mitchell (NBC): 'What is the future of our nations, given the different definitions and the different interpretations of issues such as democracy and human rights?'

Raúl Castro: 'In the recognized institutions, there are 61 international instruments on human rights. Andrea, do you know how many countries in the world comply with all these 61 human and civil rights included in these instruments? What country complies with them all? I do. None. None, whatsoever. Some countries comply with some rights; others comply with others. And we are among these countries. Out of these 61 instruments, Cuba has complied with 47. There are countries that may comply with more, there are many that comply with less. The issues of human rights cannot be politicized, that is not correct.'[19]

Castro went on to mention just three of the human rights in Cuba, such as the right to quality, free healthcare, the right to free education, and the right of women 'to get equal pay as men for equal work'.

I could only find one paper which briefly reported on these remarks by Castro: *The Guardian* of London.[20] And yet, many newspapers jumped with glee on this simplistic notion of alleged human rights abuses in Cuba.[21]

*The National Post* ran an Associated Press story reporting on the press conference. Here are the first two paragraphs:

> HAVANA — Cubans were glued to their televisions on Monday, many watching in a state of shock as President Raul Castro faced tough questions

from American journalists who challenged him to defend Cuba's record on human rights and political prisoners.

In a country where publicly questioning the authority of Castro and his brother and predecessor Fidel is unthinkable for most, and where the docile state-run media almost always toe the party line, the live broadcast was must-see TV. Some also marveled at tough questioning of President Barack Obama, simply unaccustomed to seeing any leader challenged in such a way.[22]

This account neatly fits into the usual narrative: Cubans are shocked by the open questioning of their dictator by the fearless American journalists.

### 16.3 Fidel Writes About Obama

For the most part, only fleeting references are made to Fidel, which may be plugged into the previously-formulated social construction of the man who has been demonised perhaps more than any other for more than a half century. Although Fidel did not meet with Obama, he did write a response to the speech Obama delivered to the Cuban people, afterwards. Fidel's article was described the next day in the *Washington Post* as 'scathing' and 'a long and somewhat rambling recounting' of the Bay of Pigs invasion, and as 'A little disorganized.'[23] *The New York Times* described Castro's article as 'a 1600-word missive,' and an 'admonition,' and said Fidel 'chastised Mr. Obama, 54, for his youth and for failing to recognize' the major accomplishments of the revolution.[24]

The notion that Fidel criticized Obama for his youth was fabricated. What Fidel wrote was: 'Obama was born in August of 1961, as he himself explained. More than half a century has transpired since that time.' Later on he said, '... pensions and salaries for all Cubans were decreed by [the Revolution] before Mr. Barack Obama was 10 years old.'[25] This is *hardly* chastising Obama for his youth.

What Fidel did was to respond to how Obama urged Cubans to 'forget the past, leave the past behind, let us look to the future together...' Indeed, it's easy for the perpetrator to say, 'forget the past,' but less so for the country which has been the victim of an invasion, bombings, poisonings, chemical and biological weapons attacks, hundreds of assassination attempts, and a relentless economic embargo.

### 16.4 Lectures on 'Democracy'

Another presupposition by the press, of course, is that Cuba is a one-party communist dictatorship which compares unfavorably to western democracies such as Canada and the US. So well-engrained is this notion that it hardly bears mentioning, but some still do. For example, small daily and weekly writer Gwynne Dyer wrote that '... when Fidel Castro retired after 42 years and handed power to his brother [Raúl Castro] in 2008, Western embassies in Havana (minus the United States, of course) arranged for various "experts" from their countries to visit Cuba and explain how things were done in a real democracy—which they fully expected that Cuba would shortly become.'[26] He went on to mention 'the long dictatorship of the Castro brothers,' and said, 'I now think the regime will probably survive until and unless the US Congress finally ends the embargo and exposes Cuba to the full force of international capitalism.'

This neatly sums up a number of presuppositions which require no evidence: the Castro brothers were and are dictators, who hand over power to their appointees; Canada is 'a real democracy,' and Cuba is not, *etc.*

Obama stated in a press conference with Raúl, 'We continue, as President [Raúl Castro] indicated, to have some very serious differences, including on democracy and human rights.'

In an editorial, the *Globe and Mail* stated that: 'If Mr. Castro truly wants to normalize relations with the US, he must begin by opening his fist and extending his hand to democracy.'[27] This was in the context of discussing alleged human rights violations in Cuba. It's an example of the more subtle accusations and assumptions.

In an otherwise somewhat exceptional guest column, which reviewed historical Cuban-American relations fairly accurately, even academic Jeffery Sachs offered that, 'Cuba can and should aim for Costa Rican-style social democracy, rather than the cruder capitalism of the United States.' Here, of course, Sachs confuses the albeit-related economic system (capitalism) with the electoral system (social democracy). The US is a capitalist economic state, with an allegedly-democratic political system, although many would take issue with this latter notion.[28]

It's abundantly clear to even the casual observer that our 'western-style democracies' are anything but. What we have, in fact, more closely approximates an oligarchy or plutocracy (rule by the few and the rich, respectively) rather than a democracy. Even the basic requisite for a democracy—majority rule—is seldom attained, as a cursory examination of the popular vote in recent decades demonstrates. Additionally, the unsavory characteristics of 'western-style democracies' are the very reason for their rejection by Cubans, who have ample knowledge of them, historically. For example, as Professor Isaac Saney notes,

> While in other countries, economic wherewithal [wealth] is necessary for—and does lead to—political power, in Cuba this is not the case. Those who have the most money do not have political power, as they have no support among the masses and, thus, do not offer up candidates in the elections.[29]

What Cubans know is that so-called 'multiparty elections' are the Trojan horse of politics, or, the 'democracy of exploiters,' as Fidel Castro has put it, allowing the US government to bribe and buy its way into office through one power-hungry comprador or another. In Third World elections the US has openly or covertly run a favoured candidate, directed massive funding toward its preferred candidate, and threatened economic or military repercussions if its candidate is not elected. Once elected the candidate and his or her party run a client government at the beck-and-call of its American sponsors, just as the domestic equivalent is at the behest of his or her corporate backers. It's patently ridiculous to debate this point, since it is a matter of open historical record throughout the Third World over much of the past century.

The presupposition of 'capitalist democracies' in the West does not stand up to scrutiny. Canadian Prime Minister Justin Trudeau was elected in 2015 with a majority government, for example, while receiving only 39% of the popular vote, owing to the out-dated first-past-the-post electoral system in Canada. Hence, 61% of the population voted for other Parties. Trudeau promised in his electoral campaign that the 2015 election would be the last election under that model, but reneged on this promise 18 months into his term when it became clear that his Liberal Party most likely would not fare well under a more democratic system of Proportional Representation. As for the US, Hillary Clinton received almost three million more votes than Donald Trump in their 2016 presidential race, and yet Trump was elected president. So much for majority rule in these two countries.

Relatively speaking, in comparison the Cuban political system is a model of democracy. As authors such as Arnold August and law professor Isaac Saney have described in intricate detail, contrary to conventional wisdom, Cubans have developed an elaborate, representative and inclusive democracy which has an exemplary level of voluntary participation.[30] The media simply are not open to these points of view, choosing instead to parrot exclusively the views of the US Administration, with its distorted perspectives and Cold War caricatures. The fact that Obama went to Cuba to end the last vestiges of the Cold War just adds to the irony.

## 16.5 Lectures on the Economy

As regards the Cuban economy, one is left to conclude, as do the media, that the problem is Fidel Castro. No mention was made, for example, of the collapse of the Soviet Union, which was Cuba's largest (almost exclusive) trading partner, accounting for 85% of trade, up until 1989. the USSR provided 95% of Cuban oil imports, for example. Cuban per capita income dropped by 39% following the Soviet collapse.[31]

The media said the embargo isn't working, it hasn't accomplished what it was established for.

'There's been an evolution where most of the younger [Miami] Cubans now are much less attached to the embargo, and many are saying that it hasn't worked and it would be easier if we just had normal relations with our cousin and sister-in-law in Cuba. The great resentment among Cuban-Americans against the Cuban regime – and the notion that the embargo could bring it down – that was a strong factor in the 1960s and 1970s.'[32]

This was echoed in the *New York Times*: 'while many members of older generations who remained on the island have a visceral connection to the revolution and all that followed, their children and grandchildren may have little memory of the roots of resentment toward the United States.'[33]

Luciani, writing in the *Financial Post*, said: 'Apologists blame the US embargo for Cuba's wretchedness. But it is not a blockade. Other countries trade with Cuba. Washington's Cuba policy is just a convenient excuse for a wrecked economy where most public resources are funnelled to an outsized military and bureaucracy.'

### 16.6 The Real Reason For the Embargo

The press reports that the reason for the embargo is to pressure Cuba to improve its Human Rights, or because of pressure from angry Miami Cubans, or, to pressure Cuba to democratize. The real reason for the embargo is so shocking, so unspeakable, that it must never be broached in the corporate media, except perhaps in a brief account or statement from someone who can be dismissed as a demented conspiracy theorist. The real reason the US continues its merciless punishment of Cuba is what Noam Chomsky calls, 'the threat of a good example.' It's also called the 'rotten apple theory,' or in a distorted version for more popular consumption: 'the Domino theory.' William Blum has called it 'the unforgiveable revolution.'

When a leader tries to do something for the poor and downtrodden of his country, instead of serving Washington and the IMF and other powers that be, there will be demonising and economic squeezes and coup attempts.[34] If all else fails, the US invades. It is worth quoting Chomsky at length on this because he cites US policymakers themselves, who are a trifle difficult to dismiss as mere conspiracy theorists.

> No country is exempt from U.S. intervention, no matter how unimportant. In fact, it's the weakest, poorest countries that often arouse the greatest hysteria...The weaker and poorer a country is, the more dangerous it is as an example. If a tiny, poor country like Grenada can succeed in bringing about a better life for its people, some other place that has more resources will ask, 'why not us?' ... If you want a global system that's subordinated to the needs of US investors, you can't let pieces of it wander off .... Take Chile under Allende ... Why were we so concerned about it? According to Kissinger, Chile was a 'virus' that would 'infect' the region with effects all the way to Italy .... This 'rotten apple

> theory' is called the domino theory for public consumption .... Sometimes the point is explained with great clarity. When the US was planning to overthrow Guatemalan democracy in 1954, a State Department official pointed out that 'Guatemala has become an increasing threat to the stability of Honduras and El Salvador. Its agrarian reform is a powerful propaganda weapon: its broad social program of aiding the workers and peasants in a victorious struggle against the upper classes and large foreign enterprises has a strong appeal to the populations of Central American neighbors where similar conditions prevail.' ... In other words, what the US wants is 'stability', meaning security for the 'upper classes and large foreign enterprises'.[35]

Thus, Chomsky replies to those who argue that the US only intervenes over access to natural resources, as it has openly done in the Middle East. He goes on to quote from members of the US administration who spoke more openly about their goals and objections in earlier times.

> Arthur Schlesinger had transmitted to the incoming President Kennedy his Latin American Mission report, which warned of the susceptibility of Latin Americans to 'the Castro idea of taking matters into one's own hands.' .... The dangers of the 'Castro idea' are particularly grave, Schlesinger later elaborated, when 'the distribution of land and other forms of national wealth greatly favors the propertied classes' and 'the poor and underprivileged, stimulated by the example of the Cuban revolution, are now demanding opportunities for a decent living'. In early 1964, the State Department Policy Planning Council expanded on these concerns: 'The primary danger we face in Castro is ... in the impact the very existence of his regime has upon the leftist movement in many Latin American countries .... The simple fact is that Castro represents a successful defiance of the US, a negation of our whole hemispheric policy of almost a century and a half'[36]

One can see here explicitly that this concern and the Cuban example are central to a Chomskian analysis of international affairs and specifically US foreign policy, whether or not one directly relates them specifically to the Propaganda Model, as I very briefly have done above. Little or nothing has changed in the intervening decades, since the Cuban Revolution ousted the US Mafia, which was stunningly portrayed by director Francis Ford Coppola in his film *The Godfather*, as the very epitome of capitalism. Similarly, these results comply with the findings of other contemporary writers such as Chris Hedges, Stephen Kinzer, William Blum, etc.

Clearly, Cuba under the Castro brothers' leadership has not met any of the needs of American capitalism, other than functioning as Cold War bogeymen. Chomsky writes,

[T]he assigned functions of Third World countries are to be markets for American business, sources of resources for American business, to provide cheap labor for American business, and so on…the main commitment of the United States, internationally in the Third World, must be to prevent the rise of nationalist regimes which are responsive to pressures from the masses of the population for improvement in low living standards and diversification of production; the reason is, we have to maintain a climate that is conducive to investment, and to ensure conditions which allow for adequate repatriation of profits to the West.[37]

## 16.7 One-Party Rule

Obama, and the media that reported on him, repeatedly take advantage of a technique called *presupposition*, in Critical Discourse Analysis terms, in which their particular perspective is privileged and alternative views are precluded. We saw this above in the way Luciani categorized as 'apologists' someone who holds a different perspective on the Cuban Embargo. The 'one party domination' presupposition is another case in point. In fact, the Communist Party is prohibited from taking part in elections, under the Cuban Constitution,[38] and opposition movements flourish within the dialectic of the revolution. Opposition and 'disagreement with the government' does not present a problem: it is those who are actively working in the hire of a foreign power to overthrow the Cuban government whose actions are—quite rationally and reasonably—prohibited and subjected to Cuban laws.

To provide some perspective, think of how all governments have laws prohibiting treason, with jail sentences as a result of convictions. Think about the Canadian government's reaction to the FLQ crisis in October 1970, for example, when the War Measures Act was invoked nationally, and 400 Quebecois were jailed, in response to two kidnappings, one murder and some bombings by a few dozen people in Quebec.[39]

Finally, in terms of this brief chapter, I wish to point out these virtually unreported words of US Treasury Secretary Jacob J. Lew, from March 2016. He is elaborating on how Obama has loosened restrictions on travel to Cuba by Americans. Here is what he said:

Individuals may now travel to Cuba without being attached to a US-based organization coordinating the trip, 'provided that the traveler engages in a full-time schedule of educational exchange activities intended to enhance contact with the Cuban people, support civil society in Cuba, or promote the Cuban people's independence from Cuban authorities and that will result in a meaningful interaction between the traveler and individuals in Cuba.'[40]

The words, 'support civil society in Cuba,' are Newspeak or code words for opposing the Cuban government. The next words, 'or promote the Cuban people's independence from Cuban authorities,' make this explicit. In other words, Americans may now travel to Cuba if they engage in actions which are traitorous to the Cuban government.[41]

## Notes and Bibliography

[1] This chapter is a revised version of a paper presented to the 15th International Symposium on Social Communication, Centre for Applied Linguistics, Santiago Cuba, January 2017.

[2] Cf. Noam Chomsky (2017), *Requiem for the American Dream: The 10 Principles of Concentration of Wealth & Power* (New York: Seven Stories Press). With Peter Hutchison, Kelly Nyuks & Jared Scott.

[3] Cf. William Blum (1998), *Killing Hope* (Montreal: Black Rose Books).

[4] Cf. Stephen Kinzer (2006), *Overthrow: America's Century of Regime Change from Hawaii to Iraq* (New York: Henry Holt and Co).

[5] Naomi Klein (2007), *The Shock Doctrine: The Rise of Disaster Capitalism* (Toronto: Random House).

[6] Matthew Alford (2010), *Reel Power: Hollywood Cinema and American Supremacy* (London: Pluto Press).

[7] *On the Media*, WNYC Studios. https://www.wnyc.org/shows/otm/.

[8] For an excellent, outrageous example of this, see Patrick Luciani (2016), 'How Cuba was destroyed,' *The Financial Post*, 2 March.

[9] Aviva Chomsky (2015), *A History of the Cuban Revolution*, 2nd Edition, West Sussex, John Wiley and Sons, p.28.

[10] AP, Havana (1959), 'Castro Victory Sounds Death Knell for Cuban Gambling,' *The Globe and Mail*, 5 January, p. 3.

[11] James P. Winter and Robert Everton (2006), 'Fidel Castro, Jimmy Carter, and George W. Bush in the Canadian Media: A Critical Analysis,' *The Fifth Estate Online*, June; James Winter (2007), *Lies the Media Tell Us*, (Montreal: Black Rose Books).

[12] Julie Hirschfeld Davis and Damien Cave (2016), 'Basking in Cuban Welcome, Obama Marvels at His Visit's Significance,' *The New York Times*, 21 March.

[13] Ibid.

[14] Damien Cave (2016), 'Obama Urges Raised Voices in Cuba's Hushed Discussions of Race,' *The New York Times*, 24 March.

[15] Julie Hirschfeld Davis (2016), 'Along With Obama, the 21st Century Visited Cuba,' *The New York Times*, 28 March.

[16] Jim Rutenberg (2016), 'A Victory Lap and a Wink at a Meeting in Havana,' *International New York Times*, 29 March.

[17] Ibid.

18. Julie Pace and Michael Weissenstein (2016), 'Leaders Clash During Havana Meeting,' *Globe and Mail*, 22 March.
19. *Granma* [English] (2016), 'A New Chapter in Relations Between Cuba and the United States,' transcript, 24 March. http://en.granma.cu/cuba/2016-03-24/a-new-chapter-in-relations-between-cuba-and-the-united-states
20. Alan Yuhas (2016), 'Castro Defends Cuba: "No One Country Complies With All Human Rights,"' *The Guardian*, 21 March.
21. I'm in agreement with Isaac Saney on this point. Many, if not all of these prisoners are convicted of treason, or 'working with a foreign power to undermine the government.' The international reporting bears 'no resemblance to the actual issues or evidence presented.' See Isaac Saney (2004), *Cuba: A Revolution in Motion*, Nova Scotia, Fernwood Publishing p. 69.
22. AP (2016), 'Cubans Stunned as U.S. Journalists Grill Castro on Human Rights: "It's Extraordinary to See This,"' *The National Post*, 22 March. http://news.nationalpost.com/news/world/cubans-shocked-as-u-s-journalists-grill-castro-on-human-rights-its-extraordinary-to-see-this
23. Karen DeYoung (2016), 'Castro: We don't need Obama's 'presents',' *The Washington Post*, 29 March.
24. Azam Ahmed (2016), 'In a 1,600-Word Missive, Fidel Castro Criticizes Obama's Efforts in Cuba,' *The New York Times*, 29 March.
25. Fidel Castro (2016), 'Brother Obama,' *Granma*, 28 March.
26. Gwynne Dyer (2016), 'Obama in Havana,' *Campbellford EMC*, 24 March.
27. Editorial (2016), 'Close, but no Cigars,' *The Globe and Mail*, 22 March.
28. Jeffery Sachs and Hanna Sachs (2016), 'What will the new normal look like?' *The Globe and Mail*, 23 March.
29. Saney, *Cuba: A Revolution in Motion* p. 89.
30. Ibid pp. 54-55. Also, Arnold August (1999), *Democracy in Cuba and the 1997–98 Elections*, Havana, Editorial Jose Marti; and Arnold August (2013), *Cuba and its Neighbours: Democracy in Motion* (Halifax, Fernwood Press).
31. Saney, *Cuba: A Revolution in Motion*, p. 21.
32. Raymond Espinosa (2016), 'For Cubans, There's No Looking Back Now,' *The National Post*, (AP), 19 March.
33. Julie Hirschfeld Davis (2016) 'Along With Obama, The 21st Century visited Cuba,' *The New York Times*, 27 March.
34. Venezuela under Hugo Chavez is perhaps the best recent example of this, where business and US interests objected to his government with riots, general strikes, and a coup. These activities continue under his successor, Nicolás Maduro.
35. Noam Chomsky (1993), *What Uncle Sam Really Wants* (Tucson, AZ, Odonian Press).
36. Noam Chomsky (2003), 'Cuba in the Cross-Hairs: A Near Half-Century of Terror,' 24 October, www.commondreams.com, excerpted with permission from Noam Chomsky (2003), *Hegemony or Survival: America's Quest for Global Dominance* (New York: Metropolitan Books).

[37] Peter Mitchell and John Schoeffel, eds. (2002), *Understanding Power: The Indispensable Chomsky*, New York, p.64.
[38] Saney, *Cuba: A Revolution in Motion* p.64.
[39] For an elaboration, see James Winter (2007), *Lies the Media Tell Us* (Black Rose Books, Montreal).
[40] Reported by Teresa Welsh (2016), 'More People Can Now Travel To Cuba,' *US News And World Report*, 15 March.
[41] After the election of Donald Trump in 2016, there was speculation that Trump would reverse Obama's Cuban policies. An announcement was expected in June, 2017. See Mythili Sampathkumar, 'Donald Trump to reverse Barack Obama's Cuba policies after breakthrough of decades-old stalemate,' *The Independent*, May 30, 2017. https://www.independent.co.uk/news/world/americas/us-politics/donald-trump-cuba-barack-obama-diplomatic-relations-raul-castro-communist-island-caribbean-a7763316.html

# CHAPTER 17

# Thinking the Unthinkable about the Unthinkable – The Use of Nuclear Weapons and the Propaganda Model

Milan Rai

In January 2017, Britain's leading liberal newspaper criticised a new, heavy-handed, system of press regulation, brought in under the Crime and Courts Act (2013). *The Guardian* argued: 'A press that is free to investigate and criticise is essential for good governance.'[1] Similarly, US Supreme Court Judge Lewis F. Powell Jr. once argued that, as no individual can obtain for themselves the information needed for the intelligent discharge of their political responsibilities, the press performs a crucial function in 'effecting the societal purpose of the First Amendment' of the US Constitution. The media does this by enabling the public to exert 'meaningful control over the political process'.[2]

This reflects both the self-image of the mainstream media and the image that it projects.

---

**How to cite this book chapter:**
Rai, M. 2018. Thinking the Unthinkable about the Unthinkable - The Use of Nuclear Weapons and the Propaganda Model. In: Pedro-Carañana, J., Broudy, D. and Klaehn, J. (eds.). *The Propaganda Model Today: Filtering Perception and Awareness*. Pp. 263–277. London: University of Westminster Press. DOI: https://doi.org/10.16997/book27.q. License: CC-BY-NC-ND 4.0

In contrast, Edward S. Herman and Noam Chomsky and offer a Propaganda Model (PM) of the mainstream media, in which the 'free press' serves the societal purpose of 'protecting privilege from the threat of public understanding and participation.'[3] This purpose is achieved through what Herman and Chomsky describe as 'brainwashing under freedom.'[4] Herman and Chomsky accept that, in the US and UK, the state does not directly control the output of the media or academia or other channels of indoctrination. Thought control is not achieved through police action, torture, or terror. Chomsky explains:

> A totalitarian state can be satisfied with lesser degrees of allegiance to required truths. It is sufficient that people obey; what they think is a secondary concern. But in a democratic political order, there is always the danger that independent thought might be translated into political action, so it is important to eliminate the threat at its root. Debate cannot be stilled, and indeed, in a properly functioning system of propaganda, it should not be, because it has a system-reinforcing character if constrained within proper bounds. What is essential is to set the bounds firmly. Controversy may rage as long as it adheres to the presuppositions that define the consensus of elites, and it should furthermore be encouraged within these bounds, thus helping to establish these doctrines as the very condition of thinkable thought while reinforcing the belief that freedom reigns.[5]

The PM suggests that media and the intellectual culture within the capitalist democracies are impacted in a multiplicity of ways by power..

For example, during the Vietnam War, the mainstream debate was between those liberals like Arthur Schlesinger who opposed the war, and those hawks like Joseph Alsop who predicted victory. Schlesinger believed the US was headed for defeat, adding: 'we all pray that Mr Alsop will be right.'[6] Chomsky pointed out that Schlesinger's opposition to the war was tactical, not moral or legal. Alsop and Schlesinger would have been united in supporting the war, if it could be brought to a successful conclusion. Given that they were at opposite ends of 'responsible opinion,' Chomsky suggested that it was of great importance 'to note that each presents what can fairly be described as an apologia for American imperialism.'[7] Both believed that the United States had the right to impose its will on others by force. In their debates, neither side questioned that presumption. Crucially, neither side stated that belief explicitly. It was assumed without argument. Questioning it became unthinkable.[8]

One possible test of the Propaganda Model is the ultimate national security issue: nuclear weapons. There has been fierce debate and controversy in Britain over many decades concerning Britain's possession and retention of nuclear weapons. The PM predicts that the very fierceness of the mainstream debate will have had a 'system-reinforcing character' because it kept itself within 'proper bounds.'

Chomsky has described the system of ideas that rules the propaganda machine as a 'state religion,' within which there are two basic principles. Principle 1: The Holy State[9] is Good. Policymakers may make errors, they may act out of ignorance or stupidity, and occasionally a 'bad person' may gain power, but the policymaking establishment as a whole has noble intentions. Principle 2 follows from Principle 1: Any action taken by the Holy State, however violent, is defensive in nature.[10]

According to Principle 2, Britain's possession of nuclear weapons must be defensive in nature, and British nuclear weapons policy must be defensive in nature – whatever the evidence.

Chomsky once wrote: 'A useful rule of thumb is this: If you want to learn something about the propaganda system, have a close look at the critics and their tacit assumptions. These typically constitute the doctrines of the state religion.'[11] Mainstream critics practice what Chomsky calls 'feigned dissent,' appearing to be critical of established power, but in fact reinforcing it.[12]

Let's sample the outer edge of 'responsible opinion' in the recent nuclear weapons debate in Britain. In *The Guardian* in 2013, there was a harsh critique of the British nuclear weapons arsenal from perhaps the most anti-militarist of the paper's columnists of the time, Simon Jenkins. On 25 September 2013, Jenkins described the commitment to retaining British nuclear weapons as 'irrational,' 'mad,' 'hare-brained,' 'hypocritical,' 'absurd,' and 'nonsense.' The former editor of *The Times* added that the British nuclear deterrent 'made no sense.' Jenkins explained the basis of his scorn: Britain's nuclear weapons 'bear no reference to any plausible threat to Britain that could possibly merit their use.'

Jenkins argued that nuclear weapons were 'an irrelevance' in the face of the enemies that Britain was likely to be facing on the battlefield – 'Enemies immune to nuclear weapons and heavy armour, enemies who hurl grenades and wield Kalashnikovs made in 1947.' This was a tactical critique rather than a principled one.[13] Jenkins would have supported the retention of nuclear weapons if they had been 'relevant' in defeating the enemies Britain faced.

A few years earlier, the London *Independent* had staked out its position as the most critical voice in the British mainstream media on British nuclear weapons. On 2 May 2005, an editorial argued that, during the Cold War, 'nuclear weapons acted as a deterrent to aggression by other states,' but the collapse of the Soviet Union had now 'made the deterrence argument obsolete.'

A few days later, on 6 May 2005, one of the *Independent*'s most left-wing columnists, Johann Hari, continued the disarmament campaign, suggesting that 'Britain is extremely unlikely to ever use our nuclear warheads.' The crucial question he posed was: if the al-Qa'eda terror network ever gained possession of nuclear weapons, 'what good would our deterrent be? Who would we nuke in response?' Deterrence is about nuclear retaliation against a nuclear weapon state. In the absence of a state actor, it loses meaning, according to Hari.

A few months later, on 6 November 2005, the *Independent*'s understanding of nuclear policy was spelled out in a briefing entitled 'Nukes – do they still protect us?' Cole Moreton wrote: 'Trident is a deterrent... so that anyone who threatens this country knows they will suffer greatly in return.'

In these and other mainstream criticisms of the British nuclear arsenal, we find a coherent set of ideas:

- Nuclear weapons are for 'deterrence.'
- Deterrence is about retaliation.
- Nuclear retaliation is only rational or credible if it is against a hostile nuclear weapon state - to ward off invasion or nuclear attack by that state.

When we go back to the fierce debates about British nuclear weapons in the late 1950s and early 1960s, and through much of the 1980s, we discover that mainstream critics back then also accepted these assumptions as the basis for the discussion. Among them were former military leaders such as Field Marshal Lord Carver, who saw 'no military logic' in nuclear weapons.[14] If we move from military figures to philosophers, we find a similarly disciplined discussion in *Dangers of Deterrence: Philosophers on Nuclear Strategy*, published in 1983. Editors Nigel Black and Kay Pole, for example, contribute 'A Sceptical Look at the Nuclear Debate' that does not look, sceptically or otherwise, at the underpinning assumptions of the debate around nuclear weapons. In this they are typical of much of the mainstream critique of nuclear weapons at the time. Black and Pole write:

> Deterrence rests on three expectations: that the enemy will behave rationally, that the threat which daunts him now will continue to be the most daunting he could face, and that he will not find technical means by which he could counter-deter that threat. Now taking these in reverse order, there are reasons to believe that the USSR is actually finding ways to deter the launching of medium-range weapons at her from Western Europe...[15]

In other words, deterrence is about enemies who are nuclear weapon states. Elsewhere in the book, there are a few glancing references to challenging material (see below), but, taken as a whole, this volume reinforces the idea that deterrence is solely concerned with 'threatening nuclear weapon states with nuclear retaliation in order to prevent a nuclear attack on oneself.'

We can restate the ideas about deterrence uncovered above in the following way:

1) The British government possesses nuclear weapons solely in order to defend the territory of Britain from nuclear attack.

2) The British government possesses nuclear weapons solely in order to threaten that it can and will retaliate after a nuclear attack on the territory of the UK. In other words, British nuclear weapons are focused on hostile nuclear weapon states.
3) This credible threat of retaliation makes it much less likely that a hostile nuclear weapon state will launch a nuclear attack on the UK.
There is an underlying assumption here:
4) Britain has not actually used its nuclear weapons. They have lain idle as rainy-day insurance against a worst-case superpower crisis.

These four assumptions have been accepted by and embedded in the mainstream critique of British nuclear weapons. They make up the public idea of 'deterrence.' They are fundamental assumptions held by all parties to the mainstream debate about nuclear weapons in Britain. In this case, 'feigned dissent' involves making criticisms which still take these assumptions as the starting point for discussion, without ever even stating them explicitly, let alone testing them against the evidence.

When the critics hold the same unspoken bedrock judgements, they become the boundaries of thinkable thought.

When tested against the evidence, three of the four assumptions about deterrence are contradicted by the available facts.

This essay connects two kinds of 'unthinkable.' One is the kind of 'unthinkable' predicted by the Propaganda Model.

For the general public in Britain, the idea of using nuclear weapons is so deeply unacceptable, so taboo, that it is 'unthinkable' in a different way. Of course, two nuclear weapons were dropped by the United States on Japan in August 1945, killing somewhere in the region of 100,000 civilians, but the popular perception in Western societies is that, since Nagasaki, nuclear weapons have not been used.

This is a myth.

For some uncomfortable reality, we can turn to Daniel Ellsberg, once a high-level US military analyst, who in 1969 leaked the 'Pentagon Papers,' the top secret internal history of the Vietnam War. Ellsberg wrote in 1981:

> The notion common to nearly all Americans that 'no nuclear weapons have been used since Nagasaki' is mistaken. It is not the case that U.S. nuclear weapons have simply piled up over the years – we have over 30,000 of them now, after dismantling many thousands of obsolete ones – unused and unusable, save for the single function of deterring their use against us by the Soviets. Again and again, generally in secret from the American public, U.S. nuclear weapons have been used, for quite different purposes: in the precise way that a gun is used when you point it at someone's head in a direct confrontation, whether or not the trigger is pulled.[16]

Ellsberg detailed a number of US nuclear threats, writing that 'in the thirty-six years since Hiroshima, every president from Truman to Reagan, with the possible exception of Ford, has felt compelled to consider or direct serious preparations for possible imminent US initiation of tactical or strategic nuclear warfare, in the midst of an ongoing, intense, non-nuclear conflict or crisis.'[17] These included US Secretary of State John Foster Dulles' secret offer to French Prime Minister Bidault of three tactical nuclear weapons in 1954 to relieve the French troops besieged by the Indochinese resistance at Dienbienphu, and US President Dwight D. Eisenhower's secret directive to the US Joint Chiefs of Staff during the 1958 'Lebanon Crisis' to prepare to use nuclear weapons, if necessary, to prevent an Iraqi move into the oilfields of Kuwait.[18]

There is now a considerable literature documenting US threats to use nuclear weapons, or consideration of nuclear use as a live policy option, in a range of crises. The literature around 'nuclear diplomacy' is not restricted to those critical of the nuclear arms race.[19] The website of the Office of the Historian of the US State Department contains this paragraph in its 'Milestones in History' series:

> Atomic diplomacy refers to attempts to use the threat of nuclear warfare to achieve diplomatic goals. After the first successful test of the atomic bomb in 1945, officials immediately considered the potential non-military benefits that could be derived from the American nuclear monopoly. In the years that followed, there were several occasions in which government officials used or considered atomic diplomacy.[20]

Some of these 'occasions' are then spelled out involving actual US nuclear threats or serious presidential consideration of what is referred to as 'nuclear coercion.' The examples given are: the Berlin Blockade of 1948–49 (when B-29 atomic bombers were deployed threateningly); the Korean War (there were several 'occasions,' including the deployment of nuclear B-29s); and the Vietnam War (when 'President Nixon briefly considered using the threat of the bomb to help bring about an end to the war in Vietnam').

So the use of nuclear weapons as a means of coercion, the threatened use of nuclear weapons, has not been 'unthinkable' for the US government.

It may be worth mentioning that all the examples mentioned by the State Department historians involved threatening non-nuclear weapon states: USSR in 1948–49; North Korea and China in 1950, 1951 and 1953; and North Vietnam in 1969. The Soviet Union exploded its first atomic bomb in August 1949, three months after it abandoned the Berlin blockade. China's first nuclear test was in October 1964, over a decade after the Korean War incidents. North Korea did not achieve nuclear weapon status until 2006. North Vietnam never developed or acquired a nuclear weapon.

If the use of nuclear weapons is generally 'unthinkable,' the use of nuclear weapons against non-nuclear weapon states must be even more 'unthinkable' for the public.

When we turn to the British record, we find that the British government has used its nuclear weapons repeatedly in just the ways described.

For example, Iraq has been threatened with British nuclear weapons on at least four occasions.

In 1961, Britain manufactured a crisis in the Persian Gulf to send the message that it intended to remain a power in the region despite its military withdrawal. As part of a huge military deployment aimed at threatening Iraq, nuclear-capable Scimitar aircraft were sent to the Gulf on board a British aircraft carrier,[21] and strategic nuclear bombers were placed on alert in Malta.[22] British intelligence insider Anthony Verrier later described the incident as an 'act of deterrence, in which the nuclear weapons system played a central, concealed role... directed against [Egyptian president Gamal Abdel] Nasser and, by extension, Russian ambitions in Arabia.'[23]

Thirty years later, nuclear weapons formed part of the US and British military intervention against Iraq. On 10 August 1990, just eight days after the Iraqi invasion of Kuwait, and months before British forces deployed in strength for the assault in January, a British tabloid newspaper, the *Daily Star*, reported: 'Whitehall sources made it clear that the multinational forces would be ready to hit back with every means at their disposal... [including] using tactical nuclear weapons against [Iraqi] troops and tanks on the battlefield.' On 30 September 1990, the *Observer* reported (on its front page) a warning from a senior British army officer with 7th Armoured Brigade: if there were Iraqi chemical attacks, British forces would 'retaliate with battlefield nuclear forces.' On 26 October 1990, the *Daily Mail* reported: 'One senior minister said, "If we were prepared to use tactical nuclear weapons against the Russians, I can't see why we shouldn't be prepared to use them against Iraq."' On 13 November 1990, the senior *Guardian* journalist, Hugo Young, wrote that he had heard a minister say that the war against Iraq might have to be ended with 'tactical nukes.'

British nuclear threats were not restricted to anonymous leaks. On 15 January 1991, the British Prime Minister, John Major told the House of Commons that he did not 'envisage needing to use the sanction' of nuclear weapons against Iraq.[24] Major did not rule out the use of British nuclear weapons as unthinkable against a non-nuclear weapon state. His choice of words indicated that it was a live policy option. *The Guardian* carried this report of a statement by the British Foreign Secretary, Douglas Hurd, on 4 February 1991: 'Mr. Hurd said that if Iraq responded to an allied land assault by using chemical weapons, President Saddam [Hussein] would be certain to provoke a massive response – language the U.S. and Britain employ to leave open the option of using chemical or nuclear weapons.'

Those confrontations took place under Conservative governments.

In February 1998, in the context of a crisis over UN weapons inspections, a Labour Foreign Secretary, Robin Cook, told the House of Commons that if the Iraqi dictator Saddam Hussein were to use chemical or biological weapons in retaliation for a US-UK assault, 'he should be in no doubt that, if he were to do so, there would be a proportionate response.'[25] In other words, Cook threatened that Britain or the US would use weapons of mass destruction, either nuclear, chemical or biological weapons.

In the run-up to the 2003 attack on Iraq, there were more nuclear threats from the Labour administration. British Defence Secretary Geoff Hoon told the House of Commons Defence Select Committee, on 20 March 2002, that states like Iraq 'can be absolutely confident that in the right conditions we would be willing to use our nuclear weapons.'[26] On 24 March 2002, Hoon appeared on ITV's *Jonathan Dimbleby* show and insisted that the government 'reserved the right' to use nuclear weapons if Britain or British troops were threatened by chemical or biological weapons.[27] When asked about these nuclear threats in a House of Commons debate on 29 April 2002, Hoon said: 'ultimately, and in conditions of extreme self-defence, nuclear weapons would have to be used.'[28] Hoon refused to clarify what he meant by these words.

Iraq is not the only country to have been menaced by British nuclear weapons. Until 1969, the British strategic nuclear force was composed of 'V-bombers' (Valiant, Vulcan and Victor aircraft). In the 1950s and 1960s, V-bombers made hundreds of flights not just around the British Isles but around the British Empire. They were not restricted to defending the home territory from Soviet invasion. For example, in 1962, V-bombers attended independence ceremonies in Uganda and Jamaica.[29] Three Victors were sent to Jamaica again in 1966 (by a Labour government this time). They were there for 'more than decorative purposes,' according to Andrew Brookes, historian of the V-bomber force and himself a former Vulcan pilot.[30]

According to Brookes, the strategic nuclear Vulcans at RAF Waddington were committed in 1963 to 'dealing with conventional trouble in the Middle East,' while their sister Victors in Cottesmore and Honington 'looked after the Far East.'[31]

The deployment of V-bombers to the Middle East or to East Asia amounted to nuclear intimidation, whether or not they carried nuclear weapons on any particular mission, because they were strategic nuclear bombers. There is a parallel with the deployment of US nuclear B-29s during the Berlin Blockade or the Korean War.

To take another example, V-bombers from Bomber Command were sent out to Singapore in December 1963, after the 'Confrontation' with Indonesia had begun. Brookes, the RAF historian, reports that the bombers were retained in the country beyond their normal term, 'positioned to be seen as ready to eliminate Indonesia Air Force capabilities if they launched air attacks.'[32] Brookes does not say whether this 'elimination' was to be conventional or nuclear in nature. British Air Chief Marshal Sir David Lee later commented of the nuclear-capable Victors: 'Their potential was well known to Indonesia and their presence did not go unnoticed.' Lee added: 'the knowledge of RAF strength and competence created a wholesome respect among Indonesia's leaders, and the deterrent effect of RAF air defence fighters, light bombers and V-bombers on detachment from Bomber Command was absolute.'[33]

We now know that when the first V-bombers went out to RAF Tengah in Singapore at the end of 1963, there was a storage unit there for 48 Red Beard nuclear bombs, and the squadron soon began low-altitude nuclear bombing exercises, no doubt signalling British intentions to Indonesia.[34]

So we see that the British state has repeatedly used nuclear weapons (under both Labour and Conservative administrations) 'in the precise way that a gun is used when you point it at someone's head in a direct confrontation, whether or not the trigger is pulled.'

From the threats against Iraq, a non-nuclear weapon state in 1961, 1991, 1998 and 2003; from the strategic nuclear bomber deployments right across the British Empire; from the V-bomber commitments to the Middle East and East Asia (all entirely non-nuclear weapon states in 1963); and from the intimidation of Indonesia in the mid-1960s, we learn the true meaning of 'deterrence.'

The true meaning of 'deterrence' is: creating a 'wholesome respect' among the natives in far-off lands that Britain wishes to dominate; preventing non-nuclear weapon states from using weapons or launching attacks that might even up the military odds; if necessary, finishing off a non-nuclear weapon state too tough to defeat by conventional means.

There is a remarkable consistency across the decades in the attitude that it is entirely acceptable to use British nuclear weapons to intimidate and coerce other states, particularly non-nuclear weapon states.

How is it that this material, all readily available as part of the public record, does not form part of the discussion around nuclear weapons? Somehow, these facts, and their implications, have not been expressed in the mainstream debate about nuclear weapons. In fact, they cannot be expressed, and they cannot be thought about. This history is 'unthinkable.'

If we return to the four underlying assumptions of what 'deterrence' means, we discover from this self-censored history that:

1) British nuclear weapons have not been solely focused on defending the territory of the UK. From the very beginning, they have not been just about defence, or just about the UK. From the 1950s, British nuclear weapons have been used to intimidate countries around the world.
2) British nuclear weapons have not just been a response to, and aimed at, nuclear weapon states. British nuclear weapons have often been used to menace non-nuclear weapon states. In other words, British nuclear weapons have not just been about nuclear retaliation, they have also been about nuclear intimidation and coercion.
3) It is not true that Britain has not used its nuclear weapons, and that they have lain idle as rainy-day insurance against a superpower crisis. Britain *has* used its nuclear weapons. It has often used them to threaten other countries during direct confrontations.

This has been part of British nuclear policy since the beginning.[35] All of this is a matter of public record, and yet these important facts and statements did not enter or influence the fierce debates about British nuclear weapons possession in the 1950s, 1960s and 1980s, or in the period since the replacement of the Trident nuclear weapons system came onto the agenda. The evidence of British nuclear threats against non-nuclear weapon states did not disturb the very narrow notion of 'deterrence' that was debated so passionately.

Returning to *Dangers of Deterrence*, mentioned above, Jeff McMahan (then a member of CND) made a relevant contribution entitled 'Nuclear Blackmail' (today it might be called 'Nuclear Extortion' to avoid a racist undertone). McMahan ruled out the risk of nuclear coercion of a non-nuclear weapon state in peacetime as 'largely unreal'. 'Even in times of open military conflict,' he went on, 'nuclear threats against non-nuclear countries may not be a serious option for nuclear-armed countries.' McMahan's 'most realistic scenario' would be one in which a nuclear weapon state begins an aggressive war against a non-nuclear weapon state and got 'bogged down'. The aggressor may then, 'in desperation, resort to nuclear threats in an attempt to cut [her or] his losses and gain a favourable settlement.'[36] Quite similar to the October-November 1990 threats against Iraq.

One curious aspect of McMahan's abstract and theoretical discussion of this topic is that, when writing his chapter, he was aware of Daniel Ellsberg's list of actual nuclear threats. McMahan does not refer to Ellsberg's list anywhere in the main body of the essay, but he does in three footnotes. One sentence refers vaguely to 'the various nuclear threats which successive US governments have made since 1945.' The reference (footnote 4) is to Ellsberg's list of historical cases.[37] McMahan does not discuss any of the history Ellsberg sets out, but he does consider two cases not listed by Ellsberg: the Hiroshima-Nagasaki bombings, and US nuclear threats against the USSR (a nuclear weapon state) during the Arab-Israeli War of 1973.

This is an excellent demonstration of the way the propaganda system works, according to the Propaganda Model. McMahan consciously suppressed shocking information critical to the topic he had decided to address – nuclear coercion of non-nuclear weapon states. He did so, we can presume, not because he was ordered to do so by the state or some other authority, but because of an internalised sense of the 'right' way to discuss this topic. This is a case of voluntary self-censorship rather than authoritarian censorship – 'brainwashing under freedom.' McMahan suppressed the information (Ellsberg's list of US nuclear threats) not by pretending it did not exist, but by treating it as something unworthy, or barely worthy, of attention. This is part of a larger pattern in the mainstream media and academia. Chomsky explains that:

> the enormous amount of material that is produced in the media and books makes it possible for a really assiduous and committed researcher to gain a fair picture of the real world by cutting through the mass of misrepresentation and fraud to the nuggets hidden within.[38]

Herman and Chomsky expand:

> That a careful reader, looking for a fact can sometimes find it, with diligence and a skeptical eye, tells us nothing about whether that fact received the attention and context it deserved, whether it was intelligible to most readers, or whether it was effectively distorted or suppressed.[39]

You may have noticed that in the section on the 1991 nuclear threats against Iraq, there were quotes from a number of British newspapers. Herman and Chomsky comment:

> That the media provide some information about an issue... proves absolutely nothing about the adequacy or accuracy of media coverage. The media do in fact suppress a great deal of information, but even more important is the way they present a particular fact – its placement, tone, and frequency of repetition – and the framework of analysis in which it is placed.[40]

Let's take each of these four propaganda devices in turn, in relation to McMahan's chapter: placement, tone, frequency of repetition, and framework of analysis.

Placement: McMahan, in this case, knew of Daniel Ellsberg's list of US nuclear threats and its relevance to his topic, but decided not to give any details of the list, and placed his direct references to Ellsberg's list (which tended to contradict his argument) in the least-visible section of his essay, the footnotes.

Tone and frequency of repetition: there are, in total, three (plain, factual) sentences directly mentioning Ellsberg's list - in three separate footnotes. In the main text, there are two indirect references to Ellsberg's list, separated by 23 pages. We have already noted the first (two-sentence) reference to the list, which is brief and offhand. The other (even more indirect) reference to Ellsberg's list comes in the final paragraph, which poses a number of questions that need to be investigated regarding 'those [unspecified] nuclear threats which have been made.'[41] The tone is flat, academic, and questioning, unexcited.

Framework of analysis: The overall picture within which these references appear is fairly summed up by the final words of the chapter: 'the claim that the possibility of nuclear blackmail poses a serious threat to non-nuclear countries should be treated with scepticism.'[42]

When we examine the newspaper reports (some of them front-page stories) about the British nuclear threats against Iraq in 1990–1, the most common features are: lack of repetition of the disturbing reports (almost immediately, it's as if they never surfaced) and a consistent framework of analysis for reporting both Iraq and nuclear weapons in which British nuclear threats against a non-nuclear weapon state are inconceivable and unthinkable. So the facts are sometimes reported, sometimes prominently, but they disappear as soon as they appear.

The PM's predictions of media performance are borne out by the behaviour of recent mainstream critics of nuclear weapons, and by the way in which the long history of British nuclear threats has been edited out of history in the long, often intense debate about nuclear weapons. Mainstream criticisms of British nuclear weapons have colluded with the suppression of important relevant history and have created a narrow, irrelevant definition of 'nuclear deterrence.' By focusing on abstract questions raised by possible future retaliation, the mainstream critics have helped to divert attention from the concrete reality of actual, often recent, nuclear intimidation by the British state.

## Notes and Bibliography

[1] 'The Guardian view on section 40: muzzling journalism,' *Guardian*, 10 January 2017.
[2] Justice Powell, dissenting opinion, No. 73-1265 Saxbe v. *Washington Post Co.*, 417 U.S. 843 (1974).
[3] Noam Chomsky (1989), *Necessary Illusions*, London, Pluto, p. 14.
[4] Noam Chomsky and Edward S. Herman (1979), *The Washington Connection and Third World Fascism*, Montréal, Black Rose Books, pp. 66–83.
[5] Chomsky (1989), *Necessary Illusions*, 48.
[6] Arthur Schlesinger (1967), *The Bitter Heritage: Vietnam and American Democracy 1941–1966*, Boston, MA, Houghton Mifflin Company, p. 57. Cited in Noam Chomsky (1969), *American Power and the New Mandarins*, Harmandsworth, Penguin Books, p. 240.
[7] Noam Chomsky (1970), letter, *Listener*, 15 January, 88.
[8] Schlesinger's response to Chomsky demonstrated his inability to escape the limits of the thinkable, as Chomsky observed in a subsequent letter. *Listener*, 29 January 1970, 150; *Listener*, 19 February 1970, 252.
[9] Generally, someone's Holy State is the nation-state to which they belong as a citizen. Sometimes it is a foreign nation-state, such as the Soviet Union for Communists in times past, or Israel for what are called 'supporters of Israel.' Chomsky wrote in 1983: 'To a remarkable extent, articulate opinion and attitudes in the U.S. have been dominated by people who describe themselves as "supporters of Israel", a term that I will also adopt, though with much reluctance, since I think they should more properly be called "supporters of the moral degeneration and ultimate destruction of Israel", and not Israel alone.' Noam Chomsky (rev.ed.1999 [1983]), *Fateful Triangle: The United States, Israel, and the Palestinians*, London, Pluto Press, p. 40.

[10] 'The aggressive and militant actions of every state are invariably justified on grounds of "defense". Thus Hitler's aggression in Eastern Europe was justified as defense against "a dagger pointed at the heart of Germany" (Czechoslovakia), against the violence and aggressiveness of the Poles, against the encirclement of the imperialist powers that sought to strangle Germany; and his invasion of the Low Countries and France was also "defensive", a response to the hostile acts of France and England, bent on Germany's destruction. If we had records, we would probably discover that Attila the Hun was acting in self-defense. Since state actions are always justified in terms of defense, we learn nothing when we hear that certain specific actions are so justified except that we are listening to the spokesperson for some state; but that we already knew.' Noam Chomsky (1987), *On Power and Ideology: The Managua Lectures*, Boston MA, South End Press, p. 99.

[11] Noam Chomsky (1988), *The Chomsky Reader*, James Peck (ed.), London, Serpents Tail, p. 126.

[12] Noam Chomsky (1988), *Language and Politics*, C.P. Otero (ed.), Montréal: Black Rose Books, p. 376.

[13] Jenkins had a secondary criticism: 'Meanwhile their possession by Britain is a blatant invitation to nuclear proliferation, making opposition to an Iranian bomb hypocritical.' This is also a tactical rather than a principled critique.

[14] Field Marshal Lord Carver was a member of the Canberra Commission, set up by the Australian government in 1995, which also included US General Lee Butler, responsible until 1994 for all US strategic nuclear forces. A later US equivalent was the Nuclear Security Project, formed in 2007 by former US Secretary of State George P. Shultz, former US Secretary of Defence William J. Perry, former US Secretary of State Henry A. Kissinger and former US Senator Sam Nunn. Both initiatives called for a world without nuclear weapons, on the basis of thoroughly establishment political assumptions.

[15] Nigel Black and Kay Pole (1983), 'Introduction: A Sceptical Look at the Nuclear Debate,' in *Dangers of Deterrence: Philosophers on Nuclear Strategy*, ed. Nigel Black and Kay Pole, London: Routledge & Kegan Paul, p. 8.

[16] Daniel Ellsberg (1981), 'Introduction,' in E.P. Thompson and Dan Smith, (eds.), *Protest and Survive* (New York: Monthly Review Press).

[17] Ibid.'

[18] Ellsberg cites these references for the Dienbienphu claim: Prime Minister Bidault in the film *Hearts and Minds*, and in Roscoe Drummond and Gaston Coblentz (1960), *Duel at the Brink*, New York, Doubleday, pp. 121-22; Richard Nixon (1978), *RN*, New York: Grosset & Dunlap, pp. 150-55. For Lebanon, Ellsberg cites Barry M. Blechman and Stephen S. Kaplan (1978), *Force Without War: U.S. Armed Forces as a Political Instrument*, Washington DC:,Brookings Institution, p. 238, p. 256.

19. For an early mainstream study, see Blechman and Kaplan, *Force Without War*. Three book-length works are: Joseph Gerson (1986), ed., *The Deadly Connection: Nuclear War and U.S. Intervention* (Philadelphia, PA: New Society Publishers); Michio Kaku and Daniel Axelrod (1987), *To Win A Nuclear War: The Pentagon's Secret War Plans* (Boston, MA: South End Press); and Joseph Gerson (2007), *Empire and the Bomb: How the U.S. Uses Nuclear Weapons to Dominate the World* (London: Pluto Press).
20. 'Atomic Diplomacy,' Office of the Historian, U.S. State Department, https://history.state.gov/milestones/1945-1952/atomic, accessed 3 July 2017.
21. Adel Darwish and Gregory Alexander (1991), *Unholy Babylon: The Secret History of Saddam's War*, London, Gollancz, 1991, p. 33.
22. Andrew Brookes (1982), *Force V: The History of Britain's Airborne Deterrent*, London, Jane's, p. 141.
23. Anthony Verrier (1983), *Through the Looking Glass: British Foreign Policy in an Age of Illusions*, London, Jonathan Cape, p. 171. 'Russian ambitions in Arabia' is code for the forces of independent Arab nationalism generally, including in Iraq.
24. HC Deb (1990–91) 183 col. 726.
25. HC Deb (1997–98) 306 col. 905.
26. 'UK "prepared to use nuclear weapons"', BBC News online, 20 March 2002, http://news.bbc.co.uk/1/hi/uk_politics/1883258.stm, accessed 5 July 2017.
27. Richard Norton-Taylor (2002), 'Bush's nuke bandwagon,' *Guardian*, 27 March.
28. HC Deb (2001–02) 384 col. 665.
29. UK Ministry of Defence (1963), *Statement on Defence 1963*, London, HMSO, para. 59.
30. Brookes, *Force V*, 140.
31. Ibid, 140.
32. Ibid, 138.
33. David Lee (1984), *Eastward: A History of the RAF in the Far East, 1945–70*, London, HMSO, p. 213.
34. Tom Rhodes (2000), 'Britain Kept Secret Nuclear Weapons In Singapore & Cyprus,' *Sunday Times*, 31 December.
35. For a brief discussion of the relevant nuclear doctrine, see Milan Rai (1995, rev. ed.), *Tactical Trident: The Rifkind Doctrine and the Third World* (London: Drava Papers).
36. Jeff McMahan (1983), 'Nuclear Blackmail,' in *Dangers of Deterrence: Philosophers on Nuclear Strategy*, Nigel Black and Kay Pole (eds.), London, Routledge & Kegan Paul, pp. 94–97 *passim*.
37. Strictly speaking, the footnote is connected to the very next sentence, which waters the statement down to: 'U.S. governments have *apparently* made use of nuclear threats on several occasions' (emphasis added). McMahan (1983), 'Nuclear Blackmail,' 87.

[38] Noam Chomsky (1982), *Towards a New Cold War: Essays on the Current Crisis and How We Got There*, London, Sinclair Browne), p. 14.
[39] Edward S. Herman and Noam Chomsky (1988), 'Propaganda Mill: The Media Churn Out the "Official Line"', *The Progressive*, June 1988, 15.
[40] Ibid, 15.
[41] McMahan, 'Nuclear Blackmail,' 110.
[42] Ibid, 110.

CHAPTER 18

# Conclusion

Joan Pedro-Carañana, Daniel Broudy and Jeffery Klaehn

This book has tested the three main hypotheses that Edward S. Herman and Noam Chomsky propose for empirically validating the Propaganda Model (PM). Authors have provided qualitative and quantitative evidence based on case studies and comparative analyses, evaluated the influence of the five filters, identified propaganda tactics and strategies and proposed ways of extending and improving the model. We shall explain next how this volume has addressed each of the main hypotheses.

### 18.1 First Hypothesis

The analyses featured in this volume have confirmed the first hypothesis that predicts that when the interests of the economic and political elites are strong, when there is consensus among them and oppositional forces are weak and disorganized, the most influential media (both analog and digital) will strongly support such consensus and their projects for imperial, class and racial domination both nationally and internationally.

Contributors have presented evidence of such a propagandistic role in the online and offline mainstream news coverage of the so-called 'war on terror'

---

**How to cite this book chapter:**
Pedro-Carañana, J., Broudy, D. and Klaehn, J. 2018. Conclusion. In: Pedro-Carañana, J., Broudy, D. and Klaehn, J. (eds.). *The Propaganda Model Today: Filtering Perception and Awareness*. Pp. 279–286. London: University of Westminster Press. DOI: https://doi.org/10.16997/book27.r. License: CC-BY-NC-ND 4.0

and 'humanitarian interventions', nuclear weapons and deterrence, the economic crash, the policies of austerity, inequality and poverty and race relations in the United States and Cuba. Contributors have analysed the demonisation and defamation of emergent social movements and political forces, as well as the media support of the 2002 coup in Venezuela while criminalizing protest in Mexico. As predicted by the PM, comparable events are considered newsworthy or not depending on the vested interests of powerful actors; there are worthy and unworthy victims, worthy and unworthy malefactors. Even the dramatic reporting on climate change in a crucial period for both the environment and humans meets the expectations of the PM. Concrete interests are not analysed with scrutiny. The need for a macro-transformation to move towards new socio-economic systems not based upon accelerated usage and consumption of natural resources is similarly not highlighted.

We have also featured applications of the PM to forms of media and content not previously analysed within this theoretical framework, particularly the entertainment industry. Through the study of television, professional sports, videogames, online media platforms, social networks and search engines, and the Hollywood film industry, authors have argued that the PM with a broadened analytical range of media remains to be a strong conceptual tool for explaining and predicting media performance.

The authors acknowledge a greater difficulty to measuring the PM hypotheses in entertainment media, but applied textual and political economy analyses to identify different types of entertainment products in relation to elite consensus. In order for their presence in the media, these types include: (a) Those which are overtly supportive of establishment goals; (b) Those that initially appear to criticize the political system but, on closer reading, provide it with fundamental support; (c) those that do genuinely challenge Western systems of hegemonic power but are explicitly marginalized by the corporate media mechanisms of control; (d) Those that are genuine cases of breaking through the filtration system, which invariably occur for irregular reasons and/or with serious caveats and little promotion.

A Propaganda Model for Television contextualizes the PM and provides a critical evaluation of the programming that surrounds television news. It considers the involvement of major corporations, the State, the military and other elite institutions and actors in TV shows and posits that most of the contents promote the basic tenets of neoliberalism: consumerism, selfish individualism, priority of the physical image, hierarchical organization of economic and social activities, entrepreneurial attitude, profit-making, jingoism, technocracy, war, the belief that everybody lies and that human nature is intrinsically bad, and the proposal of individual solutions to social problems.

A content analysis of both Google results and the *New York Times* has demonstrated that stigmatizing terms are used far more often to disparage professional athletes, particularly NFL players, than to describe team owners; by contrast, benevolent terms are used far more often to describe team owners than to describe players. It is worth noting that the *New York Times* was even slightly more favorable to NFL team owners than Google was.

Even though there is much more diversity on the internet than in a single newspaper (*New York Times*), the level of plurality is diminished by the mediation of Google search engine, as it operates as a power-law. Although there are possibilities for smaller media to compete and obtain visibility, the selection and ordering of the results respond to hierarchical criteria which tend to favor sites belonging to established, dominant institutions, at the expense of new and less well-established sites, and thus for innovation and diversity.

From the perspective of the first hypothesis of the PM, an important innovation ought to be observed. Even though internet media are important channels for the dissemination of commercialism and right-wing propaganda, the ongoing technological revolution also provides opportunities for critical citizens and social movements to spread their messages across geographical boundaries with unprecedented speed. Far from the one-sidedness of both techno-utopian and techno-dystopian views, contributors reflect dialectically on propaganda in the new digital communications systems. Authors apply the elements of the PM to corporate media as components of a larger System of social and ideological influence and coercion, and examine responses through digital and physical activism carried out by actors against the prevailing political order.

In other words, digital technologies have allowed for both a tighter cultural control of citizens by elites as well as opportunities for social movements, new political forces and individual citizens to create and distribute their communication. For the first time in history, most people have the possibility of creating contents and introducing more plurality into the public sphere. However, it is the traditional media that are now dominating the internet. Corporate and State actors have more economic resources and are better organized, but organized social movements have used collective intelligence to deliver creative and critical messages and achieve an important level of influence. Citizens can respond to a tweet from politicians, but they might as well be ignored. Celebrities are most widely followed, but new politicians and journalists in favor of change have more followers than traditional politicians. Thus, the study of the internet requires further analysis of the relation between digital labour (users) and digital capital, the Left online and the Right online, everyday users and online celebrities and influencers.

Contributors have provided empirical and political economy analysis of the power relations affecting the internet and of the functioning and contents of online media. They discovered that the communication practices of alternative movements have a noteworthy impact on the cyber-sphere, although they are usually limited to 'hot moments' of protests and dissent. However, the fact is that a small elite of users usually dominates most online visibility and attention. In addition, social networks reproduce abundantly the contents of the mainstream media, while the mainstream media does not include so many of the contents created by citizens and social movements (especially the critical-transformative messages). Still, digital media are fundamental for social movements to make powerful discursive interventions in moments of crisis. They can do so by exploring the contradictions, utilizing specific software, platforms and institutions, and using creativity and humour. The exceptions to the PM are, therefore, important in developing greater understanding for the possibilities of change. The potential for contestation is acknowledged since power relations are contradictory and are affected by change.

The propaganda role of the media systems has been confirmed empirically in several geographical areas, including the United States, the United Kingdom, Canada, Germany, Latin America, and Spain. We can, therefore, confirm the validity of the PM to explain news reporting in other countries different from the US where the original PM analysis was conducted.

## 18.2 Exceptions

The media in some countries have experienced overtures in which a wider diversity of opinions enjoyed their space. This is consistent with the first hypothesis of the PM: when there is no elite consensus, the media will tend to portray all the sides of the elite conflict and even allow more voices. This is what happened in Spain where the new political party Podemos was given more time on air to criticize the government. By doing this, media companies were trying to force the government to resist pressure from global digital giants (such as Netflix, Google, and Amazon) and favor national industries. The media had strategies to discipline and delegitimize Podemos, such as producing flak and accusing it members of being communists and receiving funds from Venezuela and Iran. However, their leaders did receive significant space when they were building the party.

Previously, the 15-M movement was often vilipended and misunderstood by the media, but it did also have space to express its views. In addition, the 15-M (and Podemos to a certain extent) was able to shape the online environment for some time and achieve a lot of visibility by sharing a great number of discourses. As the PM holds, when the interests of the elites are divided, when the burden for the practices of a part of the elites (especially corruption) is not to be accepted by another part of the elite, and when strong social and political movements with a communication strategy emerge, the media will tend to become more open and include more diverse views. The media frames still remain mainly within elite interests (reflecting the different sides), but there are more possibilities for journalistic autonomy, and this opens a window of opportunity for radical forces to develop strategies of critical intervention in the media. It is, thus, important to focus on national and local factors, which include the political tradition, the existence of strong social movements, the degree of hegemony exercised by neoliberalism, the State and global capitalism as well as the openness of the cultural and ideological context.

Elite differences, social and political movements for change, national and local contexts, and the innovative and creative use of the digital media are important factors to understand the functioning of the traditional and new media and exploring the possibilities of meaningfully intervening in them. It is worth highlighting the capacity of human agency, especially collective action, to influence the media system and eventually transform it. Herman and Chomsky did not reflect thoroughly on the role of social movements and civil society, but the underlying assumption is that even though propaganda tends to be effective, there are always resistance and movements for change. Chomsky has emphasized that polls show systematically that the general population in the US holds rather diverging views on important topics to those held by the elites. The System establishes determinations, but there are also degrees of freedom in which creative and transformative communication and action can have a meaningful impact.

## 18.3 Second Hypothesis

It has also been demonstrated that the five operative principles or 'filters' that comprise the model (ownership, advertising, sourcing, flak and dominant ideology) have a strong impact on media systems that are guided by market forces rather than by direct State control (second hypothesis).

It has been shown in accordance with the perspective of the PM that the main online and offline media outlets are controlled by large concentrations of corporate power that are interconnected with States and governments. Such corporations are characterized by their secrecy. Moreover, financial capital has further penetrated the media sector and is exercising increasing control over the editorial lines and the production of contents. It has been shown that internet technologies have made it easier to commodify stories. Deregulation by policy-makers has been fundamental in the marketization of both the internet and traditional media.

Advertising also plays a key role since the most important social networks, search engines, and online media depend on advertising revenues. Native advertising, branded content, and product placement have become pervasive. Individualized ads based on Big Data contribute to the culture of commercialism and its acceptance to the detriment of privacy. On television, about a quarter of total broadcast time consists of commercials.

The sourcing filter may adopt different forms depending on the media product. There is a preponderance of the traditional conventions and rules of production that guide producers towards safe sources and predictability. Large corporations, entertainment industries, traditional news organizations, and State actors (including the military) are the main sources of influence in both the online and offline environments. In addition, bots are often used to manipulate the cyber-sphere, especially in politics.

Traditional forms of flak have reached a new level of presence on the internet and often appear as hate speech. Corporate organizations, politicians, parties, movements and individuals often attack people who hold different ideas. This influence on the cyber-sphere can be conducted overtly or covertly and is often done through bots. The capacity to deliver flak obviously depends on resources and organization. The persecution of Snowden and Assange as well as the prosecution of Manning provides evidence on the severity of flak when important information affects the System negatively.

The fifth filter presents a variety of dimensions that are related to the dominant ideologies. News reporting, entertainment, and the internet tend to be influenced by dominant ideologies and usually reproduce them. Neoliberal ideology, with its commercialism, entrepreneurialism, individualism, and cynicism are amplified by online algorithms, videogames, and TV shows. The Orwellian language of the 'war on terror', 'humanitarian interventions' and 'them vs. us' also finds abundant space to generate fear, hatred, and unquestioning conformity. It is also important to note that this volume has included evidence on the renewed influence of anti-communism. In spite of the fall of the Soviet Union, the media continue to accuse social and political forces in favor of change of supporting communism and, specifically Bolivarian Castro-communism in the case of Podemos.

When analyzing the media from a dialectical perspective, it is noticed that where there is commercialization there are also social actors that share technologies and communication without a profit motive. Internet users do sometimes block advertising and use their critical skills to search for alternative media products. Citizens sometimes defend themselves collectively against flak and promote new cultural frameworks and forms of sociability and systemic organization based on equality, freedom, and solidarity. Their influence is limited, but it cannot be underestimated. As Herman and Chomsky have emphasized, governments consider the general population their main enemy; one that has to be persuaded (or coerced) to accept the social order.

The five filters of the PM have a stronger influence in both the analog and the digital media than in the past. Thus, they are relevant for analyzing new media production. However, the question remains whether there are more important factors that come into play, especially in the functioning of the internet. It could be that the first hypothesis on media contents is validated, but that the explanatory principles are insufficient. Is the PM exhaustive? Some contributors have suggested extending the PM as follows:

## 18.4 The Propaganda and Security System

The propaganda and security system refers to the nexus of decision-making power. It involves the interconnection between State and corporate actors that makes investment and political decisions, setting the framework for public policy. The System develops tactics and strategies to protect from critical forces and prevent change. It includes material actions as well as the management, dissemination, and control of information. Attention has been paid to the practices of distortion, omission, and misdirection of information put into practice by the System. It involves organisational and bureaucratic entities, government and corporation 'spin doctors' and 'PR' agents, think tanks, NGOs, co-opted elite journalists and even academia. It also involves surveillance and actors from within the so-called 'deep state' such as the intelligence services as well as online corporations based on Big Data. By taking into account the larger context, the PM considers the actors that produce propaganda in first place and who work to shape the media environments.

## 18.5 Agency: Social Movements, Journalists, Audiences-users

An exhaustive analysis of the media can be conducted by combining the structural approach of the PM with the topic of agency. In the relations between structure and agency, one can observe the degree of adjustment and contradiction between both dimensions of social reality. It is, thereby, possible to identify the forces in conflict and the disruptive factors that might be explored for promoting changes in the media systems. The historical agents of change can be identified and media strategies can be developed. Social and political movements and organizations are important, we have argued, because they can expand the limits of debate in the media. They often resist against the worsening of the state of affairs. When they errupt on the public stage during key moments of history, they can contribute to a democratization of mentalities and societies with lasting effects.

The PM views the role of journalists as overwhelmed by the constraints of the filters. It is held that journalists tend to internalize the editorial values of their employer. Our volume has provided evidence from sociological research of journalism that confirms this. This process of institutionalization of journalists does not follow a behaviourist pattern, but is instead instilled through socialisation and fear – and resistance does take place. Many critical journalists have surely been fired and received other forms of flak, but journalists, especially when they are well-organized, do sometimes question the ownership and organisational structures, the influence of advertisers and the limitations and precariousness they experience. The power relation is asymmetrical, but unions of journalists and professional organizations can wield some influence. Journalists can also feel encouraged to exercise a critical autonomy if there are strong social currents that demand and defend such autonomy. The volume has also shown that some 'journalist stars' transmit alternative information that is widely demanded.

The existence of a strong demand for alternative information and for 'journalist stars' shows that audiences are important in media production. However, citizens are more effective when organized to communicate in the media or to promote media reform through social movements.

The role of social movements, audiences-users, and journalists is understood here in the framework of the power relations *vis á vis* the structures that constrain the possibilities of agency. There is a clear imbalance in the power relations, but the small and seemingly insignificant do sometimes bring about important changes.

## 18.6 Third Hypothesis

The third hypothesis predicts that critical studies and commentary on media performance will tend to be ignored and marginalized. Our volume addresses this hypothesis and shows that Journalism Studies tend to avoid subjecting journalism to a critical analysis that highlights structural power inequalities. This is not achieved through censorship. Instead, the academic system orients human capacities and financial resources towards large-scale, data-intensive research projects. These projects avoid being critical of the media and the role of journalists and focus instead on minor and de-contextualized micro-practices. The academic system rewards these projects with funding and publications in monopolistic profit-driven publishers. In other words, academia also has a political economy.

## 18.7 Final Remarks

This volume has analysed both analog and digital media from the perspective of the PM. The three main hypotheses of the model have been confirmed in both news and entertainment products. Areas of extension and improvement have also been addressed and explanations for exceptions have been provided. The propaganda and security system as well as critical-transformative social movements are relevant factors to include in media analysis. The role of media professionals and audiences-users is also to be taken into consideration. The interplay between structure and agency in the framework of the existing, unequal power relations can be seen as key to critical media studies.

We looked back through history to identify the continuities and the changes. We focused on the social totalities, their parts and their contradictions to understand the relations of and the possibilities for democratic change. The PM still provides a fundamental, critical analytical tool to explain the functioning of hegemonic media systems in the twenty-first century. It aligns well with other theoretical and methodological approaches and is grounded in the perspective of providing a critical analysis that enables eventual transformation of both society and the media in a more egalitarian, free, democratic, and fraternal direction.

# Editors

**Dr Joan Pedro-Carañana**, works at the Communication Department at Saint Louis University, Madrid Campus. Joan holds a European PhD in Communication, Social Change and Development from Complutense University of Madrid, Spain (2015), and has been a visiting Scholar in Universidad del Norte and Universidad Minuto de Dios in Colombia, as well as in Complutense. His research interests revolve around the role of culture, communication and education in the reproduction and change of societies. He is co-editor of *Talking Back to Globalization: Texts and Practices* (Peter Lang, 2016), with Brian M. Goss and Mary R. Gould. His work has been published in international journals such as the *International Journal of Communication*, *Global Media Journal*, *Synaesthesia: Communication Across Cultures*, *Fifth-Estate-Online - The International Journal of Radical Mass Media Criticism*, *OBETS: Revista de Ciencias Sociales*, *Historia y Comunicación Social* and *Revista Latina de Comunicación Social*. Joan has also been active in a variety of social movements and is a contributor of *OpenDemocracy*, *Rebelión* and other online magazines. His work can be found at https://slu.academia.edu/JoanPedro.

**Dr Daniel Broudy** is Professor of Rhetoric and Applied Linguistics in the Graduate School of Intercultural Communication at Okinawa Christian University. As a former imagery analyst with the US Army and current member of Veterans for Peace, he draws upon his military experience and doctoral training in psycholinguistics to develop courses in communication and the rhetoric of the visual. His research focuses on systems and techniques of mass manipulation in state and corporate public relations. Recent edited collections include *Under Occupation: Resistance and Struggle in a Militarized Asia-Pacific* (CSP, 2013) and *News from Somewhere: A Reader in Communication and Challenges to Globalization* (Wayzgoose Press, 2015). His most recent book is the coauthored *Okinawa Under Occupation: McDonaldization and Resistance to Neoliberal Propaganda* (Palgrave, 2017).

**Dr Jeffery Klaehn** holds a PhD in Communication from the University of Amsterdam (2007) and completed a second PhD, in Sociology, at the University of Strathclyde in 2012. His writings on the Propaganda Model have been published in the *European Journal of Communication, Sociology Compass, Journalism Studies, Synaesthesia: Communication Across Cultures,* and *International Communication Gazette.* He has edited six books, including *Filtering the News: Essays on Herman and Chomsky's Propaganda Model* (Black Rose, 2005), *Bound by Power: Intended Consequences* (Black Rose, 2006) and *The Political Economy of Media and Power* (Peter Lang, 2010). His ongoing series of interviews with comic book writers and illustrators have been published in the *Journal of Graphic Novels and Comics, ImageText: Interdisciplinary Comics Studies, Studies in Comics,* and the *International Journal of Comic Art.* He teaches in the areas of social theory, communication, cultural studies, media and pop culture. More information about his work can be found at: http://uva.academia.edu/JefferyKlaehn.

## Contributors

**Dr Matthew Alford**, FHEA, is a Teaching Fellow at the University of Bath, England and his research focuses on the relationship between entertainment, political power, and propaganda in the United States. Dr Alford produces a multimedia project called *The Writer with No Hands*, which won the Tablet of Honor at the Ammar Film Festival in Tehran. His first book *Reel Power: Hollywood Cinema and American Supremacy* was published by Pluto Press and subsequently translated into Chinese.

**Dr Miguel Álvarez-Peralta** is Professor of Political Communication and Global Media Structure at the UCLM School of Journalism, in Spain. His research interests focus on the dialectical dependence of public opinion and cultural hegemony on the media system's structure, and the potentials of social networks for advancing political change. He has been Fellow Researcher at the Department of Romance Languages at Harvard University (2012–2013). Alvarez-Peralta graduated in Media Studies at UC3M and Computer Engineering at UCM, where he got his PhD in Mass Communications Research. He has been political analyst and campaign consultant of the party *Podemos*, where he coordinated the office for media policies (2015–2017).

**Dr Tabe Bergman** is a lecturer in the School of Film and TV Arts at Xi'an Jiaotong-Liverpool University, in Suzhou, China. His PhD is from the University of Illinois at Urbana-Champaign. He has published refereed articles on Dutch and American journalism in prominent journals and presented papers at top international conferences. His book, *The Dutch Media Monopoly* (VU University Press, 2014), is recommended by leading scholars, including James Curran and Robert W. McChesney.

**Dr Aurora Labio-Bernal** is Tenured Lecturer at University of Seville (Spain). She is Director of the Media, Communication Policies and Democracy in the European Union research group (DEMOC-MEDIA, http://www.democmedia.com) and author of the book *Comunicación, Periodismo y Control Informativo* (2006, Barcelona) and the report entitled *Medios de Comunicación y protección de la Infancia en contexto de crisis humanitarias* (2009, Save the Children). Her research on Political Economy of Communication, Global Groups and Journalism. She is currently working with a Visiting Research Fellowship at the Communication Media Research Institute (University of Westminster) and the Communication Policies Observatory, Institute of Communication (InCom), Autonomous University of Barcelona.

**Dr Christian Fuchs** is a professor at the University of Westminster. He is co-editor of the journal *tripleC: Communication, Capitalism & Critique*. His research focuses on critical theory and the critical study of the role of media, communication(s) and the internet in society. He is author of the following English monographs: *Social Media: A Critical Introduction* (2nd edition 2017), *Critical Theory of Communication: New Readings of Lukács, Adorno, Marcuse, Honneth and Habermas in the Age of the Internet* (2016), *Reading Marx in the Information Age: A Media and Communication Studies Perspective on Marx's 'Capital Volume I'* (2016), *Culture and Economy in the Age of Social Media* (2015), *Digital Labour and Karl Marx* (2014), *OccupyMedia! The Occupy Movement and Social Media in Crisis Capitalism* (2014), *Foundations of Critical Media and Information Studies* (2011), *Internet and Society: Social Theory in the Information Age* (2008).

**Dr Yigal Godler** is a post-doctoral fellow at the Edmond J. Safra Center for Ethics at Tel-Aviv University (Israel). He earned his doctoral degree from the Department of Communication Studies at Ben-Gurion University of the Negev in Beer-Sheva (Israel). In the next academic year (2017–2018), Yigal will be joining the Department of Media Studies and Journalism at the University of Groningen (Netherlands), as an Assistant Professor. His main research interests include the sociology of journalism, journalistic fact-finding and the political economy of the media. Yigal's work has appeared in *Journalism: Theory, Practice and Criticism*, *Journalism and Mass Communication Quarterly*, *Journalism Studies*, *Journalism Practice* and *Critical Sociology*.

**Dr Jesse Owen Hearns-Branaman** holds a PhD from the University of Leeds' Institute of Communications and has over eight years of experience teaching communications, linguistics, media, and cultural studies classes at various universities in the UK and China. He was lead lecturer and seminar leader for the 'Cross-Cultural Communication' and 'British Culture and Media' modules for two years at the University of Nottingham campus in Ningbo, China. More recently he has served as lecturer at University of Sheffield for a module titled

'Journalism and Language,' examining the socio-linguistics of mass mediated communication. He has previously lectured in the Graduate School of Language and Communications, National Institute of Development Administration, Bangkok, Thailand. He is currently Assistant Professor of International Journalism at the United International College of Hong Kong Baptist University and Beijing Normal University located in Zhuhai, China. He also produces music under the name Blue Third World and Homeland Security, creating three albums since 2001.

**Dr Andrew Mullen** is a senior lecturer in International Relations and Politics in the Department of Social Sciences at Northumbria University in Newcastle-upon-Tyne in Britain. His research interests include the history and politics of European integration; the history and politics of the British Left; international political economy; Western foreign policy; the media and propaganda; and political communication. His publications include *The British Left's 'Great Debate' on Europe* (Continuum, 2007); *The 1975 Referendum on Europe* (Imprint Academic, 2007); *The Political Economy of the European Social Model* (Routledge, 2012); *The Battle for Hearts and Minds on Europe: Anti- and Pro-European Propaganda in Britain since 1945* (MUP, forthcoming); and *Labour and Europe: Developing a New Perspective* (MUP, forthcoming). He has his own website (www.andymullen.com) and can be contacted at andrew.mullen@northumbria.ac.uk.

**Dr Barry Pollick** earned his PhD in Communication Studies from Kent State University in 1998 and works as Professor of Communication at University of Maryland University College (UMUC) in Okinawa. He has worked as a journalist for newspapers in Cleveland, Ohio and has authored and co-authored several scholarly papers on public speech and the mass media. He is co-author of *Rhetorical Rape: The Verbal Violations of the Punditocracy* (Waldport Press, 2010). He works as Transition Facilitator in Insignia Federal Inc. teaching Marines transitioning to civilian life how to write resumes and answer job interview questions. He coordinates a Japanese-English linguistic exchange program in Okinawa and researches cross-cultural approaches to negotiating truth claims.

**Milan Rai** is Editor of *Peace News*, a paper committed to 'nonviolent revolution', and an activist trainer. He's the author of *Chomsky's Politics* (Verso, 1995), *War Plan Iraq* (Verso, 2002), *Regime Unchanged: Why the War on Iraq Changed Nothing* (Pluto Press, 2003), and *7/7: The London Bombings, Islam, and the Iraq War* (Pluto Press, 2006). He has contributed to *The Cambridge Companion to Chomsky* and to *Noam Chomsky* (edited by Alison Edgley). Active in the British peace movement since the 1980s, he's been a member of the National Council of the Campaign for Nuclear Disarmament, and an inmate in HMPs Pentonville, Wormwood Scrubs, Lewes and Wandsworth. He is also a coordinator for *Peace News Summer Camp*, a grassroots activist gathering held annually since 2009.

**Professor Piers Robinson**, PhD is Chair in Politics, Society and Political Journalism in the Department of Journalism Studies, School of Social Sciences, University of Sheffield. He researches propaganda, organised persuasive communication and the role of media during conflict. His books include the *Routledge Handbook of Media, Conflict and Security* (2017), *Pockets of Resistance: Media, War, Theory and British Reporting of the 2003 Invasion of Iraq* (2010) and *The CNN Effect: The Myth of News, Foreign Policy and Intervention* (2002, Routledge).

**Professor Francisco Sierra Caballero** PhD is the General Director at CIESPAL, Senior Researcher and Professor of Communication Theory in the Department of Journalism at the University of Seville, Spain. He is also Director of the Interdisciplinary Research Group on Communication, Politics and Social Change (www.compoliticas.org) and Editor of the *Journal of Studies for Social Development of Communication* (REDES.COM) (www.revista-redes.com). He is President of the Latin Union of Political Economy of Information, Communication and Culture (www.ulepicc.net). He has written over 20 books and more than 50 scientific articles in journals of impact. Furthermore he has been professor at prestigious universities and research centers in Europe and Latin America.

**Dr Miyume Tanji** is an honorary lecturer at the College of Asia and the Pacific at the Australian National University. Born in Sapporo, she has studied and taught International Relations and Politics at Sophia University, the Australian National University, Murdoch University, Curtin University of Technology and University of New South Wales. Her main interest is in protest and social movements in Okinawa and Japan, as well as international relations. Recent books include *Myth, Protest and Struggle in Okinawa* (Routledge, 2006); and *Okinawa Under Occupation: McDonaldization and Resistance to Neoliberal Propaganda* (Palgrave, 2017). She has served as Guest Editor (with Greg Dvorak) for the special issue 'Indigenous Asias,' for *Amerasia Journal, Asian American/Pacific Islander/Transcultural Societies* (2015). Recent articles include 'Militarised Sexualities in East Asia' (with Vera Mackie) in Mark McClelland and Vera Mackie (eds), *Routledge Handbook of Sexuality Studies in East Asia*, (Routledge, 2015), 'Japanese Wartime Occupation, War Reparation and Guam's Chamorro Self-Determination' in *Under Occupation: Resistance and Struggle in a Militarised Asia-Pacific*, (Cambridge Scholars Publishing, 2013) and 'Rethinking Resistance in Everyday Okinawa: Diaspora, Transformation and Minor Literature,' *Asian Studies Review* (2012).

**Dr James Winter** is Professor of Communication and Social Justice at the University of Windsor, Canada. He is the author of *Lies The Media Tell Us*, (Black Rose Books, 2007); *MediaThink* (Black Rose Books, 2002); *The Big Black Book: The Essential Views of Conrad and Barbara Amiel Black* (Stoddart, 1997), with Maude Barlow; *Democracy's Oxygen: How Corporations Control the News* (Black Rose Books, 1996); *Common Cents: Media Portrayal of the Gulf War and Other Events* (Black Rose Books, 1992); and is the editor of *Silent Revolution: Media, Democracy, and the Free Trade Debate* (University of Ottawa Press, 1990); *Press Concentration and Monopoly* (Ablex, 1988), with three others. He was the founder of the University of Windsor chapter of Cinema Politica, in 2009, and the founding editor and publisher of Flipside, a muckraking alternative online webzine, from 1995–2000.

**Dr Florian Zollmann** is Lecturer in Journalism at Newcastle University. Previously he acted as a Lecturer in Media and Director of the Archbishop Desmond Tutu Centre for War and Peace Studies (Liverpool Hope University). He holds a PhD in Journalism Studies from the University of Lincoln. His PhD thesis assesses US, UK and German press coverage of US/Coalition 'counter-insurgency' operations in Iraq. Florian is currently contracted to write a monograph—applying the Herman-Chomsky Propaganda Model on international news coverage of human rights issues during a range of contemporary conflicts—for Peter Lang (New York, forthcoming). Additionally, he is conducting research on the ethical implications of propaganda and surveillance in liberal democracies and press-state relations in the twenty-first century new media environment. Florian's research has been published in international academic journals and edited collections. With Richard Lance Keeble and John Tulloch, he jointly edited *Peace Journalism, War and Conflict Resolution* (Peter Lang, 2010). Florian is a board member of the Institute of Communication Ethics. He is writing a bi-monthly report on media affairs for the German magazine *Publik-Forum* and is an op-ed contributor for the Latin American multimedia platform *TeleSUR*.

# Index

**Symbols**

9/11   93, 94, 148, 163, 167
15-M movement   111, 112, 116
21st Century Fox   228
1950s   46, 151, 250–251, 266, 270–272
1960s protests   96, 272
2008 financial crisis   193–221

**A**

ABC (American Broadcasting Corporation)   160
*ABC* (Spanish newspaper)   130–136
academia   22, 57, 59–61, 224, 264, 272, 285, 286
Acosta, Jim   252–253
advertising   2, 23–24, 29, 46, 54, 63, 71, 72, 74–77, 86, 113, 114, 120, 123, 145, 154–155, 161–162, 167–170, 176, 215, 216, 226–227, 232, 243, 251, 283–284
Afghanistan   97, 229, 250
African slave-miners   87

agenda-setting   22–23, 113, 174
Albaek, Erik   41, 50
Alford, Matthew   145–158, 250
algorithmic amplification of online ideologies   84–85
algorithms   10, 73–74, 84, 86, 117, 284
al-Qa'eda   265
Alsop, Joseph   264
Álvarez-Peralta, Miguel   107–124
Amazon   76, 111, 282
American Enterprise Institute   98
anti-communism   2, 54, 56, 64, 72, 85, 109, 110, 126–127, 154, 217, 229, 251, 284
  in Spain   125–141
  revived in the neoliberal era   126–128
anti-systems   136
*Apprentice, The*   164
Arab-Israeli war (1973)   272
Arab Spring, the   81, 116
*arcanae imperii*   101
aristocrats and aristocracy   6, 96
Assange, Julian   96–98, 102, 104, 284
astrology   146, 147

Atlantic Institute for Market Studies   251
atomic diplomacy   268
atrocities, instrumentalisation of   231
atrocity-shaming   230–231
AT&T   99, 101, 102
attention, information 'barely worth',   272
audience(s)   3, 26, 63, 75–78, 86,
        112–114, 117, 119–120, 151–152,
        167, 218, 227–228, 239, 243, 245,
        285–286
austerity   11, 13, 15, 71, 126, 136,
        193–221, 280
austerity-lite   195, 213, 214

# B

Bahrain   232
Balkanisation of the Middle East   231
Balkans   231
banking bailout
  Spain   116, 123
  UK   194–195, 199, 202, 210, 213,
        215, 217
bankruptcies   114
'basic Western benevolence'   229
Batista, Fulgencio   250–251
Bay of Pigs invasion   254
BBC   155, 163, 194, 209, 210–215, 217
Benghazi 'massacre'   231
Bennett, Lance   55
Bergman, Tabe   159–172
Berlin Blockade (1948–9)   268, 270
Bernays, Edward   7, 96
Big Data   71–92, 115, 120, 283, 285
*Bitter Paradise: The Sell-Out of East
        Timor* (1997)   149–150
Black Lives Matter   249–262
bloodbath(s)   230, 231
Blum, William   249, 257, 258
bogeymen   258
Bolton, John   98
Bosnia   229, 230
Bourdieu, Pierre   29, 87
Boyd-Barrett, Oliver   108, 153
brainwashing under freedom   264, 272
Brin, Sergey   73, 227
Britain   85, 193, 193–221, 264–265, 266,
        269, 269–271, 275
British Empire   270, 271

British nuclear arsenal   265–277
  mainstream criticism of   266
Broudy, Daniel   1–18, 93–106,
        279–286
Brzezinski, Zbigniew   8
Bush, President George W.   130
business models
  decline of traditional   110
  on internet   226
BuzzFeed   228

# C

Cambodia   152
Cano, Robinson   175
capital   9, 109, 161, 241
  accumulation   4, 10, 113
  influence on media sector   283
capitalism   6, 11, 13, 33, 56, 87, 108, 110,
        121, 161, 165–166, 202, 213, 225,
        251, 255, 258
  and laws of competition   74
  attention economy of   118
  cognitive   12
  contradictions of   218
  corporate   22
  digital   86–88, 89, 116
  global   94, 102, 109, 115, 250, 282
Carmelo, Anthony   175
Carter, President Jimmy   251
cascading activation model   55
Castro brothers   250, 251, 255, 258
  Castro, Fidel   135, 254–255, 256, 258
  Castro, Raúl   252–254, 255
causal nexus between journalists'
        attitudes and news content   40
CBC   149
censorship   4, 61, 84, 115, 167,
        272, 286
Central America   239, 241, 251
Channel 4   194, 209–211, 215
Channel 5   194, 215
Chavez, Hugo   130, 131, 239, 241, 261
*Chavismo*   132
*Chavista(s)*   132
China   34, 268
Chinese hardware-assemblers   87
Chinese news   34
Chomsky, Aviva   251

Chomsky, Noam   1, 2–3, 7, 11, 25–27, 30–32, 38, 39, 45, 47, 54–59, 62–63, 71, 75, 77–78, 80, 83, 88, 93, 95–96, 101, 107–109, 112, 114, 120, 126, 127, 128, 137, 145–149, 151–154, 159, 166, 173–175, 177, 181, 184, 193, 212–214, 216–218, 223, 230, 238, 246, 249, 251, 257, 258, 264, 265, 272, 274, 279, 283, 284
chronic traumatic encephalitis (CTE)   173
CIA, the   23, 27, 61, 103, 147, 163, 245
Cincinnati   180
cinema   145–158
citizen activism   96, 129, 281–282
citizenship   5, 8–11, 100, 112, 274
civil liberties   93, 102, 134
Cleveland   40, 180
click-bait   114
Clinton, Hillary   61, 80–82, 104, 256
Clinton, President Bill   148
coercion   7, 8, 14, 30, 62, 281
  and propaganda messages   59
COINTELPRO   98
Cold War, the   64, 138, 163, 164, 217, 231–232, 265
  ideology of   229, 246, 256
'Collateral Murder'   97, 104
collusion   274
colonialism   111, 237, 238
colonialist profile of global powers relations'   111
Comcast   101, 102, 160, 170
commercialism   165, 170, 227, 281, 283, 284
commercial logic   117, 136, 215, 216
commercials   161, 162, 169
commodification   12, 89, 113
Communication Studies   2, 7, 38, 224
communism (see also anti-communism)   56, 128, 130, 131, 135, 136, 138, 246, 284
Comte, Auguste   6
concentration process   114
*Confidencial, El*   128
conglomeration   111, 225, 228
  media   242
  television   160

consent
  engineering of   7
  forms of   4
  manufacturing of   2–3, 63, 127, 238
conservative interests   39, 169
conservative media   11–13, 75
  in Spain   136
Conservative Party (UK)   194, 195, 211, 217, 269
conservatives, cultural   164
conspiracy theories   153, 245
  and criticism of US Cuban Policy   257
  concerning Hillary Clinton   82
  vs institutional ideologies   31–33
constitutional rights   100, 263
consumerism   7, 13, 159–172, 167
control mechanism(s)   72, 94
  anti-communism as   217
  neoliberalism as   164
*Convertir la indignación en cambio político*   129
cookies   226
Coppola, Francis Ford   258
Corbyn, Jeremy   81, 85, 116, 127, 213, 217
corporate-government-media-military nexus   6, 95, 249, 284
corporate media   12, 14, 53, 55, 57, 63, 94, 95, 224, 229, 250, 280
  consolidation   99
corporate oligopoly   127
  in Mexican media   242
corporate propaganda   93
corporate-State powers   4, 9
Costa Rica   255
counter-intelligence
  activities   94, 97
  policy   96
  revelations   101
  systems   98
coups
  attempts   257
  in Venezuela   237–248, 261
credibility
  of media workers   30
  of Spanish journalism   111, 112
Creel, George   7
Crime and Courts Act (2013)   263

crisis
  in journalism  46
  media, in situations of  78
  next dot-com  74
  of progressive politics  14
  situations of  83, 99, 107, 109, 282
*Crisis of Democracy, The* (1975)  8, 96
Critical Discourse Analysis (CDA)  259
critical linguists  33
crowdfunding  116
crowdsourcing  116
Crowley, P. J.  97
'crystallisation of public opinion'  7
*CSI* (TV series)  165
Cuba
  democracy in  134, 256
  lectures on democracy to  254–257
Cuban-American relations  255
Cuban-Americans  257
Cuban Embargo  251–252, 254–259
Cuban Revolution (1959)  250–251, 257, 258
cybernetic communications  94
cyber-pessimism  116–117

# D

*Daily Mail*  269
*Daily Mirror*  78
*Daily Show, The* (1996-)  150, 154
*Daily Star*  269
*Daily Telegraph*  194, 208
Darfur  229
deception  58, 62
deep state  59, 285
'defector'  98
demagoguery  24
*Democracia Real Ya*  129
democracy  6–8, 14, 28, 77, 96, 100, 104, 110, 132, 134, 239, 240, 243, 253, 255, 258, 264
  and Google  84
  hijacking of  8
  liberal  61, 97
  and media, role of  4–5
  social  110, 255
  threats to  11, 96, 101, 246
  utilitarian  96, 103
*Democracy Now*  4

Democratic Revolution Party  245
democratization  10, 225, 285
demonisation  137, 231, 246, 250, 254, 257, 280
Department of Defense  163
deregulation  109, 160, 162, 216, 283
deterrence  280
de Vreese, Claes H.  41, 42, 50
digitalization  113, 224
digital technology  3, 225, 227, 281
disclosure (of documents)  97, 99, 131
*Dispatches*  194, 209–211
disruption of the established order  137
distortion  38, 56–59, 62, 80, 85, 228, 239, 240, 242, 249, 256, 257, 273, 285
dominant ideology  72, 109, 127, 146, 154, 164, 184, 229, 283
domino theory  257–258
Donsbach, Wolfgang  39
double-standards  246
DTT (Digital Terrestrial Television)  111
Dulles, John Foster  268
dystopia  10, 281
  Comtian (see Comte, Auguste)  6

# E

Easterbrooke, Gregg  175
East Timor  149, 152
ECHELON  98
economic crisis  62, 71, 81, 111, 200–201, 243
Edwards, David  154
egalitarian
  distribution of media power, historical  8
  role of media  4–5
Egypt  232
Eisenhower, President Dwight D.  268
elite-driven paradigm, the  55–56
elite(s)  3, 6, 8, 10, 12, 14, 22, 39, 64, 94, 101–102, 108, 150, 164, 167, 169, 170, 174–175, 179, 181, 186
  ability to frame terms of debate  102
  consensus  111, 112, 214, 280, 282
  and media compliance  213–214
  corporate  5, 184
  differences  109
  institutions  33
  interests  22–24, 27, 56, 95, 96, 112

journalists   285
knowledge   28
   national and global   191–277
   perspectives   8, 33, 96, 186
Elite 'System', the   94–96
Ellsberg, Daniel   267–268, 272–273, 275
Ellul, Jaques   167
*engaño populista, El* (2016)   135
Enlightenment, the   5, 6
entertainment film   145–158
Entman, Robert   55
entrance-barrier costs   113
escapism   167
European Union (EU)   34, 111, 240
Executive internet 'kill switch'   99
Executive Orders   97, 99

# F

Facebook   23, 71, 73, 75–77, 79, 83, 84, 110, 112, 114–115, 120, 170, 226
*Face the Nation*   99–100
fascism, new forms of   24, 83
Federal Bureau of Investigation (FBI)   23, 151
Federal Communications Commission   102, 160
Feinstein, Dianne   99–100
fifth filter   56, 64, 85, 109, 113–114, 126, 127, 137, 146, 151, 153–154, 167, 184, 217, 284
*Figaro, Le*   127
filter bubble, the   87, 113
filtering   30, 94, 229
financial crisis (see 2008 Financial Crisis)   112, 116, 137, 164, 193–219
financialization   71, 109, 114, 209
*Financial Times*   208, 211, 212
first filter   63, 145, 154, 155, 161, 167, 214–216
fit to print   9, 72, 101
flak   2, 4, 24, 31, 54, 63, 72, 80–82, 112, 118–120, 146, 153, 217, 282–285
Flickr   71
focus groups   27
Fort Apache   132
fourth filter   63, 113–114, 146, 149, 155, 167, 217

Foxconn   87
fragmentation   113, 225
   of Spanish politics   126
framing   31, 108, 116, 230
Fraser, Nancy   12
freedom of speech   84, 115
free-market capitalism   13, 250
free-market democracy   229
free press, the   244, 264
Freud, Sigmund   7
Friedman, Milton   250
Fuchs, Christian   71–92, 118, 226

# G

Gaddafi, Muammar   60, 231
gamification   116
gatekeeping models   223
Germany   11, 23, 39, 275, 282
Gitlin, Todd   11
Glasgow Media Group   194, 212
globalization   95, 109, 246
*Global Media Giants* (2016)   127
global village   10
Godler, Yigal   21–24, 37–51
Golding, Peter   225
Goodell, Roger   179
Goodman, Amy   4
Google   23, 71, 73–76, 84, 113, 117, 170, 176, 185, 226–227, 281
   monoply in search   84
Google Tax   111
Gramsci, Antonio   6, 110, 184
Great Depression, the   215, 216
Great Recession, the   193–221
Greenwald, Glenn   97–99, 101
*Guardian, The*   82, 194, 212, 215, 217, 263, 265
guided market system   95

# H

Hallin, Daniel   48, 55
Havana   250, 253–255
Hawaii   249
HBO   111, 154, 155
Hearns-Branaman, Jesse Owen   25–36
Hedges, Chris   258

hegemonic forces and control  98, 100, 112, 177, 181
hegemonic information  237–248
hegemonic media  5, 120, 286
hegemony  7, 10, 21–24, 110, 153, 174–175, 280, 282
  unconscious  26
  (US)  246
Henry Jackson Society  59, 208
Herman, Edward S.  iii, 1, 2–3, 7, 11–12, 14, 25, 27, 30–31, 33, 38–39, 45, 47, 54–56, 59, 62, 71–73, 75, 77–78, 80, 83, 85, 88, 93, 95, 107–109, 112, 114, 120, 126–128, 137, 145–155, 159, 166, 173–175, 177, 179, 181, 184, 185, 193, 213–214, 216–218, 228, 230, 238, 246, 264, 273, 279, 283–284
  interview with  21–24
high-intensity conflict  231
Hindman, Matthew  227
Hollywood  12, 15, 61, 147–148, 152, 154, 163, 250, 280
House of Commons  204, 269, 270
*House* (TV series)  165
*Huffington Post*  208, 228
Hulu  169
humanitarianism  224, 229–231
human terrain system (HTS)  61
Hussein, Saddam  269–270

I

ideological domination  7, 72, 109, 223–246
ideology  13, 14, 28, 29, 33, 54, 81, 83–86, 127, 224, 228–231, 283
  free-market  109, 126
  institutional  31–34
  Marxist  110, 251
  power and hegemony  21–24
  professional  26
  tools of  6
  user-generated  85
ideology filter  25, 56, 64, 251
Iglesias, Pablo  113, 116, 128–137, 140
'illegal' disruptions to counter-intelligence policy  96

imperialism  12, 15, 237–248
Independent Television (ITV)  194, 210, 270
indexing hypothesis  55
indigenous peoples  4, 242, 246
*indignados*  111, 128
individualism  120, 280, 284
indoctrination  101, 264
inequality  4, 21, 23, 83, 84, 218, 280
  increasing  8–9, 24, 210, 214
  programmes focusing on  210
  social  12, 184
  unprecedented  224
inequity  4
infection  94, 257
inflated salaries  176–177, 179, 183, 189
Information Age, the  97, 100
infotainment  112
Instagram  71
institutional structures  29, 37, 43, 48
internalised values  58, 184, 272
  by journalists  29, 175, 189
  by TV workers  164
international relations  3, 200
internet media  109, 281
internet service providers (ISPs)  102
internet (the)  9, 10, 23, 169, 170, 175, 226, 232, 281, 283, 284
  celebrants  224, 225, 233
  and democracy  116, 170
  and digital media  69–141
  geared towards corporate interests  227
  and newspapers, decline of  177
  promise of the  23, 225
interventionism  238
Iran  34, 131–133, 138, 250, 282
Iran nuclear crisis  34
Iraq  246, 250, 268–274
  British threats against (1990–1)  269, 272, 273
Iraq War (2003)  229
ISIS  231

J

James, Lebron  175
Jefferson, Thomas  6, 175
Jennings, Peter  12

journalism
  as democracy's watchdog   40
  routines of   27, 29, 45–48
Journalism Studies   14, 27, 38, 46, 286
journalists
  ideological views of   39
  stars   285

## K

Kansas City   184
Kellner, Douglas   174, 186
Kennedy, President John F.   258
Keynesianism   13, 195, 218
kibbutz   4, 37
Kinzer, Stephen   249, 258
Klaehn, Jeffery   1–19, 21–24, 26, 108, 112, 152–153, 185–186, 279–286
Klein, Naomi   196, 250
Kohl, Herb   227
Korean War, the   268–270
Kosovo   229–230
Krugman, Paul   13
Kuhn, Thomas S.   108
Kuwait   148, 268–269

## L

Labio-Bernal, Aurora   125–141
Lansky, Meyer   250
Lasswell, Harold   7, 230
Latin America   4, 11, 133, 135, 138, 237–248, 258, 282
Latin American Mission   258
Lazarsfeld, Paul   7
leaker(s)   98–100
Lebanon Crisis (1958)   268
Lee, Sir David   270
left   12
  parties in Spain   129
  rebranding of   14
  scapegoating of the   85
  and social media   83
'left-wing' (term)   43
Lew, Jacob J.   259
liberal democracies   54, 60, 61–62
liberalism   14
liberal media   12–13, 39
liberal politics   167

liberal view of media   108
Liberty Global   228
Libya   229, 231, 232
Limbaugh, Rush   186
Lippmann, Walter   7
local factors   108, 109, 282
López, Ian Haney   95
Luciano, Lucky   250

## M

Machiavelli, Niccolò   6–7
Maduro, Nicolás   130–131, 239, 241, 261
Mafia, US   250, 258
Main Core   98
mainstream media (MSM)   5, 9, 12, 22, 33, 38, 54, 55, 59, 62, 63, 78, 80, 85, 94, 103, 128, 136, 137, 148, 166, 186, 224, 238, 239, 240, 244, 246, 263, 264, 265, 272, 281
Major, John   269
*Make a Move: Turning Outrage into Political Change*   129
management of the public mind   7
*Manifiesto Mover Ficha*   129
manipulation   2, 55, 56, 58, 104, 117, 137
  of information   55, 58, 62, 237, 240
  of perceptions   58
Manning, Chelsea (Bradley)   96, 97, 100, 102, 284
*Manufacturing Consent: The Political Economy of the Mass Media* (1988)   2–3, 7, 11, 39, 53, 55, 71, 93, 109, 111, 193, 223, 238
  2002 edition   217
Mao Zedong   85
market-driven efficiencies   101
Marxian analysis   3–4
Marxism   110, 131, 136
Marxist thought   119
  economics   13
  ideology   251
Marx, Karl   79–80
May, Theresa   84
McCarthyism   56
McChesney, Robert   10, 26, 47, 101–102, 224–225, 227, 233
McMahan, Jeff   272–273

media
  left-liberal   212, 214, 218
  left-wing   147, 216, 218
    in Spain   112
  right-wing   83, 85, 97, 147, 153, 212, 217
media behaviour   2, 31, 38–40, 112, 228
media compliance   213–214, 217
media concentration   8, 23, 26, 54, 154, 160, 227, 228, 243–244, 246
  online   23, 225, 227
media consolidation   94, 99
media effects   31, 168
Media Lens   154
media performance   2, 3, 5, 11, 14, 15, 22–23, 27, 32, 33, 94, 102, 108, 218–219, 274, 280, 286
Media Reform Coalition   228
media spheres   55
mediated lobbying   80–82, 86
Meir, Golda   148
Mélenchon, Jean Luc   116
Mellado, Claudia   44–45
Mexico   168, 238, 242–246, 280
Michaels, Jim   102
Middle East, the   152, 231, 258, 270–271
Miliband, Ed   217
militarization   224, 243, 245
Miller, Mark Crispin   161
'miracle of the market', the   72, 217
miseducation   6
misrepresentation   2, 272
Mitchell, Andrea   253
mobile devices, propagation of   113
mobile phones   71
Mob, the   250
moderation in democracy   8, 96
Monedero, Juan Carlos   130–132, 134–135
monopoly   184, 226
  in online economy   23, 77, 226
Morales, Evo   130, 133–134
*Movimiento Al Socialismo*   134
Mullen, Andrew   22, 185, 193–221
*Munich* (2005)   148
Murdoch, Rupert   215–216, 228
Murdock, Graham   225

# N

*El Nacional*   132
Nasser, Gamal Abdel   269
National Broadcasting Company (NBC)   160, 253
National Football League (NFL)   174, 177, 179–185, 187
National Newspaper Editors Association (AEDE)   111
national security   83, 94, 97, 99, 246, 264
National Security Agency (NSA)   23, 94, 98, 99
national security state   101, 250
NATO   230–231
*Necessary Illusions: Thought Control in Democratic Societies* (1989)   193
'need to know'   100
neoliberal ideology   13–14, 83, 84, 93, 164, 165, 169, 218, 284
neoliberalism   8, 11, 12, 71, 72, 109, 148, 164, 195, 200, 215, 217, 280, 282
  and anti-communism   126–128
  as control mechanism   164–165
  progressive   12
Netflix   111, 169, 282
network television   145
new digital media environment (NME)   223–224
New Labour   194–196, 202, 204, 213, 215, 217
news and journalistic practices   45–48
  practices   32
News Corp   215
newspapers   1, 11, 22–23, 26, 33, 43, 44, 46, 73, 76, 85, 118, 146, 174, 176, 177, 179, 228, 253
  decline of advertising revenue   74
  in Spain   113, 126, 127
  in UK   194–221, 273–274
  reporting on Mexico and Venezuela   237–248
Newspeak   260
*New York Times*   11, 34, 73, 164, 169, 174–186, 189, 249, 252, 254, 257, 280, 281

NGOs   57, 59–61, 197, 285
Nicks, Denver   97
Nixon, President Richard   147, 239, 268
'no nos representan'   128
North America   22, 174
North Dakota   4
'Nuclear Blackmail'   272
nuclear coercion   268, 271, 272
nuclear deterrent   265–274
nuclear weapons   152, 263–277

# O

oath (of secrecy)   99
Obama, Barack President   97, 98, 102, 115, 249–262
objectivity   29, 31, 114
*Observer, The*   194–196, 269
official enemies   27, 34, 146, 147, 166
online ideology   84
online social networks (OSN)   10, 113–118, 120
open source   114
Operation Condor   238
Operation Mass Appeal   61
Operation Rockingham   60
oppression   4, 96
*Oprah Winfrey Show*   163–164
O'Reilly, Bill   97
organisational culture   27
'Over The Top' companies   111
overthrowing leaders in countries   249
ownership in media   2, 8, 12, 13, 22, 26, 28, 33, 38, 39, 63, 71–73, 95, 110, 117, 126, 127, 145, 154, 155, 160–161, 163, 164, 167, 168, 189, 214, 215, 227, 246, 251, 283, 285
ownership of sports teams   173–190, 280–281

# P

Page, Larry   73, 227
paired examples   38, 151, 152, 166
*El País*   114, 124, 128–132, 130, 135–137, 239
Panama   250
*Panorama*   194, 209–211

Parents Television Council   163, 164
Partido Popular   118, 126
Partido Socialista Obrero Español (PSOE)   110, 126, 129, 133, 134
partisan bias   39, 43
PATRIOT Act   98, 103
patriotism   96, 97, 167
Patterson, Thomas E.   39–40
pay-walls   114
peace operations   239
Pedro-Carañana, Joan   viii–18, 21–24, 80, 109, 110, 118, 279–286
peer-to-peer economy   114
Pentagon Papers, the   267
Pentagon, the   147, 239, 241, 245, 267
People's Party (PP)   126
perpetual war   4
Persian Gulf crisis (1961)   269
Philippines, the   250
philosophical dialectic   88
Pittsburgh   180, 181, 184
players (sports)   174–189, 280–281
pluralism   115, 133, 134
plutocracy   255
Podemos   85, 107–141 282, 284
   and 'axis of evil'.   130, 132, 134, 138
   birth of, in two-party context   128, 129, 132
   and explicit communism   128, 130, 131, 136
   Iran connection   132
   revival of anti-communism   126–128
   said to heap praise on countries like Cuba   134
policy-media interaction model   55
political contest model   55
political economy   2–3, 5, 95, 116, 165, 193, 218–219, 225, 280, 281, 286
   of the press   26, 28, 166
   of US television   159
political science   3, 108
Pollick, Barry   173–190
popular communication   238
populism   116, 128, 131, 135–136
   authoritarian   83, 85
   and communism   128
   and democracy   109, 136
*Populist Deception, The*   135

post-9/11   93, 94, 102, 165
postcolonial   111
Powell Jr, Lewis F.   263
PP   131, 133
practices, focus on   14, 26–27
*Pravda*   11
presuppositions   253, 254–256, 259, 264
priming strategies   113
PRISM   98
privatization   195, 202, 210
professionalism   3, 25, 26, 30–31, 33
  journalistic   28–29
profit orientation of the mass media   38, 54, 71, 145, 214
profit(s)
  crisis of print media   110, 112, 251
  maximisation (of)   3
  motive (absence of)   284
  sources of   110
progressive neoliberalism   14
Propaganda Model (PM), the
  American television   159–172
  Britain (2008 financial crisis)   193–221
  dismissed as conspiracy theory   26, 29, 31
  corporate market power and ideology   223–236
  democratic approach of   22
  filtering out   30, 33, 94, 95
  internet and digital media age   71–92, 107–124, 232
  limitations to   25–36, 55–57, 109–113, 146–156
  media coverage of sports team owners and players   173–190
  political economy of media   3–4
  propaganda production   57–63
  reactions to and marginalisation of   2–3, 14, 54–55
  screen entertainment   145–168
  and sociology of journalism   25–36
  and System Security 'filter'   93–116
prosumers   86, 115, 117, 226
protecting privilege   264
proxy-intervention   231

Public Broadcasting Service (PBS)   155, 160
public broadcast system   110
public discourse   13, 93–95, 101–104, 190, 237
public media   110, 111, 160
public relations (PR)   60, 177, 184, 185, 230
public sphere   5, 72, 80, 83, 95, 113, 118, 225, 246, 281

R

'rabble', the   6
Račak massacre (1999)   230
race relations in Cuba   249
RAF Waddington   270
Rather, Dan   12
Reagan, President Ronald   72, 109, 239, 268
realm of legitimate debate   27
red scares   56
refugee crisis (2014–15)   231–232
regime change (agendas)   60–61
regulation   167
representation (in media)   151
  of Presidents Chávez and Maduro   239
residue   72, 145, 146, 153
Responsibility to Protect (R2P) doctrine.   231
Robertson, John W.   224
Robinson, Piers   53–67
Rockefeller, David   8
role conceptions   40–45, 50
'rotten apple' theory   251, 257–258
Russia   24, 60, 136, 269
Russo-phobia   24
Rwanda   148, 229

S

Sachs, Jeffery   255
Sanders, Bernie   80, 85, 127
Saney, Isaac   255, 256, 261
Schieffer, Bob   99
Schiller, Herbert   100
Schlesinger, Arthur   148, 258, 264

*Science of Coercion, The* (1994)   60
second filter   63, 75, 145, 154–155, 161–162, 167, 216
secret interventions   224
selection of sources   31, 113, 114
self-censorship   25, 30, 63, 271, 272
SHAMROCK, Operation   98
Sierra Caballero, Francisco   237–248
Silicon Valley   12
Sixteenth Century, the   6
smartphones   114
Snowden, Edward   87, 97–100, 100, 102, 284
  branded as 'thief'   98
social democracy   110, 255
socialisation   14, 28, 29, 175, 285
  journalistic   14, 26, 29–31
  primary   29
  secondary   25, 26, 29
social media   72–79, 87, 110, 116, 117, 166, 227, 228, 234
sociological theory   25
Somalia   229
sourcing   25–27, 55, 63, 78, 184, 196, 198, 204, 216–217, 283
Soviet threat   229, 246
Spain   107–141, 282
  democracy in   129, 132, 137
'spectator democracy'   7
sphere of legitimate consensus   31
Spielberg, Steven   148
spin doctors   59, 63, 285
*Spinwatch*   59
splitter   99
spoiled athlete   175–176, 180
spoiled owner   175, 185
sports   15, 146, 173–191, 280
Srebrenica massacre   230
Stalin, Joseph   85
standards, ethical reporting   26, 31, 33
State-Corporate nexus   6
state propaganda   30
status quo   23, 94, 101, 102, 126, 169, 214, 238
STELLARWIND   98
Stiglitz, Joseph   13
stimulus   194

stimulus (economic)   217
Streisand Effect   117
subjectivity of journalists   27
subprime crisis   111, 114
Suggs, Terrell   175
Sumak Kawsay   4
super-structural aspects   126
surveillance   10–11, 75, 84, 87, 93, 99, 101, 103, 170, 226, 285
surveillance-industrial internet complex,   87
Syria   229, 231
  'opposition'   231
System Security   93–106
System, the   95–100, 127, 150, 155, 283–285
  protecting the   100–102

## T

Tanji, Miyume   93–106
targeted advertising   71, 74–77, 226
tax avoidance and tax evasion   201, 202, 209, 211, 213–214, 217–218
technicism   224
techno-dystopian views   281
technological change   9, 46, 48, 73, 224, 225, 281
technological standards   226
technologies   84, 98, 120, 170, 224–227, 281, 283–284
  expected and actual uses of   10
  and TV   165–166
techno-utopian discourse   9, 281
Televisa   168, 242, 243, 244
television   23, 30, 73, 120, 147–148, 159–172, 173, 176, 189, 194, 214–215, 217, 280
  advertising   75
  austerity, coverage of   204–211
  and democracy   165
  Mexican   242–245
  Spanish   111–113, 117, 119
television industry   159–162, 164, 167–170
texts, interpretation of media   26, 34, 155, 195, 280

textual analysis   151
Thatcher, Margaret   109, 215
'they don't represent us'   128
think tank(s)   57, 59, 61–62, 63, 132, 195, 204, 285
third filter   63–64, 146, 155, 166–167, 184, 216–217
Third World   246, 256, 259
*Time*   104, 114
totalitarianism   246
totalitarian state(s)   7, 9, 30, 85, 264
treason   97, 98, 259, 261
Trending Topic   114, 117, 119
Trident weapons system   266, 272
Trilateral Commission, the   8, 96, 103, 130
Trudeau, Justin   256
Trump, (President) Donald   13, 24, 80–82, 102–103, 127, 253, 256, 262
*TV Nation*   155
twentieth century   6, 26, 57, 96, 117, 136, 225, 250
twenty-first century   24, 62, 107, 286
Twitter   71, 75, 76, 80–82, 85, 110, 112, 113, 117, 120
  flak against Twitter stars   118–120
  and news lifecycle   114–116
Twittersphere   118–120

## U

Ukraine   232
Underdog Effect   117
unions   151, 184, 195
United Kingdom   136, 216, 228, 264, 267, 269–270, 282
United States of America (USA)   7, 11–12, 22–23, 32, 34, 39, 95, 97, 101, 103, 109–110, 127, 148, 152, 193, 238, 240–241, 246, 252–260, 264, 267, 280, 282
  'the indispensable nation'   93, 102
unthinkable, the   117, 214, 263–277
UN weapons inspections   60–61
*USA Today*   185
user-generated content   78, 226

user-generated ideology   84–85
user tracking technology   226
USSR (Soviet Union)   71, 85, 109, 127, 240, 256, 265–266, 268, 272, 274, 284

## V

values (see internalisation of values)   58
Van Dalen, Arjen   41–45, 50
V-bombers   270–271
Veblen, Thorstein   23, 49
Venezuela   126
  in Spanish politics   130–135, 137
  media coup in (2002)   239, 241, 246, 280
  'permanent war' against   238–242
Verizon   101
victims
  'unworthy'   150, 242, 246, 280
  'worthy'   242, 280
videogames industry   154
Vietnam War, the   56, 147, 150, 249, 264, 267, 268
viralisation   116
virus theory (of socialism)   251
Vocento   130

## W

Wall Street   12, 13
Walt Disney Company   160, 162
War Measures Act   259
war on drugs   229
war on terror   63, 163, 279, 284
war party, the   24
Washington Consensus   229
*Washington Post*   254
Watergate   8, 147
wealth tax   194, 202, 210, 213–214, 217–218
  media response to   211–213
weapons
  chemical and biological   254
  nuclear   11, 151, 263–277, 280
Weapons of Mass Destruction (WMDs)   58, 60–61, 63

Web 2.0   223
western-style democracies   255
*West Wing, The* (1999–2006)   148
whistleblowers   98, 99, 102, 209
White Helmets   60, 61
White House, the   127, 147, 148
WikiLeaks   97, 104, 232
Wikipedia   71, 104, 116
Williams, Raymond   95
Winter, James   249–262
wiretapping   101
Wolfsfeld, Gadi   55
Wolin, Sheldon   101
workers' cooperatives   4, 13

world order   100
  new–   103
World Wide Web   71, 224

# Y

Yemen   232
young people   112, 129, 203–204
YouTube   71, 83, 111, 170, 220, 226
Yugoslav Wars, the   230

# Z

Zollmann, Florian   223–246